Set fire to the capitalist stage[1]

1 Emmanuel, Arghiri (1976) "The Multinational Corporations and Inequality of Development.", International. p. 763. Social Science Journal, Vol. 28 No. 4, pp. 753-772, UNESCO, 1976.

Anti-Imperialist Marxism (AIM)

Volume 3

CRITICAL THEORY WORKSHOP'S AIM series provides a platform for scholarly research and popular-form essays from around the world that challenge the widespread assumption, including within the Western left, that there is no real-world alternative to capitalism. Refusing to shy away from serious scholarly engagements with actually existing socialism, it opens up the spectrum of analysis to explore histories and contemporary developments that have either been ignored or misrepresented. In order to do so, it promotes innovative, non-Eurocentric research that overcomes the siloing effects of the disciplines and the ideological horizons of imperial knowledge production in favor of resolutely internationalist scholarship that deploys an anti-imperialist framework of analysis. The overall objective is thus to foster non-dogmatic theoretical work that has real use-value, precisely because of its relevance to concrete struggles for a more egalitarian and sustainable world.

Unequal Exchange

Past, Present, and Future

Published by *Iskra Books* © 2025

10 9 8 7 6 5 4 3 2 1

Iskra Books
iskrabooks.org
Olympia, US | London, England | Dublin, Ireland

Iskra Books is a nonprofit, independent, scholarly publisher—publishing original works of revolutionary theory, history, education, and art, as well as edited collections, new translations, and critical republications of older works.

979-8-3306-1254-3 (*Jacketed Hardcover*)
979-8-3306-1334-2 (*Softcover*)

British Library Cataloguing in Publication Data
A catalogue record for this book is available from the British Library

Library of Congress Cataloging-in-Publication Data
A catalog record for this book is available from the Library of Congress

Editing by Sedeer el-Showk, David Peat
Cover Design by Ben Stahnke
Book Design and Typesetting by Alessandro Zancan

Unequal Exchange

Past, Present, and Future

Torkil Lauesen

Iskra Books

Olympia | London | Dublin

Contents

Editor's Note xiii

The Legacy of Arghiri Emmanuel xv

Introduction xv

Outline of the Book xvi

1 The Historical Context of the Theory of Unequal Exchange 1

Emmanuel—A Man of the 20th Century 4

The Mutiny 5

In Relation to Patrice Lumumba 7

In Paris 11

2 The Political Economy of Unequal Exchange 15

Primitive Accumulation 16

The Commodity 17

The Double Character of Exchange-Value 19

The Value of Labor-Power and Surplus Value 22

The Price of Labor-Power—The Wage 25

The Globalized Value of Labor-Power 28

Cost-Price 33

The Circulation of Capital 34

From Surplus Value to Profit 37

Formation of the Average Rate of Profit 38
The Transformation from Value into Market Price 41
The Appropriation and Distribution of Value 43
Superprofits 44
Value as Price 47
Unequal Exchange 49
On Exploitation 52
Neoliberal Lessons for Dependency Theory 55
Neoliberal Globalization 56
Global Production Chains 60
Labor Arbitrage 64
The Global *Value* Chains 68
The 'Happy' and 'Sour-faced' Smiley Curves 69
Bright and Dark Value 73

3 How to Measure Unequal Exchange? 79
The Value of Labor-Power 87
Productivity 89
The Size of the Unequal Exchange 97
Gernot Köhler Method 106
Andrea Ricci Contribution 111
Jason Hickel and Colleagues' Contributions 117
The Wage Value of Appropriation Through Unequal Exchange 120
Unequal Exchange on the Individual Level 124
The Balance 125
Peeling to the Apple Core 128
The Political Economy of a T-Shirt 129

The Advantages of the Individual Perspective 131

4 The Political Consequences of Unequal Exchange: The Break in International Solidarity 133

The Imperial Mode of Living 140

The History of the Imperial Mode of Living 146

More Than Our Chains to Lose 151

There Will Come a Day... 157

5 Profit and Crisis 161

The Political Economy of Trade Balance 164

Debt—Pushing the Problem into the Future 166

6 Over- and Under-development in Capitalism 169

Polarized Development 174

Over- and Under-development 181

Appropriate or Underdeveloped Technology? 184

The State in the Transition Period 186

Lenin and the New Economic Policy 188

Mao, Deng, and Neoliberal Globalization 189

The Need to Continue the Development of the Productive Forces 194

7 Ecology and Unequal Exchange 197

Emmanuel's Contribution 198

Ecological Unequal Exchange 200

8 Resisting Unequal Exchange 205

The History of Resistance 207

The American World Order 209
The Rise of the Third World 210
The Tricontinental Conference 214
Demand for a New International Economic World Order 215
Learning from Arghiri Emmanuel 219
The Rise and Fall of Neoliberalism 220
The South African Example 222
The Emerging Multipolar World-System 226
South–South Alliances 227
BRICS 229
The Principal Contradiction 230
The Decline of US Hegemony 231
The Rise of China 234
Just Another Imperialist Power? 237
The Contradictions of the Multipolar World-system 241
Trump's Counteroffensive 245
The Resistance from the Global South 248
Crisis and Revolution in the Global North 250

9 The Transformation Towards Socialism on the National and Global Levels 255
The Transitional State and the World Revolution 257
Advanced Socialism 262
Crisis and Revolution in the Global North 265

References 267

List of Tables

Table 2.1 38

Table 2.2 40

Table 2.3 51

Table 2.4 52

Table 3.1: Hourly Wages (USD) 84

Table 3.2: World Trade by Region, 1948-1982 98

Table 3.3: Imports to Developed Market Economies 99

Table 3.4: Exports to Developing Market Economies 100

Table 3.5: EEC Dependence on Raw Materials from Developing Countries (in 1972) 101

List of Figures

Figure I 23

Figure II 36

Figure III 37

Figure IV 42

Figure V: The Global Industrial Workforce, 1950-2010 59

Figure VI: Exchange Value Added in Global Production Chains 72

Figure VII: The Buying Power from Dark Value Drains Embedded in the iPad and the iPhone 4 128

Figure VIII: BRICS+ GDP (PPP) in world economy as from 1990 to 2022 230

Editor's Note

Many of the Arghiri Emmanuel documents referenced are available online at the Arghiri Emmanuel Archive. See 'References' section for links or visit https://unequalexchange.org/category/digital-archive/.

The Legacy of Arghiri Emmanuel

Introduction

ARGHIRI EMMANUEL WAS BORN IN 1911 and passed away in 2001. The Indian economist Jairus Banaji called him "the last great left-wing theoretician of the 20th century."[1] This book aims to explore his work, but also to place it in a twenty-first century context, as his ideas continue to cast light on the development of capitalism in its decline.

I read *Unequal Exchange* after its publication in English by Monthly Review Press in 1972. The political implications of unequal exchange on the international solidarity of the working class, presented in the book, were similar to the ones promoted by the organization—Communist Working Circle—I belonged to at the time.[2] In that *milieu,* there were not many with such a perspective, and as such we reached out to Emmanuel in 1974 and maintained contact by letters and occasional visits until he passed away.[3]

After many years of insufficient interest in the political economy of imperialism, there has, in recent years, been a growing interest in the work of Emmanuel, reflected in many articles and books and the republishing of his main work, *Unequal Exchange: A Study of the Imperialism of Trade.*[4] The reason for the decline of interest in the theory of unequal exchange in the last decades of the 20th century and the first of the 21st century was not that it has become irrelevant. On the contrary, the flow of value by unequal exchange accelerated as industrial production on a huge scale was outsourced to low wage countries. Instead, the reason for the lack of interest was neoliberal ideological dominance, also penetrating deep into left wing movements and their intellectual production. With the ongoing decline of neoliberalism and U.S. hegemony, the dis-

---

1 Banaji, Jairus (2024) "Arghiri Emmanuel (1911-2001)", *Historical Materialism*.

2 See my introduction to the republishing of Communist Working Group (1986), *Unequal Exchange and the Prospects of Socialism* (2025, Washington: Iskra Books).

3 Lauesen, Torkil (2023) "Emmanuel and Us".

4 **Ed. Note:** Republished by Monthly Review Press in July 2025, with a new foreword by Torkil Lauesen.

course of anti-imperialism has made a comeback, and so has the interest in the political economy of imperialism. That is welcome.

The growing interest in unequal exchange theory has also led to the formation of the Emmanuel Association. Its website has a rich digital archive of documents from Emmanuel's personal archive.[5] The Association has also been the driving force behind the establishment of an archive of his left papers, at the International Institute of Social History in Amsterdam.[6]. On January 29-30, 2026, the Association is hosting a conference on the work of Emmanuel. In 1974 we first made contact with Emmanuel, and so, after fifty years of "living with Emmanuel's political thinking" it is fitting to "close the circle" and sum up his work.

Outline of the Book

In chapter 1, I present Emmanuel's biography, as it is important for the development of his ideas. Before embarking on an academic career at the age of fifty, Emmanuel had practical expertise not only in economics, from working in Greece and then the Congo Free State, but also in political activism, sometimes under dramatic circumstances.

In chapter 2, I present the theory of unequal exchange. Since it is based on Marx's conception of value and the accumulation process of capital, I explain unequal exchange by following its development, from the simple "cell" in capitalism—the commodity—through the production and circulation processes, and international trade, thereby mirroring Marx's structure in *Capital*. From there, I proceed by bringing the theory into the 21st century. I do this by drawing on new material from Emmanuel's personal archive, dependency theorists such as Samir Amin, Ruy Mauro Marini, Andre Gunder Frank, Immanuel Wallerstein, and contemporaneous theorists such as, Donnald Clelland, John Smith, and Andrea Ricci.

In chapter 3, I deal with the size of unequal exchange. First, the question of how to measure it. The discussion of the different calculation methods reveals the factors which have an impact on the size of unequal exchange. Then I will discuss the most important empirical studies of unequal exchange. What is the actual size of unequal exchange? How has it developed in the past two centuries?

5 https://unequalexchange.org/category/digital-archive/

6 The Emmanuel Association website: "Who was Arghiri Emmanuel?", https://unequalexchange.org/who-was-arghiri-emmanuel/.

To what extent can it explain the polarization of the world-system in terms of living conditions?

In chapter 4, I look at the political consequences of unequal exchange for the international solidarity of the working class.

Emmanuel's work was much more than the theory of unequal exchange. In 1974 he published *Profit and Crises*, which deals with the fundamental contradictions in the capitalist mode of production.[7] As capitalism is entering a deep structural crisis, this work is becoming more relevant than ever. In the beginning of the 1980s Emmanuel was preoccupied with the connection between the transfer of technology by multinational companies and the development of the productive forces in the Global South, predicting the rise of China.[8] He also was preoccupied by the significance of dollars as world money, the role of the state and more specific political issues, such as settler colonialism. All these questions were, of course, not isolated, but interlinked as a coherent conception of how capitalism works. In chapter 5, I deal with Emmanuel's theory of the fundamental contradiction in the capitalist mode of production: between the need to expand production and the attendant level of consumption power generated by production, which is insufficient to realize profit through the sale of goods.

In chapter 6, I explain how the mechanism of unequal exchange became the historical solution to the contradiction in capitalism, creating a polarized dynamic of over-development in the center and under development in the periphery. The chapter also tells the story of how neoliberal globalization of production changed that pattern. And how, subsequently, China managed to break the polarizing dynamic in capitalism, signalling profound changes in the economic and political balance in the world-system.

Chapter 7, I deal with the ecological aspects of unequal exchange, which Emmanuel mentions in passing. With the growing significance of ecological and climate problems, the school of ecological unequal exchange has developed from the 1980s and onwards.

Chapter 8 deals with resistance to unequal exchange, historical and present. This is basically the history of anti-imperialism, but it is seldom told as the story of resistance to unequal exchange, as the concept, to a large extent, has been marginalized by Western Marxism, due to the political implications for the western working class.

---

7 Emmanuel, Arghiri (1984) *Profit and Crises*. London: Heinemann, 1984.

8 Emmanuel, Arghiri (1982) *Appropriate or underdeveloped Technology?* Chichester. London: John Wiley & Sons, 1982.

In the final chapter 9, I open up for a discussion on the future development of capitalism and a possible transfer towards socialism within this century. How is it possible to end the curse of unequal exchange on humanity? How is it possible to develop a mode of production which generates a more equal world and one in balance with nature? Since I am not a utopian idealist, I try to do this on the basis of the existing conditions in the world-system. Taking into account the existing world economy and the existing political forces, what can the first practical steps be?

1

The Historical Context of the Theory of Unequal Exchange

To paraphrase Mao Zedong: Where do correct ideas come from? Do they drop from the sky? No, they come from social practice, the struggle for production, the class struggle, and scientific work.[1] There is a close link between what goes on in the world—historical development—the projects of classes and states, and theoretical and political debates.

What characterized the historical development of "the long 1960s" (1955–75) that brought forth the theory of "unequal exchange"? One major event was the decolonization process in the wake of the Second World War. The two World Wars cleared the way for the soon-to-be new hegemon after the decline of the British Empire: the United States. The decline of the European colonial empires and the rise of the Soviet Union as a balancing force against the rise of the United States created a "window of opportunity" for national liberation movements in the colonies, in what became known as the Third World.

The postwar U.S. pushed for decolonization to open the former European colonies for U.S. investment and trade—the transformation from colonialism to neocolonialism. Meanwhile, the Soviet Union saw the creation of new states opposed to colonialism as possible new allies against Western capitalism.

The Asian and African countries from the first wave of decolonization participated in the Bandung Conference in Indonesia in 1955. They stressed the importance of independence from both East and West and the development of their national economies. The Bandung Conference was not a new Communist International that strived for the socialist world revolution as the COM-

1 Tse-tung, Mao (1963) "Where Do Correct Ideas Come From?" in *Mao: Four Essays on Philosophy*, p. 134, Beijing: Foreign Languages Press, 1963.

INTERN had done since its formation in 1919. It was the expression of the national liberation struggles against colonialism, which in some instances meant communist forces taking the lead.

The new global hegemon had to make sure that the decolonization process ended in "free enterprise" for U.S. capital and not with socialist-orientated states linked to the socialist bloc. Therefore, from around 1965 to 1975, the main contradiction in the world was between the U.S. and the different anti-imperialist liberation movements and socialist-orientated states. The Vietnam War became the symbol of this contradiction.

The rise of socialist-orientated projects in the Third World, from China and Vietnam in the East to Cuba and Chile in the West, produced new theoretical and political debates, most prominently around the Chinese interpretation of Marxism in the form of Maoism, but also from other Third World revolutionaries. These included Che Guevara and Fidel Castro in Cuba, Frantz Fanon in Algiers, Ho Chi-Minh and Nguyen Giap in Vietnam, Amílcar Cabral in Guinea-Bissau, and Eduardo Mondlane in Mozambique.

The revolutionary spirit of China, Vietnam, Cuba, and other countries had a strong impact on anti-imperialist theory. Before the 1960s, the Marxist understanding of imperialism was almost exclusively based on V. I. Lenin's writing from around the time of the First World War, especially *Imperialism as the Highest Stage of Capitalism* from 1917.[2] In the late 50s, things began to change. New perspectives emerged, both from Third World revolutionaries and from academics. The latter were mostly connected to the so-called "New Left" and criticized both the capitalist world-system and existing socialist projects.

The U.S. representative of this strain of thought was Paul Baran, a professor at Stanford University and a leading figure in the journal *Monthly Review*, founded in 1949. Baran defined monopoly capitalism as a transnational rather than a national phenomenon. This reflected the development of capitalism in the US after the Second World War. A special feature of transnational monopoly capitalism was the underdevelopment of the Third World. In 1957, Baran's book *The Political Economy of Growth* was published. In 1966, *Monopoly Capital* was released, written by Baran together with *Monthly Review* editor Paul Sweezy.

Baran did not write about "unequal exchange" or Third World "dependency". His main interests were monopoly capital, investment, and profit, but his underlining of underdevelopment as a consequence of global capitalism

2 Lenin, V. I. (1917) *Imperialism as the Highest Stage of Capitalism*, in Lenin: *Selected Works*, Vol. 1. Moscow: Progress Publishers, 1963.

posed a serious challenge to mainstream economists, who insisted that Third World countries would develop, if only they followed the example of the Western world.

Baran's work was of importance to those theorists of imperialism who rose to prominence in the 1960s: Andre Gunder Frank, Samir Amin, Immanuel Wallerstein, and Arghiri Emmanuel. After a meeting with Baran in 1964, Gunder Frank wrote that Baran's systematic investigation of capitalist development and underdevelopment—defining them as two sides of the same coin—had opened the door to a new understanding of world history, the present, and the future.[3] Che Guevara was also an admirer of Baran. In 1960, he welcomed him to Cuba to discuss underdevelopment and related economic questions.[4]

The renewal of imperialism theory in the U.S. centered around the journal *Monthly Review*, including theorists such as Sweezy and Harry Magdoff. Later, Immanuel Wallerstein, who had studied liberation movements in Africa, developed his world-system theory. In Latin America, several academics such as Celso Furtado, Anibal Pinto, and later Ruy Mauro Marini began to formulate the theory of "dependency." Dependency theory described imperialism as a system with a center, the "metropole" consisting of North America, Western Europe, and Japan, and an exploited "periphery", the Third World. Third World countries supplied the metropole with raw materials and tropical agricultural commodities produced by cheap labor, while the metropole had political and economic control. The development of the periphery was deemed impossible within the capitalist world-system. Development in Third World countries would only become possible if there was a revolution that cut off the pipeline of value transfer to the metropole.

Gunder Frank, who was living in Chile, wrote an essay in 1963 on the connection between development and underdevelopment.[5] From Africa, the Egyptian Samir Amin presented his thesis: *The Origins of Underdevelopment: Capitalist Accumulation on a World Scale* in 1970.[6] Besides dealing with the issue of unequal exchange in international trade, Amin put forward the thesis of a law

---

3 Sweezy, Paul and Huberman, Leo. eds. (1965) *Paul Alexander Baran (1910–1964): A Collective Portrait,* p. 99. New York: Monthly Review Press, 1965.

4 Ibid., pp. 107–8.

5 Frank, A. G. (1966) 'The Development of Underdevelopment', *Monthly Review* Vol. 18, No. 4, pp. 17–31.

6 Amin, Samir (1970) *L'accumulation a l'echelle Mondiale: Critique de la theorie du sous-development.* IFAN-Anthropos. Dakar/Paris. In English: Amin, Samir (1974) *Accumulation on a World Scale.* New York: Monthly Review Press, 1974.

of globalized value resulting in an imperialist rent in favour of central powers. According to Amin, the wage differences between North and South workers generate an unequal exchange. However, Arghiri Emmanuel was the first to rigorously and systematically emphasize the crucial role of wage differences as a fundamental cause of unequal exchange in trade between nations. Having been in the Congo from 1937-41 and again 1946-60, Emmanuel presented his theory of unequal exchange in Paris in 1963. All of these theorists used "unequal exchange" in the world market as part of their understanding of how imperialism transfers value, showing how ideas are historically determinate, rather than a product of the mind of an individual genius. Here, let's focus on Emmanuel and his specific context.

Emmanuel—A Man of the 20th Century

Emmanuel was born 1911 in Patras, Greece, At the time Greece was in the semi-periphery, if not the periphery, of the capitalist world-system. His mother worked as a teacher, which was remarkable at that time in conservative Greek Catholic society. His father had a business selling textiles. Emmanuel's childhood was at the time of the first wave of revolutionary uprisings in the periphery: the Taiping rebellion in 1911 and the Russian revolution in 1917. It was also the era of inter-imperialist rivalry. Greece took part in the Balkan wars (1912-13) and was also drawn into the First World War and subsequently into yet another war, the Greco-Turkish War from 1919 to 1922.

The world economic crisis of 1929 hit Greece severely, leading to continued mass emigration. Emmanuel studied at the High School of Economics and Commerce in Athens from 1927 to 1932 and then at the Faculty of Law until 1934, from where he went on to work in a trading firm in Athens. At the time, the political situation was unstable in Greece, as in the rest of Europe, with fascism on the rise. In 1936, Prime Minister Metaxas initiated a 'self-coup' and established a fascist, anti-communist regime. In the midst of these events Emmanuel's father died in 1937, and as the eldest son, he became responsible for the well-being of his mother and sisters. To raise money, Emmanuel decided to emigrate. Most Greek emigrants went to the United States. However, this flow was restricted in the 1930s by US anti-immigration laws, and Emmanuel was not very fond of the U.S., so he decided to go to Belgian King Leopold II's colony in the Congo, then known as the Congo Free State, where some friends of the family had settled and established a small textile import business in Stanleyville.[7] Immigrants from southern Europe, such as Greeks, were generally perceived as not entirely "white" by the Belgian settlers in the Congo. Emmanuel's experiences in the Congo provided him with illustrative practical examples of settler colonialism which he used in his later writings. The extreme difference in wages between Africans and European settlers and the brutal racist Belgian regime were a microcosm of the center-periphery division in the world-system.

The Mutiny

Back in Greece, despite the leader Metaxas's fascist ideology, he did not side with the Axis powers, due to his conservative royalist nationalist feelings, so the Germans occupied the country in May 1941. The Greek king George II, accompanied by the Metaxist administration, fled to Egypt where they established a government-in-exile. In Greece, the starvation winter of 1941-42 and the brutal occupation killed half a million, driving many to join the resistance movement E.A.M. [National Liberation Front], whose driving force was the Communist Party of Greece. They fought a successful guerrilla struggle against the Nazi-occupation on the Greek mainland and on the island of Crete. In 1942, inspired by the E.A.M. resistance, Emmanuel left the Congo to volunteer for the Greek Liberation Forces in the Middle East. He became a naval officer on a ship based in Alexandria in Egypt, hoping to engage in the struggle against Nazi Germany. However, the Greek forces in the Middle East were controlled by the Metaxist government. In coordination with the British forces, they wanted to "spare the army" to be ready to fight against E.A.M. to regain control over Greece when the war against Germany ended. The majority of the 30,000 Greek soldiers in the Middle East supported E.A.M.. In order to control them, thousands were interned in British prison camps in the region. The Greek communists were seen as a greater danger than the Nazis by the Greek ruling class and their British counterparts. This was a prelude to the Greek Civil War.

In April 1944, Emmanuel took an active part in the mutiny of marines and soldiers against the right-wing Greek government being installed by the allies in Cairo. The mutiny was a protest against the passivity of the government, who did not want to engage the army and navy against the Germans.

The revolt began on April 4 in Alexandria. Sailors' Revolutionary Commissions were formed in support of E.A.M. on five navy ships and in the naval shore establishment. A large part of the navy and army units joined it. However, the

7 Details of this section from conversation with Emmanuel's daughter Catherine Emmanuel, 6.9.2024.

ships were stormed and recaptured by Greek officers loyal to the government-in-exile, with the assistance from British military forces. Eleven seamen were killed, others wounded, and many were taken prisoner, among them Emmanuel. They were charged with high treason, and subsequently sentenced to death by a Greek court-martial in Alexandria. Emmanuel gave a speech in court on behalf of the accused. It is seventeen-page-long passionate "apology", in which he accuses the accuser of treason against the Greek people and praises the E.A.M. for their heroic struggle. It is not the speech of a frightened young man facing a death sentence but of an angry revolutionary:[8]

> Gentlemen Judges: When this trial began, we had, like you, made the decision not to take part in the debates, not to defend ourselves; we knew that two things were going to take place in this trial; a comedy would be played out and a crime would be committed. Both could just as well have been done without us [...]
>
> And despite this we still agreed to participate in this trial and if not to defend ourselves at least to speak. We told ourselves that for us there was one more fight here and that we know how to fight both when we have weapons and when we don't. We told ourselves again that we are going to break this monologue, yes, whether you like it or not, we are going to break it [...]
>
> Whether you like it or not, you will soon be spreading the deep impression that the superb words of little Fournari made on you a few minutes ago, when he shouted to you in his honest and childish voice: "[...] and if you do not kill me, and if I live another hundred years, and if a hundred times the need arises again to revolt and raise arms against traitors to save my country, I will not hesitate to do so." This voice you will have a hard time stifling. You can shut forever the mouth that uttered these words. But tonight, and every day when you think of talking about this trial you will suddenly feel with fear that your aplomb has diminished, you will realize that you are slipping, that you are losing your steps as if you had suddenly entered an unknown, improbable and incomprehensible territory. For such is the power of truth and moral courage [...]
>
> We were accused of having detained three warships in the port and thus even indirectly benefiting the enemy. How and why these three warships were stopped in the port of Alexandria is known to everyone and I will explain it to you shortly. But I ask you: Who then gives advantage to the enemy? The one who immobilizes three warships for three weeks or the one who immobilizes tens of thousands of fighters who ask to be sent into combat for three years [...]
>
> I came to fight—also to give something to the total struggle of our people, to the struggle of all people for freedom. And instead of finding the pure air of faith and fraternity of a legion of liberators, I found the infected and suffocating atmosphere of a nursery of praetorians. Instead of finding the anti-fascist army I dreamed of, I found an army infected by a band of political adventurers, fifth columnists and vulgar traitors, who were slowly and systematically carrying out their horrible crime against our homeland. The veil was torn, and I saw clearly. I realized in a flash precisely why the Greek Armed Forces of the Middle East had been created [...] Establish a body of mercenary praetorians and thus prepare the dynamic means of their political survival once they arrive in Greece after the liberation. At the top of the conspiracy was a clique of proven fascists who aimed

8 Emmanuel, Arghiri (1944) Apology. Translated By Daniel Williams.

> and are aiming at the establishment after the war of a fascist and plutocratic dictatorship with Georges Glyxbourg, the son of Constantine the Boche, at the head (uproar [...]). Around them a clique of bankrupt politicians, long accustomed to getting tangled in the murky waters of petty mayoral politics [...]
>
> In its path of betrayal and vassalage, the Government of Cairo was moving further and further away from the Greek people [...] Since the first moments of its creation, the E.A.M. embraced the overwhelming majority of the Greek people, this people thirsty for the fight to leave the conqueror. In no other country, with the sole possible exception of Yugoslavia, has the liberation movement taken on such a universal form. It was no longer the underground action of conspirators, it was the cosmogonic spasm of an entire people who do not accept the chains of slavery [...]
>
> The more the Popular revolutionary movement strengthened in Greece, the more asserted the reaction in the Middle East and the deeper the pit of our national split became. The reaction in the Middle East had to lead the fight on two fronts: 1) Strike by any means the popular liberation movement growing in Greece. 2) Politically appropriate the Greek forces of the Middle East in order to be sure to use them to impose themselves in Greece when the moment of the final combat with the E.A.M. would come. To achieve the first she used two means: a) The conspiracy of silence b) Collaboration with the invader.[9]

Emmanuel and his comrades received a death penalty for treason. However, by the end of 1945, Emmanuel was granted amnesty and instead sent to a British prison camp in Sudan. While in the prison camp, he wrote a textbook on dialectic materialism for his fellow prisoners.[10] For sure he had become a Marxist. In March 1946 he was released, but with his record and the defeat of the communists in the Greek Civil war, the prospect of finding work in Greece was limited, so he went back to the Congo.

In Relation to Patrice Lumumba[11]

In the Congo in the late '40s, he directed different commercial and building enterprises. In the '50s the anti-colonial liberation movement was on the rise in Africa. There was the Kenya Land and Freedom Army (aka Mau Mau) rebellion in 1952-57, the African National Congress (ANC) in South Africa organized protests and civil disobedience up through the 1950s, and Ghana became inde-

9 Translation by Daniel Williams.

10 Emmanuel's personal copy of this book was supplied by Catherine Emmanuel to the Emmanuel Archive at the International Institute of Social History (IISG), in Amsterdam.

11 See also Ilonga, Héritier (2024) "Arghiri Emmanuel, the law of unequal exchange, and the failures of liberation in the DR the Congo", and Ilonga, Héritier (2024) "Arghiri Emmanuel, the Free Republic of the Congo, and socialism—not capitalism—first", *ROAPE*, Vol. 4 and Vol. 11, September 2024.

pendent in 1957 with Kwame Nkrumah as president. On the global level, the Chinese communists had proclaimed the People's Republic of China in 1949, and the Bandung conference gathering the newly independent countries in Asia took place in 1955. In the Congo, this trend was reflected in the formation of different anti-colonial movements. A prominent figure in this development was Patrice Lumumba. Emmanuel became engaged in Congolese politics, reflected in his articles in the newspaper *Le Stanleyvillois*.[12] These dealt with political and economic questions, which hint at themes later to be developed in *L'Échange inégal* [Unequal Exchange] (1969) and *Le Profit et les crises* [Profit and Crises] (1974).

Emmanuel lived in Stanleyville, which became a stronghold for Patrice Lumumba. On May 22, 1960 Lumumba's party, the Congolese National Movement (*Mouvement National Congolais*, MNC), won the first general elections in the country, which was then still known as the Belgian Congo. On June 24, 1960, Lumumba assumed the role of Prime Minister in the newly established government. Independence from Belgium was declared on June 30, 1960, with the country renaming itself the (Free) Republic of the Congo that year. Emmanuel became an advisor to the Lumumba government, preparing the economic policy for an independent Congo. A week after independence, on July 6, 1960, Emmanuel held a speech at a dinner party at the Hotel Stanley in Stanleyville, addressed to the Provincial President of the MNC. In this quite personal speech, Emmanuel publicly declared his support for Lumumba:

> I wondered if you have an accurate idea of what the condition of an anti-colonialist white person within a colonial society represents: Rejected by his own clan, and unable to enter deep into the indigenous society, where he encounters incomprehension and mistrust, he finds himself in an untenable position, at odds with the world. It is a drama of every day and every moment [...] the wall of colonialism that stood between you and us, prevented our fingers from shaking [...] Our gaze was not as direct before June 30 as it was after. It was the opaque smokescreen of colonialism that troubled it. If you knew, you who are jubilant today for having been freed from the colonialist yoke, if you knew the joy that is ours, to have been freed from an even more terrible yoke, to have been freed from ourselves, from our complexes, from this inversion of values, in which we struggled without a way out [...] If we do not feel responsible for the specific crimes of colonialism, we certainly feel responsible for its aberration. This monstrous aberration of our Western civilization of the last three centuries, which has wasted so many ideals and so much good will [...] I will not sleep peacefully until colonialism is erased not only from the earth, from all lands, but also from the thoughts and memories of men. This is why we are answering your call. The path you have chosen is the right one: Drive out colonialism as an institution, be understanding of men. Punish, if necessary, the great exploits of the colonialists, forget the small deeds and gestures of the whites under the old regime, these small miscellaneous facts which constituted the inseparable corollary of a lifestyle imposed by colonialism. In this way, you can count on us.

12 These can also be found as part of the Emmanuel archive at IISG.

> Long live the MNC of the Eastern Province.
>
> Long live the Republic of the Congo.[13]

The Congo had been declared independent, and Lumumba had won the election and formed a government, but that government surely was not in full control of the state apparatus. On the contrary, Emmanuel's statement had provoked the settler-controlled police and intelligence service. Shortly thereafter, on July 16, 1960, an arrest order was issued for Emmanuel:

> Whereas Mr. EMMANUEL Arghiri, born in Patras, (Greece), on July 22, 1911, holder of the status of permanent resident, is undesirable and by his presence and conduct compromises and threatens to further compromise tranquility and public order; Whereas it is undesirable on the basis of information received from the Belgian Government and foreign Governments; Whereas through his subversive activities, his declarations and speeches he constitutes a threat to the internal and external security of the Republic of the Congo, to tranquility and public order; Whereas in particular by his activities he is attempting to place the Republic of the Congo under the direct or indirect domination of a foreign Government; that to do so he has, among other things, helped to foment unrest, create and maintain a state of mind in rebellion against legal powers, provoke the excitement of law enforcement against their hierarchical superiors and established powers. Arrest: Mr. EMMANUEL Arghiri, permanent resident awaiting expulsion, is placed at the disposal of the government for the duration of the expulsion procedure. He will be immediately incarcerated at Stanleyville Central Prison.[14]

On the same day, Emmanuel was abducted and deported to Nairobi, together with another Greek citizen, Georges Yannakis, on a British military aircraft. Simultaneously, the Belgian government declared Emmanuel a threat to public safety. From Nairobi Emmanuel had to fly to Paris, where he sent a telegram on July 18 to Lumumba, informing him on the arrest, deportation, and his wish to return to the Congo:

> To: Patrice Lumumba, Prime Minister and Kasongo President of the National Assembly:
>
> STANLEYVILLE BELGIAN COLONIALISTS KIDNAPPED US ON JULY 16TH TAKEN
>
> AWAY BY FORCE ON ENGLISH MILITARY PLANE TAKEN TO NAIROBI UNDER
>
> ESCORT ENGLISH SOLDIERS STOP NO DECISION ON EXPULSION WAS
>
> COMMUNICATED TO US STOP THE ONLY PAPER WE HAVE SEEN IS AN ORDER
>
> FOR PROVISIONAL ARREST SIGNED BY BADJOKO STOP THE ONLY ACTIVITY
>
> THEY ARE ABLE TO ACCUSE US OF IS CLOSE COLLABORATION WITH MNC
>
> STANLEYVILLE STOP WE ENERGETICALLY ASK FOR YOUR PERSONAL

---

13 Emmanuel, Arghiri: (1960) "Speech given by Mr. A. Emmanuel, at the M.N.C. banquet, on July 6, at the Stanley Hotel, in Stanleyville, in response to the speech of the Provincial President of the M.N.C."

14 Arrest order, Ibid.

INTERVENTION WE WANT TO RETURN TO THE CONGO THAT WE LOVE PRAY

ANSWER US PARIS 61 RUE GRENELLE

YANNAKIS STOP EMMANUEL[15]

However, the telegram never reached its intended recipient. Emmanuel subsequently followed up with a letter to Lumumba, dated July 21, 1960, which also got lost. The arrest, deportation, and missed communications underscore the limited control Lumumba exercised over state institutions at the time. In the chaotic situation developing in the Congo, Lumumba only managed to reply to Emmanuel on November 12, 1960:

Georges YANNAKIS and ARGHIRI Emmanuel

Gentlemen,

Your registered letter dated July 21, 1960, reached me only today. I do not understand this long delay.—I deeply regret your departure from Stanleyville, a departure provoked by the intrigues of the Belgian colonialists.—I know your loyalty to our people and I deplore the humiliating measures to which you have been subjected.—I mark my words that you shall return to Stanleyville where you will only have friends.—I will do everything in my power to ensure that you live in the Congo in good conditions.—I am looking forward to seeing you again, please accept, Gentlemen, the assurance of my distinguished consideration.

P.E Lumumba,

Prime Minister of the Republic of the Congo.[16]

With this in hand, Emmanuel tried to get a visa to return to Congo, but no Congolese embassy would issue a visa to him. A few months later, on January 17, 1961, Lumumba was executed by rebels under command of Belgian soldiers. Despite Lumumba's death, further correspondence from the Congolese central administration followed. Letters dated February 11, May 2, and December 20, 1961 invited Emmanuel to return to the Congo. Emmanuel continued to advise the independence movement on economic matters. In his paper dated June 27, 1961, on the Congolese economy's transition from a colony to an independent state, there is the first formulation of "unequal exchange"[17]:

Colonialism maintains the colonized countries in the system of monoculture or some export crops and the extraction of raw materials. This is the clearest part of colonialist exploitation, an exploitation which is carried out not only for the benefit of the colonizer but on behalf of all the industrial countries [...] When an industrialized country exchanges its products with an underdeveloped country, it actually exchanges one hour of national labor for 5, 10 or 15 hours of labor in the other. This exchange rate

15 Emmanuel, Arghiri (1960), Telegram to Patrice Lumumba.

16 Lumumba, Patrice (1960) Letter to Emmanuel, dated 12 November 1960.

17 Emmanuel, Arghiri (1961) "Analysis of the Congo's economy". Unpublished paper.

in turn prohibits the underdeveloped country from carrying out its own capitalization and emerging from underdevelopment. This cycle must be broken.[18]

In Paris

Emmanuel ended up in Paris with nothing but the clothes he was wearing. He had lived in the Congo most of his adult life. It was there that he had his business, his house, and his friends. As late as 1967, he wrote directly to Sese Seko Mobutu, who had become president in the Congo in 1965, and asked for permission to return, but in vain.[19] While in the Congo, Emmanuel had some relation to Paris. From 1957 to 1960 he was enlisted at L'École du Louvre as a student in art history. However, now stuck permanently in Paris, at the age of fifty, he changed his mind concerning studies, switching from art history to political economy. He entered the École Pratique des Hautes Études to study socialist planning under Charles Bettelheim. Perhaps he had plans to acquire knowledge of economic planning and return to an independent Congo. Or perhaps he had developed some ideas on international trade through his business experience on which he wanted to elaborate.

The political developments in the Congo were negative. It soon became a neo-colony of Belgium and US mining interests. However, the anti-imperialist movements in general continued their progress in the Third World. The Cuban revolution in 1959, the Algerian war of liberation in 1954-62, the victory of the Vietnamese over France in Dien Bien Phu in 1954, the continued liberation of South Vietnam, the resistance against Portuguese colonialism in Africa, and so on. If you were to put pins on a map of the world to show every significant anti-imperialist movement at the time, it would quickly become evident that the prospects were positive in the '60s. This development on the ground was reflected in Marxist theory. Studies of imperialism and anti-imperialism blossomed. One school was "dependency theory". It described imperialism as a system consisting of a center or imperial core of North America, Western Europe, and Japan, and an exploited periphery—the Third World—which supplied the metropole with raw materials and tropical agricultural commodities produced by cheap labor. Emmanuel became part of this flux in theoretical understanding.

After less than two years of studies, in 1963, Emmanuel introduced the no-

18 Ibid.

19 Emmanuel, Arghiri (1967) Latter dated June 1967 to Mobuto. Emmanuel archive, ISSG Amsterdam

tion of "unequal exchange" in an article.[20] The second publication on "unequal exchange", "El Intercambio Desigual", appeared in the February 1964 edition of *Revue Economica*, a Cuban journal.[21] Emmanuel received a doctorate ("de 3ème cycle") in sociology from the Sorbonne based on his thesis "Lĕchange inégal" in 1968, the year of the student revolt in Paris. His thesis appeared in 1969 in book form, published by Maspero. In the following years, *Lĕchange inégal* [*Unequal Exchange*] was translated into English, Spanish, Portuguese, Italian, and Serbian. In the '70s, literally, hundreds of articles in academic journals and left-wing magazines discussed Emmanuel's groundbreaking critique of David Ricardo's classic theory of international trade and its modern versions. A controversial point in Emmanuel's book was the political consequences of unequal exchange. The idea was that the workers of rich countries benefit from the transfer of surplus value from the workers of poor countries. As a result, Emmanuel got many academic relations but few political friends.

On the personal level, his life also took a turn in Paris. In 1961 he married Nicole, and they had a daughter, Catherine, in 1971. With his PhD thesis in place in 1968 and its publications by the prestigious publisher Maspero in 1969, Emmanuel's academic career was launched. His career was rather short, since he was already 58 years old. He was appointed Associate Professor at the University of Paris I in 1969. In the same year, he became Director of the Economics Department, UER of Geography and Social Sciences, at the University of Paris VII, and from 1972 he was Director at the International Economic Relations Department at the Institute of Economics and Social Development Studies (IEDES), until his retirement in 1981.

After retirement, Emmanuel continued to study and publish on the subject of development and underdevelopment. He especially emphasized the role of the transfer of technology for the development of the productive forces in the Third World. His book *Appropriate or Underdeveloped Technology?* was published in French 1981 and soon translated to English.[22] The book envisioned the rise of China and caused much debate, as Emmanuel stated that multinational corporations' outsourcing of industrial production to the Third World was historically progressive since it developed the productive forces through the transfer of technology. Emmanuel stated: "*Capitalism is bad but underdevel-*

20 Emmanuel, Arghiri (1963) "Échange inégal", Revue "Problemes de Planification", No. 2. Paris, 1963.

21 Emmanuel, Arghiri (1964) EL INTERCAMBIO DESIGUAL, in Revue Economica, La Havane, Fevrier, 1964.

22 Emmanuel, Arghiri (1982) *Appropriate or Underdeveloped Technology?* John Wiley & Sons, Chichester. London 1982.

oped capitalism is worse."[23]

A personal tragedy, his wife's sudden death in 1990 at the young age of 53, had a huge impact on Emmanuel in the last part of his life. He died in 2001 and was buried at the Cimetière du Montparnasse in Paris besides his wife. His friend and assistant from the university years, Claudio Jedlicki, and Emmanuel's colleague Serge Latouche held speeches at the funeral. Jedlicki also became caretaker of Emmanuel's archive. At the time—the heyday of neoliberal globalization—few were interested in the political economy of imperialism, and Jedlicki did not manage to find an institution interested in Emmanuel's papers. However, things have changed. In the past decade, there has been a growing interest in Emmanuel's work. In 2021, the Emmanuel Association was established, dedicated to spreading the knowledge of Emmanuel's ideas. The association has a website with articles by and about Emmanuel. In 2024, the association, together with Emmanuel's daughter Catherine, signed a contract with the International Institute of Social History in Amsterdam to host Emmanuel's archive.

The course of Emmanuel's life as a political activist and his theoretical academic work reflects the 20th century. His childhood and youth were characterized by wars, fascism, and capitalist economic crises. He spent nineteen years of his adult life in one of the most brutal colonial regimes. He took an active part in the national liberation struggle of the Congo, and he lived in Paris during the 1968 rebellion. These first-hand impressions and experiences during the first fifty years of his life were an important basis for the ideas he developed in the latter part of his life. As Mao explains in his essay "On Practice":

> Knowing is through perception and experience from lived practice, to arrive at the thought, to develop concepts, and arrive step by step at the comprehension of the internal contradictions of objective things. It is to develop a logical knowledge capable of grasping the development of the surrounding world in its totality, in the internal relations of all its aspects.[24]

23 Ibid.

24 Tse-tung, Mao (1937) On Practice, in Tse-tung, Mao, *Selected Works*. Vol. I. Foreign Languages Press: Peking, 1965.

2

The Political Economy of Unequal Exchange

EMMANUEL'S EXAMINATION OF FOREIGN TRADE AND UNEQUAL EXCHANGE was a direct extension of Marx's *Capital*. It is firmly based on Marx's perception of value and the accumulation process of capital. Marx had plans to investigate foreign trade more closely in a fourth volume of *Capital* but never got to write it. In the preface to his *A Contribution to the Critique of Political Economy* written in 1857, Marx wrote:

> I examine the system of bourgeois economy in the following order: capital, landed property, wage-labour; the State, foreign trade, world market.[1]

Of the planned six volumes of *Capital*, only the first was published during Marx's lifetime. The second volume appeared in 1885, and the third in 1894, both compiled by Friedrich Engels. What is called the fourth volume, *Theories of Surplus Value* was edited by Karl Kautsky and published in 1904. Marx's intentions were to conclude the critique of political economy with a volume of *Capital* which examined the accumulation of capital on the world scale. Unfortunately, Marx did not manage to complete this project.

In short, the work *Capital* as envisioned by Marx is incomplete and, in the later parts, very fragmented. Capitalism cannot be isolated to the sphere of production, which is the focus of the first volume. The accumulation of capital is a process of production and circulation—on the global level. Emmanuel picked up this loose thread of Marx's incomplete project.

Like Marx, Emmanuel's theory of international trade was based on a critique of the classic political economists, in this case David Ricardo (1772-1823).

1 Marx, Karl (1859). *A Contribution to the Critique of Political Economy*. Preface. Moscow: Progress Publishers, 1977, with some notes by R. Rojas.

Emmanuel sought to critique Ricardo's theory of comparative advantage, according to which international trade benefits all participants. However, before we turn to how capitalism works at the global level today, we must begin with the Marxist theory of capitalism in general, and in particular the theory of value, since it is upon this foundation that Emmanuel built his theory.

Primitive Accumulation

Capitalism did not fall from the sky. It grew inside the feudal mode of production, nourished by its contradiction. Marx and Engels write in the *Manifesto of the Communist Party:*

> We see then: the means of production and of exchange, on whose foundation the bourgeoisie built itself up, were generated in feudal society. At a certain stage in the development of these means of production and of exchange, the conditions under which feudal society produced and exchanged, the feudal organisation of agriculture and manufacturing industry, in one word, the feudal relations of property became no longer compatible with the already developed productive forces; they became so many fetters. They had to be burst asunder; they were burst asunder.[2]

The disintegration of feudalism and the creation of the prerequisites of the capitalist mode of production are referred to by Marx as "primitive (or 'original') accumulation"—primitive because the birth of capitalism cannot be explained by the law of accumulation of the capitalist mode of production itself. The accumulation of value which constituted primitive capital was not a result of capitalist exploitation of wage labor but of violence and open theft.

In the chapter "The so-called primitive accumulation" in *Capital* Marx describes it as the process of creating the basic conditions of capitalist production: at one pole, the creation of "free" propertyless laborers, unencumbered with the means of production; at the other, the creation of the owners of money, means of production and means of subsistence, whose only aim is to increase the sum of value they possess—in short, the capitalists.[3]

The original capital was generated by the plunder of the colonies in the Asian and American continents, combined with the trade and exploitation of slaves from Africa in the 16th and 17th century. Marx writes:

> The discovery of gold and silver in America, the extirpation, enslavement and entombment in mines of the aboriginal population, the beginning of the conquest and looting of the East Indies, the turning of Africa into a warren for the commercial hunting of

2 Marx, Karl and Engels, Freidrich (1848) *The Communist Manifesto*, in Marx and Engels, *Selected Works* Moscow: Progress Publishers, 1970, p. 40.

3 Marx, Karl (1867) *Capital* Vol. I, part VIII, Progress Publishers, 1962. Moscow.

> blackskins, signalised the rosy dawn of the era of capitalist production. These idyllic proceedings are the chief momenta of primitive accumulation. On their heels treads the commercial war of the European nations, with the globe for a theatre [...]
>
> The different momenta of primitive accumulation distribute themselves now, more or less in chronological order, particularly over Spain, Portugal, Holland, France, and England. In England at the end of the 17th century, they arrive at a systematical combination, embracing the colonies, the national debt, the modern mode of taxation, and the protectionist system. These methods depend in part on brute force, e.g., the colonial system. But they all employ the power of the State, the concentrated and organised force of society, to hasten, hot-house fashion, the process of transformation of the feudal mode of production into the capitalist mode, and to shorten the transition. Force is the midwife of every old society pregnant with a new one. It is itself an economic power.[4]

As primitive accumulation and the exploitation of the colonial areas were a condition of the breakthrough of industrial capitalism, they also created a world-system which, from its establishment, was polarized in a center-periphery structure, laying the foundation of the future transfer of value by unequal exchange.

The Commodity

Marx's critique of capitalism is based on an analysis of the commodity. Commodities can be thought of as the cells of the capitalist system. In the commodity, we find the DNA of capitalism. It contains the contradictions that drive the system from a simple exchange of goods in a medieval town square to today's globalized capitalism. In *Capital*, Marx unfolds the logic of capitalism in increasing complexity, from the commodity cell to the full body of capitalism.

The mechanism of unequal exchange does not deviate from the laws of capitalist development put forward in the three volumes of *Capital* but relies on them and uses them to explain the dynamics of capitalist trade and production at the global level. I will follow how Marx's concept of value unfolds from the contradiction in the commodity to the sphere of nation states, international trade, and finally to the current form of globalized capitalism. I will focus on how the international transfer of value—imperialism—became the mode in which the contradictions in capitalism could move ahead, developing the productive forces and giving the system a dynamic development up through the twentieth century, and how it is approaching its limits in the twenty-first century.

A commodity is a product of human labor, made by an independent producer with the intention of exchanging it. Emmanuel writes:

---

4 Ibid., p. 703.

> [...] behind the comparison between commodities, lies hidden a comparison between the different labors needed to produce them.
>
> If man ever troubled to compare things so unlike each other as a canoe and cow, it is solely in order to be able to pay as correctly as possible for the labor of those who had produced each of them, when these producers had become independent of each other [...]
>
> Reducing complex to simple labor is not an effect of the market; it results from production carried on with the market in view. It is obvious that without the market there would be neither abstract labor nor value, but that does not mean that these are determined by the market.[5]

A commodity has two forms of value: use-value and exchange-value. Its use-value is defined as its ability to satisfy a physical or psychological need, such as a raincoat or a teddy bear. The use-value is mainly of interest to the buyer. No matter how different their use-value is, commodities have something in common, which makes them comparable on a certain level of abstraction in quantitative terms. This commonality is what Marx calls value—or more specifically *exchange-value* (to distinguish it from *use-value*). Exchange-value is defined as the quantitative relation between commodities no matter how different they are. Thus, for example, one smartphone may equal twenty pairs of sneakers.

The exchange relation between different commodities varies according to the circumstances under which the exchange occurs. Commodity exchange may thus immediately appear to be rather accidental. However, this is not the case. What all commodities have in common is that they are produced by human labor for exchange on the market. The exchange-value is a manifestation of the value which the commodity has by virtue of being a product of human labor. What is actually compared at the commodity exchange is not the exchange-value itself, but the human labor inherent in the commodity.

Both use-value and exchange-value are rooted in human labor. Use-value is related to the concrete labor necessary to produce a commodity: sewing, welding, etc. Use-value and concrete labor are qualitative in nature and satisfy needs. Exchange-value relates to abstract labor—or the consumption of human labor-power—which is quantitative in nature, measuring the time, energy, and skills needed to produce the commodity. Of particular importance is the socially necessary labor time, which is the time required to produce a commodity based on the average quality and intensity of labor and the available technology. Thus, abstract labor forms the basis of the value of the commodity, which is compared to the value of other commodities when exchanged.

---

5 Emmanuel, Arghiri (1972) *Unequal Exchange: A Study of the Imperialism of Trade*, pp. 3-5. New York: Monthly Review Press, 1972.

Thus, commodity exchange is not a relation between objects or things. Whether something is a commodity does not depend on certain physical qualities but on the social relationship between seller and buyer. This exchange of values appears to be a relation between things, but it is in fact a social relation between people. Engels writes:

> Political economy begins with commodities, with the moment when products are exchanged, either by individuals or by primitive communities. The product being exchanged is a commodity. But it is a commodity merely because of the thing, the product being linked with a relation between two persons or communities, the relation between producer and consumer, who at this stage are no longer united in the same person. Here is at once an example of a peculiar fact, which pervades the whole of economics and has produced serious confusion in the minds of bourgeois economists: economics is not concerned with things but with relations between persons, and in the final analysis between classes; these relations, however, are always bound to things and appear as things.[6]

We can neither touch nor see value as such. We can only touch and see the commodities that have value. Value can be measured in labor time or in quantities of other commodities, but it is not a quality physically embedded in commodities. It is not an intrinsic quality which has been injected into the commodity by productive labor. As Marx put it, "*So far no chemist has ever discovered exchange-value either in a pearl or a diamond.*"[7] The ultimate test of value is the market: whatever can be sold is a commodity. It has use-value for the buyer, and it is on the market that the exchange-value unfolds. Value becomes an exchange-value on the market; in the sphere of production, value is only a *possibility*. No sale, no value. The term *exchange-value* was not chosen randomly by Marx.

The Double Character of Exchange-Value

Not only does the commodity have a dual character in the form of use-value and exchange-value, but exchange-value itself also has a dual nature. Its magnitude can be measured in two distinct ways. Externally, it is the market exchange ratio of commodities: two coats in exchange for a chair, equivalent to say 100 dollars—a market price. Intrinsically, it is the quantity of socially necessary abstract labor—a number of hours at a certain level of skill. In Marx's famous words:

> 20 yards of linen = 1 coat or = 10 lbs. tea or = 40 lbs. coffee or = 1 quarter corn or = 2 ounces gold or = ½ ton iron or = &c. [...] The value of a single commodity, the linen, for

6 Engels, Friedrich (1859) *Review of Karl Marx: Critique of Political Economy*, In Marx and Engels *Collected Works*, vol. 16, p. 476. Moscow: Progress Publishers, 1976. Emphasis original.

7 Marx, Karl (1867). *Capital*, Vol. I: Part I: Commodities and Money, Chapter One: Commodities, section 4: 'The fetishism of commodities and the secret thereof', p. 53. Moscow: Progress Publishers. 1962.

> example, is now expressed in terms of numberless other elements of the world of commodities. Every other commodity now becomes a mirror of the linen's value. It is thus, that for the first time, this value shows itself in its true light as a congelation of undifferentiated human labour. For the labour that creates it, now stands expressly revealed, as labour that ranks equally with every other sort of human labour, no matter what its form, whether tailoring, ploughing, mining, &c., and no matter, therefore, whether it is realised in coats, corn, iron, or gold.[8]

These two representations of exchange-value, expressed as money, are the price of a commodity and the wage for the labor time needed to produce it.[9] Marx writes:

> The value (the real exchange-value) of all commodities (labour included) is determined by their cost of production, in other words by the labour time required to produce them. Their price is this exchange-value of theirs, expressed in money.[10]

It is human labor in the production process that is the source of value. However, the specific determination of the actual exchange-value occurs on the market. The blood, sweat, and tears of living concrete labor in production is transformed by the process of the market into the dead social objectivity of exchange-value—a market price.

The fact that all commodities are products of human labor is what makes it possible to relate them to one another. Thus, value reconciles the production sphere and the circulation sphere in capitalist accumulation. Both are necessary for the realization of value. In the preface to the first volume of *Capital* published in 1867, Marx announced his plans for four volumes: one on capitalist production, one on the circulation of capital, one on "the varied forms assumed by capital in the course of its development," and one on "the history of the theory." In a letter to Engels, dated July 31, 1865, Marx wrote that the volumes were to be considered as an "artistic whole."[11] If one only reads the first volume, one's impression might be that production is essential and circulation secondary. However, Marx was very clear about the relationship between production and circulation in the valorization of capital:

> Capital cannot [...] arise from circulation, and it is equally impossible for it to arise apart

---

8 Marx, Karl (1867) *Capital*, Vol. One, Part I: Commodities and Money, Chapter One: Commodities, Section 3 - The Form of Value or Exchange-Value, B. Total or Expanded Form of Value, 1. The Expanded Relative Form of Value. Moscow: Progress Publishers, 1962.

9 I will return to the importance of this dual character of exchange-value, for international transfer of value on page 69.

10 Marx, Karl (1857) *Grundrisse*, Notebook I—The Chapter on Money. New York and London: Penguin Books in association with New Left Review, 1973.

11 Marx, Karl (1865) Letter to Engels, dated July 31, 1865. In Karl Marx & Freidrich Engels: *Collected Works*, Vol. 42, p. 173. Moscow: Progress Publishers, 1975.

from circulation. It must have its origin both in circulation and not in circulation.[12]

In the polemic with Charles Bettelheim in the book *Unequal Exchange*, Emmanuel explains the relation between production and circulation in the process of specifying and distributing value in society:

> Exchange is not, as Bettelheim supposes, something that complements production at a level external to the latter, and at most a condition for capitalist production; it is an essential moment of this production.[13] Once we assume the existence of private ownership, it is not value that leads to exchange, but exchange that necessarily results in value.[14] Can production be dissociated from exchange? I do not think it can, and I consider that the reproach Bettelheim brings against me, that I situate exploitation in the sphere of circulation and exchange, is ill-founded, since no such "sphere" exists in reality, and every phenomenon is organically included in the entire system of social production relations, in which production and exchange are inextricably interlinked [...]
>
> This surplus product, though the condition and presupposition for exploitation, does not in itself constitute exploitation. The latter begins not with the creation of surplus product but with its **appropriation**.
>
> Now, appropriation, in the context of the distinction just made, is a matter of exchange, not of production. It begins with the contract for the purchase of labour power, made between the capitalist and the worker. This contract Marx himself describes as an act of exchange [...]
>
> We know at this stage only the worker's nominal wage, whereas exploitation depends on his real wage, which will not be known until after the circulation and realization of the product.
>
> After the contract comes the act of production in the true sense. During this act nothing happens by way of exploitation. The exploitation engendered by the preliminary contract of employment is in suspension, kept on ice, so to speak. Finally comes the phase of circulation and the exchange of the product, in the course of which not only does the "subject," the agent, of exploitation change, since the surplus-value produced is partly transferred from one "subject" to another—from the industrialist to the rentier, or to the merchant, or to the banker, etc., and also from one branch to another and from one country to another—but also the volume, of exploitation changes, since the total amount of surplus-value is modified by the prices at which the workers' consumer goods will be sold. **Exploitation is not a fact of production but of appropriation**.[15]
> [16]

---

12 Marx, Karl (1867). *Capital*, Vol. I: "Part II, Ch. 5: Contradictions in the General Formula. p. 268. Moscow: Progress Publishers, 1962.

13 Cf. Marx, *Grundrisse* (Principes d'une critique de l'economie politique), Pleiade edition of Oeuvres de Karl Marx: Economic (Paris, 1968), 2: 258.

14 Cf. Marx, Notes de Lecture, Pleiade edition of Oeuvres de Karl Marx: Economie, 2: 17.

15 This argument was suggested to me by Ricardo Guastini, Professor at the University of Genoa.

16 Emmanuel, Arghiri (1972) *Unequal Exchange: A Study of the Imperialism of Trade*, pp. 327-329. New York: Monthly Review Press, 1972. Emphasis original.

The Value of Labor-Power and Surplus Value

Labor is the common measure of the value of all commodities. However, the commodity that is purchased via wages is not an ordinary commodity. To the capitalist, the commodity labor-power has one quality which is different from the qualities of all other commodities. The use-value of labor-power, for the capitalist, consists of producing commodities whose exchange-value exceeds the costs of the labor-power required to produce them. In order to exploit labor-power in this way, capitalists must own means of production. What the capitalist buys is the labor-power of the worker: the strengths, the energy, the knowledge, and the commitment for a specific quantity of time. To maintain this power, the worker needs a certain supply of substances. The value of the labor-power is the amount of labor necessary to produce these substances. However, the two quantities—the labor-power and its value—are not equal. The labor time and energy the worker delivers are more valuable than the value of the substances the worker needs to be able to deliver the labor-power. Just as with other commodities, the value and use-value of labor-power are different. Labor-power's use-value for capital is its capacity to produce an amount of commodities, the exchange-value of which is greater than the exchange-value of labor-power itself. This difference is what Marx called surplus value—which is the source of profit.[17]

For our further investigation, we can divide the workday into two periods: one in which the worker reproduces the value of their labor-power and another in which they create surplus value.[18] The rate of surplus value depends on the extent of the second period. The rate of surplus value therefore indicates the level of exploitation of labor-power:

> The rate of surplus-value is defined in terms of hours as: the time of surplus-value divided by the time required to reproduce the value of labor-power.

Alternatively, the rate of surplus value, in terms of money, the universal equivalent for all other commodities, can be defined as:

The "variable capital" equals the wage. It is labelled "variable" because it changes size during the accumulation process. One hour of labor can produce

17 The Marxist concepts of value and surplus value are of no interest to workers or capitalists. What they are interested in are prices, wages, and profit. These concepts are certainly also of interest to us; however, in order to understand how these forms of appearance of value are generated and divided, we need to explain the basis for these forms of presentation.

18 Marx, Karl (1867) *Capital*, Vol. 1: Part III. Chapter Nine: The Rate of Surplus-value, pp. 162-164, Moscow: Progress Publishers, 1962.

$$\textit{Rate of Surplus Value} = \frac{\textit{Surplus Value}}{\textit{Variable Capital}} \qquad \left(s' = \frac{s}{v}\right)$$

Figure I

commodities that have more value than the value of one hour of labor (i.e., than the value of the substances needed to produce one hour of labor). But the value of labor is not only measured hours. It is also a question of intensity and productivity—sweat and skills. We have to define those properties:

> Intensity of labor means the output of a unit of labor with a given set of equipment. It is important not to confuse this concept with productivity, which increases with the increase in the equipment available—new technology. More intense labor produces more use-values and more value (more labor-power goes into the commodities); more productive labor produces more use-values but the same value (the same amount of labor-power goes into the commodities).

There are basically three ways capital can increase the rate of surplus value and thereby the potential volume of profit:

1. **Increase the absolute surplus value** by an extension of working time and/or the intensification of work, in relation to the required working hours to reproduce the "basket of goods" which forms the value of labor-power.
2. **Increase the relative surplus value** by a productivity increase as a result of new technology or more effective management forms, which reduces the "necessary working hours for the reproduction of labor" share of the total working hours.
3. **Extract super-surplus value** by lowering the value of the wages below the level of reproductive costs, even beneath the subsistence level, and thus the "necessary working time" share of the total working hours.

The concept of "super-exploitation" originates from Ruy Mauro Marini (1932–1997), a Brazilian economist known as one of the creators of "Dependency Theory". In his book *Dialéctica de la Dependencia,* he describes how the breakthrough of industrialization in England in the nineteenth century was dependent on imports of cheap food products, produced through the super-exploitation of labor in countries such as Ireland and the countries of Latin America. This export-oriented capitalism in the periphery created a dynamic capitalist development in the center and underdevelopment in the periphery. Marini defines super-exploitation as:

> [...] the intensification of work, the extension of the working day, and the expropria-

> tion of part of the labor necessary for the worker to replenish his labor-power— [...] In capitalist terms, these mechanisms (which, moreover, can and usually do occur in combination) mean that labor-power is remunerated below its value, and thus amount to a super-exploitation of labor.[19]

The "intensification and extension of the working day" equals Marx's absolute surplus value. However, it is the last form in the list—the expropriation of the labor needed for replenishment—which is of special interest here. Marini is referring to wage depression in the colonial areas (to below the value of labor-power) when he mentions expropriating the part of the labor necessary for the laborer to reproduce his labor-power. Marini furthermore draws the interesting conclusion that the super-exploitation of labor-power in the periphery changes the pattern of the extraction of surplus value in England from being dependent on absolute surplus value (longer and more intensified labor) to relative surplus value (greater productivity) due to the dynamic development of industrial capitalism in the second half of the nineteenth century. Marini writes:

> Beyond facilitating the quantitative growth of these countries, Latin-American's participation in the world market will contribute to shifting the axis of accumulation in the industrial economy from the production of absolute surplus-value to that of relative surplus-value; that is, that accumulation will come to depend more on increasing labor's productive capacity than simply the exploitation of the worker. It is this contradictory character of Latin American dependency, which determines the relation of production of the capitalist system as a whole, that should draw our attention.[20]

The development of the productive forces in the center due to colonial super-exploitation increased the relative surplus value considerably. However, the working class in the center managed to get its share of the gains from the increased productivity by raising their level of wages through class struggle in the second half of the 19th century.[21]

In a letter to Samir Amin, Emmanuel wrote:

> I note in passing and with pleasure a sentence on page 121 where you state that the rate of surplus-value measures the relationship of power between the workers and the capitalists. This is my most intimate conviction. On page 51 you say that monopoly makes the phenomenon of the labour aristocracy possible. I don't know what you mean exactly by that. On page 85, you return to this subject by speaking of "mechanisms which enable monopoly capitalism to ensure a continuous growth of wages at the centre". If you mean to say that not only do the external surpluses enable the monopolies to provide this growth, but that the monopolies as such react in a more realistic and positive

---

19 Marini, Ruy Mauro (1974) *The Dialectics of Dependency*, ed. Amanda Latimer and Jaime Osorio, page 131-132. New York: Monthly Review Press. 2022.

20 Ibid., pp. 120-121.

21 Lauesen, Torkil (2018) *The Global Perspective, Reflections on Imperialism and Resistance*, Montreal: Kersplebedebm, 2018, p.54.

> way than competitive capitalism to workers' demands, it seems to me that this is indeed correct.[22]

There is no necessarily built-in relationship between a rise in productivity and an increase in wages; who gains is a question of class struggle.[23]

I will return to the importance of super-exploitation as a generator of surplus value in contemporary global capitalism, based on low wage labor arbitrage.[24] First, however, I will address the relation between the value of labor-power and the development of highly differentiated wage levels in global capitalism.

The Price of Labor-Power—The Wage

Labor-power is not like other commodities. There is no factory that produces labor-power. Labor-power does not produce labor-power. Labor-power is generated in the private sphere of society—mostly. The commodity that capital purchases for the wages is not the worker's labor but the labor-power, the skills and energy that enables the worker to produce commodities for a certain number of hours. In order to gain and regain these skills and energy the worker needs to consume a certain "basket" of commodities, produced in the capitalist sphere. In addition an amount of service such as care, cooking and cleaning is provided by the household. The value of this "basket" of commodities and services defines the value of labor-power.

However, the value that labor-power produces in the form of commodities is not equal to the value of commodities in the basket. The labor time a worker can put in is longer than the time needed to produce the commodities the worker must consume in order to perform this labor. The difference constitutes the source of profit realized by the sale of the commodity on the market.

---

22 Among the papers found in Emmanuel's archive is a long undated response to Samir Amin with comments to the manuscript of Amin's book: *L'accumulation a L'echelle Mondiale* [*Accumulation on World Scale*]. The Book was published in 1970; hence, the letter must be from before. There is no introduction in the document so maybe some pages are missing. The text starts rather abruptly with comments about the connection between wages and productivity. This letter (indeed, all his letters) is not listed in Emmanuel's own CV and biography. This quote is from p. 7 in the document.

23 For a historical account for the development of wages in the late nineteenth century in England, see: Lauesen, Torkil. (2018). *The Global Perspective, Reflections on Imperialism and Resistance*, pp. 52-55. Montreal: Kersplebedeb, 2018.

24 Smith, J. (2016). *Imperialism in the Twenty-first Century*. New York: Monthly Review Press, 2016.

But what defines this "basket of goods" and how is its price (being also the price of labor-power, the wage) determined? Marx distinguished between two factors determining the value of labor-power: the bare reproduction costs of labor-power and what he called the "historical and moral element." The bare reproduction costs of labor-power relate to the costs that are necessary to keep the working class alive, fit to work, and able to have children who become new workers. In simple terms, they are the costs necessary for food, clothes, and shelter. When a worker receives a wage that covers only the bare minimum of what is necessary to reproduce the ability to work, it is often called a subsistence wage. This was basically the wage paid up until the mid-19th century. It could vary because of natural conditions, such as climate, soil fertility, and so on, but it was more or the less the same globally. However, the development of industrial capitalism in Europe, in combination with the European colonial empires and the large-scale trade union struggle, broke that pattern.

In addition to the "basket" of essentials Marx added the "historical factor":

> The number and extent of his so-called necessary wants, as also the modes of satisfying them, are themselves the product of historical development, and depend therefore to a great extent on the degree of civilisation of a country, more particularly on the conditions under which, and consequently on the habits and degree of comfort in which, the class of free labourers has been formed. In contradistinction therefore to the case of other commodities, there enters into the determination of the value of labour-power a historical and moral element. Nevertheless, in a given country, at a given period, the average quantity of the means of subsistence necessary for the labourer is practically known.[25]

In other words, the historical and moral element of the value of labor-power is a product of class struggle—national and international, historical and current. This class struggle and its entire historical and economic basis determines the wage level, and through this process also the level of surplus value (which depends on the value of labor-power) and hence the profit-rate for capital.

The long history of capitalism, the creation of a world divided into a center and periphery by colonialism and imperialism—together with the limited international mobility of labor—helps explain the development of differences in wages globally. In the imperialist core, the price of labor-power (the wage) is relatively stable over time within a specific country. There are norms, rules, laws, and union regulations about the length of the working day, working conditions, overtime, minimum wages, piece rates, etc. which makes the variability of wages comparatively limited. A similar tendency cannot be seen internationally.

The relative stability of the wage levels in time and their variation with place

25 Marx, Karl (1867). *Capital*, Vol. 1: "Part II, chapter six: The buying and selling of labour-power", p. 121. Moscow: Progress Publishers, 1962.

in the world-system stands in contrast with the price for other commodities, which varies significantly over time but is relatively stable from place to place. The prices for copper and wheat, for example, go up and down almost daily, but they do so across the world. There is a world market price for most commodities, with labor-power as a significant exception. Within countries, especially imperialist ones, there is a tendency for wages for the same kind of work to balance out. Globally, however, the differences remain huge.

Emmanuel writes:

> From remotest antiquity to the beginning of the 19th century, the wage has, in real terms, hardly varied in any country; from the beginning of the 19th century up to the present it has, in certain countries, moved slowly and steadily upwards. Such a constancy in certain periods or certain countries, such an evenness and duration of a one-dimensional movement in certain other periods and other countries, are contrary to the endogenous economic determinations which are plastic and multiform. An extra-economic (institution) vector alone can generate them.
>
> At any rate, on the international plane, the multiplicity of wage rates is inconsistent with the existence of a market since the essential function of the market is precisely to secure one price for each item. Now in the case of wages, this disparity continues without the slightest attenuation, even when, here or there and in certain epochs, the labour-factor enjoys a relatively important mobility. Neither the great immigration of Europeans into the United States during the 19th century and the beginning of the 20th, nor the contemporary considerable immigration of North Africans, Portuguese, Greeks, etc., into the developed countries of Western Europe after the last war, have given rise to the slightest tendency towards the equalization of wages between the countries of origin and the host countries.
>
> [...] There is no relevance between the conjunctural fluctuations of employment in different countries and the comparative rates of wages in these same countries. For example: during the 1929-34 crisis, unemployment in the United States was 36.47% of the active population against 13.42% in France and only 7% in Italy. Yet the American wage remained, during the worst of the crisis, two to three times that in France and three to four times that in Italy.
>
> We can conclude that the determination of wages is more a political than an economic process. Its variations reflect the fluctuations of the relations of power between social classes. This extra-economic institutional determination makes possible a lasting gap between the price and value of labour power.
>
> However, these two magnitudes continue to be connected to each other in a dialectical interaction. A wage greater than the value of labour power, if it prevails for a long time, ends by driving upwards this value itself, since the extra consumption which it allows ends by being transformed into vital needs—what Marx calls a second nature—and, hence, by being incorporated into the real cost of reproduction of the labour force.[26]

The "moral and historical element" in the determination of the value of

---

26 Emmanuel, Arghiri (1975) 'Unequal Exchange Revisited', pp. 49-50. IDS Discussion Paper No. 77 Institute of Development Studies, Sussex University, Brighton, UK.

labor-power is sometimes used to explain the difference in wages on the global level. However, there is no "moral" component, which legitimizes a higher wage for the workers in Europe than for the proletariat in the Third World. If the difference between wages at the Volvo factory in Gothenburg in Sweden and Durban in South Africa is due to a "historical and moral component" then the history is colonialism and imperialism and the "moral component" is racism.[27]

The Globalized Value of Labor-Power

As mentioned before, Marx never gave a coherent and comprehensive account of the theory of value and the formation of wages at the international level, although he considered it an integral part of the critique of political economy. When Marx formulated his conception of "the historical and moral element" of the value of labor-power, capitalism consisted of rather distinct national economies. Up through the 20th century, a global market of trade and capital investment developed, and under neoliberalism, production itself became globalized, linking labor-power in the North and South together in production-chains under the command of multinational firms. With the industrialization of the Global South, in the past half century, the level of technology and management regimes has also become increasingly similar on a global level. The *value* of a commodity is based less on varied and isolated national conditions. The value is based on global conditions. Thus, labor-power also has a globalized value.

Amin writes in his 1973 article, "The End of a Debate":

> The essential contribution made by Emmanuel is undoubtedly the discovery of the pre-eminence of international values. Our world longer consists of juxtaposed national systems carrying on "external" relations with each other (even if these are important), as was the case until quite recently. Rather it constitutes a unity—a whole—the world capitalist system. [...] Emmanuel has gradually drawn these conclusions; the system is defined in the abstract by the great mobility of goods and capital and by a relative immobility of labour. This means that commodities are not first of all national commodities, and then, exceptionally or marginally, international. On the contrary, it means that commodities are primarily worldwide [...]
>
> We are among those who consider that the publication of échange inégal' [Unequal Exchange] by Arghiri Emmanuel marks an important date in the theory of international trade and, beyond that, in the theory of unequal relations of domination/dependence between the center and the periphery of the world capitalist system. The fact that Em-

27 Lauesen, Torkil (2024a) Scandinavian Imperialism, *Journal of Labor and Society*, No. 27, 2024. pp. 29-23, pp. 58-61. Amin, Samir (1973) The End of a Debate. IDEP, September 1973. Dakar. Also published in: Amin, Samir (1977) *Imperialism and Unequal Development*, Essays, pp.181-252. New York: Monthly Review Press, 1977.

> manuel's argument was rejected out of hand by conventional economists is quite understandable, since the Ricardian theory of international trade is consistent with the subjective theory of value. In fact, that was the only exception to Ricardian internal logic, based on the labour theory of value as Emmanuel was the first to point out and—very clearly.[28]

The development of a *global* value of commodities and labor—opposed to different national values—is an important question in the political economy of imperialism. Samir Amin explains the formation of global values in "The End of a Debate" in a very accessible way, so I will quote him at length:

> Within Emmanuel's context in which the capitalist mode of production governs the specific activities of the partners, capital mobility shows a tendency towards equalizing the profit rate throughout the world while remunerations to labour, which is immobile, vary from one country to another according to historical conditions. Hence the transformation of international values (the only meaningful ones) into international prices (again the only meaningful ones) implies the transfer of value from some nations to others. Since all products are international commodities, the same quantity of labour used up in different parts of the world and incorporated in the products also gives rise to a single world value although labour power is not an international commodity as it does not move beyond national boundaries.
>
> Emmanuel is quite right in stressing this point; the labour-hour of the African proletarian is equal to that of the European proletarian since the product of the labour of either one are international commodities. In reply to Palloix who is surprised at the comparison of the value generated by an hour of labour in the two places, Emmanuel says "how does one compare—an hour of African labour with that of a Detroit worker? Well, in the same way that one labour-hour of a Detroit worker is compared with the labour hour of a New York barber" [...]
>
> At this stage, we simply want to show that the assertion of the preeminence of international values is the very essence of the theory in question, Emmanuel's critics have in fact clearly noted this and it is precisely this preeminence that they question or categorically reject. On this point, Palloix writes: "Is there an international value, which is the basis of world prices, in the same way as there is a national value: Emmanuel assumes that the world is the only reality. On the contrary, it seems that the only reality is the existence of economic blocs: U.S.A., Europe, Asia, Latin America."[29] And Bettelheim writes:
>
> > "Within every national capitalist social formation, the law of value ensures the extended reproduction of the material conditions of production, the specific form of domination by the capitalist mode over the ether modes, [...] a given level of wages. In the capitalist world market, the law of value guarantees the extended reproduction of the material conditions of world production, the specific forms of domination/subordination of the different social formations, the unequal rates of development [...]

---

28 Amin, Samir (1973) The End of a Debate. IDEP, September 1973. Dakar. Also published in: Amin, Samir (1977) *Imperialism and Unequal Development*, pp. 181-252. New York: Monthly Review Press, 1977.

29 Palloix, Christian (1969) l'impérialisme et l'échange inégal, *l'Homme et la Société* N° 12, 1969, p. 21.

> The level of wages peculiar to each social formation cannot be determined by the world level of development of productive forces; in fact, it is basically related to the specific combination of productive forces/production relations peculiar to each social formation."[30]

The position here is quite categorical, and it seems to us to be mistaken. Further on, we shall show how we deal with the dialectic between world level and national levels of development of productive forces and how we use this dialectic to determine the wage at the centre and at the periphery of the system.

In any case, this position nullifies the question to be solved. If we follow Bettelheim in accepting that wages are autonomously determined in each social formation, we can no longer have a theory of international trade. We must then accept Ricardo's theory of comparative advantages, i.e., make an exception to the labour theory of value. It is not even possible to speak of the effects of the law of value at the world level. This is no longer meaningful, and we can no longer speak of international commodities. In the last analysis, this position means regarding the world-system as a juxtaposition of national systems. Each of the latter being autonomous, it is clear that their trade relations cannot be analyzed in objective terms but must be seen in terms of subjective theory, which can here be applied, as opposed to the national context which is governed by objective value.

This position was certainly not one adopted by either Marx or Lenin. In fact, Marx considered that the import of American wheat in England in the 19th century lowered the value of labour power in that country. Hence already, he regarded "subsistence foods" (corn) as international commodities. Precisely for this reason, Marx considered that the development level of world productive forces, a development which made it possible to obtain wheat more cheaply in the New World, determines the wage and the rate of surplus-value in England. Similarly, Lenin clearly upholds the pre-eminence of the world-system: this is reflected in his praise of Bukharin's work, [...] Bukharin's shortcoming was not that he gave pre-eminence to the world-system, but that he made the mistake of characterizing this system, like the capitalist mode of production, by the triple international mobility of commodities, capital and labour ("the tendency towards the equalization of the wage rate" which we have pointed out). In other words, Bukharin regards the world-system as an extension of the capitalist mode of production on a world scale: hence its tendency to uniformity.

The preeminence of world values therefore constitutes the very essence, the core of the affirmation of the unity of the world-system, the condition for this unity. The adjective, "international" derived from "the economic theory of international trade" is indeed inappropriate and should be replaced by the word "world." [...]

Unity has never been synonymous with homogeneity. There is diversity and inequality within the unity of the world. Things seem to be clear-cut at the centre of the world capitalist system: social formations are close to the pure capitalist mode of production. At its periphery, the preeminence of world values is overshadowed by the apparently heterogeneous nature of social formations: only apparently, since here again, there is no juxtaposition of the capitalist mode with the pre-capitalist modes. The nucleus of the problem is to understand the meaning of the domination by the capitalist mode over the other modes, the domination being the basis of this unity. But this analysis does not derive from "economies" but from historical materialism. It is through the alliances

30 Bettelheim, Charles (1969) Débat sur l'impérialisme, rapports internationaux et rapports de classe. *Politique Aujourd'hui*, N° 12, p. 87, 1969.

among classes peculiar to each formation and to the world-system that this integration within the unity of the world takes place [...]

There is perhaps a reason for this persistent "dualistic" vision, to which in contrast we present the unity of the world-system. The fact is that this unity is very recent. It is true that the roots of the world-system go back to the beginning of mercantilism, four centuries ago; it is true that the system's contribution was accelerated two-fold by imperialism as from the end of the last century. However, the process of transformation of the relations between the capitalist mode and the other modes of production, (which were originally "periodic" and "marginal"), upon the emergence of domination relations which have radically altered the non-capitalist modes and have reduced them to a simple form, a "shell" whose content has since become a relation of sale of labour power, is a process which was at first, slow but, recently quickened its pace. It is possible that in the thirties, the producers at the periphery were still largely small commodity producers. We are convinced that they are no longer so and that today, they are mostly proletarians and sellers (although indirectly) of their labour power. A thousand social facts prove it every day. There are certainly important errors of political strategy arising from this inconsistency between the present reality and the picture which is still based on the reality of yesterday.[31]

In his 2010 book *The Law of Worldwide Value*, Samir Amin still considers this his major contribution to the political economy of imperialism:

My major contribution concerns the passage from the law of value to the law of globalized value, based on the hierarchical structuring–itself globalized–of the price of labor-power around its value [...] this globalized value constitutes the basis for imperialist rent.[32]

It is crucial to distinguish between the value and the price (wage) of labor-power. As mentioned, labor-power is not an ordinary commodity produced by capital, but one generated in complex social relationships. Its value is determined by historical development as well as the contemporary class struggle, family structure, and so on. This means that labor-power is reproduced under very different conditions in the South and North, but it is nevertheless brought together through global production and consumption. The port worker who loads containers in Shanghai creates as much value as the port worker in Rotterdam who unloads them, assuming that the work has the same intensity and uses the same technology. However, the price of labor-power—the wage—varies due to the different historical backgrounds, different social relations, political conditions, and the limited mobility of labor, as Amin writes:

Capitalism is not the United States and Germany, with India and Ethiopia only "halfway" capitalist. Capitalism is the United States and India, Germany and Ethiopia,

---

31 Amin, Samir (1973) The End of a Debate. IDEP, September 1973. Dakar. Also published in: Amin, Samir (1977) *Imperialism and Unequal Development*, pp. 187-191. New York: Monthly Review Press, 1977.

32 Amin, Samir. (2010). *The Law of Worldwide Value*, p. 11. New York: Monthly Review Press, 2010.

> taken together. This means that labor-power has but a single value, that which is associated with the level of development of the productive forces taken globally (the General Intellect on that scale) [...] You have to be consistent. You cannot invoke "inescapable" globalization when it suits you and refuse to consider it when you find it troublesome! However, though there exists but one sole value of labor-power on the scale of globalized capitalism, that labor-power is nonetheless recompensed at very different rates.[33]

The "bare reproduction cost" and the "historical and moral component" of the value of labor-power are not two distinct, isolated, and different elements. The class struggle may incorporate new elements in the "bare reproduction cost," and repression can pressure the wage below that level. The wage may vary below as well as above this global value of labor.

The combination of the historical development of highly different wage levels between the Global North and South and the constitution of a global value of labor-power has several consequences. It entails different rates of surplus value. The combination of globalized value and low wages in the South is the basis of the extraction of what Marini calls super-surplus value, which generates super-profits for capital and relatively low commodity prices for a North wage level. Thus, the difference between the value of labor and the price of labor causes a transfer of value from the South to both capital and labor in the North.

As capitalism has developed over centuries in the process of colonialism and the formation of a center-periphery world-system, capital accumulates on the global level. In this way, value and its mediations—in prices of production and market prices—increasingly become the ground on which market exchange is generalized globally.

During fifty years of neoliberalism, capitalism advanced the global law of value concerning commodities while simultaneously fostering mechanisms that violate and negate it concerning one specific commodity, the wage—the price of labor-power. Through this, capital can produce by using low wage labor in the Global South and sell the resulting commodities to high wage labor in the Global North. Super-exploitation is a violation of the global value of labor-power, which leads to unequal exchange at the expense of low-wage countries. This anomaly is a necessary condition for the accumulation processes of world capitalism. It is thus not an accidental feature but instead is reliant on sustained political suppression of labor movement in the periphery and restrictions on the international movement of labor.

Hence, we see the development of a global law of *value* of goods and labor. However, the *price* of labor, the wage, varies, due to the history of class struggle.

33 Ibid., p. 84.

It is the class struggle in capitalism, dividing the social product into profits and wages, which is the driver in the development of unequal exchange. The core of the theory of unequal exchange is the Marxist concept of value. The depression of wages in the periphery by colonialism and imperialism and the rise of wages in the center by successful trade union struggle, based on colonial exploitation, are the basis of unequal exchange. The international law of value, combined with the history of colonialism, is the key to understanding the exploitative relations between the center and the periphery, relations which are hidden behind the appearance of the price structure of commodities in the world market. The central point is not the exchange on the market, but the difference between the global value of labor and the local prices of labor-power.

So, what is the global value of labor-power in terms of size? As Marx explained in the quote above concerning the value of labor-power in a country:

> The necessary wants [...] are themselves the product of historical development, [...] depend on the degree of civilization. Nevertheless, [...] at a given period, the average quantity of the means of subsistence necessary for the labourer is practically known.[34]

If we apply this to the global level, we can determine the global value of labor-power as the global average wage at a given time period. The average wage is calculated according to the number of workers on certain wage levels in all parts of the world, taking into consideration skill and intensity of the labor-power. (I will return to the specific size in the next chapter.) A given level of wages compared to the global value of labor-power indicates whether you are in the center or periphery of the world-system. Historically the difference in wage levels between center and periphery has steadily widened. Around 1800, wages around the world were at more or less subsistence level. Today, in 2025, the difference in wages between the USA and China is around 6:1 and between Sweden and Bangladesh 50:1.

Following this discussion of the value and price of labor-power, I return to the transformation of value into commodity prices and the transformation of surplus value into profit. The first step is the formation of the cost-price.

Cost-Price

The individual capitalist is not interested in surplus value (s) and the rate of surplus value but in how much profit the total amount of invested capital yields. Therefore, what actually interests the capitalist is the wage (v) and other costs of

34 Marx, Karl (1867) *Capital* Vol. 1: Part II, Chapter Six: The Buying and Selling of Labour-power, p. 121. Moscow: Progress Publishers, 1962.

production (c). Marx writes:

> The value of every commodity produced in the capitalist way is represented in the formula: V=c+v+s. If we subtract surplus-values (s) from this value of the product there remains a bare equivalent or a substitute value in goods [...] This portion of the value of the commodity, which replaces the price of the consumed means of production and labour-power, only replaces what the commodity costs the capitalist himself. For him it, therefore, represents the cost-price of the commodity.[35]

How this cost-price is distributed between constant and variable capital does not interest the capitalist. To him, the profit is the yield of the aggregate capital. Surplus value, in its assumed capacity as the offspring of the aggregate advanced capital, is converted into profit.[36]

It should be noted that it is the wage and profit rate which determines the cost-price and not the other way round. Emmanuel observes:

> Wages are differentiated by geographical areas and independently of ups and downs in commodity prices. They are rigid and remarkably stable in time. During the last twenty years the price of coffee, copper, and sugar has fluctuated in a range of one to three and sometimes even more than that. No corresponding change or anything like it has been recorded in the wages paid in the countries producing these goods. All through these evolutions and even revolutions in prices, the worker in Guinea, Uganda, Brazil, or Katanga has gone on receiving his subsistence wage, which can be estimated, without much margin of error, at five cents an hour, whereas his American or European counterpart has in the same period been earning 20, 30, or 40 times as much, depending on the particular country and not at all on the movement of prices. During this same period the capitalist in Guinea, Uganda, Brazil, or Katanga had, of course, his ups and downs; yet, taking one year with another, he ended up with something not too far from the average international rate of profit [...]
>
> In the days when wages varied from one country to another only as 1 to 2, or even 1 to 3 or 1 to 4, it was perhaps legitimate to suppose that fluctuations on the commodity market could be the underlying cause of these variations. When, however, wages vary at the rate of 1 to 20 or 1 to 30, and vary only in space, while possessing extreme rigidity in time (in which only a slow and linear trend is to be observed, with hardly any variation), we are indeed compelled to recognize that they probably vary in accordance with laws peculiar to themselves and that, consequently, they really are the independent variable of the system.[37]

The Circulation of Capital

Let us take a look at the full circle of capital accumulation.

---

35 Marx, Karl (1883) *Capital*, Vol. 3: pp. 25-6. Moscow: Progress Publishers, 1962.

36 Ibid., p. 36.

37 Emmanuel, Arghiri (1972) *Unequal Exchange: A Study of the Imperialism of Trade*, pp. 66 and 70. New York: Monthly Review Press, 1972.

The capitalist invests partly in buildings, machinery, raw material etc.—in short, in the production apparatus. This part of the capital is called constant capital, because it does not change in value during the accumulation process. The capitalist also invests partly in labor-power. This part of the capital is called variable capital, because it forms the basis of the creation of new value in production. Thus, the factors of production which the capitalist acquires by investments are divided into two main parts, which both are equally vital: variable capital and constant capital.[38]

The circulation of capital can be divided into the sphere of production and the sphere of circulation. In the latter, commodities are bought and sold. Both spheres are dependent on one another: there is no circulation without production, and there is no point in producing without circulation. The concept of value unifies the production and circulation spheres, which are both necessary in capitalist accumulation.

For sure, the labor-power in the sphere of production is a precondition for surplus value, but the commodities have to be sold on the market to turn the surplus value into profit: the accumulation of capital.

The concept of "unequal exchange" is often criticized for focusing on circulation —international trade—instead of the sphere of production, where the exploitation of labor is assumed to take place. However, this perception is wrong, both regarding the theory of unequal exchange and the Marxist theory of exploitation in general. Emmanuel writes in a polemic with Charles Bettelheim:

> Bettleheim [...] exchange-value [...] is merely a phenomenal form of "value" created in production, appearing at the level of circulation and accompanying the commodity as an intrinsic quality, like a substance that has, so to speak, been injected into the commodity by productive labor [...] Exchange is not, as Bettelheim supposes, something that complements production at a level external to the latter, and at most a condition for capitalist production; it is an essential moment of this production.[39] Once we have assumed the existence of private ownership, it is not value that leads to exchange, but exchange that necessarily results in value.[40] (For)

The first phase of the circulation of capital consists of capitalists acquiring means of production and buying labor-power. The second phase consists of using the means of production and the purchased labor-power to produce

38 Marx, Karl (1867). *Capital*, Part III, Chapter eight: Constant Capital and Variable Capital, pp. 142-149. Moscow: Progress Publishers, 1962.

39 Marx, Karl (1857) *Grundrisse*. Pléiade edition of Oeuvres de Karl Marx: Economie. Vol. 2, p. 258. Paris 1968.

40 Emmanuel, Arghiri (1972) *Unequal Exchange. A Study of the Imperialism of Trade*, pp. 325 and 327. New York: Monthly Review Press, 1972. Original emphasis.

commodities. The third phase of the circulation of capital consists of trading commodities. In this phase, the capitalist collects the surplus value created in the production process as profit.

The capitalist must be able to sell the commodities that have been produced on the market, at a price that includes both the expenses for constant and variable capital plus the surplus value, which can then be used either to start the circulation of capital anew (with expanded possibilities) or for consumption.[41] The total circulation of capital appears as follows:

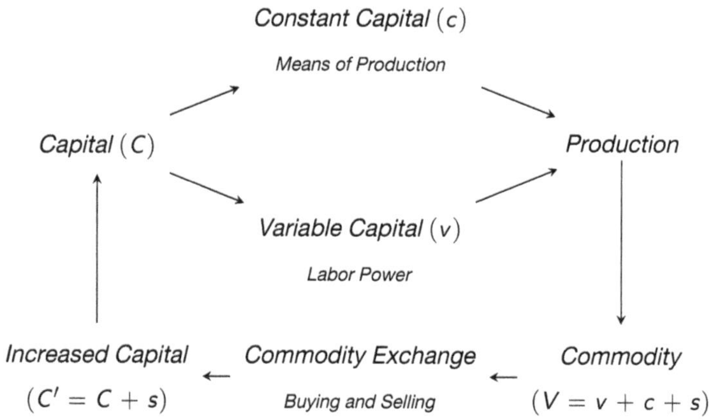

Figure II

In Marx's words:

> The conversion of a sum of money into means of production and labour-power, is the first step taken by the quantum of value that is going to function as capital. This conversion takes place in the market, within the sphere of circulation. The second step, the process of production, is complete so soon as the means of production have been converted into commodities whose value exceeds that of their component parts, and, therefore, contains the capital originally advanced, plus a surplus-value. These commodities must then be thrown into circulation. They must be sold, their value realised in money, this money afresh converted into capital, and so over and over again. This circular movement, in which the same phases are continually gone through in succession, forms the circulation of capital.[42]

---

41 Marx, Karl (1867). *Capital*, Vol. I: Part VII. Chapter twenty-four: Conversion of Surplus-value into Capital, p. 400. Moscow: Progress Publishers, 1962.

42 Marx, Karl (1867). *Capital*, Vol. I: p. 529. Moscow: Progress Publishers, 1962.

$$\textit{Rate of Profit} = \frac{\textit{Surplus Value}}{\textit{Aggregate Capital}} \qquad \left(p' = \frac{s}{C}\right)$$

Figure III

Although the price of a commodity can differ from its value, it is determined by the value in the final instance. According to neoclassical market economists, prices are determined exclusively by supply and demand on the market. This is, however, only the final touch. Commodities need to be produced and reproduced to keep accumulation running. If capitalists do not recover the cost of production plus a profit on the market, they will not produce the commodities again, and accumulation ceases. The price they need is what Howard Nicholas calls "reproduction prices."[43] The size of this price cannot be determined by market forces, since the formation of the market price is what we want to explain. Freya Brown formulates the problem nicely:

> We cannot use prices to measure inputs, for prices are what we are trying to explain in the first place! The only thing common between all the inputs of a commodity is labor. Thus, in any economy based on commodity production, the prices of commodities will in the final instance be fundamentally tied to the (socially necessary) labor time embodied in those commodities.[44]

Let us see how surplus value and value is transformed into profit and market prices.

From Surplus Value to Profit

Just as the worker is interested in the size of the wage more than in the concept of value, the capitalist is interested in profit more than the concept of surplus value. Profit, as we have seen, is dependent on production costs in general, or what is called the cost price.

The relation between the surplus value and the total capital used for production defines the profit rate (p'), as shown in the formula:

The profit rate depends both on the rate of surplus value and on the relation between constant and variable capital. A rise in surplus value brings a rise

43 Nicholas, H. (2011). *Marx's Theory of Price and its Modern Rivals*. Palgrave Macmillan. Houndsmills, 2011.

44 Brown, F. (2011). Summary and Review: "Marx's Theory of Price and its Modern Rivals" by Howard Nicholas.

in the profit rate. The relation between constant and variable capital is labelled capital's organic composition. It depends on the ratio between the amount of labor-power and the means of production. This relationship varies from industry to industry. The organic composition is low when variable capital makes up a large part of total capital, and it is high when constant capital makes up a large part of total capital. An example for an industry with a high organic composition of capital is the petrochemical industry, which relies largely on constant capital. An example of an industry with a low organic composition of capital could be nursing or the care-service industry, which relies (relatively) largely on variable capital.

The following table 2.1 illustrates the immediate relation between capital's organic composition and the profit rate. The higher the organic composition, the lower the profit rate; the lower the organic composition, the higher the profit rate.[45]

Table 2.1[46]

	Aggregate Capitals $C = c + v$	Rate of Surplus Value $\frac{s}{v}$	Surplus Value s	Value of Product $V = c + v + s$	Rate of Profit $p' = \frac{s}{C}$
I	$80c + 20v$	100%	20	120	20%
II	$70c + 30v$	100%	30	130	30%
III	$60c + 40v$	100%	40	140	40%
IV	$85c + 15v$	100%	15	115	15%
V	$95c + 5v$	100%	5	105	5%

Formation of the Average Rate of Profit

As the table above shows, capital investments of the same size but with different organic compositions can, in theory, generate very different rates of surplus value and therefore very different profit rates. However, this is not what happens in practice. If it were, capital would flock to industries with a low organic

45 Marx, Karl (1883). *Capital*, Vol. 3, Part IV, Ch. 20. 'Historical Facts about Merchant's Capital', p. 155. Moscow: Progress Publishers 1962.

46 Source: Marx, *Capital*, Vol. III, p. 155.

composition, yet this is not the case. We know that the average long-term profit rates of different industries are very similar. But why? Capital always moves toward industries that promise the highest profits. If there is increased demand for the products of a certain industry, their prices will rise and so, in turn, will the profit rate. This attracts capital formerly invested in other industries and leads to the growth of this particular industry. Often the consequences are overproduction and oversupply, falling prices, a lower profit rate, and capital moving elsewhere. Unequal profit rates between different industries cause the constant movement of capital and balance out the rate of profit between different industries to reach an average. In other words, competing capitals ensure that the average, long-term profit rates of different industries are very similar. This also means that a given amount of capital will, in the long run, create similar profits no matter what industries it is invested in or how it is divided between constant and variable capital.

This can be explained through the first step of the transformation of value into price—the conversion of the value of commodities into a price of production. The price of production of a commodity consists of the cost price (variable plus constant capital) plus the average profit in relation to the total capital used in its production. This can be summarized in the following formula:

$$\text{Price of production} = \text{cost price} + (\text{total capital invested} \times \text{average rate of profit})$$

The price of production of a particular commodity is not the same as its value. At first glance, these two categories might seem the same. However, the formation of the average profits leads to a transfer of value between different production spheres, with different organic composition, and hence different relative size of the surplus value. However, the combined price of production of all commodities is the same as the combined value of all commodities. In addition, combined profits are the same as the combined surplus value created in production. The price of production must not be confused with the market price, to which it is only sometimes coincidentally equal. The market price is the price a commodity is actually sold for on the market. Market prices are adjusted by supply and demand, the existence of monopoly, and so on. The goal for each commodity is to reach a market price that consists of its cost price times the average rate of profit as a share of total capital. This allows production, and therefore the accumulation of capital, to continue.

Let us see how the average rate of profit affects the numbers in the table above. If we put total capital at 100 and the rate of surplus value consistently at 100% and we assume that the whole capital turns over in one circulation, then the new numbers indicate the formation of the average rate of profit. See table

2.2.

Table 2.2[47]

	Total Capital	Surplus Value	Value	Average Rate of Profit	Price of Production	Deviation of Price of Production from Value
	C	s	V	P'	PP	$PP - V$
I	$80c + 20v$	20	120	22%	122	+2
II	$70c + 30v$	30	130	22%	122	−8
III	$60c + 40v$	40	140	22%	122	−18
IV	$85c + 15v$	15	115	22%	122	+7
V	$95c + 5v$	5	105	22%	122	+17

The average rate of profit:

$$\frac{20\% + 30\% + 40\% + 15\% + 5\%}{5} = 22\%$$

As the table indicates, the amount of labor-power required in different industries (and therefore the organic composition of capital), as well as the surplus-value differ widely. When profits are distributed, surplus value is transferred from industries with a low organic composition to industries with a high organic composition. This is of no relevance for capitalists. However, for a Marxist analysis of capitalism, it is important to account for this transfer. Some Marxist economists have called this transfer "unequal exchange in the general sense" but this must not be confused with Emmanuel's use of the term (which we will consider below). To speak of unequal exchange in this context can be misleading. The value transfer described above is inherent in the logic of capital. The fact that the profit rate is distributed among all industries, so that capitalists can make profits in each of them, whatever the organic composition of capital is, is a structural necessity in capitalism. It allows capitalists to compete in the market and to develop the productive forces. If commodities were priced according to

47 Table 2.2 is identical to the one in *Capital*, Vol. III, p. 157. However, Marx has divided the constant capital c into fixed and flowing parts in order to prove that this does not have any consequence. Therefore, it has been omitted here in order not to complicate the matter unnecessarily.

their value, instead of according to the price of production, investments in mechanization would come to a halt. Capitalists would only invest in labor-intensive industries with greater variable capital and a low organic composition. The pharmaceutical industry would disappear, and woodworking would prosper.

The Transformation from Value into Market Price

In the transformation from value to price of production and then to market price, we can—as discussed above—conclude that value is not linked to the specific commodity, a substance injected in the production process and then in some way transmuted into price of production. This perception of value as a sort of physical thing in itself is a common misconception, even in Marxist circles. However, this is not the case; value is a social relation which unfolds itself in different forms, in the interaction between seller and buyer on the market, between different capitals, and between national economies in the capitalist mode of production on world scale.

Inside a developed capitalist country, labor is mobile enough to guarantee that the rate of surplus value will be similar across different industries. The market prices of commodities depend on the price of production (where the profit rate is equalized), not on the cost price (c+v). Market forces provide a final adjustment based on the current supply and demand of the commodity. The transformation from value into market price can be summarized in figure IV:

We can conclude that it is not the supply and demand on the market that determine the size of profits and wages, but the opposite. It is the wages and profits which are the independent variables in the system, and these determine the prices of commodities.

Andrea Ricci emphasizes the relation between labor-power and final market price through the concept of exchange-value:

> The dual nature of abstract labour is reflected in the dual nature of the exchange-value, as exchange-value created in production (hours of work) and exchange-value realized in circulation (as the market price), which manifests itself in the real confrontation occurring in the process of market exchange between seller and buyer concerning supply price and demand price, the real cost of production, and the final price of the commodity.[48]

Andrea Ricci adds:

> The former (labour time) is hidden and invisible inside the production process, while the latter appears in the form of the market price of commodities. In their equivalence,

48 Ricci, Andrea (2021) *Value and Unequal Exchange in International Trade*, p. 81. New York: Routledge, 2021.

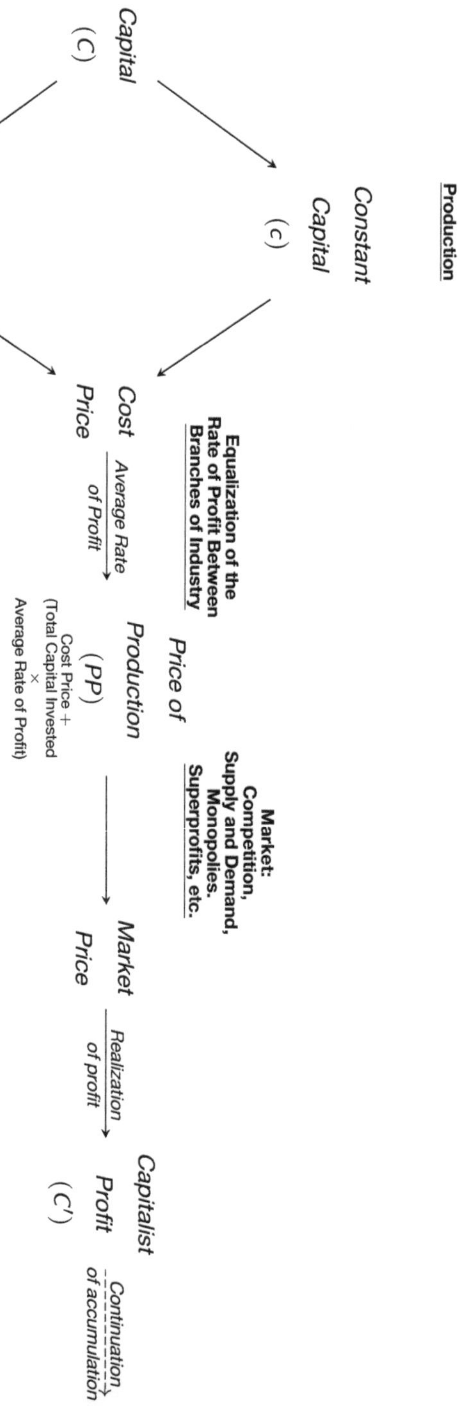

Production
Capital
(C)
Constant
Capital
(c)
Variable
Capital
(v)
Class Struggle
Equalization of the
Rate of Profit Between
Branches of Industry
Cost
Price
Average Rate
of Profit
Price of
Production
(PP)
Cost Price +
(Total Capital Invested
×
Average Rate of Profit)
Market:
Competition,
Supply and Demand,
Monopolies.
Superprofits, etc.
Market
Price
Realization
of profit
Capitalist
Profit
(C′)
Continuation
of accumulation

Figure IV

the socially necessary labour in production and the socially necessary labour in circulation are reunited, defining the magnitude of value of the commodity as a given quantity of objectified abstract labour.[49]

The Appropriation and Distribution of Value

The transformation of value into price occurs on the market—in other words, in exchange. If we look at value only in the realm of production, we turn value into an essence that flows from the minds and bodies of workers into the specific commodities they produce. But, as we have seen, value is the result of social relationships. Exploitation occurs throughout the entire circulation of capital, that is, during the production of commodities as much as during their exchange. Surplus value is created in production, but it is acquired and distributed in exchange. It is in exchange that human labor appears as the only possible measure of the different commodities, that is, as the basis of value. It is the sphere of circulation—the market—that distributes the value created by human labor between industries, countries, and individuals. Among capitalists, the average rate of profit balances out. Value is transferred from industries with low organic composition to industries with high organic composition. Finance and trade capital can acquire value without being involved in production at all. Between capitalists and workers, the distribution of value follows a simple principle: profit for the capitalists and wages for the workers. Value is moved and allocated because of competition and class struggles, national and global.

As Marx put it,

> From the possibility that profit may be less than surplus-value, hence that capital [may] exchange profitably without realizing itself in the strict sense, it follows that not only individual capitalists, but also nations may continually exchange with one another, may even continually repeat the exchange on an ever-expanding scale, without for that reason necessarily gaining in equal degrees. One of the nations may continually appropriate for itself a part of the surplus labour of the other, giving back nothing for it in the exchange, except that the measure here [is] not as in the exchange between capitalist and worker.[50]

At this point, I would like to draw attention to deviations in the transformation of value into price and hence the realization of profit at an average rate, as shown in the figures and tables above. In real existing capitalism, we can observe differences in the rate of profit. Certain sectors and firms can get extraordinarily high profits.

---

49 Ibid., p. 82.

50 Marx, Karl (1857) *Grundrisse*, p. 872. London: Penguin books, 1973.

Superprofits

Statistics on international rates of profit are rather problematic. This is partly because the information on which the statistics are based is unreliable, as tax and book-keeping conditions may lead to the rates of profit quoted not being in accordance with the "real" rates. In addition, detailed information is seldom found in the statistics regarding how the rates of profit that are quoted have been calculated. However, the available statistics—although vitiated by uncertain factors—mainly confirm the tendency to an equalization of profit, laid out by Marx in *Capital,* as a general rule in the capitalist mode of production. Capital is attracted to sectors and markets where profits are high and moves out of sectors and markets with low profit rates. This tendency is strengthened by the mobility of capital. However, it is countered by different forms of monopoly in technology and market access.

In his writings on imperialism in 1916, Lenin spoke of superprofits, meaning profits substantially over the average profit in a given time period. The basis for this divergence was colonialism and monopoly capitalism.

Monopolies take different forms. Some have to do with the production sphere and monopolistic ownership of a certain technology that produces a commodity more efficiently, protected by patent and copyright laws. Others have to do with the circulation sphere: branding, a certain privileged access to a market or raw material that others do not have. Some have to do with being a "first mover"; for example, outsourcing production to a low wage country in the 1980s.

Monopolists get superprofits by selling commodities for more than their price of production (i.e., the price that equalizes the rate of profit) at the expense of lower profits for the other capitalists. English capital had already gained superprofits in the second half of the nineteenth century through its monopoly on industrial production and on colonial trade in many regions of the world.[51] Marx writes about superprofits on the international and national level.

> Capitals invested in foreign trade can yield a higher rate of profit, because, in the first place, there is competition with commodities produced in other countries with inferior production facilities, so that the more advanced country sells its goods above their value even though cheaper than the competing countries. In so far as the labour of the more advanced country is here realised as labour of a higher specific weight, the rate of profit rises, because labour which has not been paid as being of a higher quality is sold as such.

51 Marx, Karl & Engels, F *On Colonies, Industrial Monopoly & the Working Class Movement.* Introduction Cope, Z and Lauesen, T. Montreal: Kersplebedeb, 2016

> The same may obtain in relation to the country, to which commodities are exported and to that from which commodities are imported; namely, the latter may offer more materialised labour in kind than it receives, and yet thereby receive commodities cheaper than it could produce them. Just as a manufacturer who employs a new invention before it becomes generally used, undersells his competitors and yet sells his commodity above its individual value, that is, realises the specifically higher productiveness of the labour he employs as surplus-labour. He thus secures a surplus-profit.[52]

The advantage of having a new technology or being a "first mover" on the national level is temporary; however, superprofits on the international level in connection with imperialism seem to have remained as a constant feature. Marx explains in the following passage:

> As concerns capitals invested in colonies, etc., on the other hand, they may yield higher rates of profit for the simple reason that the rate of profit is higher there due to backward development, and likewise the exploitation of labour, because of the use of slaves, coolies, etc. Why should not these higher rates of profit, realised by capitals invested in certain lines and sent home by them, enter into the equalisation of the general rate of profit and thus tend, pro tanto, to raise it, unless it is the monopolies that stand in the way. There is so much less reason for it, since these spheres of investment of capital are subject to the laws of free competition [...] The favoured country recovers more labour in exchange for less labour, although this difference, this excess is pocketed, as in any exchange between labour and capital, by a certain class.[53]

Lenin took up in 1916 where Marx left off:

> Super profits have not disappeared; they still remain. The exploitation of all other countries by one privileged, financially wealthy country remains and has become more intense. A handful of wealthy countries – there are only four of them, if we mean independent, really gigantic, "modern" wealth: England, France, the United States and Germany have developed monopoly to vast proportions, they obtain super profits running into hundreds, if not thousands, of millions, they "ride on the backs" of hundreds and hundreds of millions of people in other countries and fight among themselves for the division of the particularly rich, particularly fat and particularly easy spoils.[54]

In the Second Congress of the Communist International (Comintern) in 1920, Lenin went as far as to state: "Super-profit gained in the colonies is the mainstay of modern capitalism."[55]

Samir Amin spoke of "generalized monopoly capitalism" in the '70s, when referring to capitalism's current phase. When he speaks of monopolies, it is not

---

52 Marx, Karl (1883) *Capital. A Critique of Political Economy*. Vol. II, Chapter 14 p. 163. 1894. Edited by Freidrich Engels. New York: International Publishers, 1959.

53 Ibid.

54 Lenin (1916). *Imperialism and the Split in Socialism*, p. 105.In Lenin, *Collected Works*, Vol. 23, pp. 105–120. Moscow: Progress Publishers, 1964.

55 Lenin (1920, July–August). "Supplementary Theses" (Attached to Lenin's "Preliminary draft theses on the national and colonial questions").

just corporations dominating industries. It means networks that dominate the entire productive system. Small- and medium-sized firms serve as suppliers to the monopolized production chains, which take a significant share of their profits. The profits made by Foxconn from the production of Apple products between 2005 and 2015 amounted to between 2 and 3 percent of the sales price; the profits made by Apple were 30 percent.[56] Another example is the many textile factories in countries like Bangladesh, Pakistan, India, Nepal, Indonesia, Cambodia, and Eritrea, which produce for the "fabric-less" brand-companies, like Nike, Adidas, H&M, Zara, and Hugo Boss. Suppliers in Global South often produce exclusively for a particular corporation in Global North. If that corporation threatens to relocate its production, the supplier is likely to go out of business—it is easy to understand the pressure that can be exerted.

Emmanuel was of the opinion that an equalization of profit rates take place not only at the national level but also on the global level. In contradistinction to the (lack of) mobility of labor, the mobility of capital is sufficient to generate a tendency towards the equalization of its rate of remuneration. In his model of value transfer through unequal exchange, he also assumes an equalization of profit rates (as we will see later). The reason he assumes this is to keep all factors, except the wage, equal, to emphasize the effect of a rise in wages in one country. However, it is not a prerequisite for a value transfer by unequal exchange that the profit rate is equalized, as Emmanuel writes:

> It follows, that to refute the theory of unequal exchange it is not enough to show that there are monopolies and that the rates of profit are unequal. It must be shown too that there exists an inverse functional link between the rates of wages of one region and the rates of profits of the same region. We have no reason to believe in the existence of such a function.
>
> As Somakni puts it: " [...] whereas the wages run apart along national lines, profits run apart mainly along different lines (per industry or branch), irrespective of the proportion in which these industries or branches are introduced in the different countries and there is no precise relevance between the rationale of variations of relative levels of wages and that of variations of relative levels of rates of profit [...] There is no evidence of the existence of a profit rates gap as deep as one of wage rates and especially of a profit rates gap being systematically correlative to the wages gap. This allows us to rule out the idea either that the circumstances which depress the wages in a country could tend to depress the profits too, or that the low wages of certain countries entail "constantly and systematically" higher profits in these same countries. The best approximate analyses of national rates of profit between advanced and under-developed countries are those of J.H. Dunning on the average rates of profits realized in various countries by British investments abroad. (Studies in International Investment, London 1970). The scale of

---

56 Drahokoupil, Jan Andrijasevic, Rutvica and Sacchetto, Devi (eds.) (2016) *Flexible workforces and low profit margins: electronics assembly between Europe and China.* page. 158. European Trade Union Institute (ETUI) Brussels, 2016.

> growing rates of profits is distributed quite erratically among low wages countries and high wages countries." (Salari, Sottosviluppo, Imperialismo, Einaudi, Turin).
>
> Lastly, we can add that, in any event, possible disparities in the rates of profit, even if they move in the right direction, are of another order of magnitude than the disparities of wages, so that it is excluded that the one offsets or diminishes the others.[57]

The profit-*rate* is not determined in the specific firm, but in a wider context at the global level. Today, international trade is not just an exchange of commodities produced by capitalist firms in different countries, as was primarily the case when Emmanuel formulated his thesis in 1969. With the globalization of production in the form of outsourcing and transnational productions chains, the controlling "brand-firm" located in the Global North, gets a higher profit rate than the producing firms further along the chain in the Global South. In this case, the inequality of exchange not only is not reduced but is in fact aggravated, since the Global North "charges" its sales not only with its super-wages but also with its superprofits.

There is no theoretical reason why the imperialist transfer of value, based on low wage labor-power, cannot take place both in the form of superprofit to capital and as cheap commodities to consumers in high wage countries. The division of social product in profits and wages is determined by class struggle on the national and international level.

However, let's continue the examination of the generation of prices of commodities and labor-power in the capitalist mode of production.

Value as Price

Historically, money emerged as the necessary intermediary of exchange in the marketplace long before the breakthrough of capitalism. However, it is first in capitalism that the exchange of commodities through the use of money is generalized in society.

Marx, in his analysis of money in *Capital,* first assumes that gold is the money-commodity for "the sake of simplicity," not from some theoretical necessity.[58] Gold and silver coins represented only a first stage of the historical development of money in capitalism, followed by paper notes and credit money, though these were not yet universally adopted at the time of Marx. Marx was

57 Emmanuel, Arghiri (1975) 'Unequal Exchange Revisited', page 53-54. IDS Discussion Paper No. 77, University of Sussex, Brighton. UK. !975.

58 Marx, Karl (1867) *Capital* Vol. II. Chapter 20: Simple Reproduction—Part 4, XII. The Reproduction of the Money Material. Moscow: Progress Publishers, 1962.

fully aware that money as a medium of circulation can just be a symbolic commodity, devoid of any intrinsic value, representing a given amount of value by social recognition in the form of guarantees from the national bank. The so-called *gold standard*, the possible exchange between bank notes and an amount of gold, to guarantee their value, was the basis for the international monetary system from the 1870s until 1971, when the United States unilaterally terminated the convertibility of the US dollar to gold.

The advantage of using gold instead of paper money or plastic cards in Marx's analysis is that in a unit of gold we can still recognize the measure of the abstract socially necessary *labor time* for its production. For example, one ounce of gold equals 100 kilograms of wheat in terms of labor-power. Money, in the form of metal pieces, paper notes, or plastic cards issued by banks, has a production cost close to nothing. But the national bank guarantees that you can exchange your money with commodities on the market. This guarantee is built on trust in the banks and in the performance of the national economy in general.

In terms of the price of a commodity, we again see the two sides of exchange-value. Andrea Ricci sums it up:

> In a capitalist economy, therefore, money simultaneously represents the visible mode of appearance of both measures of the exchange-value of a commodity, directly as extrinsic measure and indirectly as intrinsic measure. In other words, both the market exchange ratio of one commodity with other commodities, and the abstract labour time objectified in them, appear in the exchange in the form of a given amount of money.[59]

Until now we have assumed that the two forms of measurement of exchange-value (first as the price of commodities at the market and second as the labor time it took to produce them) were equivalent in terms of exchange. But what if the price of labor-power is determined in a different way than the price of the commodities they produce? What if the wage is determined on the national level, and commodity prices are determined on the global level?

It is only with the formation of international trade and production that the law of value reaches its final stage, as Marx writes in *Theories of Surplus Value*:

> But it is only foreign trade, the development of the market to a world market, which causes money to develop into world money and abstract labour into social labour. Abstract wealth, value, money, hence abstract labour, develop in the measure that concrete labour becomes a totality of different modes of labour embracing the world market. Capitalist production rests on the value or the transformation of the labour embodied in the product into social labour. But this is only [possible] on the basis of foreign trade and of the world market. This is at once the pre-condition and the result of capitalist

59 Ricci, Andrea (2021) *Value and Unequal Exchange in International Trade*, p. 121. New York: Routledge, 2021.

production.[60]

Let us see how the law of value works out at the global level.

Unequal Exchange

As mentioned above, Marx never properly outlined theories of the world market and international trade. But there are fragments in *Capital* which indicate what effect a possible differentiation in wages between countries could have upon international prices. In Vol. I, Marx mentions that the value of labor-power varies not only in time but also, as mentioned above, between different countries as they have a different "historical element," however:

> ..in a given country, at a given period, the average quantity of the means of subsistence necessary for the worker is also given.[61]

From the middle of the 19th century onwards, we see a difference developing in the *subsistence necessary for the worker* between the center and periphery of the capitalist world-system.

Such a difference has consequences on the prices of commodities, as Marx writes:

> In the case of a partial, or local, rise of wages—that is, a rise only in some branches of production—a local rise in the prices of the products of these branches may follow.[62]

We have here Marx's indications of what can happen in international trade. However, the first coherent theory of international trade in the spirit of *Capital* was formulated 100 years later by Arghiri Emmanuel.

Emmanuel referred to value transfer from one country to another as unequal exchange on the world market.[63] The basis of unequal exchange is the historically constituted difference in wage levels between the imperialist countries and those which were then called the Third World.

Colonialism engulfed the planet, according to Emmanuel, by expanding international trade through importing raw materials and agricultural products

---

60 Marx, Karl (1883) *Theories of Surplus-Value*, chap. XXI, page 858. Moscow: Progress Publishers, 1976.

61 Marx, Karl (1867) *Capital*, Vol. I, Part II, Chapter Six: The buying and selling of labour-power", p. 121. Moscow: Progress Publishers, 1962.

62 Marx, Karl (1962) *Capital* Vol. II, p. 345. Moscow: Progress Publishers, 1962.

63 Emmanuel, A. (1972) *Unequal Exchange: A Study of the Imperialism of Trade*. New York: Monthly Review Press, 1972.

and exporting industrial goods, and this developed into an ongoing unequal exchange of value.

The supply of cheap agricultural products and raw materials (for example, cotton) from the colonies in the second half of the nineteenth century made it possible for English capitalism to reduce the value of its workers' labor-power (reduce the cost of reproduction of labor-power) and thus increase surplus value (profit) while, at the same time, increasing their wages (the price of labor-power). In turn, this favored a dynamic mode of capital accumulation in the imperialist center, which was dependent on the expanding consumption power of the working class.

By contrast, super-exploitation—the remuneration of labor below its value (reproduction cost)—became the model used by capital in Latin America, Asia, and Africa in the export sector, supplying raw materials and food to the imperialist center. The capitalist in the periphery was not dependent on the consumption of a domestic market, as long as Northern and Western Europe and the United States demanded their production; hence, super-exploitation became the most prominent way of increasing profits in the reproduction of capitalism in the periphery of the world-system.

Marini's concept of super-exploitation in the colonies and Emmanuel's explanation of the wage rise in the imperialist center, as the drivers of unequal exchange between center and periphery, supplement each other nicely. Both Marini and Emmanuel see the deviation of the wage from the value of labor as the generator of unequal exchange.

By the 1880s, the unequal relationship between the center and periphery had been cemented. While only subsistence wages were being paid in the latter, wages became significantly higher in the former. This was the result of two simultaneous processes: the struggle of the working classes in the center for better pay and living conditions, and the oppression and exploitation of those in the periphery.

Let us see what different wage levels mean for Marx's theory of the formation of prices of production. We suppose two countries, A and B. In table 2.3 we have equal wage levels and in table 2.4 we have different wage levels. First, we suppose that the rate of surplus value and the rate of profit in the two countries are equal. This means that the mobility of the labour-force and the capital is sufficient for an equalization.

The organic composition of the production in the countries A and B is the same (c and v is 100 in both countries). This has been done to make "other things equal"—to eliminate the possibility that a higher organic composition should be the cause of any transfers of value. This means that, in this case, the value and price of production coincide. Finally, we suppose that the entire capital turns over at the same speed in both countries. Thus, the exchange relationship between the two countries is equal.

Table 2.3

Country	Constant Capital	Variable Capital	Surplus Value	Cost Price	Value	Rate of Profit	Average Rate of Profit	Price of Prod.
	c	v	s	$c + v$	$c + v + s$	$\frac{s}{C}$	P'	$(c + v) + P' \times C$
A	100	100	100	200	300	50%	50%	300
B	100	100	100	200	300	50%	50%	300
					= 600			= 600

In table 2.4, the wages in country A have risen by 50%, which leads to less exploitation and less surplus value domestically. This has consequences for the exchange of commodities between the two countries.

Equal quantities of labour-power are used in the two countries. It is only the price for the labour-power which is not the same and, therefore, the value of the production in the two countries is the same. The rate of surplus value 's' is different in the two countries, but the average rate of profit is the same. Because the price of labour-power is different, we get different prices of production even though there is the same quantity of human labour and the same quantity of value in the two countries.

Whereas the commodities in table 2.3 were equally exchanged by 300 to 300, the wage increase of 50% in table 2.4 (which is moderate compared to the real differences) results in an unequal exchange: 333 1/3 for 266 2/3. Country B is down 300—66 2/3 = 33 1/3 as compared to an equal exchange. And country A gains 333 1/3—300 = 33 1/3. In the case of a complete exchange of commodities between country A and country B, country A would gain 33 1/3 + 33 1/3 = 66 2/3. At the same time, the wage increase in country A means that the overall average rate of profit falls from 50 per cent to 33 1/3 per cent. However, in "historical capitalism" this tendency has been countered by higher profit rates in country A and lower in B, due to the different forms of monopoly, mentioned above.

Table 2.4

Country	Constant Capital	Variable Capital	Surplus Value	Cost Price	Value	Rate of Profit	Average Rate of Profit	Price of Prod.
	c	v	s	$c + v$	$c + v + s$	$\frac{s}{C}$	P'	$(c + v) + P' \times C$
A	100	150	50	250	300	20%	33.33%	333.33
B	100	100	100	200	300	50%	33.33%	266.67
					= 600			= 600

As seen from table 2.4, unequal exchange involves both export and import. On the export side, it results from the difference between the international value created by domestic labor in the production of exported commodities and the international value realized in money from their sale on the world market. On the import side, it is the difference between the international value created by foreign labor in the production of the imported commodities and the sum of international money given in payment for them by domestic purchasers. Therefore, transfers of value in international trade derive from the difference between value created in production in one country and value realized in circulation in another country.

On Exploitation

The values of commodities is measured in terms of quantity of labor, which takes place in the sphere of production; however, the appropriation of value takes place in the sphere of circulation, through exchange on the market.

Exploitation is an appropriation of other people's labor. This is true whether it is a person's exploitation of another person or one country's exploitation of another. The products of human labor are commodities or services and, therefore, the appropriation of human labor is the appropriation of these commodities and services. Consequently, all exploitation between countries is ultimately based on an unequal exchange of commodities and services. This may either be reflected by a deficit in the balance of trade, which means that the imperialist country imports more commodities than it exports according to current world market prices, or by inequality in the actual price formation. As Emmanuel argues:

> To simplify still further: one country can only gain something at the expense of another by taking more goods than it provides or by buying the goods it obtains too cheaply and selling those it provides at too high a price.[64]

It is no accident that the U.S. has the largest trade deficit in the world—773.4 billion USD in 2023.[65]

In a developed capitalist mode of production, the transfer of value takes different forms. As we have seen, value is transferred from lines of industry with a low organic composition to lines with a high organic composition. Finance and trade capital can gain value without even being directly attached to the sphere of production. Value is transferred from countries with a low wage level to countries with a high wage level. All these transfers of value can only be understood if capitalist circulation is considered as a whole. The basis of the surplus value—the surplus-labor—is performed in production, and the appropriation and distribution of the surplus value take place in the trade in commodities.

Because exploitation through unequal exchange takes place in the interactions on the world market, the smaller industrial countries in the core—like the Scandinavian countries—that lacked colonies could join in and ride on the wave of the big colonial powers. Denmark connected to the British Empire in the second half of the 19th century by delivering agricultural products to the British working class. Sweden linked to Germany by delivering raw materials, such as iron, copper, and timber, to the rapidly expanding industrial power.[66] Through the movement of capital and goods between the colonial powers and the other industrial countries, each of them got its share in the worldwide unequal exchange. The share of the cake did not depend on the size of imperial possessions but on the industrial potential and wage levels in each of these countries. We have only to compare the standard of living of Sweden, Denmark, and Canada, on the one hand, with that of Portugal, Italy, or even France before World War II, on the other.

This is also why this dismantling of colonialism after the Second World War was not the end of imperialism, but its expansion. By the middle of the twentieth century, the anachronistic character of colonialism, under pressure from the United States to free international trade, had rendered it obsolete in this form. The former colonial empires adjusted themselves to the new situation without

---

64 Emmanuel, Arghiri (1975) 'Unequal Exchange Revisited', p. 56. Institute of Development Studies, University of Sussex, Discussion Paper No. 77, August 1975.

65 World Population Review, US Trade Deficit by Country 2024.

66 Lauesen, Torkil (2021) *Riding the Wave, Sweden's Integration into the Imperialist World-system*, pp. 35-43. Montreal: Kersplebedeb, 2021.

too much grief, letting the economic laws of international trade attribute to each of them the benefits of unequal exchange.

The fact that a person takes part in production as a wage-laborer does not necessarily mean that the person is exploited or that the worker cannot exploit other people. Wage-labor is a *sine qua non* of capitalist exploitation, but it is not enough. The exploitation depends on the actual ratio between the "necessary labor" (the wages) and the "surplus labor" (the surplus value). Thus, if you can appropriate more value by buying commodities with your wages than the value you produce as a wage worker, you are *not* being exploited, but you are exploiting—if we take the global perspective.

In principle, there is nothing new about this. In *Grundrisse,* Marx deals with the fact that laborers could benefit from other laborers' products being sold below their value to the extent that these products were part of their consumption. He writes:

> As regards the other workers, the case is entirely the same; they gain from the depreciated commodity only in relation (1) as they consume it; (2) relative to the size of their wage, which is determined by necessary labour. If the depreciated commodity were, e.g. grain—one of the staffs of life—then first its producer, the farmer, and following him all other capitalists, would make the discovery that the worker's necessary wage is no longer the necessary wage; but stands above its level; hence it is brought down. [...][67]

Engels did not doubt the possibility of the British' proletariat exploiting the colonial proletariat.

> [...] the English proletariat is actually becoming more and more bourgeois, so that this most bourgeois of all nations is apparently aiming ultimately at the possession of a bourgeois aristocracy and a bourgeois proletariat alongside the bourgeoisie. For a nation which exploits the whole world this is of course to a certain extent justifiable.[68]

And in a letter to Kautsky he wrote:

> You ask me what the English workers think about colonial policy. Well, exactly the same as they think about politics in general: the same as the bourgeois think. There is no workers' party here, you see, there are only Conservatives and Liberal-Radicals, and the workers gaily share the feast of England's monopoly of the world market and the colonies.[69]

Thus, the fact that wages of a certain size can contain more value than the labor performed in order to get those wages is not something new. It is a question

---

67 Marx, Karl (1857-61) *Grundrisse,* Foundations of the Critique of Political Economy. Notebook IV: The Chapter on Capital, The General Rate of Profit, p. 439. London: Penguin, 1973.

68 Engels, F (1858) "Letter to Marx, dated 7 October 1858", In Marx and Engels, *Selected Correspondence*, p. 110. Progress' Publishers, Moscow, 1965.

69 Engels, F (1882) "Letter to Kautsky, dated 12 September 1882", In: Marx and Engels, *Selected Works*, p. 678. Moscow: Progress Publishers, 1970.

of calculations, not of principles.

As mentioned above, Emmanuel's theory of unequal exchange has been criticized for focusing too much on the circulation of goods and disregarding production. But the theory concerns more than just trade: it points to the heart of the conflict between capital and labor, which is reflected in the global differences in wages and differing degrees of exploitation. Emmanuel knew very well that the basis for value was created in production, but it is in exchange that value is realized. Exploitation is the result of the full circle of capital accumulation, which encompasses both production and circulation. No interpretation of Marx's theory of value can disregard the role of the market in the transfer of value. It is through the market that value is acquired and distributed, both between different capitals and between capital and labor. Emmanuel adapted the theory of value to international trade, something that most of his critics have not even tried to do. However, the development of capitalism continued with a new division of labor and the globalization of the production process itself.

Neoliberal Lessons for Dependency Theory

When the political group I belonged to—Communist Working Group—was studying Unequal Exchange in the late 1970s, we were wondering why capital did not move much more industrial production to the Global South to take advantage of low wages. We discussed this with Emmanuel in 1982, who cited several practical, technical, cultural, and political reasons. Transport and communications barriers posed huge obstacles to manage and control production at a distance. The trade unions in the center still had the strength to resist outsourcing, and the social democratic-led states had the ambition to regulate multinational companies.[70] The polarizing dynamic in global capitalism from the second half of the nineteenth century and up through the twentieth century led the "dependency" theorists of the 1970s to conclude that the industrialization of the Third World was impossible within the imperialist system. They assumed that a substantial domestic market for consumer products had to be developed before a substantial industrialization could occur. Third World countries had to delink to unblock the development of their productive forces, as Russia in 1917 and China in 1949 had tried. Third World countries would continue to supply raw materials, tropical agricultural products, and simple, labour-intensive industrial commodities; their economies would remain dependent, and they would continue to constitute the periphery of a world-system still dominated by capital-

70 Lauesen, Torkil (2023). "Emmanuel and Us".

ist states. However, the development of the production forces and capitalism's need to expand accumulation changed all that. History moves in leaps. Capitalist development knocked down the barriers to industrialization of the Global South. Its need to expand and its hunger for profit led it to outsource industrial production on a massive scale from the Global North to the Global South.

Neoliberal Globalization

Emmanuel began to develop his ideas of unequal exchange while living in the Congo from 1937 until 1960 and formulated his thesis in the mid-'60s. However, from the late '70s and over the next three decades, a transformation of historical dimensions of the international division of labor took place. It not only changed and expanded international trade but also globalized the capitalist production process itself.

Neoliberal globalization was based on the development of the productive forces in terms of information handling and communication (computers, cell phones, etc.), new management forms (such as "just in time" production), and the huge reduction in transport costs because of the introduction of the standard shipping container and corresponding handling equipment in sea- and airports. These developments of the productive forces made it possible to control and manage production globally. The distance between the place of production and the market became less relevant, and hence also the need for the geographic proximity of a high level of consumption to generate or sustain an industrialization process.

The political side of this transformation of the global division of labor was the introduction of neoliberalism, a showdown with the attempts of the state to control capital. Capital supposedly hates the state, as it interferes with business and demands taxes, but equally capital cannot live without a state. The state is the necessary "over-capitalist" that administers the system to prevent it from crashing. The state, through its monopoly on the use of violence, maintains "social peace" and protects property rights. The state is also the central entity in capitalism's international political institutions. Transnational capital is therefore not detached from the nation-state. The U.S. government looks after the interests of U.S. corporations first, the German government after the interests of German ones, and so forth. Nation-states provide political and military means for national bourgeoisies to compete with one another in the struggle over global market share and investment opportunities.

In the '60s, capital concentration reached the point where the revenue of some corporations exceeded that of smaller nation-states. The national-state administration of economics, finance, and trade became more and more a straitjacket for capital. The pressure on capital culminated in the early 1970s. In terms of the economy, the "oil crisis" erupted in 1973. There was high inflation and stagnation in both production and consumption, a phenomenon referred to as "stagflation." The West experienced its first serious recession since the Second World War. This crisis revealed that Keynesian methods were no longer effective in protecting the nation-state from economic crises.

However, capitalism was still a vital mode of production and was not out of options to expand. If millions of people in the Third World and the socialist bloc could be firmly integrated into the capitalist labor-force and world market, imperialism could be reinforced. However, this new "spatial fix" required a weakening of the nation-state. The "social state" was no longer part of the solution for capital but part of the problem. This was partly because welfare programs demanded a share of the capitalists' profits via taxes, but mainly because the control of the nation-state was a barrier to transnational capital global ambitions, which was the key to a revived imperialism. If transnational capital wanted not only to invest and trade globally but also to relocate production from the Global North to countries where low wages could be enforced, it had to free itself from state restrictions. This was the reason behind neoliberalism's attack on the "social state" and trade unions in the '80s.

Neoliberal political leaders, such as Ronald Reagan in the US and Margaret Thatcher in Britain, launched an all-out attack on government regulation, public welfare programs, and the redistribution of wealth via taxes. They ensured capital's free mobility, privatized the public sector, and limited trade union power. They demanded a shift from the "social state" to the "competition state." This meant that the state's main task was to compete with other states to create the best conditions for capital. From regulating and controlling transnational capital, the state has now moved on to serve it.

From the very beginning of industrial capitalism up to the 1970s, the countries of the periphery mainly served as sources of raw materials and tropical agricultural products. In the 1950s, industrial goods made up only 15% of the exports of all Third World countries combined. By 2009, the number had risen to 70%.[71] Industrial production had, at a rapid speed, been moved from the Global North to the Global South.

The liberalization of goods, labor, and capital markets, the reduction of transport costs and shipping times, and the spread of new information and com-

71 UNCTAD (2009), *Handbook of Statistics, 1980–2009*. New York & Geneva: United Nations.

munication technologies have all contributed to the emergence of a new model of organization of production on a global scale. This new industrial paradigm has replaced the old vertical and spatial integration of production with a new horizontal integration under the control of large multinational corporations, based on the dispersion of the manufacturing cycle between firms and countries around the globe and aimed at minimizing costs.

In total, the global labor force engaged in capitalist production rose from 1.9 to 3.1 billion people between 1980 and 2011. That is an increase of 61 percent. Three quarters of this workforce live in the Global South. Together, China and India account for 40 percent of the world's labor force.[72] India joined the World Trade Organization (WTO) in 1995, China in 2001, and the former Soviet republics and countries of Eastern Europe were integrated into the global capitalist market around the same time. This meant an expansion of capitalism of a historic magnitude, comparable to the abolition of feudalism.

Figure V illustrates the changes in the global division of industrial labor between 1950 and 2010. In 1980, the numbers of industrial workers in the Global South and Global North were about equal. In 2010, there were 541 million industrial workers in the Global South, while only 145 million remained in the Global North.[73] The center of gravity for global industrial production no longer lies in the Global North but in the Global South.

Agriculture in the South has also undergone big changes. Agricultural production has been integrated into the global market, and a new rural proletariat has emerged, involved in the production of tropical timber, vegetable oil, coffee, tea, fruits, meat, and fodder. More effective means of transport and "cold chains" have radically transformed the global market for fruits, vegetables, and flowers. These are now available in all shapes and forms year-round for customers in the North. Eighty percent of the workforce in this so-called "non-traditional agricultural sector" consists of women.[75] The market itself is controlled by a handful of global distributors.

Outsourcing is not limited to industrial and agricultural labor. It is also a major factor in the service industry. Services that can be moved *are* moved. Mumbai, for example, has become the global center for IT services. Labor costs

72 ILO (2011) *World of Work Report 2011.* Geneva: International Labour Organization, 2011.

73 Intan Suwandi and John Bellamy Foster (2016), "Multinational Corporations and the Globalization of Monopoly Capital", *Monthly Review*, vol. 68, no. 3 (July–August 2016), p. 124.

74 Smith, John (2011) *Imperialism and the Law of Value,* Global Discourse, vol. 2, no. 1, 2011.

75 ILO (2002) Decent Work and the Informal Economy. *Report* 6. Geneva: International Labour Organization (2002), p. 36.

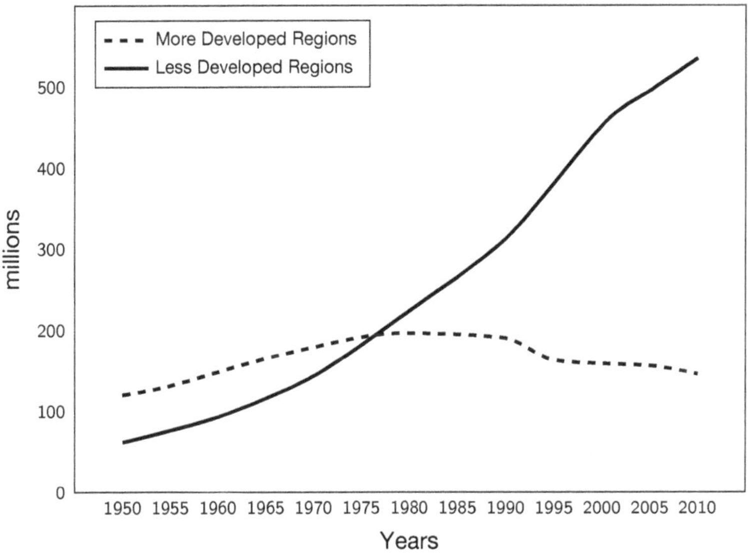

Figure V The Global Industrial Workforce, 1950-2010[74]

for an Indian software engineer, programmer, or data assistant are a fraction of what employers would have to pay in North America or Europe. Telephone call centers, accounting, design, and printing are also increasingly being moved to the South.

In the 1990s, it became popular to describe Western societies as "post-industrial." Immaterial labor, meaning labor related to knowledge, information, communications, service, creativity, and what has been dubbed the "experience and entertainment economy" became increasingly important. We are a far cry from a "post-industrial" world, however: computers, screens, smart phones, and all the other consumer goods we use in ever increasing quantities are produced by actual people. Globally, there are *more* industrial workers today than four decades ago, not less. While the labor is done in the South, it is still controlled by the North, which handles finance and trade, and enforces property rights. Economists have characterized the present phase of globalization as one "in which production and the realization of value are more delinked geographically than ever before."[76]

76 Milberg, William and Winkler, Deborah (2013) *Outsourcing Economics: Global Value Chains in Capitalist Development.* Cambridge University Press, Cambridge. 2013, pp. 12–13.

Global Production Chains

In the nineteenth century, goods were typically produced within a factory, where raw materials were turned into a finished product. In the twentieth century, especially after the Second World War, more and more parts of products were produced elsewhere. Big corporations began to use suppliers, but most of them still operated in the same country. International trade was still dominated by raw materials and finished products.

Today, the journey from idea to finished product happens increasingly along *global chains of production*.[77] These first rose to prominence in the 1970s, when they were used in the production of shoes, clothes, and toys. It didn't take long before the principle was applied to the production of pretty much everything, from heavy machinery to advanced electronics. Each step in the production process is moved to where conditions are best for the corporations involved. If these optimal conditions change, production moves again. The first links in the chain—finance, research and development, and design—are placed in the center, which also controls the overall process. Production takes place in a multitude of factories in peripheral countries, where labor costs are low. It is also here that all the intermediate stages of processing and assembly are done. The final stages, branding and marketing, are done in central countries, where a major portion of the products is sold, hence realizing the value, which is distributed between profit for capital and cheap commodities for consumers.

Today, the parts of a new car on the market might have been produced in twenty different countries, and even its assembly might have been divided between different locations. BMWs are assembled not only in Germany but also in China. Ford assembles cars in Mexico, Volkswagen in Brazil, and Toyota all across Asia. Nike shoes and clothes are produced at forty different locations in South and Southeast Asia. They are designed in the US, and prototypes are made in Taiwan. With the help of advanced computer technology, blueprints for mass production are then sent to China, Vietnam, Indonesia, South Korea, and India. The finished products end up, for the most part, in North America and Europe, where they are marketed and sold. This is an example of a fairly simple chain of production. Others can be much more intricate. Computers produced by Dell include about 4,500 different parts, produced in three hundred different locations.

---

77 The term "global commodity chain" was introduced by Hopkins, Terence K. and Wallerstein, Immanuel (2013) Commodity Chains in the World-Economy Prior to 1800. *Review* (Fernand Braudel Center), vol. 10, no. 1 1986, pp. 157–170.

A good example of a so-called "fabless" (no fabrication) company is Apple. Apple develops, designs, and sells products but outsources all of the manufacturing. Apple is one of the world's most valuable companies; in 2024, it had a stock market value of over 3 trillion USD. Most of the money does not come from production but from patents. A 2010 report on Apple's iPhone production, commissioned by the Asian Development Bank Institute, states: "It is almost impossible to define clearly where a manufactured product is made in the global market. This is why on the back of iPhones one can read 'Designed by Apple in California, Assembled in China.'"[78]

This information tells us very little about the actual production process. The parts for Apple products are produced by companies such as Toshiba and Samsung in different locations across Southeast Asia. They are then shipped to Shenzhen in China, where the Foxconn company, whose headquarters is in Taiwan, owns gigantic factories. In the Longhua factory, where iPhones and other Apple products are assembled, four hundred thousand Chinese laborers work, sleep, and eat. Laborers in the Shenzhen factories work twelve hours a day, six days a week.[79] Apple executives in California call Foxconn's factory town "Mordor," after the ghastly region in J.R.R. Tolkien's *Lord of the Rings*.[80] If we follow the chain of production further, we find Congolese miners working under lethal conditions to retrieve the minerals used in electronic components. The Congolese miners, the Chinese workers, and the California executives are all connected by chains of production, yet their standards of living are worlds apart.

Global chains of production can be roughly divided into two categories:

The first is the *producer-driven* chain of production: transnational corporations coordinate a network of production sites where single parts are manufactured and assembled in the locations that offer the best conditions. In a 2011 study, Timothy Kerswell offered a detailed description of chains of production in the automobile industry.[81] Once upon a time (when the term "Fordism" was used to describe an entire era's form of industrial production), an automobile

---

78 Xing, Yuqing and Detert, Neal (2010) "How the iPhone Widens the United States Trade Deficit with the People's Republic of China", *ADBI Working Paper 257*. Asian Development Bank Institute, Tokyo 2010.

79 Duhigg, Charles and Bradsher, Keith (2012) "How the U.S. Lost Out on iPhone Work", *New York Times*, January 22, 2012.

80 Aschoff, Nicole (2015) "The Smartphone Society", *Jacobin*, no. 17 (March 2015), p. 2.

81 Kerswell, Timothy (2911) *The Global Division of Labour and Division in Global Labour* (Ph.D. thesis). Queensland University of Technology 2011, p. 192.

was assembled in a factory along an assembly line. Today, the automobile industry is a textbook example of how "lean and flexible" chains of production function. Parts for a Ford car, for example, come from seventeen different countries, are delivered "just in time," and are assembled in various locations around the world.

The other type of chains of production is the *consumer-driven* one, the trademark of global supermarket chains such as Tesco and Walmart, as well as big fashion brands like Nike, Adidas, Zara, Hugo Boss, Vero Moda,[82] and H&M. These companies outsource the production of goods for mass consumption to suppliers in the Global South "at arm's-length." The suppliers are responsible for production, while the corporations are responsible for design, branding, marketing, distribution, and sale.

The fact that the global chains of production are controlled by corporations based in the Global North is the reason for the superprofits they generate. It allows monopolies to claim significant shares of the value created in the suppliers' factories. The profits made by Foxconn from the production of Apple products between 2005 and 2015 amounted to between 2 and 3 percent of the sales price; the profits made by Apple were 30 percent.[83] Suppliers in the Global South often produce exclusively for a particular corporation in the Global North. The "brand" company from the North has the power to put pressure on the producing company in the South and appropriate a bigger share of the profit. Once upon a time, transnational corporations had offices in various countries. In fact, this was the original definition of a transnational corporation. Today, a transnational corporation is simply a corporation that has the power to control and coordinate economic activities in various countries. Corporations based in the US, Western Europe, or Japan do not compete with companies in Mexico or Bangladesh. Nor do the industrial zones of the Global South currently threaten the power of North American, European, and Japanese corporations. Companies in the Global South are simply *used* by corporations in the Global North. Their only competitors are other companies in the Global South. The same is true for the corporations of the Global North: Nike vs. Adidas, Apple vs. Microsoft, and so on.

Globalization of production, in the form of production chains, has changed the structure of international trade. The flows of intermediate and semi-finished goods, within transnational companies, have significantly in-

82 **Ed. Note:** A Danish womenswear brand.

83 See, for example, Drahokoupil, Jan and Andrijasevic, Rutvica and Sacchetto, Devi (eds.) (2016), *Flexible workforces and low profit margins: electronics assembly between Europe and China.* Brussels: European Trade Union Institute (ETUI) (2016), pp. 158, 167.

creased their share in the imports and exports of each country.[84] International trade increased tenfold between 1980 and 2007, and it has been estimated that transnational corporations' networks of production accounted for roughly 80 percent of this.[85] The sometimes fictive pricing of this inter-firm trade, and the multiple crossing of borders before a product reaches the final market, makes the traditional method of calculating imports and exports less indicative of countries' real trade positions.[86]A more accurate picture of net trade flows is given by exports and imports measured in terms of value added, which are compiled by UNCTAD.[87]

William Milberg has noted that "many 'manufacturing' firms now do no manufacturing at all, providing only brand design, marketing, supply chain logistics and financial management services."[88] He explains how this is directly linked to falling import prices, which have been essential for maintaining high profit rates.[89] Milberg also links finance capitalism in the North to the low prices for products manufactured in the South. Reduced production costs brought increased profit shares that were "retained and reinvested." The correlation between financialization in the North and the creation of value in the South is expressed in the fact that the corporations most dependent on cheap imports are also the most financialized in terms of shareholder value.[90] As Steve Knauss concludes:

> The expansion of finance, as with marketing, logistics coordination, and other prominent types of unproductive labor commonly seen in the North in recent decades, provides a strong indication that transfers of value remain a prominent feature of global political economy in the 21st century.[91]

In the past 75 years, "development economists" have been telling Third World countries that industrialization will allow them to catch up with the rich

---

84 Hickel, Jason (2021), *The Divide.* United Kingdom: Left Book Club 2021. p. 225.

85 UNCTAD (2013), *World Investment Report 2013.* New York & Geneva: United Nations (2013), p. 35.

86 Ricci, Andrea (2021) *Value and Unequal Exchange in International Trade*, p. 14, New York: Routledge, 2021.

87 UNCTAD (2018) UNCTAD-Eora Global Value Chain (GVC) database.

88 Milberg, William (2008) Shifting Sources and Uses of Profits: Sustaining US Financialization with Global Value Chains. *Economy and Society*, vol. 37, no. 3. 2008, p. 425.

89 Milberg, William and Winkler, Deborah (2013) *Outsourcing Economics: Global Value Chains in Capitalist Development*, Cambridge: Cambridge University Press, 2013, pp. 107–108.

90 Milberg, William (2008) "Shifting Sources and Uses of Profits: Sustaining US Financialization with Global Value Chains", *Economy and Society*, vol. 37, no. 3. 2008. pp. 439, 445.

91 Knauss, Steven (2015), "Unequal exchange in the 21st Century." Unpublished paper, p. 29.

countries; all the poor countries had to do was emulate Europe and North America. But the current industrialization of the South cannot be compared to the industrialization of Europe and North America more than a century ago. Circumstances are entirely different. The industrialization of the North was made possible by tariff barriers and a strong domestic market. It was made possible by colonialism and imperialism. The current industrialization of the South is entirely dependent on exports. There are no industrial monopolies in the South. On the contrary, the industrialization of the South is characterized by fierce competition. The monopolies based in the North (the "big brands") can choose between numerous suppliers. Furthermore, the South has no periphery to exploit, and the vast majority of the profits go to the North. It is very difficult for the workforce of the South to gain higher wages: there exists a large reserve army of labor, millions of unemployed men and women desperately seeking employment, and migration laws make it difficult for them to move to countries where wages are higher. Finally, the reserve army of labor in the South do not have the "undiscovered continents" to settle in, as the Europeans did.

When industrial jobs were moved to the South, wage levels from the North did not move with them. Industrialization brought some countries in the South a higher GDP, but this mainly benefited new upper and middle classes, as for example in India. The industrialization of countries like Mexico, Brazil, and South Africa is not paving the way to a life resembling that of the majority European or North American working classes. It is impossible to export the goods produced in the South for low prices to the North and establish a consumer society in the South at the same time, as Marini explained (discussed above). The industrialization of the South depends on the purchasing power of the North. While capitalist development in the North was characterized by a balance between supply and purchasing power, no such balance exists in the South. Nor can it within the current world-system. The low wages of the South require the creation and maintenance of a large reserve army of labor.

Labor Arbitrage

The globalization of production is characterized by the outsourcing of production to low-wage countries. To explain this process, the economist John Smith uses the term "labor arbitrage."[92] Arbitrage is an economic term that describes trading to take advantage of differences in the price of a commodity (in this case,

92 Smith, John 2011) "Imperialism and the Law of Value." *Global Discourse*, vol. 2, no. 1 (2011), p. 17. Stephen S. Roach was the first to use the term "global labour arbitrage."

labor-power) in different markets (in this case, low-wage and high-wage countries). Arbitrage allows a corporation to make a profit by buying cheap labor-power on one market and selling the products they produce on another market where the wages are higher. The more unequal the markets are, the higher the profit. There are hardly any markets more unequal than those for labor in the Global North and the Global South.

Labor arbitrage takes two forms: first, production is moved to low-wage countries. Second, labor is imported from low-wage countries. The first is by far the most important because the mobility of labor is limited by migration laws, as the militarized borders of the European Union and the US make painfully obvious. However, on the other hand, in the last two decades we have seen a new dynamic in the international division of labor: the exportation of labor-power.

Industries that cannot easily move, for example agriculture, construction, or the care and service industries, do what they can to import cheap labor. Migrant workers toil in the fields of the US and on European construction sites. Truck drivers from the Philippines and Bangladesh take care of logistics in Denmark at a fraction of local wages, sleeping and living in their vehicles. Countries such as Saudi Arabia, Kuwait, and other Gulf States have become entirely dependent on the import of low-wage labor. Migrant workers are brought into the country when they are needed and sent away when they are not. This is particularly pronounced in the construction and service industries. The skylines of Dubai and Qatar have been built by workers from Bangladesh, Nepal, and the Philippines. William Robinson has described their situation: "Neither employers nor the state wants to do away with immigrant labor. To the contrary, they want [...] its maximum exploitation together with its disposal when necessary."[93]

The export of labor power, through international labor migration, involves high vulnerability regarding the human rights and the working condition of the migrant workers. Workers who emigrate from their country of origin are subjected to restrictive migratory regimes regardless of whether they are considered legal or "illegal" immigrants. The legal immigrant workers in the U.S. pay taxes without receiving social benefits. The workers categorized as "illegal" regardless of the labour market demand are subjected to conditions of super-exploitation, discrimination, and xenophobia. This situation not only obscures the significant contributions that migrants make to destination economies and societies but also contributes to criminalizing them and turning them into "public enemies," with important political dividends for the neoliberal far right.[94]

---

93 Robinson, William (2008) *Latin America and Global Capitalism. A Critical Globalization Perspective*, Baltimore:Johns Hopkins University, 2008, p. 313.

In recent years, the migration of labor has been included as a form of unequal exchange by Immanuel Ness in his book, *Migration as Economic Imperialism:*

> [...] the stark reality of neoliberal migration and imperialism [lies in] its continuity rooted in unequal exchange between the Global North and the Global South which originated in the European colonial project of resource extraction over the last three centuries.[95]

It might seem a contradiction in terms to add migration of labor as a form of unequal exchange, since the prerequisite for unequal exchange is the relative free mobility of capital and trade of goods together with the restricted mobility of labor by national borders, which upholds the difference in wage-levels. However, the migration of labor-power adds to the unequal exchange in two ways.

First is the import of the commodity of labor-power, with the poor country footing the bill for its upbringing and education. The costs of social reproduction, schooling, and training were assumed by the families of the migrants and the social capital fund administered by the state in the country of origin. These costs tend to be much more onerous than the accumulated remittances that are returned to the country of origin. This implies that, contrary to what is proclaimed by the World Bank and other institutions at the service of the interests of the United States and other imperialist powers, remittances—and therefore labour migration—do not represent a North-South subsidy, but precisely the opposite: a South-North subsidy, which is to say, a disguised modality of unequal exchange.[96]

Second, historically—and today—there are forms of labor migration which, so to speak, *take the difference in wage-level with them in the migration process.* Historically, European settlers took their relatively high wage-levels with them as they settled in the periphery of the world-system in past centuries, incorporating North America, Australia, and New Zealand into the center by more or less eliminating the original population. European settlers also turned South Africa, Namibia, Rhodesia, the Belgian Congo, Kenya, Algeria, and Palestine into small versions of the polarized world-system by creating a

---

94 Delgado Wis, Raúl (2022) "Imperialism, Unequal Exchange, and Labour Export." In Zak Cope (ed.), Immanuel Ness (ed) *The Oxford Handbook of Economic Imperialism*, Oxford, 2022, pp. 254-255.

95 Ness, Immanuel (2023) *Migration as Economic Imperialism: How International Labour Mobility Undermines Economic Development in Poor Countries.* Polity Press, Cambridge 2023. p. 16.

96 Delgado Wise, R., and S. Gaspar. 2018. 'Claves para descifrar la arquitectura de la globalización neoliberal: Exportación de fuerza trabajo e intercambio desigual'. In *La Globalización Neoliberal en Crisis*, edited by José Luis Calva, Mexico: Juan Pablos, pp. 159–186.

sharply divided labor force in terms of wage, together with apartheid-structured societies, all fundamentally based on brutal racism.

Similarly, in the migration from the periphery to the center, the labor force perpetuates the low remuneration. For African slave labor, there was no wage at all. For the Chinese and Indian contract labor in the U.S, the remuneration was far below that of the European settlers. We see similar patterns today. The legal and illegal migrants of labor from Latin America, Africa, and Asia to the center receive much lower wages than the homegrown labor force, a difference upheld by racist attitudes and structures in the center.

As the difference between the global value of labor and different wage levels of labor is the central point in the theory of unequal exchange, it makes sense to relate it to the migration of labor. Value can be transferred through the price-structure, when countries with relatively low wages exchange goods with countries with relatively high wages, but value can also be transferred through the migration of labor-power from the periphery to the center in order to produce goods and perform services, from child and elder care to prostitution, at a lower wage than is earned by the resident working class.

The driver of labor migration is that the low wage in the North is still significantly higher than what they could earn at home. According to the World Bank, each of the 210,000 Bangladeshi immigrants who resided in England in 2013 sent, on average, 4,058 USD to their families in Bangladesh. That same year, the average income of a worker in Bangladesh's textile industry was 1,380 USD. This means that a Bangladeshi immigrant worker in the UK could save three times more money than what a Bangladeshi worker in the textile industry could earn.[97] However, part of the money sent home by the migrant workers is used for the generation of future migrant workers.

The global market for labor is determined by global labor arbitrage, which is directly linked to both the limited mobility of labor and the vast reserve army of labor that is created and maintained in the Global South. According to the World Bank, "international wage price gaps exceed any other form of border--induced price gap by an order of magnitude or more."[98] Labor arbitrage allows a form of exploitation that is not directly dependent on political or military oppression and can simply rely on the global labor market. This does not mean,

---

97 Smith, John (2015) *Marx's Capital and the Global Crisis*. Paper presented at 'Imperialism: Old and New Conference', New Delhi, p. 6.

98 Clemens, Michael Montenegro, Claudio and Pritchett, Lant (2009) "The Place Premium: Wage Differences for Identical Workers Across the US Border." Background Paper to the *2009 World Development Report* (Policy Research Working Paper 4671). World Bank. New York, 2009, p. 33.

however, that oppression and violence have disappeared. They are necessary to maintain state power, global chains of production, and the division of the labor market. One of the most important functions of the state today is to control the movement across its borders—not of commodities and capital, but of people.

The Global *Value* Chains

The new international division of labor not only takes the form of global *production* chains but also of global *value* chains. Emmanuel's theory of unequal exchange was a critique of David Ricardo's classic comparative cost theory of foreign trade. Ricardo's classical example was Portuguese port wine traded against linen from England. International trade was the exchange of commodities produced *inside* different countries. However, the export-oriented industrialization of the Global South and the creation of global chains of production have added new forms of unequal exchange. These are more intricate than swapping raw materials and agricultural products for industrial products, which characterized most of the unequal exchange until the end of the 1970s and still exists. The Global North still imports agricultural products, such as coffee, tea, cacao, bananas, soy, etc., and minerals on a huge scale from the Global South.

However, the global production chains imply a new form of global value transfer. In these value chains, the contradiction between use-value and exchange-value in the commodity—the DNA of the cell in capitalism—reappears, now unfolded, at the global level. On one side, we have export-orientated "production economies" in the low wage countries in the Global South, focusing on exchange-value. On the other side, we have the "consumer economies" in the relatively high wage countries in the Global North, focusing on appropriating use-value.

In these global value chains, we also meet again, the double form of measurement of the exchange-value, unfolded at the global level. On the one hand, we have the different commodities standing in quantitative relation to each other. For example, one smartphone equals 5 pairs of sneakers equals a thousand dollars. On the other hand, the exchange-value of the commodity can be measured in the socially necessary labor time it takes to produce it. This period of time can also be quantified as the price of labor—the hourly wage.

However, in globalized capitalism, we have a situation where the *prices* of commodities tend to be globalized, except for one commodity—that of labor-power. The market price of labor-power—the wage—differs by a factor approximately 1:10 between the Global South and North, despite the globalization of the *value* of labor-power, which we can define as the average global wage. This difference between the market prices of labor in South and North and the globalized value of labor, in the global production chains, leads to a transfer of value from South to North in the value chain.

In other words: the basis of the value transfer is the difference between the exchange-value expressed by the market price of the commodity and the exchange-value of the commodity, calculated by the socially necessary labor time remunerated at average global wage. This value transfer is mediated by the price structure of labor-power and commodities in the world market.

The 'Happy' and 'Sour-faced' Smiley Curves

We can visualize the difference between the two forms of exchange-value. One, a 'happy' smiley curve, shows the value added along a production chain, generating the *market price* of a commodity. Another, a 'sour-faced' smiley curve, shows the value added at each step in the chain in terms of the globalized value of labor-power.

In neoliberal economic theory, the formation of the market price (for example, of a computer) is described as a production chain in which each step adds "value" to the product. In the first steps, when financing and management have control of the whole process, development and design are handled in the Global North, where wages and costs are high, so there is much "value" added; hence, the curve starts at the high end. Then the chain of production moves to the South, where low-wage labor produces the components of the product and assembles it; hence little "value" is added, and the curve falls. Finally, when the product returns to the North and requires branding and marketing to be sold, there is again a lot of "value added." A curve illustrating "value added" in terms of market prices, along this chain, looks like a happy-face smiley [Figure **??**].[99] According to the 'happy' smiley curve, the biggest part of the product's "value" is created in the North. However, this curve only reflects one form of measurement of the exchange-value—the market price. It does not visualize the *value* of the labor-power it takes to produce the product. The value of labor is not just a Marxist concept handy for analyzing capitalism. The necessary social time it takes to produce a commodity is a real existing expression of exchange-value in real existing capitalism. Let me explain.

---

99 Dedrick, J., Kraemer K. L., & Tsai T. (1999). ACER: An IT company learning to use information technology to compete. P.156. Center for Research on Information Technology and Organization, University of California.

Despite disagreements among economists of different stripes, they all seem to agree that production costs entail two main elements: raw materials, machines, factories, etc. (which Marx calls constant capital) and wages (which Marx calls variable capital). However, what determines the price of all these elements? Here, economists begin to disagree. As mentioned above, neoliberal market theory simply states that the prices of goods and services are determined by what consumers are willing to pay—supply and demand. If a product can be sold for a price that is higher than the production costs, someone makes a profit.

For Marxists, on the other hand, it is not the market that determines the price, but the cost of production. This is the first step in the transformation of value into market price. So, what determines the cost of production? Simply adding up the costs of raw materials, wages, etc. is not an answer, because we want to understand why they cost what they cost. As mentioned above, what all the necessary parts in the production process have in common is that they can be traced back to the consumption of labor-power.[100] We also explained above that labor-power is a very peculiar commodity; although it has a globalized value, its price—the specific wage—is determined by class struggles, historical and current, on both the national and the international level. These struggles cause huge variations in global wages.

If the question of surplus value is not particularly important to capital, wages and working hours certainly are. Capital understands that long and intensive working hours and low wages are sources of profit. Furthermore, as we noted concerning capital's organic composition, what matters to the capitalist is the *overall* production costs, not the ratio between constant and variable capital (and thereby surplus value). A sweatshop in Bangladesh does not necessarily generate more profit than an automated robot factory. It is not the raison d'être of capitalism to squeeze surplus value out of workers. This is, under the given circumstances, simply a consequence of all that really matters to the capitalist—namely, selling something for more than what it costs to produce it. This is where profit comes from in the mind of the capitalist.

From a Marxist perspective, however, price is not the same as value. Some commodities are sold for less than their value and others for more. Price determines the profit rate but also the distribution of value and surplus value, both between capital and labor (in the form of profits for the former and wages for

---

100 I am aware of the so-called "transformation problem," which consists in the assertion that Marx "failed" in his explanation of prices of production to transform the inputs (c + v) into prices of production. However, I do not think there is a problem. To transform inputs into prices would have been to explain prices in terms of prices. Instead, Marx sticks to the concept of value (average socially necessary labor time) in the formation of prices of production.

the latter) and between fractions of capital with different organic compositions (via the average profit rate). The transformation of value into price is therefore highly dependent on the political relationship between capital and labor, as well as between different fractions of capital. The redistribution of value and surplus value through market prices not only occurs between workers and fractions of capital within a single country but also globally, as a result of transnational movements of capital, trade, and production chains.

Marx's theory about the transformation of value into price assumed an integrated market for goods, capital, and labor. Such markets tend to form a single price for a single commodity, balance out profit rates, and pay the same wage for the same kind of labor. This is what we see domestically in the US, the EU, and Japan, and in the trade between them. The global market is different: it is an integrated market with respect to the movement of capital and goods, but not with respect to labor. Therefore, the wages paid for the same kind of labor can differ widely. This also applies to global production chains. Depending on where labor is carried out, its impact on the price of a product is very different. The surplus value of labor in one part of the world (the Global South) raises profits and consumption ability (via cheap prices) in another part of the world (the Global North). The "value added" in the "happy" smiley curve includes not only the value created by a company in its home country but also the value created elsewhere and usurped by capital and consumers via the price for which a commodity is sold on the global market. "Value added" is in reality value *captured*. In short, the basis for the profits made by companies and high consumption power in the North are created in the South.

In neoliberal economic theory, this fact is not recognized; on the contrary, lower wages mean less "value added." Therefore the "value added" curve in a global production chain running from North to South and back again has the shape of a "happy" smiley. However, it is not a curve of "value added" in Marxist terms but a curve illustrating the formation of prices of production. If we apply Marx's conception of value, the curve looks different. If you draw a curve for value added during the production of a computer or a pair of sneakers following Marx's theory, it will look like a "sour-faced" smiley, the exact opposite of the curve drawn by neoliberal economists. This does not mean that their curve is "wrong." It simply illustrates the creation of price, while the "sour-faced" smiley illustrates the creation of value in terms of labor time. The reason for labor in the Global South being much cheaper than labor in the Global North is not that labor in the South creates less value. The reason is that laborers in the South are more oppressed and exploited.

Andrea Ricci's definition of "Unequal Exchange" as the difference between

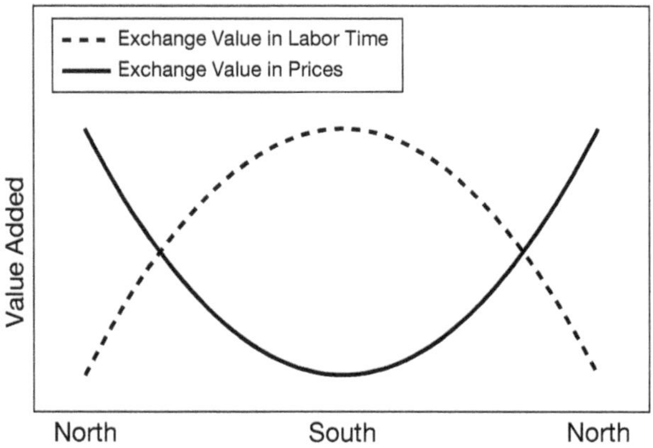

Figure VI Exchange Value Added in Global Production Chains

two measures of value of the same commodity, one expressed in terms of market exchange ratio (price) and one in terms of labor time, explains the two smiley curves well:

> Consequently, behind every extrinsic measure of the exchange-value of a capitalist commodity, consisting of the visible market exchange ratio it has with another commodity [the happy smiley], there is always a corresponding intrinsic measure consisting of the abstract labour time objectified in them [the sour-faced smiley]. This intrinsic measure, however, is not visible and is expressed externally in the form of extrinsic measure [i.e., the wage]. The existence of two measures of the exchange-value, one extrinsic and visible, the other intrinsic and invisible, makes possible the discordance between them.
>
> The quantitative correspondence between intrinsic and extrinsic measures of the exchange-value defines an equivalent exchange. When, on the other hand, the two measures diverge, there is non-equivalent exchange. In the equivalent exchange, the market exchange ratio between the commodities is defined by the respective abstract labour time objectified in each of them in production. By contrast, in non-equivalent exchange, a given amount of objectified abstract labour time is exchanged with a different amount of abstract labour time objectified in the production of the other commodity. In the latter case, we have value transfer in trade, since market exchange ratio and relative objectified abstract labour time differ from each other.
>
> Unequal exchange, therefore, derives from the discrepancy between the two measures of the exchange-value. These two measures, in turn, originate from the dual nature of exchange-value as a reflection of the dual nature of abstract labour as the substance of value. [...] In the definition given here, the unequal exchange concerns the difference between two measures of the same magnitude of value, represented by the given exchange-value of the commodities, once expressed in terms of market exchange ratio and once in terms of labour time. [...] [U]nequal exchange is the result of the non-equivalent conversion of the two units of measurement used to determine the same magnitude of

a given exchange-value.[101]

Unequal exchange arises in the divergence between value production and value realization on the world market.

Andrea Ricci continues, and sums up this interaction between the economic law of capitalism and the historical development of capitalism:

> In fact, with the rise of the global capitalist economy, underdeveloped countries are somehow objectively forced to participate in international trade, because they lack the technological, organizational, and social capacity to produce in an autonomous and independent way a wide range of consumer and investment goods necessary for their economic modernization. Unless radically questioning the model of capitalist economic and social development, the alternative poor countries face is between the subordinate access to capitalist modernity through their dependent integration in the global market or remaining in a pre-modern situation of secular economic and social stagnation. [...] In short, therefore, the exploitation of the poor countries by the rich countries through trade is an ordinary phenomenon in capitalism produced by the spontaneous operation of the international law of value, from which it is only possible to escape through conscious political and social actions aimed at breaking with the neoliberal logic of free trade, both within peripheral societies and at the level of the global world economy [...]
>
> In addition to the objective and purely economic action of the international law of value, resulting from the integration into the world market, the condition of subordination and dependence of peripheral economies is enhanced by additional non-economic factors. These are represented by the forms of direct exploitation of a colonial or neocolonial character imposed by imperialist powers and transnational corporations, based on political and military domination, overexploitation of indigenous labour power, and monopolistic control of natural, technological, and financial resources.[102]

Bright and Dark Value

Another picturesque presentation of value transfer by unequal exchange is given by the late sociologist Donald A. Clelland (1935-2021). Coming from Wallerstein's world-system tradition, he was inspired by Emmanuel in his analysis of value transfer in global production chains. Clelland distinguishes between the visible "bright value" (accounted costs) and the invisible "dark value" (unaccounted cost):

> Bright value is the "normal" form of extraction in which the flow is from peripheral labor and capitalists to core capitalists. Bright value is based on normal bookkeeping in which all paid out costs are worked out and recorded [...] The multinational corporation has

101 Ricci, Andrea (2021) *Value and Unequal Exchange in International Trade*, pp. 83-84. New York: Routledge 2021. (The words in square brackets are mine)

102 Ibid., pp. 126-127.

> increased its outsourced transaction "costs" by externalizing its production chain as a trade chain. It does so in order to reduce costs, thus obtaining "transaction benefits". Much of the value added at various steps in the chain is added to the surpluses collected toward the end of the chain. In other words, commodity chains are "degree of monopoly chains", designed to transfer surplus from competitive capitalists to quasi-monopolist capitalists, generally higher up the chain and in the core.[103]

In mainstream economics, a country's GDP is supposed to indicate the value of what it produces, but what country can claim the value of a smartphone, a pair of sneakers, or a Barbie doll produced in global chains of production? If the GDP indeed measured a country's production, then countries such as Liechtenstein, with a GDP of 89,400 USD per capita, Bermuda, with 85,000 USD per capita, and Luxembourg, with 102,000 USD per capita, would be among the five most productive countries in the world. China, with a GDP of 15,400 USD per capita, would be number 104, and Vietnam, with a GDP of 6,400 USD per capita, number 161.[104]

The reason for the high GDPs of countries such as Bermuda and Liechtenstein is not that their populations work so hard and are so incredibly productive but that these countries function as tax havens and provide offshore banking services. Simply put, they allow capital to grow. GDP figures are often criticized for disregarding both what are known as externalities (such as pollution and the exploitation of non-renewable resources) and reproductive labor (such as unwaged domestic work), but the single biggest problem with the figures is that the production of many commodities is no longer confined to any one country.

The basis of the high GDP in the Global North is the capture of what Clelland calls dark value.:

> Inspired by the recognition by physicists that imperceptible "dark matter" and "dark energy" account for 90 percent of the universe, I term this invisible surplus flow to consumers dark value, a hidden force that fuels the structure and expansion of the capitalist world-system. Unlike bright value that is accumulated as profit by the capitalist, the second type of surplus drain is collected by buyers in the form of cheap commodity prices. Because these transfers are externalized from economic accounting, a full calculation of dark value would require analysis of millions of surplus drains that are derived from unpaid household labor, under-paid labor, under-valued resources, and savings through uncosted human and environmental externalities. Dark value is deeply embedded in every economic transaction or commodity, making it the silenced partner that renders every bright value drain more profitable. Dark value is distinctive in three ways. First,

103 Clelland Donald A. (2014) Theoretical Conceptualization of Bright Value in Global Commodity Chains.

104 Smith, John (2016) *Imperialism in the twenty-first century*. "The GDP Illusion", p. 260, New York: Monthly Review Press, 2016). All numbers are from 2016. See CIA (2017), *The World Factbook*.

> these surplus drains are "free" inputs to capitalists, i.e., they are externalized from calculation of the costs of production. [...]
>
> How, then, is dark value produced? Since dark value may be found in all factors of production (capital, labor, land, natural resources, energy, knowledge), a hidden transfer occurs any time a capitalist obtains a component of production at less than the average world-market price. It is the embodiment of at least four types of hidden subsidies to commodity chains: (1) under-compensated formal labor, (2) under-remunerated or unpaid inputs from households or the informal sector, (3) cheap natural resources and (4) ecological and human externalities that are "economically free" to capitalists. Since employers have a high degree of monopoly over peripheral labor markets, their payments to labor often fall near or below household subsistence. It is these unpaid hours that are embedded in cheap core consumer prices and concealed in profit accumulation. Workers who do the same tasks with similar skills and equipment earn hourly wages that differ by as much as a ratio of fifty to one between zones, making the core working class an aristocracy of labor.[105] The core worker becomes an unwitting beneficiary of this exploitative system when he/she uses one waged hour to purchase a product that embodies many more lower-waged hours of peripheral labor.[106] The typical consumer is aware that the commodity would be more expensive if produced in the core. In that sense, dark value is not truly hidden at all, even though its actual economic value is officially denied.
>
> [...]
>
> Dark value drains occur because of the super-exploitation of peripheral labor, households and ecological resources. Once unequal exchange and surplus drains are initiated, their consequences are historically cumulative in peripheries.[107] On the one hand, bright value drains remove surpluses that might be invested in expanded reproduction and economic growth in the periphery. On the other hand, extraction of dark value threatens ecological sustainability and lowers the quality of life for worker households and women.[108]

Based on a Marxist understanding of value, the global economy resembles an iceberg. Only a small fraction is visible above the surface, while most of it remains out of sight. Clelland uses the name "dark value" to identify the latter, a reference to the term "dark matter," used by astrophysicists. In the same way that dark matter is required to explain the expansion of the universe, dark value is required to explain the expansion of capitalism. Clelland refers in this context to Emmanuel's notion of unequal exchange. But dark value is also created in indirect ways; for example, in the reproduction of labor-power. Many industrial

---

105 See Communist Working Group (1986) *Unequal Exchange and the Prospects of Socialism*, Copenhagen: Manifest Press. 1986. Updated edition: Washington: Iskra Books, 2025.

106 Emmanuel, A. (1972) *Unequal Exchange: A Study of the Imperialism of Trade*. New York: Monthly Review Press, 1972.

107 Amin, S. (1974) *Accumulation on a World Scale: A Critique of the Theory of Underdevelopment.*

108 Clelland, Donald A (2012) *Surplus Drain and Dark Value in the Modern World-System*. In Handbook of World-Systems Analysis, ed. Christopher Chase-Dunn and Salvatore Babones. Routledge. London 2012.

workers in the Global South are supported by an underpaid rural proletariat, peasants, and service workers in the informal sector who cook, clean, look after the children, etc. These groups constitute the lowest social layer in the production of dark value, making it possible for industrial laborers in the Global South to work for a dollar or two a day.

This becomes more concrete if we look at the way in which the value of a good produced in a global chain of production is attributed to GDPs. Clelland has studied the value transfer from the Global South to the Global North during the production and sale of Apple products.[109]

In a one-year period from 2010 to 2011, Apple sold over one hundred million iPads. Apple does not own a single factory, being a prime example of a "fabless" company. Apple develops, designs, and sells its products but outsources production. 748 suppliers working for Apple form a global chain of production. 613 of them are based in Asia, and 351 in China alone, where the products are assembled. Meanwhile, Apple's copyright is fiercely protected; it is the corporation that has filed the highest number of patent-related lawsuits worldwide.[110]

In 2011, an iPad in a US store cost 499 USD. Apple's overall production costs for one iPad were 275 USD. This means that Apple made a profit of 224 USD per item sold. That's 45 percent of the sales price. Out of the production costs of 275 USD, 150 USD were paid for development, design, and marketing, 92 USD for various components, and 33 USD to Foxconn, which was responsible for the production in China. Foxconn itself paid roughly 8 USD per unit in wages to its workers.[111] We can call the value added in this analysis the *bright value*, that is, the value that is visible in official statistics, calculations, and the "happy" smiley curve. Only a fraction of the value created during the production of an iPad is reflected in China's GDP, however. The lion's share is counted as part of the GDP of the US.

If we took GDP figures at face value, we'd have to conclude that even though people in China work very hard, the *visible* value of an iPad comes from US designers and advertisers. But even if you haven't read *Capital*, it is obvious that the profits that Apple takes home are largely based on the low-wage labor used to manufacture its products. Value *captured* is the much more accurate

---

109 Kraemer, Kenneth L. Linden, Greg and Dedrick, Jason (2011) *Capturing Value in Global Networks: Apple's iPad and iPhone.* Paper. Irvine, Berkeley & Syracuse: University of California & Syracuse University, 2011.

110 Clelland, Donald A. (2014) The Core of the Apple: Dark Value and Degrees of Monopoly in the Commodity Chains. *Journal of World-System Research,* vol. 20, no. 1, p. 92.

111 Ibid., p. 86.

term than value added to describe what is going on.[112] As John Smith puts it: "Despite its claim to be a measure of product, GDP measures the results of transactions in the marketplace. Yet, nothing is produced in marketplaces, the world of exchange of money and titles of ownership. Production takes place elsewhere—behind high walls, on private property, in production processes." For Smith, GDP has become "a veil concealing not just the extent but the very existence of North-South exploitation."[113]

If, in 2011, an iPad had been assembled by workers in the U.S., Apple would have paid 178 USD, not 33 USD. Add to this the production of the parts, which cost Apple 39 USD per item—had they been produced in the U.S, Apple would have paid 186 USD.[114]

The workers in the Global South who produce for Apple do not get their jobs because their productivity is lower than that of workers in the Global North. It is probably higher. The companies supplying Apple are leaders in their fields and use the most modern forms of management and technology. The intensity of labor expected from their workers would be unacceptable in the North. When, at a White House dinner in 2011, Barack Obama asked Apple's CEO, Steve Jobs, what it would take to bring the production of iPhones to the US, Jobs gave a candid answer: "Those jobs aren't coming back."[115]

On top of the unequal exchange caused by global wage differences, we have to add the ecological unequal exchange. Companies like Apple can avoid climate-related costs, so-called externalities, by moving production to places with weak environmental laws. For the production of an iPad, 12.2 kilograms of minerals and metals are needed, many of them rare ones. The production process requires 360 liters of water and releases 105 kilograms of greenhouse gases. The main ecological burden is borne by China and other Asian countries, not by consumers in the Global North. Donald A. Clelland has calculated that Apple saves about 30 USD per iPad in environmental fees by producing in the Global South instead of in the US—and the US does not even have particularly strict environmental regulations for industrial production.[116]

---

112 Kaplinsky, Raphael (2005) *Globalization, Poverty and Inequality. Between a Rock and a Hard Place.* Cambridge: Polity (2005), p. 164; Robert C. Feenstra, "Integration of Trade and Disintegration of Production in the Global Economy." *Journal of Economic Perspective*, vol. 12, no. 4 (1998), pp. 31–50.

113 Smith, John (2016) *Imperialism in the twenty-first century*. New York: Monthly Review Press (2016), p. 262.

114 Clelland, Donald A. (2014) The Core of the Apple: Dark Value and Degrees of Monopoly in the Commodity Chains. *Journal of World-System Research*, vol. 20, no. 1, p. 97.

115 Duhigg, Charles (2012) Apple's Jobs to Obama. *New York Times*, January 23, 2012.

Clelland concludes that the total dark value of an iPad, conservatively calculated, is no less than 472 USD. Producing it in the Global North would almost double the costs of production and therefore also the sales price. Without the dark value gained by production in Asia, Apple would sell fewer iPads and lose profits. But dark value does not just benefit transnational corporations: a huge part is passed on to consumers in the Global North in the form of lower prices. In other words, consumers in Global North benefit from the exploitation of workers in the Global South. For what they make in one hour of work, consumers in the Global North can buy commodities whose production requires numerous hours of low-paid (or unpaid) labor, environmental destruction, and the exploitation of valuable raw materials.[117]

To sum up: capitalism must be analyzed in its totality—in its global accumulation process. However, even in this complex process we can identify the contradiction in its "cell"—the commodity—between use-value and exchange-value. The contradiction in globalized capitalism is, on one hand, the imperative to expand production, to create more *exchange-value* in the search for more profit, and on the other hand, the lack of consumption power, created by the same production in search of *use-value* to fulfill its needs. This contradiction generated the overproduction/underconsumption crises which ravaged capitalism in the middle of the 19th century and led Marx and Engels to predict an early end of capitalism in the Communist Manifesto in 1848. However, the development of unequal exchange, the transfer of value from the periphery to supplement the consumption power in the center, became the historical, temporary solution, in which this contradiction could exist, and move ahead, creating a polarized world-system up through the twenty century and to the present.

Let's proceed by seeing how we can measure the transfer of value by unequal exchange on a global level.

---

116 Clelland, Donald A. (2014) The Core of the Apple: Dark Value and Degrees of Monopoly in the Commodity Chains. *Journal of World-System Research*, vol. 20, no. 1 (2014), p. 102.

117 Ibid., p. 105.

3

How to Measure Unequal Exchange?

THE COMMUNIST WORKING CIRCLE I was part of developed the so-called "parasite state theory"[1] in the late '60s. It was based on Lenin's writing on imperialism and opportunism in the European working class, in the contexts of the First World War and the split in the Second International.[2] We adapted—so to speak—Lenin's concepts to the Scandinavian consumer and welfare state of the '60s. The labor aristocracy was not just a layer of the working class, in the form of the ruling social democratic parties, who had administered capitalism for decades in Denmark, Sweden, and Norway, but instead more or less the working class as such constituted a privileged layer, from a world-system perspective. We wanted to consolidate the "parasite state theory" in the political economy of imperialism. Again, we turned to Lenin's book *Imperialism, the Highest Stage of Capitalism*, and in particular, his concept of "superprofit"—extraordinarily high profits from colonial investments.[3] We wanted to update Lenin's data from 1914 on foreign investments and profits and other factors related to imperialism, an exercise that had already been done by Varga and Mendelsohn in 1938.[4] We collected a huge amount of data and processed them into categories similar to Lenin's. We concluded that the profits from investment in the Third World did not have a size that could explain the difference in living standards

1 Lauesen, Torkil (2018) The Parasite State in Theory and Practice. *Labor and Society, No.* 21. (2018) pp. 285-300.

2 Lenin, V.I. (1916) 'Imperialism and the Split in Socialism'. In *On Imperialism and Opportunism,* Montreal: Kersplebedeb, 2019.

3 Lenin. V.I (1916) *Imperialism, the Highest Stage of Capitalism*. In Lenin, Collected Works, vol. 22. Moscow: Progress Publishers, 1972.

4 Varga, and Mendelsohn (ed.) *New Data for V.I. Lenin's 'Imperialism, the Highest Stage of Capitalism'* Moscow: Foreign Languages Publishing House, 1939.

between the imperialist countries and the Third World. However, our empirical studies also revealed that the difference in wage levels between the imperialist center and former colonies had expanded from five to one before the Second World War to fifteen to one at the beginning of the 1970s. We also noted a substantial increase in international trade based on an international division of labor exchanging raw materials and agricultural products from the Third World for industrial goods produced in the imperialist countries. However, it was only in 1974 that we became aware of Emmanuel's thesis of unequal exchange. We were not only interested in the mechanism of unequal exchange but also in the size of value transfer. Could the unequal exchange explain the relatively high living standard in the imperialist countries?

Several attempts have been made to calculate the overall value transfer by unequal exchange. Samir Amin spoke of 22 billion USD in 1965, and of 300 billion USD in 1980, but he didn't explain how he had reached those numbers.[5] Since then, others have developed models to measure the value transfer by unequal exchange.[6] Emmanuel did not make any specific calculations of the total size of unequal exchange, in his book he states:

> What is the quantitative importance of these transfers? Is it great or small? It is what it is. If it appears small and disappointing to some theoreticians of economic imperialism, I cannot help that, and there is nothing more to be said about it. But in fact, it is not small. Charles Bettelheim has made a simple mistake in arithmetic. The sum of the prices of the goods exported by the Third World to the advanced countries is, he says, about 25 billion USD, whereas the national income of the latter group of countries exceeds 1,000 billion USD. From this it would follow that the gain made by the advanced countries must be less than 2·5 percent. According to this method of calculation, if these prices should fall still further tomorrow, so that the Third World receives no more than 12·5 billion USD for the same amount of goods, the total gain made by the advanced countries will be cut by half. And so on and so forth, with any further reductions! The more the terms of trade of the underdeveloped countries worsen, the more negligible, according to this method of calculation, will be the gain made by the advanced countries. [...] Is it necessary, then, to reiterate that that sum of 25 billion USD represents the present

5 Samir Amin, *Accumulation on a World Scale,* p. 25. New York: Monthly Review Press, 1980.

6 Gibson Bill (1980), 'Unequal Exchange: Theoretical Issues and Empirical Findings'. *Review of Radical Political Economics,* vol. 12 no.3, pp. 15-35. Others: Webber, M. J., & Foot, S. P. H. (1984). 'The Measurement of Unequal Exchange'. *Environment and Planning A: Economy and Space, 16*(7), pp. 927-947. Williams, K.M. 'Is "Unequal exchange" a mechanism for perpetuating inequality in the modern world-system?'. *Studies in Comparative International Development* 20, pp. 47–73 (1985). Joseph, G.G. and Tomlinson, M. (1991) 'Testing the Existence and Measuring the Magnitude of Unequal Exchange Resulting from International Trade: A Marxian Approach'. *Indian Economic Review* New Series, Vol. 26, No. 2 (July-December 1991), pp. 123-148. Department of Economics, Delhi School of Economics, University of Delhi. Nakajima, A., & Izumi, H. (1995). 'Economic Development and Unequal Exchange among Nations: Analysis of the U.S., Japan, and South Korea'. *Review of Radical Political Economics, 27*(3), pp. 86-94.

> depreciated value of the Third World's exports? That its loss, and the gain accruing to the other group of countries, is not to be looked for on this side of that sum but on the far side of it? The fact that the present value is only 25 billion USD in no way prevents the plundering that arises from unequal exchange from assuming the dimensions of 200 or 300 billion. Everything depends on our estimate of the amount by which present value has been reduced.
>
> If we assume that wages account for 50 percent of the cost of these exports, and that the relevant rate of wages is one-twentieth of that prevailing in the advanced countries, a simple calculation will show us that the difference between the present value and the equivalence value is not a difference in tens of thousands, but in hundreds of thousands, of millions. If 50 sacks of coffee are at present exchanged for one automobile, whereas, in order to pay coffee plantation workers at the same rate as workers in the automobile industry, 50 sacks would have to be exchanged for 10 auto mobiles, the loss suffered by the coffee producers and the gain made by the other party in this transaction are not less than the value of 50 sacks, but nine times as much.[7],[8]

In our process of studying unequal exchange in the late '70s, my political organization decided to try to calculate the size of the value transfer by unequal exchange. The result of our studies was published in the book: *Unequal Exchange and the Prospects of Socialism*. It was written in 1979-1981 as a collective process. The manuscript was translated into English, and a group of us went to Paris to discuss its contents with Emmanuel in 1982. We wanted to present the concept of unequal exchange as concretely as possible, by providing actual figures for the value transferred to the imperialist countries. We discussed our manuscript with Emmanuel, and he was kind enough to write a preface for the book. The book was published in English in 1986.[9] In 1987, we sent a copy to Samir Amin, who also was a great source of inspiration for us. He wrote back:

> I fully appreciate your work and do share most of it (yet I think you are too "severe" with the western working class) Anyway, I hope we shall have the opportunity to discuss this. I particularly appreciated your estimate of the transfer of value S-N inherent in in the price system. This is really a good piece.[10]

In the following, I will reproduce our approach to measure the extent of unequal exchange, using the statistical figures from then, as it lays out many of the problems relating to measuring the size of the value transfer.[11] The first prob-

---

7 Hypothetical though they are, these figures are not at all fantastic. Bettelheim himself estimates that wages in the advanced countries are between 20 and 30 times as high as in the underdeveloped ones. (See his article, "Les travailleurs des pays riches et pauvres ont des interets solidaires," in *Le Monde*, November 11th, 1969.)

8 Emmanuel, Arghiri (1972) *Unequal Exchange: A Study of the Imperialism of Trade*, pp. 237-38. New York: Monthly Review Press 1972.

9 Communist Working Group (1986) *Unequal Exchange and the Prospects of Socialism*. Copenhagen: Manifest Press, 1986. Updated edition: Washington: Iskra Books, 2025.

10 Letter from Samir Amin, dated 21.1.1987. Private correspondence.

lem was to figure out a method—a formula—to calculate the size. The formula had to be an expression of the essence of unequal exchange.

If the wage rate is the exogenous and independent variable, generated by national and international class struggle, then the variation in the wage rate in one country will entail a variation in the same direction of the price of production. When countries with different wage rates exchange commodities on the world market, based on price of production, then there is an unequal exchange, in terms of labor time—a value-transfer from the low wage countries to the high wage countries. The value transfer is hidden in the formation of world market prices.

The ideal situation would be to have statistics of the number of hours of labor transfer from each country in the Third World to the imperialist center in the process of trade. This would imply knowledge of the size of the wage portion in the different exported commodities. Beside this, we needed to determine the variation of the specific national wage rates in relation to the global value of labor, defined as the global average wage, in dollars—the closest to world money you can get. The next step was to map out the trade pattern between North-Western Europe, North America, Japan, Australia, and New Zealand, on one side, and the Third World countries on the other side.

Another problem was the shortage of useful statistics. Statistics that measured the transfer of hours of labor between countries, did not exist at the time. So, the problem was how to measure the quantity of transferred labor in a uniform unit, when information on the size of the wage portion of the commodity price was not available, in addition to not having information on the intensity and productivity of labor in each country. The only available data were the figures for national wages, commodity prices, and information about international trade. None of us were academics, nor schooled in statistics, and it was long before the internet, so I spent many hours at the library of Copenhagen Business School, reading and photocopying statistics from international organizations such as the U.N., I.L.O., I.M.F., and World Bank, and reading in detail documents such as the General Agreement on Tariffs and Trade (GATT), and so on. It is evident that the figures, especially on wages in the Third World, were fraught with considerable uncertainty, so we tried to validate and supplement the official statistics, with the literature on international wage-variation, both historical wage studies and current studies of global wages.

This revealed that prior to capitalism, subsistence wages were more or less

11 See also the discussion in: Raffer, Kunibert (1987) *Unequal Exchange and the Evolution of the World-system*. pp. 193-212. New York: Palgrave Macmillan, 1987.

the global norm. It was the simultaneous process of colonialism and the breakthrough of industrial capitalism which broke this pattern. The plunder and super-exploitation of the colonies created profits, along with cheap raw materials and agricultural products, and these, in combination with the trade union struggle in the imperialist center, paved the way for higher wages in the second half of the 19th century.

> The limited information (on wages in Britain) available suggests that only after the Napoleonic wars did the level of real wages take off on the path of climb that was to take it by the end of the nineteenth century to levels never reached before. In the course of that climb it regained for the first time the level of the fifteenth century plateau [...] in 1880.[12]

A global study of wages by Cairnes in 1874 came to the following results: at that time, wages in the United States were 25-50 per cent higher than in Britain, 48-70 per cent higher than in Belgium, and about 100 per cent higher than in France. If we consider countries such as India and China, American wages were about 4-5 times as high.[13]

During the hundred years which have passed since then, this tendency has become much more emphasized. In the late 1970s, the difference in wages between the imperialist countries and the exploited countries was not 4-5 times but 10, 20, or 30 times. Table 3.1 gives an outline of the hourly wage rates in the industries of a number of selected countries, which are characteristic of both the imperialist countries and the exploited countries. The figures in the table correspond to the wage levels in the sectors in which the countries in question produce for the world market.

As can be seen in table 3.1, there are considerable international wage variations in the case of industrial workers. In the case of agricultural workers, the wage differences are even more pronounced, with agricultural workers in the Third World receiving wages which are lower than the industrial workers of the countries in question. This applies especially to the exporting plantations which produce coffee, cocoa, tobacco, tea, rubber, peanuts, bananas, cotton, and similar commodities, which are mainly consumed by the population of the imperialist countries and by the middle and upper classes of the exploited countries. Agricultural workers in the Third World are paid about 30 times less than the workers of the richest countries. Other studies at the time confirmed the main results of the statistical investigation.[14]

---

12 Glyn, Andrew and Sutcliffe, Bob (1972) *British Capitalism, Workers and the Profit Squeeze*, p. 18. London: Penguin, 1972.

13 Cited in: Emmanuel, Arghiri (1972) *Unequal Exchange: A Study of the Imperialism of Trade*, p. 46. New York: Monthly Review Press, 1972.

Table 3.1 Hourly Wages (USD)

Country	Industry		Agriculture			
	Year	Wage	Year	Wage	Paid in Cash	Part. Paid in Kind[a]
Africa						
Egypt	1973	0.22	---	---		
Kenya	1978	0.94	1977	0.23[b]	✓	✓
Nigeria	1978	0.44	1975	0.30[c]	✓	
Tanzania	1974	0.45	1974	0.26		✓
Zambia	1976	0.75	1976	0.33	✓	
Ghana	1970	0.40	---	---		
Latin America						
Argentina	1977	0.22	1977	0.18 (U)		
Bolivia	1977	0.61[c]	---	---		
Brazil	1976	1.23	---	---		
Colombia	1978	0.65	---	---		
Chile	1978	0.60	1978	0.22[c]	✓	
Ecuador	1977	0.75	---	---		
Mexico	1976	0.97	1978	0.49[c]		✓*

14 Frank, A. G (1981) *Crisis in the Third World*, pp. 179-182. London: Heinemann, 1981, and

Table 3.1 (continued)

Asia						
Bangladesh	1977	0.14 (S)[c]	1977	0.09 (S)[c]	✓	
Burma	1977	0.17	---	---		
Hong Kong	1978	0.70[c]	---	---		
India	1977	0.22	1977	0.18[c]		✓
Japan	1978	6.79	1976	1.67 (M) 1.33 (W)		✓
Pakistan	1975	0.19	1978	0.12	✓	
Philippines	1975	0.25	1975	0.11[b]	✓	
Singapore	1978	0.79	---	---		
Sri Lanka	1978	0.21	1978	0.07		✓
South Korea	1979	1.06	1978	0.86 (M)[c] 0.65 (W)[c]		✓
Turkey	1977	0.84	1977	0.80		✓**
Europe						
Denmark	1978	8.76	1978	6.51	✓	
Spain	1976	1.99	1978	1.43	✓	
France	1978	4.18	1976	2.10[b]	✓	✓
West Germany	1978	6.42	1978	3.98 (M)[c] 3.02 (W)[c]		✓
Greece	1978	1.85	---	---		
Italy	1977	3.07	---	---		
Switzerland	1979	7.23	1978	7.07 (M) 5.19 (W)	✓***	
Sweden	1978	7.52	1978	6.10 (M) 5.49 (W)	✓	✓
Great Britain	1978	3.97 (M) 2.74 (W)	1977	2.68 (M) 2.15 (W)	✓	

Table 3.1 (continued)

Oceania						
New Zealand	1979	4.29	1978	2.61[c]	✓	
Australia	1978	5.88 (M) 4.69 (W)	---	---	✓	
North America						
Canada	1979	6.34	1978	3.17[c]	✓	
USA	1979	6.66	1978	3.07[bc]	✓	✓

M = Men W = Women S = Skilled U = Unskilled

* = Day-laborers ** = Fishermen *** = Woodmen

a = Some of the wages are paid in kind. The statistics show only the amount paid in cash.

b = Besides the wages stated, free meals and free lodgings are granted.

c = The amounts shows the wages agreed to through collective bargaining. It is usually the minimum wage. In the exploited countries this figure will almost correspond to the actual wages or it may be just above.

It is evident that a table like table 3.1 is vitiated by errors and uncertainty, but other studies[15] and our own experiences from travels in the Third World confirmed the main results of the investigation.

If we use the figures in table 3.1 and weigh them with the number of industrial workers in the countries in question, the average figure representing the wages of the industrial workers appears as:

Imperialist countries: about 5.60 USD per hour

Third World countries: about 0.46 USD per hour

In 1979, it was impossible for us to find reliable figures for the number of agricultural workers in most countries and, as many of the wage figures for agricultural workers do not represent the real remuneration, we chose to estimate, on the basis of the figures available, the ratio of the number of industrial workers to agricultural workers and the ratio of the wages in industry to agriculture. We reached the following result:

15 Frank, A. G (1981) *Crisis in the Third World*, pp. 179-182. London: Heinemann, 1981.

The ratio of the number of industrial workers to agricultural workers:

Imperialist countries: 18:1

Exploited countries: 1.3: 1

The ratio of the wages of industrial to agricultural workers:

Imperialist countries: 1.4:1

Exploited countries: 2:1

Thus, the average wages of both industrial and agricultural workers can be calculated:

Imperialist countries: 5.50 USD per hour

Exploited countries: 0.36 USD per hour

Thus, wages were, in general, 15 times higher in the imperialist countries than in the exploited countries.

We used the ratio 15:1 for the wages in the imperialist countries to the exploited countries as a conservative estimate. Several things indicate that the difference in wages might have been greater. The wages which are actually paid in poor countries are often lower than the ones stated. This is due to sheer evasion of agreements and legislation on the part of the employers.[16] Furthermore, the statistics often only apply to organized laborers. In the Third World, many laborers are not organized, and they get even lower wages than the organized members of their own class. In many imperialist countries, the employer pays insurance, pensions, etc., which are not paid directly to the workers. These amounts ought to be considered as part of the wages in such calculations.

The Value of Labor-Power

However, the measurement of the value of labor-power is more complex than just measuring hours. There are also questions concerning the intensity of the work, whether it is skilled or unskilled labor, and the discussion about the pro-

16 Fröbel, J. Heinrichs and O. Kreye (1980) *The New International Division of Labour,* pp. 351-352. Cambridge: Cambridge University Press, 1980.

ductivity of labor in relation to its creation of value.

The wages paid to the industrial and agricultural workers in the exploited countries are often not enough to cover the physical reproduction costs of the labor-power. The high intensity and long working days—often 10-12 hours in "sweatshops"—have the consequence of a rapid attrition and change of labor-power. A rate of change of 5-7% each month and of 50-100% annually is not abnormal within industries and plantations in the Third World.[17] Within the electronics industries of Asia, e.g. in Hong Kong, Singapore, Malaysia, and Taiwan, young female laborers are preferred. They have essentially no family life, domestic work, or child minding duties to take care of besides their work and are therefore able to work harder and longer hours, up to sixty hours weekly. They do not participate in the maintenance of the family and can therefore manage being paid low wages. After 3-4 years of back-breaking work at the microscopes, they are worn down. Their sight and nerves can no longer comply with the demands of production for speed and accuracy, and they are fired—or as it is called, "encouraged to retire and marry." New and fresh labor-power is employed.[18] Fröbel, Heinrichs and Kreye, in their book *The New International Division of Labour*, published in German in 1977, were some of the first to observe the new wave of industrialization of the Third World. In the book, they describe the working hours:

> In most of the countries where free production zones and world market factories are in operation the standard working week is forty-eight hours. The difference between this figure and the standard working week of forty to forty-four hours in the traditional industrialized countries is only a partial reflection of the real prolongation of the working day in the new production sites in the developing countries. The high number of weeks worked in the year, the large amount of overtime and the low number of days off serve to prolong the total annual working time still further, so that the labor-force in some world market factories works up to 50% more hours per year than the traditional industrial countries. For example, working hours in manufacturing industry in Hong Kong often amount to more than sixty hours per week. In the world market factories in South Korea the usual working week of the factory worker is sixty hours. Total productive hours per year amounts to approximately 2800, compared with 1860 on the average in Federal Germany. Workers in South Korean industry are required to work seven days, eighty-four-hour weeks—i.e. a twelve hour shift each day without rest days. In Thai manufacturing industry a nine-hour working day with only one day off per month is often required.[19]

---

17 Fröbel, J. Heinrichs and O. Kreye (1980) *The New International Division of Labour*, pp. 329-30. Cambridge: Cambridge University Press, 1980.

18 Frank, Andre Gunder (1981) *Crisis: In the Third World*. London: Heinemann (1981), p. 164.

19 Fröbel, J. Heinrichs and O. Kreye (1980) *The New International Division of Labour*, pp. 353-355. Cambridge: Cambridge University Press, 1980.

Conditions have not changed since the late '70s. The intensity of labor in the Global South is not less but higher than in the Global North, and that is part of the unequal exchange, because higher intensity work creates more value, as Marx writes:

> But still, even then, the intensity of labor would be different in different countries and would modify the international application of the law of value. The more intense working day of one nation would be represented by a greater sum of money than would the less intense day of another nation.[20]

Productivity

One of the most popular explanations of the international wage differences is that they are based on similar differences in productivity. The wage is low in the Global South because the workers are less productive. This explanation is used as an objection against the theory of unequal exchange. In Bettelheim's comments, in the appendix of Emmanuel's book, he sums up this line of thinking:

> leads to making the proletarians of the rich countries "appear" to be "exploiters" of the poor ones. [...] In reality these workers are, in general, more exploited [...] than the workers in the poor countries. [...] Owing to the high level of intensity and productivity of labor in the rich countries, the wages of the workers in those countries, though nominally higher, and (to a lesser extent) higher in purchasing power than in the poor countries, generally correspond to a smaller proportion of the value these workers produce. [...] In other words, the more productive forces are developed, the more the proletarians are exploited. [...] Despite their low wages, the workers of the underdeveloped countries are less exploited. [...] While the proletarians of the industrialized countries are not subject to "superexploitation" as are the proletarians of the dominated countries, they are more intensively exploited. The capitalists are not deceived: they know that, generally speaking, it is more profitable to exploit the proletarians of the industrialized countries than their brothers in the poor countries. [...] This is why the big international companies have made the "advanced" countries their preferred sphere of investment. [...] Domination by imperialism is based above all upon the exploitation of the proletarians in the imperialist countries.[21] (Emmanuel's argument)

Bettleheim's argument is that because of the high productivity of Northern workers, only a small share of their working hours is necessary labor time, or time required to cover the reproduction costs of their labor-power. The rest is surplus labor. In the Global South, a much greater share of the workers' hours goes into the reproduction of their labor-power, hence they are subject to less exploitation.

---

20 Marx, Karl (1867) *Capital. A Critique of Political Economy.* Vol. I: The Process of Production of Capital, p. 525. Progress Publisher, Moscow: 1970.

21 Bettleheim, Charles (1972) Theoretical Comments, page 301-302. In Emmanuel, Arghiri, *Unequal Exchange: A Study of the Imperialism of Trade*, by A.New York: Monthly Review Press 1972.

The argument rests on several misconceptions, not least concerning the term "productivity" itself.

First, one has to distinguish between *productivity* and the *intensity* of labor. Bourgeois economists focus on output per worker, either in the form of the number of goods they produce or in the form of profit made from their labor. Whether the profit can be increased by raising the prices of the goods produced, or by employing new technologies, or by making management more effective, is of secondary interest. Even Marxist economists often confuse productivity and intensity. They define productivity as the amount of goods finished during a certain period of time. This does not account for why there is a difference in the number of goods produced. Is it because of new technologies? Is it because the workers are required to work harder? Is there another reason? To bring more clarity to these issues, I offer the following definitions:

Intensity is the rate of consumption of labor-power. Higher intensity means a faster wearing out of the laborers, and more produced commodities per unit of time by the same means of production.

Productivity is determined by the efficiency of the technological facilities and by the organization of production. Improving the technology and/or the organization, keeping intensity the same, results in a production of more commodities per unit of time.

Both increased intensity and increased productivity results in the creation of more use-value per unit of time. But only increased intensity creates more value per unit of time. Increased productivity just means the production of a greater quantity of commodities with the same overall value.

Concerning the relation between productivity and wages, Engels writes in a letter to Lafargue:

> [...] in what respect the wage worker gains an advantage in seeing his productivity increase, when the product of that productivity does not belong to him and when his wage is not determined by the productivity of the machine.[22]

Improvements in productivity are a result of improved technology of the capitalist production apparatus. Gains from improvements in productivity go to the capitalist as profit, perhaps superprofit, for a short period. The value and payment of the labor-power do not depend on whether the laborer operates an expensive, highly productive plant or a screwdriver. No matter how big the difference in productivity is, it cannot be a result of the labor-power in itself. As Emmanuel writes:

---

22 Engels, F. (1884) Engels, Paul & Laura Lafargue *Correspondence*, Volume. I, p. 233. Moscow: Foreign Languages Publishing House, 1959.

> They forget that with equal qualifications any difference in productivity can only result from an improved tool, i.e. equipment that is heavier and more costly (higher organic composition of capital). But since profits are proportionate to the capital invested, this equipment has already weighted the selling price of the product by a sum which the system's own logic considers to be strictly equivalent to its differential contribution. To try to increase it by the difference in salaries as well is simply to try to obtain payment for the same thing twice over.[23]

In the case of an equal amount of used labor-power—i.e., an equal wear of muscles and nerves and equal education and qualifications—an unequal result can only be explained by other factors—i.e., the quality of the means of production, which is paid through profit. The assertion that the wages of agricultural workers are determined by the fertility of the soil, and the wages of the industrial workers by the size and quality of the machinery are not only absurd but have nothing to do with reality. In a capitalist society, the product of the soil or of machinery belongs to the landowner or the industrial capitalist. Only in the case of independent producers, who own their land and tools, is there a connection between productivity and the wages of labor.

The productivity of the laborers' work does not influence his wages. However, Marx believed that increased productivity in sectors which are included in the determination of the value of the labor-power may have an influence—in a *downward* direction. This is because machines make formerly skilled work into simple, unskilled work—as happened in the industrial revolution in England in the beginning of the 19th century.

If we assume that productivity affects wages in an upward direction, it would be difficult to understand why the working class in the Third World does not benefit from the productivity increase to the same extent, as Emmanuel argues:

> [...] one could not see why the same quantity of labour of the same qualification, incorporating the same learning and training should be paid ten times more or less according to whether it is supplied some miles on this or the other side of the American-Mexican border and according to whether the name of the vendor is John or Fernandez. Of all monopolies, this one, grounded on a passport or a birth certificate, seems to me the most "un-ethical."[24]

The alleged inherent economic connection between productivity increases and wage increases is wrong. What determines the wages is the class struggle and the possibilities of wage variation which the international position of the

23 Emmanuel, Arghiri (1975) 'Unequal Exchange Revisited', p. 60. IDS Discussion Paper No. 77 Brighton, UK: Institute of Development Studies, Sussex University.

24 Emmanuel, Arghiri (1975) *Unequal Exchange, A Summary*, p. 25. Paper presented to a conference on trade at Sussex University UK. 1975.

national economies can offer. For sure, the trade unions in the Global North demand that workers should benefit from improved productivity by getting a share of the profit.

Concerning the differences in global productivity, already back in the '70s, many studies of individual enterprises and analyses of various industries showed that the rate of productivity—defined as output per head—was by and large the same in the world market industries in the Third World and in the rich countries. The multinational company Philips concluded—based on surveys in 1970 and 1978 of its enterprises in Europe, Japan, Australia, and the Third World—that the productivity (measured as produced units per laborer) is more or less the same in these areas.[25]

On the basis of a number of studies in the '70s, Deutsche Entwicklungsgesellschaft[26] concluded that the rate of productivity of the industries in Third World countries which have turned their production towards the world market is only a little lower than the rate of similar industries in Western Europe. In light of the longer working hours in the Third World, the workers have a much higher rate of performance than the workers of Western Europe.[27]

According to studies made by The United States Tariff Commission, the rate of productivity of workers in American-owned enterprises outside the US is by and large the same as the rate of productivity of workers in the same industries in the U.S. According to these studies, workers in the clothing industry in exploited countries produce just as many units per hour as their American colleagues do.[28] Certain studies even concluded that the rate of productivity of industries in the exploited countries is higher than in the imperialist countries. A study by Baerresen concludes that the productivity in American-owned enterprises in Mexico is considerably higher than in similar enterprises in the US in certain cases. For example, in the electronics industries, the Mexican rate of productivity was 10-25 per cent higher than in the US. According to Baerresen, American managers in Mexico report that South Korean labor-power is a further 10-40% more productive than Mexican labor-power. Managers in the US and Western Germany, who were the heads of Malaysian textile and electronics enterprises, unanimously stressed after a few months of production that the

25 Le Nouveau Journal (1979) 18/4. 1979.

26 **Ed. Note:** One of the world's largest private-sector development financiers, known as German Investment Corporation in English.

27 Fröbel, J. Heinrichs and O. Kreye (1980) *The New International Division of Labour,* p.356. Cambridge: Cambridge University Press, 1980.

28 Ibid.

rate of productivity in Malaysia was the same as at home. Another American study, by R. W. Moxon, also concludes that the rate of productivity in the electronics industry is generally higher in the exploited countries than in the United States.[29]

It should be stressed that in these studies the definition of productivity is the number of units produced per laborer within a given time unit. This is different from the definition of productivity given above, which reflects the technological and organizational component of production. As the rate of productivity (units produced) turns out to be the same or higher in the exploited countries, it is often due to much higher labor intensity in the Third World. Very often, many manual operations are mechanized or automated in the imperialist countries. This means that laborers in the Third World have to work much more intensively to achieve the same rate of productivity. If working processes have not been mechanized in this part of the world, it is only because the wages are so low that it currently would not be of any advantage to the capitalists to proceed with mechanization. In Third World countries, the rate of productivity is often much higher within mining and plantations than in the imperialist countries. This is first and foremost due to natural (geologic, climatic etc.) prerequisites. As the world looks today, it would be extremely costly for the imperialist countries, in terms of both labor hours and money, to produce, for example, coffee or cacao in Europe or North America. .[30]

All the examples above refer to the situation in the '70s. Today, after the outsourcing of most industrial production to the Global South in the form of globalized production chains, we can ask: how much value do millions of workers in China contribute to the Dell computers and iPhones they produce? According to mainstream economists, the answer is very little. After all, the costs involved in assembling the products in China's factories make up only a small fraction of the sales price. However, if this is seemingly such an insignificant factor, why are millions of jobs being moved to the Global South each year? Capital goes where the value is. If this is not reflected in mainstream economic theory, that's a sign of flaws in those theories concerning the creation and exchange of value, and its transformation into price. Value is mistaken for price, and productivity is defined as value added per working hour. If one accepts that logic, it may seem that Chinese workers add little value to what they produce because they are paid very little. This, then, is interpreted as low productivity—apparently,

---

29 Moxon, Richard W. (1973) Offshore Production in Less Developed Countries, p. 61, Harvard Univ., Diss., 1973.

30 Emmanuel, Arghiri (1975) 'Unequal Exchange Revisited', p.33. IDS Discussion Paper No. 77 Institute of Development Studies, Sussex University, Brighton, UK.

it does not matter that they work twelve hours a day under strict supervision in factories equipped with the latest technology. As if this wasn't preposterous enough, there are even some economists who claim that moving production to the Global South has increased the productivity of labor in the Global North, even if workers in the Global North do exactly the same work as they did before.[31] What *is* true is that the corporations they are employed by now receive more value added from their work.

Timothy Kerswell has studied productivity in the global car and textile industry. His studies show that there is no correlation between high wages and high productivity. Internationally, the car industry in Mexico has the highest productivity, Slovakia comes second, and productivity in Germany is the lowest. In the textile industry, both Brazil and Thailand have higher productivity than the US and Germany. Overall, in the industries studied by Kerswell, the labor force in the South was as productive, and in many cases more productive, than in the North.[32] This confirms that the global differences in wages cannot be explained by differences in productivity. Other factors are much more important: restrictions on the mobility of labor, an enormous reserve army of labor, and political power structures.

The extra profits temporarily yielded by productivity increases fall first and foremost to the capitalist. The fact that increases in productivity are used by the unions of the imperialist countries as an argument for higher wages through collective bargaining does not mean that productivity increases are an economic factor which regularly pushes up wages. Whether the working class succeeds in benefitting from productivity increases does not depend on the actual increases but on the relative strength of the working class and the capitalist class. The wages are not the price of the results of the work but the price of the labor-power.

Unequal exchange has nothing to do with the exchange of goods produced with low technology against goods produced with high technology (productivity as defined above). Emmanuel writes in a letter to Samir Amin:

> I have spoken here and there in my book of Third World exports from branches with a very high technological level, ultra-modern textile factories in Egypt and India, Katanga's mines, etc., which, like the others, and despite their high productivity, suffer from the inequality of exchange. I also mentioned certain stagnant branches of the developed countries (Scottish whisky, certain semi-artisanal fabrics, etc.) which benefit from the same inequality, despite the low level of productivity.

---

31 Grossman, Gene M. and Rossi-Hansberg, Esteban (2006), *The Rise and Fall of Offshoring: It's Not Wine for Cloth Anymore*, p. 15.

32 Kerswell, Timothy (2011) *The Global Division of Labour and Division in Global Labour* (Ph.D. thesis). Queensland University of Technology, pp. 43–65.

> [...] if the difference in organic compositions were to determine the scale of wages in the various branches, then the French hairdresser or taxi driver would have to earn a wage some hundred or two hundred times less than that of a French metal worker. This is absurd; not all branches have the same capacity to absorb technical progress and mechanization, but humanity, like the nation, needs all these branches and someone has to work in them.
>
> I did not dwell on the chapter on productivity, not only because I considered it irrelevant to my subject, but also because I did not suspect that the unconscious influence of marginalism was so great, and that so many economists claiming to be Marxians reasoned on the basis of productivity as a determinant of the value of labour power and wages [...]
>
> What the employer buys is not the labour, but the labour power, which is more or less productive, depending on the conditions of its use and the equipment to which the worker is attached. Labour power has no productivity. It is a neutral vital energy, and its value is already constituted before we even know where its purchaser is going to use it, in the handling of a million dollar press or a handcart.
>
> In other words, if the underdeveloped country exports oil and imports cars, it is not a question of comparing the productivity of the oil industry in the underdeveloped country with the productivity of the car industry in the developed country (an impossible comparison), but of comparing the difference between the productivities of the two countries in oil with the difference between the productivities of the two countries in cars, if the two countries were to produce both items in isolation. It is thus a question of comparing for each country its advantage over the other country in the exported item with its disadvantage over the other country in the imported item.[33]

The increase in productivity is the result of the competition between capitalists. They are constantly forced to improve the productive forces. The capitalists who produce the most and fastest at the lowest price do best in the competition. Therefore, capital tries to limit the production costs, of which the wages make up a considerable part. The result is that the industries in the Global South began to outstrip industries in the Global North. It began within shipbuilding, textile manufacturing, and certain electronics industries, where Southeast Asian low-wage industries outstripped the high-wage industries of the Western World, and then moved into all industrial sectors.

Economists have called it "social dumping": when low-wage industries, with the use of modern technology, crush the industries of the rich countries. Of these economists' hypocrisy and dual attitude to this problem, Emmanuel writes:

> When it is a question of importing coffee or bananas, which the rich countries do not themselves produce, and the low prices of which can consequently be only to the advantage of the purchasing countries, then any notion of artificially increasing prices is

33 Emmanuel, Arghiri (1969) Letter to Amin with remarks on Amin's book *Accumulation on World Scale* pp. 1-3. From the Emmanuel Archive. (Translated from French, my emphasis). Available online, see References.

> repudiated in the name of the sound principles of economic rationalism, and no allusion to the low wages of the producers is allowed, since, in accordance with these same sound principles, these wages are not the cause of prices, but their effect. When, however, by chance the poor countries decide to export products such as Indian cotton goods or Japanese transistors, which are already included in the production of a traditional branch of industry in the rich countries, then all these principles are cheerfully forgotten, and, it is discovered that it is only proper that the rich country should make up by means of artificial tariff barriers for the equally artificial difference in wages; thus brusquely and brazenly admitting that wages are not the effect of prices but their cause.[34]

This is the argument that Trump and the European Union economists use today against electric cars, solar panels, and windmills produced in China. Emmanuel continues:

> But if this conjunction causes the prices of Indian cotton goods and Japanese ships to be abnormally low, why are the prices of bananas and coffee not also abnormally low, since wages in these branches are just as exotic and productivity is undoubtedly higher than in the West? (Has anyone ever thought what it would cost to grow bananas or coffee in Flanders or the Rhineland?)
>
> "Unfair competition by means of low wages", "pauperized labor", "social dumping", etc., are expressions of which present-day writing on economic matters is full, while pure economics goes on imperturbably teaching that wages depend on prices, and not the other way round.
>
> In the days when wages varied from one country to another only as 1 to 2, or even 1 to 3 or 1 to 4, it was perhaps legitimate to suppose that fluctuations on the commodity market could be the underlying cause of these variations. When, however, wages vary at the rate of 1 to 20, or 1 to 30, and vary only in space, while possessing extreme rigidity in time (in which only a slow and linear trend is to be observed, with hardly any variation), we are indeed compelled to recognize that they probably vary in accordance with laws peculiar to themselves and that, consequently, they really are the independent variable of the system.[35]

One could add that the industrialization of the Global South has ended the discussion on productivity differences between the North and South as the reason for the difference in wage levels. The outsourcing of industry to the Global South in the past forty years is also a transfer of technology and management regimes. It is obvious that electronics or car production in Asia or Latin America is as high tech as in Europe or North America, in spite of the fact that the wage is one tenth.

---

34 Emmanuel, Arghiri (1972) *Unequal Exchange: A Study of the Imperialism of Trade*, pp. 69-70. New York: Monthly Review Press, 1972.

35 Emmanuel, Arghiri (1972) *Unequal Exchange: A Study of the Imperialism of Trade*, pp. 70-71. New York: Monthly Review Press 1972.

The Size of the Unequal Exchange[36]

Having determined the global differences in price of labor and the global value of labor, we can turn to the exchange of commodities on the world market. In the end, one country can only exploit another country by importing a total value of commodities which is higher than the value of the exported commodities. This may take place by simple plundering, as was the case during early colonialism, or it may take place by having a constant trade deficit, as Britain had during the last century and the U.S. has currently. Finally, it may take place through a distortion of the actual prices at which the commodities are sold, which is the case between the imperialist countries and the exploited countries. The imperialist countries sell their commodities at prices which are too high compared to their value, and the exploited countries sell at prices which are too low.

Table 3.2 shows the development of world trade from 1948-82 between the imperialist countries, the exploited countries, and the centrally-planned economies in absolute figures (i.e. in prices) and in percentages. I begin with statistical material from this period for several reasons. It represents the international division of labor at the time when Emmanuel presented his theory of unequal exchange, and so these materials provide the empirical background for a discussion of his theory. These were the statistics we used when we developed our method to calculate the size of unequal exchange at the time. Later, I will discuss the changes in the international division of labor, present updated statistics and show how this has affected both the form of unequal exchange and its size.

---

36 **Ed. Note:** Some of this information in this section was previously included in *Unequal Exchange and the Prospects for Socialism* (1986, Manifest Press. Republished 2025, Washington: Iskra Books).

Table 3.2 World Trade by Region, 1948-1982

Export From	Year	World Total	Export To: Developed Market Economies		Developing Market Economies		Centrally Planned Economies	
			Total	%	Total	%	Total	%
Developed Market Economies	1948	36.5	23.7	65%	11.3	31%	1.5	4%
	1956	68.4	45.9	67%	19	28%	1.7	2%
	1965	128	95.3	74%	25.9	20%	5.2	4%
	1970	224.2	172.5	77%	41.4	18%	8.9	4%
	1975	577.2	402	70%	138	24%	33.8	6%
	1980	1,260.6	894	71%	293.4	23%	61.2	5%
	1982	1,161.2	802.9	69%	289.6	25%	53	5%
Developing Market Economies	1948	17.3	11.8	68%	5.0	29%	0.5	3%
	1956	24.9	18.3	73%	5.9	24%	0.8	3%
	1965	35.9	25.6	71%	7.4	21%	2.6	7%
	1970	54.9	39.8	72%	10.9	20%	3.4	6%
	1975	209.4	146.7	70%	49	23%	10.1	5%
	1980	558.5	391.5	70%	138.9	25%	20.5	4%
	1982	486.5	312.2	64%	145.6	30%	23.7	5%
Centrally Planned Economies	1948	3.7	1.5	41%	0.4	11%	1.7	46%
	1956	10.1	2	20%	0.9	9%	7.2	71%
	1965	21.8	4.7	22%	3.3	15%	13.8	63%
	1970	32.8	7.8	24%	5.1	16%	19.9	61%
	1975	84.6	23.1	27%	13.3	16%	47.6	56%
	1980	175.1	56.4	32%	31.6	18%	85.5	49%
	1982	189	58.5	31%	41.5	22%	88.9	47%

Let us look at the importance of Third World exports to the imperialist countries at that time. From table 3.3, it can be seen that imports by imperialist countries from the Third World amounted to about one quarter of the total imports, calculated on the basis of the current world market prices. Furthermore, if this figure is compared with the national product of the imperialist countries, imports from the Third World amounted to about 4-6%. The fact that, in terms of world market prices, imports from the exploited countries make up a relatively small quantity compared with trade between the imperialist countries, and an even smaller part compared with the national product of these countries, could lead one to believe that the importance of trade with the Third World and thus of the unequal exchange was comparatively small. But nothing could be further from the truth. The opposite conclusion should be drawn, because unequal exchange is based on the disproportionately low prices of commodities from the Third World, which are also the reason for the disproportionately low trade figures. The lower the wages are, the lower the prices and the lower the trade figures will be. The argument that comparatively small trade with the Third World demonstrates that unequal exchange is relatively unimportant shows that the theory of unequal exchange has been misunderstood.

Table 3.3 Imports to Developed Market Economies

Year	Total	From Developed Market Economies		From Developing Market Economies		From Centrally Planned Economies	
		Total	%	Total	%	Total	%
1965	125.6	95.3	76%	25.6	20%	4.7	4%
1970	220.7	172.5	78%	39.8	18%	7.8	4%
1975	571.9	402	70%	146.7	26%	23.1	4%
1980	1,341.9	894	67%	391.5	29%	56.4	4%
1982	1,173.5	802.9	68%	312.2	27%	58.4	5%

It is far more interesting and more significant to look at the distribution of the exports of the Third World at that time. From table 3.2, it appears that about 70% of the exports of the Third World are sent to the imperialist countries. The internal trade between the countries of the Third World amounted only to 25-30%. Furthermore, this trade is less important for the transfer of value between the countries, as these countries have more or less the same wage level. Exports to the socialist countries—the centrally planned economies—amounted to about 5% only. Thus, the imperialist countries imported by far the majority of the cheap commodities from the Third World, and in this way, they benefited from unequal exchange and exploited the Third World.

In table 3.4, it can be seen that 60-70% of Third World imports came from the imperialist countries. Some 20-30% came from internal trade between the exploited countries, and 7-9% from the planned economies of the period. Thus, in terms of both exports from and imports to the Third World, the imperialist countries were predominant, whereas the "socialist countries"—the centrally planned economies—kept to themselves to a much larger extent.

Table 3.4 Exports to Developing Market

Year	Total	From Developed Market Economies		From Developing Market Economies		From Centrally Planned Economies	
		Total	%	Total	%	Total	%
1965	36.6	25.9	70%	7.4	20%	3.3	9%
1970	57.3	41.4	72%	10.9	19%	5.1	9%
1975	200.3	138	69%	49.0	25%	13.3	7%
1980	464	293.4	63%	138.9	30%	31.6	7%
1982	476.7	289.6	61%	145.6	31%	41.5	9%

The internal trade between the imperialist countries accounted for a considerable part of total world trade in terms of world market prices. In 1982, total world trade amounted to 1,836.6 billion USD, out of which inter-imperialist trade amounted to 802.9 billion USD. However, this trade was of less direct importance than international transfers of value between the imperialist countries and the exploited countries, because the wage differences between the imperialist countries were relatively small compared to the global wage differences.

In the beginning of the '80s, when this calculation was made, the international division of labor was very different from today. The predominant exports from the Third World were still raw materials and agricultural products, while the imperialist core exported industrial products in return. The contents of inter-imperialist trade were very different from trade between the imperialist countries and the Third World. Inter-imperialist trade was, to a large extent, an exchange of the same type of products, whereas trade with the Third World was based on the exchange of qualitatively different products. At the time, Denmark sold Bang & Olufsen electronics and bought Philips, Sony, and Grundig. West Germans bought Fiat, Toyota, and Citroën and sold VW, Mercedes, and BMW. The exchange of a large number of industrial products, such as machines and consumer goods—all produced within the imperialist core—mainly functioned to expand choices regarding aspects like shape and color.

The imperialist core was qualitatively dependent on imports from the Third World. They could not get the agricultural products, raw materials, and minerals which were necessary inputs to their industrial production from within the imperial core. Soy beans and other agricultural products were inputs in meat production, while coffee, bananas, and other tropical fruits could hardly be produced in the North. Table 3.5 shows the dependence of the European Economic Community (as it was called at the time) on raw materials from developing countries.

Table 3.5 EEC Dependence on Raw Materials from Developing Countries (in 1972)

Industry	Materials	EEC Import Dependence	Developing Countries' Share of EEC Import	Developing Countries' Share of World Export
Exhaustable Raw Materials				
Industrial Raw Materials	Copper	100%	60%	44%
	Tin	86%	85%	77%
	Iron	75%	55%	42%
	Bauxite	83%	50%	88%
	Phosphate	99%	63%	43%
	Manganese	100%	45%	51%
	Tungsten	95%	43%	50%
Energy Raw Materials	Uranium	75%	---	15%
	Petroleum	98%	98%	45%
	Natural Gas	3%	100%	5%
	Coal	11%	1%	10%

Table 3.5 (continued)

Reproducible Raw Materials				
Tropical Products	Coffee	100%	99%	97%
	Cocoa	100%	97%	98%
	Tea	100%	80%	84%
	Bananas	100%	100%	95%
	Spices	100%	100%	90%
Industrial Raw Materials	Timber	50%	29%	43%
	Leather	---	23%	23%
	Rubber	100%	100%	98%
	Cotton	---	60%	57%
	Wool	---	12%	13%
	Jute	100%	98%	95%
	Sisal	100%	100%	97%
Agricultural Products	Meat	---	35%	20%
	Oilseeds	100%	---	43%
	Fruit	---	45%	25%
	Sugar	---	99%	73%
	Corn	---	25%	10%
	Rice	---	55%	40%
	Tobacco	---	24%	21%

With these trade figures in place, we can finally estimate the size of unequal change in a single year—1980. Again, I will mention that the information on wages, the size of the labor-force, and the estimate of the wage-share of the price of the product is subject to some uncertainty. Therefore, the following is meant as an illustration of the approximate size.

According to table 3.2, the exports of the exploited countries to the imperialist countries in 1980 amounted to:

391.5 billion USD

And the exports of the imperialist countries to the exploited countries:

293.4 billion USD

Assuming that wages amount to 20% of the price of the products from imperialist countries and 15 per cent of the price of the products from exploited countries, the wage-share amounts to:

Of exports from exploited countries: 58.7 billion USD

Of exports from imperialist countries: 58.7 billion USD

According to 1974 figures from the International Labour Organization, there were about 400 million people engaged in active employment in the imperialist part of the world, and about 800 million people engaged in active employment in the non-"socialist" part of the Third World.[37]

If we assume that wages in the imperialist countries are 15 times higher than wages in the exploited countries, we can set the wage-factor in the exploited countries to 1, and the wage-factor in the imperialist countries to 15. On this basis, we can calculate the global average wage-factor:

The wage-factor of imperialist countries:

$$400 \text{ mill. workers at wage} - \text{factor } 15 = 6000 \text{ million units of wage} - \text{factor}$$

The wage factor of exploited countries:

$$800 \text{ mill. workers at factor } 1 = 800 \text{ million units of wage} - \text{factor}$$

Then the average global wage factor, representing the global value of labor, is the total number of units: 6800 million, divided by the total number of workers 1200 million:

$$\text{Average wage factor: } \frac{6800}{1200} = 5.7$$

The factor 5.7 reflects the global average wage, which is the closest we can get to the globalized value of labor.

If workers in exploited countries were paid this global average wage-factor

37 ILO (1974) International Labour Review, 1974, vol. 109, no. 5-6, pp. 422-9. ILO. Geneva. 1974.

of 5.7 instead of wage factor 1, the wage-share of the exports from the exploited countries would be:

58.7 billion × 5.7 divided by 1 = 334.7 billion USD

Meanwhile, if workers in imperialist countries were paid this global average wage-factor of 5.7 instead of wage factor 15, the wage-share of the exports from the imperialist countries would be:

58.7 billion × 5.7 divided by 15 = 22.3 billion USD

These wage shares are then added to the remaining production costs (the non-wage share) in the exploited and imperialist countries, giving the following prices of exports:

Exports from exploited countries:

$$\frac{391.5 \times 85\%}{100} + 334.7 = 667.5 \text{ billion USD}$$

Exports from imperialist countries:

$$\frac{293.4 \times 80\%}{100} + 22.3 = 257.0 \text{ billion USD}$$

Compared to this hypothetical situation of equal global wages (equal exchange), the gain of the imperialist countries from the actual, unequal exchange amounts to: From low import prices:

667.5---391.5 = 276.0 billion USD

From high export prices:

293.4---257.0 = 36.4 billion USD

Total gain in the year 1980: 312.4 billion USD.[38] - factor is a shortcut. The calculations co

By way of comparison, it may be mentioned that in 1980 the GNP of the US was 2,573 billion USD.

The amount of profit repatriated by multinationals from investments in the Third World in 1970-78 was about 100.2 billion USD.[39] This means that

39 Castro, Fidel (1981) *Speech at the Conference of the Inter-parliamentarian Union in Havana*, 15-23 August 1981, Granma 27 Sept. 1981.

the amount of value transferred by way of unequal exchange in a single year was 3 times bigger than the amount of profits from the investments of the imperialist countries over eight years.

The flow of value by unequal exchange has taken place decade after decade up through the 19th and 20th century, steadily growing in size. Using the method above, the gain from unequal exchange in 2009 was calculated as 4,900 billion USD. In spite of some uncertainties about the figures, this shows that unequal exchange is an important form of imperialism. Emmanuel writes:

> I do not claim that unequal exchange explains by itself the entire difference between the standards of living of the rich countries and the poor ones, even though, if we base ourselves on certain statistical data that are available, however fragmentary and arguable these may be, we arrive at a loss in double factoral terms (if not in terms of trade) that is enormous in relation to the poverty of the underdeveloped countries while being far from negligible in relation to the wealth of the advanced countries. Even if we agree that unequal exchange is only one of the mechanisms whereby value is transferred from one group of countries to another, and that its direct effects account for only part of the difference in standards of living, I think it is possible to state that unequal exchange is the elementary transfer mechanism, and that, as such, it enables the advanced countries to begin and regularly to give new impetus to that unevenness of development that sets in motion all the other mechanisms of exploitation and fully explains the way that wealth is distributed.[40]

In addition, we should not only focus on the quantity expressed in these yearly figures. We also have to consider the accumulated effects of unequal exchange, which has been characterizing world trade for centuries. Whether unequal exchange amounts to 250, 350, or 1000 billion dollars a year, the qualitative aspect is even more important. Earlier, we mentioned capitalism's main problem: the imbalance between the production of goods and the purchasing power needed for them to be sold. Capitalist crises always relate to overproduction—or the lack of markets, depending on the way you look at it. The constant value transfer from the South to the North ensures enough purchasing power in the North and therefore stable capitalist growth. At the same time, the development of stable national economies in the South is made impossible by the constant drain of value. Unequal exchange does not just mean a value transfer of X billion dollars a year but has been the requirement for capitalist growth in the Global North in the past century.

---

40 Emmanuel, Arghiri (1972) *Unequal Exchange: A Study of the Imperialism of Trade*, p. 265. New York: Monthly Review Press 1972.

Gernot Köhler Method

In the late '80s, the anti-imperialist struggle in the Third World declined—as the neoliberal offensive gained power in a US-led unipolar world-system—and so did the interest in the political economy of imperialism. However, with the neoliberal globalization of production and the changing international division of labor, the importance of unequal exchange only grew stronger. This was acknowledged by neither scholars nor politicians at the time. Kunibert Raffer notes that unequal exchange has "virtually vanished from academic debates during the era of neoliberalism."[41] As Marx notes: "The ruling ideas are nothing more than the ideal expression of the dominant material relationships, the dominant material relationships grasped as ideas; hence of the relationships which make the one class the ruling one, therefore, the ideas of its dominance."[42]

However, there were a few exceptions. In the 1990s, the Canadian economist Gernot Köhler, who has a background in computer science and belongs to the world-systems school, developed an alternative method to estimate the size of unequal exchange, and used computers to handle the huge amounts of data.[43]

Instead of wage differentials as the basis for measuring unequal exchange, Köhler's model used the structure of the world's currencies. Köhler writes:

> I am contending that (1) the value of money is non-homogeneous throughout the world-system (even after exchange rates have been taken into account); that (2) the currencies of low-income countries tend to be undervalued, not overvalued as many economists claim; that (3) the exchange rate system is one of the mechanisms by which high-wage countries extract value from low-wage countries; and that (4) this situation contributes significantly to unequal exchange between periphery and center countries.[44]

In international trade, when commodities are to be exchanged and the price has to be settled, the prices are expressed in the local currency and have to be set-

41 Raffer, Kunibert (2006) Differences between inequalities and unequal exchange: comments on the papers by Chaves and Köhler." *Entelequia, revista interdisciplinar*, no. 2 (2006), p. 198.

42 Marx, Karl and Engels, Freidrich (1845) *The German Ideology*, Part I: Feuerbach. Opposition of the Materialist and Idealist Outlook, *Marx-Engels Collected Works*, Vol. 5, p. 59. Moscow: Progress Publishers 1976.

43 Köhler, Gernot (1998). The Structure of Global Money and World Tables of Unequal Exchange." Journal of World-Systems Research. Volume 4. No.2 Fall 1998. p 145-168 Among Köhler' books are: *The Global Wage System* (2004), Canada: Nova Science Pub Inc.

44 Köhler, Gernot (1998) The Structure of Global Money and World Tables of Unequal Exchange, p. 145. *Journal of World-Systems Research* Vol. 4 no. 2: pp. 145-168.

tled in the trading currency. In most cases, the trade is settled in US dollars, even if the US is not involved in the exchange of the commodities, but other hard currencies such as the Chinese Yuan (CNY) or Euro (EUR) are also used. The conversion of local currency into the trading currency is done according to the current exchange rate on the financial market. For instance, in 2022, the exchange rate between USD and CNY was 1 USD for 6.73 CNY. However, the amount of commodities that one can buy for the national currency in one country does not necessarily correspond to the amount of goods that can be bought for the equivalent (according to the exchange rate) amount of local currency in another country.[45] In other words, the consumption power of different currencies is not in line with the exchange rate between those currencies. What one could buy in 2022 in China for 6.73 CNY does not correspond to the goods available in the US for 1 USD, even though the value is the same according to the exchange rate. In general, the currencies of all countries outside North America, the EU, Japan, Australia, and New Zealand, are undervalued in terms of consumption power. Köhler do not explain the reason for this systematic undervaluation of Third World currencies, but states:

> It may be asked whether the global power/wealth structure determines the global money structure or vice versa. I assume that both causalities exist. The global power/wealth structure contributes to the global money structure and the global structure of money feeds back into the perpetuation of the global power/wealth structure.[46]

We can express equality between the exchange-value of a currency and its consumption power by the concept of Purchasing Power Parity (PPP). This is a conversion factor used in economics for international comparisons of income levels between countries with different national currencies. PPP data for different currencies became available in the mid-80s as a result of the International Comparison Program by the World Bank and the United Nations.[47]

Going back to our example of China and the US, the value of Chinese Yuan expressed in PPP$ would be 3.99 CNY for 1 PPP$ (the value of 1 USD is, obviously, always 1 PPP$). In other words, CNY is undervalued (6.73 CNY—3.99 = 2.74), and that implies a loss for China in trade with the US, in real terms, or an unequal exchange. This difference between the PPP value of a currency and its exchange rate is what Köhler calls the deviation factor of a country. It is calcu-

---

45 Kravis, I.B., A. Heston and R. Summers (1978) *International Comparisons of Real Product and Purchasing Power*. Baltimore, USA: Johns Hopkins University Press.

46 Köhler, Gernot (1998) The Structure of Global Money and World Tables of Unequal Exchange. Page 151. *Journal of World-Systems Research* Vol. 4 no. 2: 145-168.

47 Kravis I.B. (1986) 'The Three Faces of the International Comparison Project'. *The World Bank Research Observer* 1(1): pp.3–26. The World Bank.

lated by dividing the Gross Domestic Product (GDP) of the country expressed in PPP$ by its nominal GDP. To illustrate this, Nemanja Lukić has given the following example:

> Let's assume that China exports commodities worth 6,730 CNY to USA, and USA exports commodities worth 1,000 USD to China. With the exchange rate of 6.73 CNY for 1 USD, in this example 6,730 CNY is equal to 1,000 USD. However, if the real value of CNY is 3.99 CNY for 1 USD as per PPP, from the point of view of China, the value of exported commodities should have been 3990 CNY meaning a loss of value worth 2740 CNY. From the standpoint of USA, it captured this difference, and when converted to USD at PPP$ rate, it amounts to a value of extra 686.71 USD.[48]

An important feature of the deviation rate (d), between the PPP-rate and the official exchange rate of a currency, is that it correlates with the core-periphery structure of global capitalism. As per Köhler, it is expected that the PPP value of the currencies of core states would oscillate around the real value and come very close to it over a long period of time. The peripheral countries would typically have permanently high deviation rates, indicating undervalued currencies.

This form of unequal exchange can be expressed in the formula:

$$T = d1d2 \times X$$

where:

- T is the amount of value transferred due to unequal exchange.
- d1 is factor d for the low-income country.
- d2 is factor d for the high-income country.
- X is the volume of exports from the low-income country to the high-income country.[49]

The difference between PPP and nominal exchange rates is called the Exchange Rate Deviation Index (ERDI). An ERDI deviation rate below one indicates that the current exchange rate is overvalued relative to PPP. An ERDI rate above one indicates that the current exchange rate is undervalued relative to PPP. A country with an overvalued currency has favourable terms of trade and benefits from value inflows in international trade.

The PPP rate is certainly a more precise representation of the consumption power of the wage in local currency, but it is not the basis on which unequal exchange rests. The division factor does not generate the difference or uphold the

48 Lukić Nemanja (2024), private correspondence.

49 Ibid.

different wage levels in the world-system. The deviation factor only corrects the undervaluation of local currencies in which the wage is paid out, due to the general dominance of the US over the financial system and its institutions. It represents an addition and precision to the transfer of value in terms of labor time, hidden in the price structure (beyond the currency exchange rates) of international trade of finished commodities and intermediate products in production chains.

With this method at hand, Köhler measured that the unequal exchange in 1965 reached 19 billion USD, and in 1980 it was 300 billion USD (which corresponds with Amin's and our estimations), and 1,750 billion USD by 1995. The biggest losers in unequal exchange in 1995, according to Köhler, were China, Mexico, and Indonesia. The biggest winners were the US, Japan, and Germany.[50] It is worth noting that Köhler's study measures only the unequal exchange in international trade of finished goods. It does not include the inter-industry trade in components within the global chains of production, which is a considerable—and growing—part of trade. About 70% of international trade involves global value chains, as services, raw materials, parts, and components cross borders.[51]

Köhler concludes:

> The subtitle of Emmanuel's book "Unequal Exchange" is "A Study of the Imperialism of Trade", where trade refers to commodity trade, not currency trade. With the help of now-available PPP data, it becomes increasingly apparent that the element of unfairness or exploitation in the notion of "unequal exchange" is not **only** a matter of unequal commodity exchange, **but also** a matter of unequal currency exchange, both being intricately linked.
>
> Emmanuel's theory of unequal exchange includes the following views:
>
> 4. Trade between low-income and high-income countries (periphery and center of the world-system) is unequal, meaning: unfair, biased against the low-income countries.
> 1. Wages in low-income countries are undervalued in relation to wages in high-income countries.
> 2. Export prices of exports from low-income countries are undervalued in relation to the export prices of high-income countries.
> 3. There is a relationship between the undervaluation of labour and the undervaluation of exports of low-income countries. Emmanuel stresses that: " [...] inequality of wages as such, all other things being equal, is alone the cause of the inequality of exchange" (Emmanuel 1972: 61) and refers to wages as "the inde-

50 Köhler, Gernot (1998) "Unequal Exchange 1965–1995." Paper. School of Computing and Information Management, Sheridan Collage (1998), pp. 7–9.

51 OECD (2023) 'Global value and supply chains'.

> pendent variable of the system" (Emmanuel 1972: 64).
>
> What causes the inequality of wages between high-wage and low-wage countries? Here Emmanuel discusses various possible influences — physiological wage, historical wage, market wage, equilibrium wage, moral element, trade-union factor, wage zones and so on. (Emmanuel 1972: 109-122) Generally, the problem is seen as an "institutional" problem.
>
> An alternative causal view, based on a structural view of global money, is that the "undervaluation of a country's currency" has two simultaneous valuation effects as a consequence of the distorted structure of global money [...] It leads to an undervaluation of labour in the low-income country relative to labour of high-income countries; and [...] it leads to an undervaluation of the exports of the low-income country relative to the exports of high-income countries.
>
> Seen this way, the unfairness of commodity trade between low-wage and high-wage countries ("unequal exchange" in Emmanuel's sense) is, **in part, caused by the structure of global money** ("unequal exchange" in the sense of "unequal exchange rates"). The distortion of global money and of the exchange rate system is shaped by the historically grown structure of the world-system (center-periphery, imperialism, "global apartheid" (Kohler 1978,1995)) and ideologically supported by neoclassical international economic theory (favouring free/unregulated currency markets).[52]

Köhler is of the opinion that the value transfer caused by the difference between exchange-value of currencies and their PPP value is **part of** the unequal exchange—not ***the*** unequal exchange.

In 2021, Hickel, Sullivan and Zoomkawala published an empirical study of unequal exchange from 1960-2017 following Köhler's method. They summed up the results in this way:

> In the 1960s, the South lost on average $38 billion a year (constant 2011 dollars), a significant sum at the time. Yet the scale of value transfer increased dramatically over the following decades, with particularly rapid growth between 1983 and 2005, during the height of the structural adjustment period and the establishment of the WTO trade system. Value transfer reached a maximum of almost $3 trillion per year before declining somewhat after the global financial crisis. In 2017, the most recent year of data, drain through unequal exchange amounted to $2.2 trillion; in other words, it was equivalent to the quantity of Northern commodities that one could buy in that year with $2.2 trillion. This represents a significant loss for the South. For perspective, $2.2 trillion is enough to end extreme poverty fifteen times over (i.e., with reference to the poverty gap at $1.90 per day in 2011 PPP, or the rough equivalent of Northern prices). For the North, this represents $2.2 trillion in savings, which can be invested in technological development, military power, etc., while maintaining high consumption levels. Aggregate value transfer over the whole period sums to a total of $62 trillion.[53]

---

52 Köhler, Gernot (1998) The Structure of Global Money and World Tables of Unequal Exchange. Pp. 156-7. *Journal of World-Systems Research* Vol. 4 no. 2: pp. 145-168. Emphasis original.

53 Hickel, J. Sullivan, D. & Zoomkawala, H (2121) Plunder in the post-colonial era: quantifying drain from the Global South through unequal exchange, 1960–2018. P. 5. *New Political*

Andrea Ricci Contribution

The Italian economist Andrea Ricci followed Köhler's footsteps regarding the method of measuring unequal exchange.[54] In his 2021 book *Value and Unequal Exchange in International Trade, The Geography of Global Capitalist Exploitation*, Ricci follows Marx's concept of value from the simple exchange of commodities in the marketplace to globalized production and exchange. Using the scattered remarks on the world market in Marx's writings, Ricci constructs, in an excellent way, the international theory of value Marx had planned to develop but was never able to complete. He then explains the formation of the different national currencies and how the exchange rate between them is influenced by differences in productivity:

> After having determined, following Marx's suggestions, the universal labour unit resulting from the average of different national labour intensities, we will see how the essential modification of the law of value is the consequence of international differences in labour productivity, which lead to different monetary expressions of the international value per unit of universal labour between countries. This modification is directly reflected in the different value of money between countries according to their level of economic development, which manifests itself in a systematically higher price level in more developed than in less developed economies.[55]

This phenomenon, called the "Penn effect" after the Penn World Table (PWT) developed at the University of Pennsylvania,[56] is a long-term, systematic overvaluation of richer countries' currencies and an undervaluation of poorer ones, compared with the level that would guarantee the international purchasing power parity (PPP) of different national currencies. If the exchange rate on the financial market is different from the purchasing power parity rate, then the terms of trade are unequal. Rich countries, with an overvalued exchange rate, are favoured at the expense of poorer countries, with an undervalued exchange rate. Ricci writes that:

> Despite the vast amount of research, no convincing explanation has succeeded in reconciling the consolidated empirical evidence of the "Penn effect" with the neoclassical

Economy 26, March 2021 1–18 (2021).

54 Others using this methods are Reich, 2007, 2014; Köhler & Tausch, 2002; Somel, 2003; Tausch, 2005; Elmas, 2009; Kohler, 2015, Raffer, 2006.

55 Ricci, Andrea (2021) *Value and Unequal Exchange in International Trade, The Geography of Global Capitalist Exploitation*, p. 11. New York: Routledge 2021.

56 The "Penn World Table" is a set of comparable national account data covering all countries in the world for a long historical period from 1950 to the present day. Penn World Table version 10.01|Groningen Growth and Development Centre|University of Groningen.

> theory of free trade. Similarly, the rare attempts to formulate a heterodox theory of international trade failed in this regard.[57]

Ricci explains the "Penn effect" in this way:

> [...] the international homogenisation of labour, resulting from the operation of the law of value on the world market, means that national differences in labour productivity are reflected in differences in the value of money between countries. The result is persistent and systematic real currency undervaluation for less developed countries and overvaluation for more developed countries. These real exchange rate misalignments lead to an imbalance in the terms of trade, resulting in unequal exchange. In international transactions, developed countries receive more economic and ecological resources than they give to developing countries because of the greater international purchasing power of their currencies. In other words, on the international market, the Global North receives more value (measured in terms of socially necessary labour) from a dollar than it spends to obtain a dollar. In the Global South, the reverse is true. Since value is materialised in use-values, the production of which requires natural resources as well as labour, this implies that the unequal exchange of value also entails the unequal exchange of biophysical resources. Behind the monetary equivalence of trade lies a real exchange inequality of both abstract wealth in terms of economic value and concrete wealth in terms of material assets. International trade thus functions as a hidden mechanism for the exploitation of both labour and ecological resources by the Global North from the Global South.[58]

What distinguishes Ricci calculations from Köhler's is that Ricci uses international trade data expressed in the *value added* to commodities from the UNCTAD-EORA Global Value Chains database rather than in gross *final value* of the commodities.[59] This allows Ricci to capture the additional flow of value generated in the intermediate stages in the global chains of production—the "intra-firm" trade in intermediate products—which is different from the traditional unequal exchange generated from international trade in finished goods.

Defining the Exchange Rate Deviation Index (ERDI) as the ratio of the PPP exchange rate to the nominal exchange rate, with XVA denoting exports in value added, the value transfers by international trade (T) for each country are calculated according to the following formula:

$T = (1 - ERDI)(XVA)$[60]

Ricci's study covers the period from 1995 to 2019, and measured a rise

57 Ricci, Andrea (2021) *Value and Unequal Exchange in International Trade, The Geography of Global Capitalist Exploitation*, p. 12. New York: Routledge 2021.

58 Ricci, Andrea (2022) Global locational inequality: Assessing unequal exchange effects, p. 1331. Economy and Space 2022, Vol. 54. NO.7, pp. 1323–1340.

59 UNCTAD-Eora Global Value Chain Database.

60 Ricci, Andrea (2022) Global locational inequality: Assessing unequal exchange effects, p. 1331. Economy and Space 2022, Vol. 54. NO.7, pp. 1323–1340.

in the value transfer from 1,334 billion USD in 1995 to 3,924 billion USD in 2019.[61] These figures correspond with the results of the Hickel, Sullivan, and Zoomkawala study mentioned above.

What is interesting in Ricci's data is the change in the relative share of the GDP that the value transfers represent in the three regions in the world-system: the center (including North America and the E.U.), the so-called emerging periphery (most importantly China), and the poor periphery (including Africa and India).

For the center, the value transfer increased from 5.4% of GDP in 1995 to 7.8% of GDP in 2018. The two peripheral regions in the world-system suffered from similar outflows of value around 20% of GDP in 1995. However, they then exhibited a divergent trend. Ricci writes:

> Since the early 2000s, the emerging periphery shows a rapid reduction in value outflows up to 6.3% of GDP in 2019. By contrast, the Poor Periphery suffered a drastic deterioration in the 1990s, followed by a period of partial reduction of value outflows which, however, in 2019 were still higher at 22.8% of GDP than at the outset. This evolution results from the new international division of labour marked by the rapid economic growth of some emerging countries, China in particular, and the economic marginalization and decline of large areas of the poorer periphery, such as Africa.[62]

Andrea Ricci's book *Value and Unequal Exchange in International Trade* is founded firmly in Marx's theory of value. Ricci expands it to international trade and explains the formation of a global value of goods and labor. In this process, Ricci also describes the development of money as the general equivalent and the quantitative measurement of value in the form of production price and market price. Finally, Ricci explains the formation of the different national currencies and how the exchange rate between them is influenced by differences in productivity. Ricci uses the difference between the currency exchange rate at the financial market and the PPP exchange rate as the basis for measuring unequal exchange.

As opposed to Köhler, Ricci considers differences between official currency rates and PPP rates to be *the* basis for the unequal exchange. I would rather uphold that the basis is the national deviations in the price of labor (wages) from the global value of labor (in practical terms, the average global wage), and the subsequent trade on the world market between countries with different wage-levels.

These wage differences have been generated by national and international

---

61 Ibid., p. 1332.

62 Ibid.

class struggle through the history of capitalism. The wage difference is the "independent variable" in the system and the "driver" in the generation of unequal exchange. Ricci sees this as a historical accident:

> He [Marx] believed that in the capitalist global economy, the poor countries suffered a condition of exploitation by the richer countries, resulting from a twofold order of reasons, distinct from each other. The first reason is inherent in the normal functioning of the law of value on a world scale, from which the unequal exchange automatically arises, and the second reason derives from specific, variable, and potentially reversible historical circumstances, such as political, economic, and financial monopolies. [...] This is the case of both the monopoly capital and neo-dependency theory and Emmanuel's theory based on the institutional higher wages in richer countries. The unequal exchange, therefore, appeared more as a historical exception to the supposed general rule of equivalent capitalist market exchange, than as the ordinary and structural result of the expansion of the capitalist system on a global scale.[63]

In Emmanuel's polemic with Bettlheim in *Unequal Exchange*, Emmanuel discusses precisely the difference in the role of class struggle and productivity in determining the level wage:

> [...] the fundamental question that divides Charles Bettelheim and myself. How are wages determined? He says that inequality in wage levels is an effect of inequality in the development of the productive forces. However, he admits, this determination is not exclusive: there are other elements affecting wage levels—class struggle, international relations of forces, and so on, which operate on the ideological and political level. All these parallel determinations nevertheless confer only a relative indeterminacy upon wages, so that it is not legitimate to treat it as an independent variable.
>
> If I did not know Bettelheim's horror of eclecticism, I would have smelt that when reading this passage. How is it possible to put on the same plane, and bring together as combined causes, on the one hand, the development of the productive forces, which at best can only mean the **possibility** of an increase in wages, and, on the other, the trade-union factor (the class struggle), which is a driving force in the increasing of wages? (see Chapter 3, pp. 120-122 in Unequal Exchange [...] I will merely add that "independent variable" does not mean undetermined variable, nor does it mean extraneous variable: it means predetermined variable. This is what Marx expresses when he says that, despite the **previous** (historical) determinations of the value of labor-power, "in a given country, at a given period, the average quantity of means of subsistence necessary for the worker is also given."[64]
>
> Bettelheim does not appear, however, to challenge this point, namely, that at each moment the existing difference in wages may determine the regulating relative prices (equilibrium prices). What he stresses is that these differences have their source in the uneven development of the productive forces, and he goes on to conclude that the "exploitation"[65] of the dominated countries is based on a certain international division of labor imposed by imperialism, which blocks the productive forces of some countries while

63 Ricci, Andrea (2021) *Value and Unequal Exchange in International Trade, The Geography of Global Capitalist Exploitation*, p. 127. New York: Routledge, 2021.

64 Marx, *Capital*, vol. 1, p. 71. (Translation corrected on the basis of the German and French Versions-Trans.)

> overdeveloping those of others. Now, if we leave out of account the trade-union factor, the development of the productive forces has in itself absolutely no effect on the value of labor-power. This is a point that I develop at some length in Chapter 3 (in Unequal Exchange). I would only add that Marx, when he studied the effect of the development of the productive forces on wages, concluded that this development, far from helping wages to rise, exerted on the contrary a strong downward pressure upon them, and he explained the reasons why: division and simplification of labor, displacement of workers by machinery, destruction of small enterprises and proletarianizing of the middle classes, increase in the organic composition of capital and, consequently, relative diminution of the share of capital devoted to wages, etc. It was in this context that Marx spoke of an absolute decline, "due to the ever-greater diminution in the quantity of commodities received by the worker,"[66] a phrase that has given birth to a certain theory of absolute impoverishment in the industrialized countries, refuted by the facts. Yet Marx was not wrong: these are indeed the effects of increasing productivity of labor, if we leave out of account the trade-union factor.
>
> But, Bettelheim may object, the trade-union factor itself cannot operate except in dependence on the level of the productive forces and can therefore not be regarded as a primary factor. Here again I must refer to my Chapter 3, where I show, on the one hand, that while development of the productive forces may form a favorable circumstance—in no way an exclusive one—for an increase in wages mediated through the trade-union factor, an increase in wages itself acts directly and through the actual working of economic laws in favor of development of the productive forces; and, on the other hand, that the two processes are not interdependent but interact dialectically.[67]

This point was also Ruy Mauro Marini's point: the super-exploitation of low wage workers in the periphery not only paved the way for a positive result of the trade union struggle in the center, in terms of higher wages, but by this it also encouraged the use of new technology, to save salary expenses, and hence development the productive forces.[68]

Instead of taking the wage level as the independent variable, Ricci wants to link unequal exchange to what he considers a structural phenomenon of the

---

65 Bettelheim disapproves of the term "exploitation" being used to describe the one-sided transfer of value from one country to another, on the grounds that Marx used this term to mean the purchasing of labor-power at its own value and not at the value that it produces. In the generic sense of the word, to exploit someone means to enrich oneself at his expense; Marx was concerned with a particular instance of this. Engels used the word to describe relations between countries, when talking about England: "For a nation which exploits the whole world [...]" (letter to Marx, October 7, 1858). On this basis, exploiters may well be exploited in their turn.

66 Marx, Arbeitslohn (The Wages of Labor), Pleiade edition of *Oeuvres de Karl Marx*: Economie, 2: pp. 155-156, 160-164.

67 Emmanuel, A. (1972). *Unequal Exchange: A Study of the Imperialism of Trade*, pp. 334-336. New York: Monthly Review Press 1972. Emphasis original.

68 Marini, Ruy Mauro (1974) *The Dialectics of Dependency*, ed. Amanda Latimer and Jaime Osorio, pp. 131-132. New York: Monthly Review Press. 2022.

capitalist world market, namely the development of the different national currencies. The basis of unequal exchange is the difference between the consuming power of the national currency, in which the wage is paid out in the periphery, and its consuming power in the "strong" currencies, in which the wage is paid out in the core—the "Penn effect."

For my part, I want to underline the dialectical relation between the economic laws that have to be fulfilled in order to keep accumulation running, on one side, and class struggle subdued, on the other side. The capitalist mode of production has its laws; we can even express these laws in algebraic formulas. However, they are not laws of nature. The laws of capitalism are the result of national and global political struggles. An enormous political apparatus stands behind these laws, and if necessary, they are secured by military intervention. The capitalist mode of production is made by humans, it consists of human relations, and it can— and will—be altered by humans.

Furthermore, Ricci's investigations lead him to conclude that the reason for these differences in exchange rates is differences in productivity, meaning that the core, in general, has higher productivity than the periphery. I do not share that conclusion, and even if I did, I certainly do not accept the proposition that it explains the huge difference in wage levels.

Exactly how are the different levels of productivity transformed into the difference between the official market exchange between currencies and the purchasing of the currencies (PPP)? I fully accept the existence of this "Penn effect," and it has a certain influence on the consumption power of the wage, but not enough to determine the huge international differences in the wage level.

It seems to me that the under-valuation of the local currencies in the Global South, compared to the "strong" dollar, euro, or yen—measured in PPP (consumption power)—is an unequal exchange which comes *on top* of the unequal exchange generated by the difference in national wage compared to the global average wage (global value). The overvaluation of the strong currencies is linked to US domination of the financial system and its institutions, and the role of the dollar as world money—the general trust, that with dollars in hand, instead of rupees or pesos, you can always get the commodities you want. Unequal exchange of *value* (hours of work) occurs when goods, produced at different wages levels, are exchanged at world market prices. So, I would stick to a method of measurement of unequal exchange based on the following:

- The existence of a global *value* of labor, which is in concrete terms, the average global *price* of labor, calculated in US PPP$.
- The existence of a variety of national prices of labor—the local wages—for

comparability also measured in US dollars, calculated in PPP$.

- Statistics of international trade of finished and intermediate products in production chains, from which it is possible to calculate the exchange of labor time, taking into consideration differences in skills, labor intensity, and productivity. Such statistics have only been available in recent years.

Jason Hickel and Colleagues' Contributions

In 2024, Hickel, Lemos, and Barbour published a groundbreaking empirical study of unequal exchange covering the years 1995–2021.[69] Using the statistics from the EXIOBASE[70] to track flows of embodied labour between the Global North and South, they were able to study, directly, the essential parameter of unequal exchange—the difference in wage levels—now also taking into account skill levels. They demonstrated that unequal exchange is driven by wage inequalities, without taking the detour through differences in currency exchange rates used by Köhler and Ricci. As Hickel, Lemos, and Barbour wrote in the article:

> Several studies have sought to quantify the scale of appropriation through unequal exchange indirectly by adjusting monetary trade volumes for North-South disparities in wages or general prices.[71] More recent research has used environmentally extended multi regional input-output (EEMRIO) models, which enable us to track the flows of resources embodied in each nation's final consumption. These studies demonstrate empirically that the core economies rely on a physical net appropriation of embodied labour and resources from the Global South.[72] However, this research has so far not directly analysed price dynamics associated with the labour time embodied in North-South trade. It has also been unable to answer questions about the extent to which North-South wage disparities and unequal exchange may be an effect of differences in the type of labour being performed, such as in terms of skill level or sector (for instance, if wage inequalities arise because the South trades low-skilled labour for high skilled labour, or primary goods for secondary goods). In this study, we use the EEMRIO model EXIOBASE to track flows of embodied labour between North and South, for the first time accounting directly for sectors, wages and skill levels (as defined by the

69 Hickel, Jason; Lemos, Morena Hanbury and Barbour, Felix: (2024)' Unequal exchange of labour in the world economy', *Nature Communications*| (2024) 15:6298, Springer Nature.

70 Exiobase: www.exiobase.eu.

71 Hickel, J. Sullivan, D. & Zoomkawala, H (2121) Plunder in the post-colonial era: quantifying drain from the Global South through unequal exchange, 1960–2018. *New Polit. Econ.* 26, pp. 1–18 (2021).

72 Dorninger, C. et al. (2021) Global patterns of ecologically unequal exchange: Implications for sustainability in the 21st century. Ecol. Econ. 179,106824(2021). And: Pérez-Sánchez, L., Velasco-Fernández, R. & Giampietro, M. (2021) The international division of labor and embodied working time in trade for the US, the EU and China. Ecol. Econ. 180, 106909 (2021).

> International Labour Organisation, ILO, described in Methods). This enables us to define the scale of labour appropriation through unequal exchange in terms of physical labour time, while also representing it in terms of wage value, in a manner that accounts for the skill level composition of labour embodied in North-South trade.[73]

By using data from EXIOBASE on global trade and production, differentiated by sector and skill level, including data for labor time in hours and wages from 1995–2021, Hickel, Lemos, and Barbour provided by far the best measurement of unequal exchange to date, both in terms of the method used and the amount of statistics. They summarize their method of calculation in this way:

> **Overview of calculations** We obtained data on labour embodied in traded goods and services flowing from North to South, from South to North, between Southern countries and between Northern countries, for the three skill levels and the five sector aggregates [...] along with the labour compensation paid against these flows. We also obtained data on labour by skill level and sector involved in domestic production and consumption within both the Global North and the Global South (i.e. labour involved in the production of non-traded goods), along with compensation paid. To calculate the Northern net appropriation of labour, we subtracted Northern flows to the South from Southern flows to the North. To calculate total Northern consumption, we summed Southern flows to the North together with flows of traded goods within the North and production and consumption of non traded goods within the North. Wages (euros/hour) for each region are calculated as the total compensation (in euros) the region receives for its exports of labour divided by its total exports of labour (in hours). To calculate labour hours per worker we divided total labour hours rendered in each region by the total number of workers employed, also obtained from EXIOBASE.[74]

The main results of the study are:

[...] The South's contribution to total global production has increased steadily over the period since 1995, across all skill categories. The largest increase has occurred in the high-skill category, with the South's contribution to high-skill production increasing from 66% of the world's total in 1995 (1.9x more than the North) to 76% in 2021 (3.2x more than the North). In fact, the South now contributes more high skilled labour to the world economy (1124 billion hours in 2021) than all the high-, medium- and low-skilled labour contributions of the Global North combined (971 billion hours in 2021). The South also contributes the overwhelming majority of labour across all aggregated sector groupings we derived from EXIOBASE, including agriculture (99%), mining (99%), manufacturing (93%), services (80%) and 'other' (89%). Despite contributing 90–91% of the total labour that goes into global

73 Hickel, Jason; Lemos, Morena Hanbury and Barbour, Felix: (2024) 'Unequal exchange of labour in the world economy.', pp. 1-2. *Nature Communications*| (2024) 15:6298, Springer Nature.

74 Ibid., p. 10.

production and the production of traded goods in 2021, including the majority of high-skilled labour, the Global South received less than half (44%) of global income, and Southern workers received only 21% of global income in that year. In other words, while global production is overwhelmingly performed in the Global South, the yields are disproportionately captured in the Global North, indicating a disproportionate command of the global product.[75]

The study also revealed that workers in the Global South consistently render more labour per worker than in the North, on average 466 hours more than their Northern counterparts (26% more). We also see that labour time per worker decreased by 7% over that period in the North, while in the South it increased by 1%.[76] So, there is no indication of lower productivity or intensity of Southern labour, which is used to explain global wage-difference by mainstream economists. Concerning unequal exchange, the article states:

> Our analysis confirms a substantial and persistent pattern of unequal exchange between the Global North and South. In 2021, the Global North imported 906 billion hours of embodied labour from the South while exporting only 80 billion hours in return (a ratio of 11:1). On average across the period, the North imported 15x more labour from the South than it exported in return. In other words, the North net appropriates large quantities of labour from the South. This net appropriation occurs across all skill categories, including high-skilled labour. On average the North imports 4x more high-skilled labour from the South than it exports, together with 17x more medium-skilled labour and 29x more low-skilled labour [...][77]

This is the essence of unequal exchange as defined by Emmanuel. Hickel, Lemos, and Barbour continue:

> The unequal exchange of labour described above is not explained by sectoral differences. We found that the Global North net-imports large quantities of labour from the South in all skill levels across all five sectors. On average, the North imported 120x more agricultural labour than it exported, 110x more mining labour, 11x more manufacturing labour, and 6x more service labour. In other words, it is not the case that the North net-imports labour in primary production from the South while net-exporting a smaller quantity of labour in secondary and tertiary production. On the contrary, the Global North relies on a net appropriation of labour from the South across all sectors, including manufacturing and services.[78]

What does all this mean for the consumption power in the Global North?

> We find that this pattern of net appropriation plays a major role in the North's consumption. In any given year, the North consumes roughly twice as much labour as it renders, thanks to appropriation through unequal exchange. In 2021, net-appropriated labour

75 Ibid., p. 3.

76 Ibid., Table 1, p.3.

77 Ibid., p. 3.

78 Ibid., p. 4.

> comprised 46% of the North's total consumption of labour. [...] the Global North have become increasingly reliant on low-skilled labour, the vast majority of which is net-appropriated from the Global South (71% in 2021). While the majority of the North's net appropriation of Southern labour is comprised of medium-skilled labour, the net appropriation of high-skilled labour nonetheless constitutes a significant feature of Northern economies. We find that Global North economies net appropriate more high-skilled labour from the Global South (52 billion hours in 2021) than they obtain and consume through North–North trade (31 billion hours in 2021).[79]

The Wage Value of Appropriation Through Unequal Exchange

If I must criticise something in this excellent study, then it is that it measures the unequal exchange against a US wage. level, instead of a world average wage level (the global level of value). Hickel, Lemos, and Barbour state:

> As previous studies have pointed out,[80] because wages and prices are an artefact of bargaining power in the world economy (plus the level of commodification, the extent of monopoly concentration, etc.) as well as dynamics of supply and demand, it is not possible to assign a "true" monetary value to labour. The most we can do is to represent labour in terms of the prevailing wages experienced by different agents in the existing capitalist world economy, purely as a point of reference. Previous studies of unequal exchange, including by Samir Amin,[81] argue that the net appropriation of hidden labour from the Global South should be represented in terms of the prevailing Northern wages; in other words, from the perspective of Northern workers and producers.[82] This is the approach we take here.[83]

I disagree. Let me explain. The unequal exchange must be measured as the deviation of national wages against the global value of labour, in practical concrete terms the global average hourly wage, which can be calculated from figures in the study to be 3.9531 EUR.[84] Anyway, Hickel and colleagues continue:

---

79 Ibid., p. 5.

80 Hickel, J.,Sullivan, D. & Zoomkawala, H (2021) 'Plunder in the post-colonial era: quantifying drain from the Global South through unequal exchange, 1960–2018', *New Polit. Econ.* 26,1–18 (2021). and Kohler, G. The structure of global money and world tables of unequal exchange. J. World Syst. Res. 4,145–168 (1998).

81 Amin, S. *Unequal Development: An Essay on the Social Formations of Peripheral Capitalism* (New York: Monthly Review Press, 1976).

82 Köhler, Gernot (1998) The Structure of Global Money and World Tables of Unequal Exchange. *Journal of World-Systems Research* Vol. 4 no. 2: 145-168.

83 Hickel, Jason; Lemos, Morena Hanbury and Barbour, Felix: (2024) Unequal exchange of labour in the world economy, p. 5. *Nature Communications*| (2024) 15:6298, Springer Nature.

First, we established the scale of net-appropriated labour time within each skill level for each year. We then multiplied the net appropriated labour time by the wages that Northern workers receive for the labour of the same skill level, rendered in the production of traded goods (ignoring goods produced for final domestic consumption). Labour is therefore compared like-for-like: for example, the appropriated quantity of low-skill labour is valued at the Northern wage for low-skill work, the appropriated quantity of high-skill labour is valued at the Northern wage for high-skill work, etc. In this way, we calculated the wage value of appropriated labour in a manner that answers longstanding questions about the degree to which this is affected by the skill level composition of exchange. Our results show that in 2021 the wage value of labour net appropriated from the South was worth 16.9 trillion EUR (in constant 2005 EUR). In other words, if Northern workers were to perform the net-appropriated quantity of labour domestically, it would cost 16.9 trillion EUR in terms of wages. [...] Over the period 1995–2021, the total wage value of net appropriated labour sums to 310 trillion EUR.[85]

Wage trends We find that the North-South wage gap is large and has been increasing over time for all skill level categories. Southern wages are 87–95% less than Northern wages at the same skill level, i.e. for equal work as defined by the ILO. Southern wages are 87% less for high-skill labour, 93% less for medium-skill labour, and 95% less for low-skill labour. The disparity is so extreme that high-skill labour in the Global South receives 68% less than low-skill labour in the Global North. Stated otherwise, for every hour of work at a given skill level, Northern workers are able to consume 8–19x more of the global product than Southern workers (8x more for high-skill labour, 14x more for medium-skill labour, and 19x more for low-skill labour) [...]

[...] These results indicate that workers in the Global South, who receive an average 1.62 EUR per hour, perform the vast majority (90%) of the labour that produces for the global economy, the vast majority (91%) of the labour that produces traded goods, and nearly half (46%) of the labour that supports growth and consumption in the Global North (net of trade). The global economy is overwhelmingly characterised by a regime of cheap labour.

These wage gaps are not explained by sectoral differences. Our results show large and growing North-South wage gaps for all skill levels across all of the sectors we analysed. In agriculture, Southern wages are 85–91% lower than Northern wages for any given skill level. In mining, Southern wages are 93–98% lower. In manufacturing, 89–94% lower. In services,83–90%.[86]

In the end of the article the authors discuss the result of the study:

Discussion The results of this study demonstrate the occurrence of large net transfers of embodied labour from the Global South to the Global North through unequal exchange in international trade and global supply chains, across all skill levels and all sectors, amounting to a total of 826 billion hours in 2021. These results illustrate several important features of the world economy. For one, it is clear that Northern economies rely substantially on net appropriation from the Global South. Net appropriated labour comprises approximately half of the total labour that provisions goods and services for

84 Ibid., p. 2.

85 Ibid., p. 6.

86 Ibid.

> Northern consumption. In other words, this dynamic doubles the total quantity of labour that is available to the economies of the Global North, which sustains their high levels of consumption and wealth, and underpins their economic growth. [...] Given this dynamic, it is clear that the North's development model cannot be universalised, as it relies on appropriation from elsewhere. Furthermore, it is unlikely that the North's current levels of aggregate consumption could be maintained under fair trade conditions [...][87]

Correct, it would be impossible to homogenise the world to current Northern consumption patterns, for simple ecological reasons. In addition, an equal exchange, based on a Northern wage level, is impossible because the South has no periphery to exploit. We need another mode of production and consumption to obtain an equal world. Hence, as mentioned above, the volume of unequal exchange should be measured on the basis of the difference between Northern and Southern wage deviation from the global average wage (global value of labor), instead of representing the "appropriation of hidden labour from the Global South [...] in terms of the prevailing Northern wages."

The discussion continues:

> Unequal exchange is understood to be driven in part by large North-South wage gaps. We find that Southern wages are 87–95% lower than Northern wages for work of equal skill. Our analysis confirms arguments by others (e.g. Ruy Mauro Marini, Samir Amin, Arrighi Emmanuel, etc.) that these wage gaps cannot be explained by sectoral differences, as they prevail across all sectors of the economy: the wages of Southern workers are 83–98% lower for work of equal skill within the same sector [...] We conclude that while Southern workers contribute the majority (90–91%) of labour that powers the world economy, they receive only 21% of global GDP. The yields of production are disproportionately captured in the Global North.
>
> It is interesting to note that our results describing the North's reliance on high-skilled labour from the South confirm statements made by the CEOs of major firms, who have claimed that the necessary quantity of high-skilled engineering labour to support their production is not available in the core states and therefore this production must be performed abroad. Apple's former CEO Steve Jobs noted that his company required 30,000 engineers; as he put it, "You can't find that many in America to hire."[88] Current CEO Tim Cook has noted that Apple's production relies on large quantities of high-skilled labour in China for advanced engineering, tooling and innovation.[89] [90]

---

87 Hickel, Jason; Lemos, Morena Hanbury and Barbour, Felix: (2024) Unequal exchange of labour in the world economy. Page 7. *Nature Communications*| (2024) 15:6298, Springer Nature.

88 Isaacson, W (2011) *Steve Jobs*. Little Brown, 2011.

89 Leibowiz, G. (2017) Apple CEO. Tim Cook: this is the number one reason we make iPhones in China (it's not what you think). Inc 21 December 2017.

90 Hickel, Jason; Lemos, Morena Hanbury and Barbour, Felix: (2024) Unequal exchange of labour in the world economy. Page 8. *Nature Communications*| (2024) 15:6298, Springer Nature.

The study does not take possible differences in productivity between the Global South and North into consideration, as the databases used do not provide such data. However, recent case studies indicate that the production of cars, electronics, solar panels, windmills, and so on is not less productive in China or Mexico compared with the US and EU.[91] The authors discuss this question in the article:

> There are several reasons to believe that physical productivity differences cannot explain the large North-South wage gaps and unequal exchange we observe. First, in the case of export industries (rather than subsistence and non-traded sectors), most production in the South is performed with modern techniques, often with technologies provided by international capital.[92] Workers in these industries have been found to produce as much or more physical output per hour than their Northern counterparts.[93] Southern production is also characterised by greater labour intensity, as workers are subject to rigid systems of control designed to maximise output to an extent that would fall foul of labour regulations in the core.[94] Second, in cases where Southern export industries do operate with less efficient technologies, productivity differences only account for a small share of the North-South wage gap and the appropriation of labour time.[95] The key fact is that Northern firms choose to use Southern labour not only because wages are cheaper per hour, but because wages are cheaper per unit of physical output.[96] Offshoring occurs precisely because the North-South wage difference is greater than any physical productivity difference. Third, physical productivities can only meaningfully be compared for identical tasks and products. For many industries and product categories, Southern production has no counterpoint in the North, because it cannot or does not occur there (such as in the case of coffee, coltan, smart phones, fast fashion, etc.). [...] In such cases, productivities cannot be compared and cannot explain wage inequalities and unequal exchange.[97]
>
> It is important to note that, in cases where physical productivity differences do exist, this is often because it is more profitable for capital to use cheaper, more labour-intensive methods than to invest in modern equipment—especially in cases where state invest-

91 See also the discussion on productivity on page 24.

92 Smith, J. (2016) *Imperialism in the Twenty-first Century: Globalization, Super-Exploitation, and Capitalism's Final Crisis.* New York: Monthly Review Press 2016.

93 Baerresen, D. W. (1971) *The Border Industrialization Program of Mexico.* Health Lexington Books, 1971.

94 Suwandi, I Jonna, R. J. & Foster, J. B. (2019) Global commodity chains and the new imperialism. *Monthly Review.* Vol. 70. 2019. and Ngai, P. & Chan, J. (2012) Global capital, the state, and Chinese workers: the Foxconn experience. *Mod. China* 38, pp. 383–410 (2012).

95 Amin, S. (1976) *Unequal Development: An Essay on the Social Formations of Peripheral Capitalism.* New York: Monthly Review Press, 1976.

96 Suwandi, I. (2019) *Value Chains: The New Economic Imperialism.* New York: Monthly Review Press, 2019.

97 Hickel, Jason; Lemos, Morena Hanbury and Barbour, Felix: (2024) Unequal exchange of labour in the world economy. Page 8. *Nature Communications*| (2024) 15:6298, Springer Nature.

> ment in technological development has been curtailed by structural adjustment programmes, or where patents prevent affordable access to necessary technologies—precisely because Southern wages are maintained at artificially low levels.[98] This arrangement benefits Northern consumers with cheaper goods and benefits Northern capital with an increased surplus. In such cases, the use of labour-intensive methods facilitates value transfer and should be understood as constituting unequal exchange. [...]
>
> Finally, our analysis does not extend to gender dynamics, including uncompensated household labour or social reproduction, which is also constitutive of unequal exchange and should be explored in future EEMRIO research.[99],[100]

At the end of the discussion, the authors write:

> It should be understood that unequal exchange is ultimately driven by the corporations and investors that control supply chains, and the states that determine the rules of international trade and finance, not by workers or consumers.

Unequal exchange takes place within the framework of the capitalist mode of production, and in that sense it is ruled by corporations and investors. However, unequal exchange is also generated by the differences in global wage levels. The class struggle in Western Europe and North America in the latter part of the nineteenth century raised the wage level of the working class. This result was made possible by the super-exploitation of the colonial proletariat, generating the dynamic of unequal exchange. Imperialism was for the benefit of both capital and the working class, and as such, it is no wonder that the majority of the Northern working class supported and still support colonialism and imperialism.

Unequal Exchange on the Individual Level

All the previously mentioned attempts to measure unequal exchange have been calculated on the global level. Here, I will look at how it works at the level of the individual wage laborer. The prerequisites and mechanisms are the same: a

98 Francis, G. & Sutcliffe, B. (1987) *The Profit System: The Economics of Capitalism* (Penguin, 1987). And Hickel, J. & Sullivan, D. (2023) Capitalism, global poverty, and the case for democratic socialism. *Monthly Review.* Vol. 75, page 99–113 (2023). This is also the argument of Marini in: *The Dialectics of Dependency.* New York: Monthly Review Press, 2023.

99 Ossome, L.& Sirisha, N. (2021) The Agrarian Question Of Gendered Labour in Labour Questions In The Global South (eds. Jha, P., Chambati, W. & Ossome, L.) Palgrave Macmillan, 2021. And: Dunaway, W. A. (ed.) (2013) Gendered Commodity Chains: Seeing Women's Work and Households in Global Production (Stanford Univ. Press, 2013).

100 Hickel, Jason; Lemos, Morena Hanbury and Barbour, Felix: (2024) Unequal exchange of labour in the world economy. Page 8. *Nature Communications*| (2024) 15:6298, Springer Nature.

difference in the *price* of labor due to the immobility of labor, and a tendency towards the formation of a global *value* of labor and goods.

The Balance

Exploitation in capitalistic relations consists of an appropriation of surplus value. So, if we look at the individual wage laborer, there is a balance between the appropriation of value from unequal exchange, through the consumption of goods produced by low wage labor, and the exploitation of labor through the extraction of surplus value in the production process.

A worker cannot benefit from capitalistic exploitation, unless the wages contain surplus value extorted from other workers. So long as the wage increases obtained by the workers of a country only represent a partial recuperation of the surplus value extorted from them by their own employers, there is no share in exploitation and no antagonism between the working classes of different nations.

However, the fact that you are a wage earner does not necessarily mean that you are exploited, when viewed in a global context. Due to the considerable difference in wages between North and South, the transformation of value into price, and the transfer of value through global production chains, it is quite possible for capital to employ labor in the North with a relatively high wage and get a profit out of it, while at the same time, this wage earner is able to consume more value than she or he creates.

Some wage workers consume more *value* (in terms of labor hours) than they create. In concrete terms, the *value* of smartphones, iPads, sneakers, t-shirts, IKEA furniture, chocolate bars, bananas, coffee, etc. produced in the Global South and consumed by workers in the Global North may be greater than the value extracted from Northern wage earners in the production process.

Already in 1857, Marx discussed the possibility of workers drawing advantages from the labor of other workers. This happens when the goods some workers produce are sold for less than their value and consumed by other workers who can afford them because of the higher wages they are paid. As he wrote in the Grundrisse:

> As regards the other workers, the case is entirely the same; they gain from the depreciated commodity only in relation (1) as they consume it; (2) relative to the size of their wage, which is determined by necessary labour. [101]

---

101 Marx, Karl (1857) *Grundrisse,* Notebook IV: The Chapter on Capital, The general rate of profit. London: Penguin, 1973.

It is certainly possible for a wage earner to consume more value than they produce. This is not a matter of morals but of mathematics. As Emmanuel writes:

> No Marxist would deny that certain wages, far from providing surplus-value, contain it. The question of whether this only happens with the 200,000-dollars annual salary of an Executive Director at General Motors, or with a Sub-Director's 100,000 dollars salary, or already with the wages of a qualified French worker at 4,000 francs a month, is a mere matter of calculation, not of conceptual analysis. In the same way, whether the "workers' aristocracy" as defined by Lenin includes 5% or 10% or 90% of the working class of this or that nation at this or that moment is not a question of principle but a matter of history and of general economic conditions.[102]

Assuming a globalized value of labor and given the difference in the price of labor (wage) between the Global North and the Global South, then being a wage laborer does not necessarily imply that you are exploited. A worker in the electronic industry in Southeast Asia and a worker in the biotech industry in North America or the EU are both wage laborers. Both create value, and both are a source of surplus value and hence profit for capital. Their labor is exploited. However, given the high wage level in the Global North, the worker can appropriate more value through the consumption of goods produced by low-wage labor than the value that is extracted from them through the labor process. As Emmanuel states:

> [...] a labour aristocracy by definition producing less value than their wages allow them to appropriate and thus becoming the objective allies of imperialism, which brings them the supplement [...][103]

I have made an estimate of the global average wage (global value of labor), across sectors and skill levels, based on the figures in the Hickel, Lemos and Barbour study. This determines the threshold above which workers begin to appropriate more value by consumption than they produce, and thereby cease to be exploited in the global context:

In 2021, a total of 9.6 trillion hours of labor went into producing for the global economy. 8.64 trillion hours came from the Global South, at an average wage of 1.62 EUR, making the southern total wage-bill:

$$8.64 \times 1.62 \text{ EUR} = 13.9968 \text{ trillion EUR}$$

0.96 trillion hours came from the Global North at an average wage of 24.95 EUR, making the northern total wage-bill:

---

102 Emmanuel, Arghiri (1975) 'Unequal Exchange Revisited'. IDS Discussion Paper No. 75, pp. 63-64. Institute of Development, University of Sussex, Brighton, England.

103 Emmanuel, A. (1986) Preface to Communist Working Group (1986), *Unequal Exchange and the Prospects for Socialism in a Divided World*, p. 9. Copenhagen: Publishing House Manifest. Republished by Washington: Iskra Books, 2025.

0.96×24.95 EUR = 23.95296 trillion EUR

Total global wage in 2021:

$13.9968 + 23.95296 = 37.94976$ trillion EUR

Global average hourly wage:

37.94976 trillion EUR/9.6 trillion hours = 3.9531 EUR/hour (4.0 USD/hour)

For comparison, the average hourly wage in the U.S. in 2022 was 42.78 USD, in Germany 43 USD, and in Denmark 46.75 USD.[104]

Therefore, a wage earner in the Global North can consume more value than she or he produces. Whether someone earns 1000 dollars or 10 dollars per hour changes the extent of the value transfer but not its nature. It is not a matter of principle but calculation. I estimate that the transition point—the income threshold at which workers can begin to consume more value than they produce, in a global context—is as low as 4 dollars per hour, which is around 650 dollars per month.

Ricci, with his method based on currency exchange rates, calculated that the inflow of value to Western Europe by unequal exchange in 2019 was 6,921 USD per capita, which is equivalent to 14.8% of GDP per capita.[105]

In all the calculations above, there are of course uncertainties and sources of error in the information on wages and the numbers of wage workers in different countries, and it should also be noted that the OECD average wage covers all wages, high and low. However, even with these caveats, we can get an approximate range of the global value of labour in money terms. On this basis, it is fair to conclude that the appropriation of value in the North through consumption—due to the relatively high wage level—is higher than the exploitation by capital through the surplus value extracted through the labor process.

In the Global South, the value consumed covers only the value of labor-power (sometimes less, called super-exploitation) Hence the exploitation by surplus value exceeds the value appropriated by consumption.

---

104 OECD (2023) Comparing Weekly Work Hours and Salaries in OECD Countries, *Visual Capitalist*.

105 Ricci, Andrea (2022), Global locational inequality: Assessing unequal exchange effects, p. 1334. *Economy and Space* 2022, Vol. 54. No.7, pp. 1323–1340.

Peeling to the Apple Core

Donald Clelland provides a specific example of the relation between different global wage levels and the consumption of Apple products, which have a globalized price level:

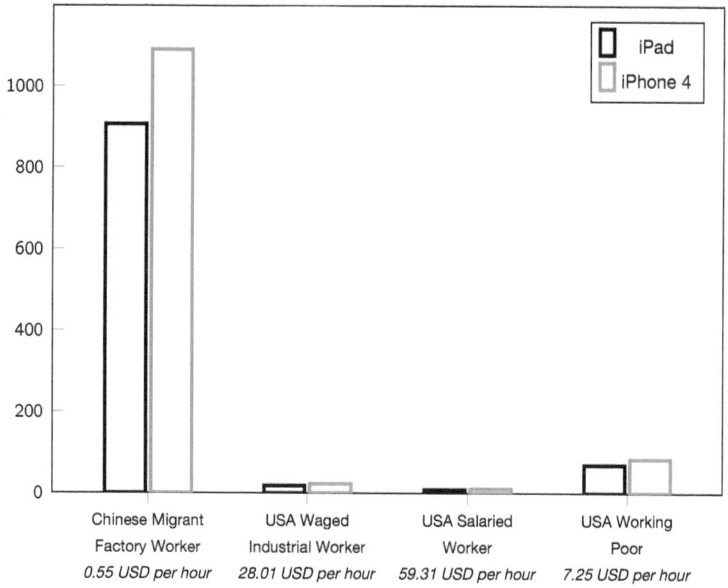

Figure VII The Buying Power from Dark Value Drains Embedded in the iPad and the iPhone 4[106]

> Let us begin with this fact: the USA is the primary market for the Apple iPhone and the iPad. By 2018, 84 percent of American households owned a smartphone, and 63 percent owned a tablet, both items routinely used by working class and professional people in the contexts of both their work and personal lives. The figure analyzes consumer outcomes by comparing labor time needed to purchase an iPhone4 or an iPad, pointing not only to the inequalities between Chinese factory workers who produced the iPhone4 and American workers who consumed it, but also to the income differentials between USA waged, salaried and poor workers. At the weighted average wage of $0.55 for migrant workers at the Shenzhen and Chengdu factories, the Chinese migrant fac-

106 Chinese migrant workers comprised 58% of the iPhone labor force, but they earned 32 to 47% less than resident urban workers (Cheng et al 2020). For that reason, I utilized the average weighted wage of migrant workers who assembled the iPhone4 in Shenzhen and Chengdu. US mean wage data is from the US Bureau of Labor Statistics (2011). **Ed. Note:** Note from Clelland, 2020.

tory laborer would need to work 907 hours to purchase an iPad or 1,089 hours to afford the iPhone4. At the average of $28.01, a USA waged industrial worker needed about 18 hours to afford the iPad or 21 hours for an iPhone (less than 2.5 workdays in both cases). The American enjoyed a consumer surplus of 889 iPad hours or 1,068 iPhone hours in comparison to the Chinese laborer. At the average of $59.31, the USA salaried worker required only 8.4 hours to buy the iPad or 10 hours for the iPhone (about a day's labor in both cases), taking advantage of a dark value consumer surplus of 899 to 1,079 hours to subsidize the purchase. In terms of income position, the working poor American earning $7.25 per hour is the closest structural parallel to the Chinese factory worker. However, that American worker could have purchased either an iPad or an iPhone with less than 8 percent of the hours required of the Chinese migrant worker. Even the impoverished American enjoyed a consumer surplus of 838 to 1,007 hours that was made available through dark value drains from low-paid Chinese migrant workers.[107]

The Political Economy of a T-Shirt

Another example that illustrates the consequences of the different global wage levels and the globalized prices of goods is the garment industry. The Swedish clothing brand Hennes and Mouritz—H&M—has no production of its own. All production is outsourced to 900 suppliers at 1,900 factories with 116,000 workers.[108] In 2016, the UN's International Labour Organization published a report on work conditions at textile factories in Cambodia, India, and Bangladesh that are suppliers to H&M.[109] The monthly wages at the Cambodian factories supplying H&M averaged 187 USD. At the factories in India, the monthly wages were 114 USD, while the monthly salary in Bangladesh was approximately 87 USD. According to the ILO report, these wage levels are enough to pay for approximately half of the basic necessities of life and a simple dwelling.

A 2010 German investigation, published in the newspaper *Die Zeit*, described the conditions in a factory where workers produced 125,000 shirts a day, half of which were sold to H&M, the rest to other Western retailers.[110] Workers at the factory earned 1.36 EUR a day for 10–12 hours work. The journalists described the price formation of a T-shirt manufactured in Bangladesh and sold

107 Clelland, Donald (2020) "Peeling to the Apple Core: Dark Value Drains at the Heart of High-Tech Mass Consumption, 2010-2020." Unpublished Paper provided by Wilma A. Dunaway.

108 Donaldson, T (2016). "H&M to source more garments from Bangladesh," *Sourcing Journal*, March 14, 2016.

109 Bhattacharjee, Shikha Silliman (2016) Precarious Work in the H&M Global Value Chain. A Report to the ILO 2016.

110 Uchatius, Wolfgang (2010) "Das Welthemd." *Die Zeit*, December 17, 2010. Here from: Tony Norfield, "The China Price," *Economics of Imperialism* (blog), June 4, 2011.

by H&M in Germany. The price of the T-shirt was 4.95 EUR in the store in Berlin. This is what this sale price represents:

1. 0.40 EUR: the cost of 400g of raw material (cotton) bought by the factory in Bangladesh.
2. 1.35 EUR: the price H&M paid per T-shirt to the Bangladeshi company.
3. 1.41 EUR: after adding 0.06 EUR per shirt for shipping costs from Bangladesh to Hamburg in Germany.
4. 3.40 EUR: after adding 1.99 EUR for transport within Germany, storefront rent, wages to sales employees, and marketing and administrative expenses within Germany.
5. 4.16 EUR: after adding 0.76 EUR net profit for H&M.
6. 4.95 EUR: after adding 19 percent VAT, paid to the German state.

This breakdown of price formation reveals that H&M paid the manufacturer in Bangladesh 1.35 EUR for each T-shirt, corresponding to 28% of its sales price. From that share, one must deduct 0.40 EUR, the cost of cotton fabric for each T-shirt. That leaves 0.95 EUR of the sales price to be split between capital and workers in Bangladesh. That covers salaries, power, materials needed other than cotton, depreciation of the machinery, buildings, and other assets, plus the local manufacturer's profit. A reasonable estimate would be that the average labor cost to produce one T-shirt is roughly 0.10–0.15 EUR. The remaining 3.54 EUR, corresponding to 72% of the sales price, is distributed in Germany. This includes 2.05 EUR for transport, sales, and marketing expenses. H&M's profit is 0.76 EUR per T-shirt, which is 5-7 times what is paid to the workers in Bangladesh who make the T-shirts. The German state receives 19% of the sales price, equivalent to 0.79 EUR, in VAT.

So, a t-shirt produced in Bangladesh is a cheap commodity for Northern consumers, one which generates profits for H&M and tax revenue for the German state. The sales tax alone is significantly higher than the wages the workers receive to produce the clothes. Among other things, this tax is used to pay for welfare benefits, such as financial support in case of unemployment, illness, etc. In Denmark, a "cash beneficiary recipient" gets the equivalent of between 1,500 USD and 2,300 USD per month. The level of social benefits is similar in Sweden. In 2018, a textile worker in Bangladesh received a salary of roughly 87 USD per month.[111]

111 Danish Ministry of Employment (2021) "Satser for 2021." And Bizvibe (2017) "Minimum Wages in Asia's Textile and Apparel Industry."

The Advantages of the Individual Perspective

One advantage of looking at unequal exchange as a balance between appropriation of value through consumption and capitalist exploitation by wage labor in the national framework is that it underlines the dynamics of the process.

The value acquired by workers in the Global North through the consumption of goods produced by low-wage workers has been growing throughout most of the 20th and 21st centuries. The unequal exchange reached its peak around 2010 and is now, for the first time in a century, declining, partly due to rising wages in China, partly due to declining North-South trade as the neoliberal world market erodes.[112] China has, in the last decade, reduced the outflow of value from around 19% in the period 1995-2007 to only 10% of per capita in the period 2007-2019.[113] That is significant, as China has a population of 1.4. billion people.

This way of looking at the unequal exchange, at the individual level, as a balance between appropriation through consumption and exploitation through surplus value, also opens up the possibility of differentiating between different sectors of the working class within each country—between the high-wage labor aristocracy and lower-waged immigrant labor in the Global North.

In conclusion, to answer the question raised at the beginning of this chapter: yes, the value transfer by unequal exchange has a size that can explain the difference in living standards of the working class between the Global North and South. It is not just the matter of the yearly flow of value; it is the historical continuity of this flow, decade after decade. And most importantly, this flow of value added to the consumption power in the North and thereby balanced the expanded production, creating a dynamic development of the productive forces in the Global North and blocking the development in the South.

---

112 Hickel, Jason, Sullivan, Dylan & Zoomkawala, Huzaifa (2021) Plunder in the Post-Colonial Era: Quantifying Drain from the Global South Through Unequal Exchange, 1960–2018. *New Political Economy,* vol. 26 no. 6, pp. 1030-1047.

113 Ricci, Andrea (2022) Global locational inequality: Assessing unequal exchange effects, p. 1334. *Economy and Space* 2022, Vol. 54. No.7, pp. 1323-1340.

4

The Political Consequences of Unequal Exchange: The Break in International Solidarity

IN THE 1970S, literally hundreds of articles in academic journals and left-wing magazines discussed Emmanuel's concepts of unequal exchange. He became a well-known academic, together with people like Samir Amin, Andre Gunder Frank, and Immanuel Wallerstein. *Unequal Exchange* is not an easy read, but it is rewarding in the same way as *Capital.*[1] Besides his systematic rigor in argument, another appealing characteristic of Emmanuel writings is that he dares to break with established left-wing orthodoxies. Already in June 1970, Emmanuel wrote in *Monthly Review*:

> The most bitter fruits of my work on L'échange inégale [Unequal Exchange] was the negative conclusion arrived at regarding the international solidarity of the working class [...] [L]oyalty to the nation transcends internal conflict of interest, on the one hand, while on the other, it grows stronger in the consequence of international antagonism. National integration has been made possible in the big industrial countries at the cost of international disintegration of the proletariat. [...] As I said in my book, when the relative importance of the exploitation which the working class suffers through belonging to the "proletariat" continually decreases as compared with that which it benefits through belonging to a privileged nation, a moment comes when the aim of increasing the national income in absolute term takes precedence over that of improving each section's share relative to that of the others. This is what the workers of the advanced countries have well understood, becoming, over the last half-century, increasingly "social democratized"—either by supporting the social democratic parties already in being or by "social-democratizing" the Communist Parties themselves.[2]

The main argument for the continuing international solidarity of the pro-

1 In 2025 Iskra Books republished our introduction to the theory of Unequal Exchange: *Unequal Exchange and the Prospects for Socialism*, to which I contributed a new prologue and epilogue. Washington: Iskra Books, 2025.

letariat was the following: it may be that workers in the Global North are less exploited than workers in the Global South, but this is no reason why they should not act together to expropriate the exploiters and recover all the surplus value in global capitalism.

This argument might be valid if all workers were donors of surplus value. But this is not the case. Today, the majority of workers in the center are no longer donors but receivers of surplus value, which can only come from the labor of workers of other nations. The problem is that even if one were to expropriate all the capitalists of the world, the value produced would not be enough to ensure equalisation from above, both in terms of income, and in terms of material resources. Global ecology cannot sustain a world living the Northern way.

Andrea Ricci sums up Emmanuel's position:

> Finally, wage growth in more developed countries acts as the ultimate cause of the continuing deterioration of the terms of trade for less developed countries, and consequently, central workers are the primary beneficiaries of the super-exploitation of the peripheral proletariat through the transfers of value deriving from unequal exchange. The latter point was by far the most provocative, and it triggered the start of a heated discussion among Marxist scholars and political activists of the North and South. Emmanuel did nothing to mitigate the political and practical implications of his thesis, but rather he stressed them in their whole scope. In fact, he argued that the increases in wages of central workers are paid for the most part by the surplus labour extracted to the peripheral workers, and to a lesser extent by the capitalists of the whole world by a reduction in the international general rate of profit. In this way, Emmanuel resumed and amplified the thesis of the "labour aristocracy" used by Lenin, who explained the opportunism of the British labour movement up to the First World War by the distribution of a small part of the imperialistic super profits to a privileged upper stratum of the working class for influencing the mass of proletariat towards collaborative positions. Actually, Emmanuel went far beyond Lenin by asserting that the phenomenon of the labour aristocracy cannot be attributed uniquely to a case of "false consciousness" induced by a corrupted fraction of the labour movement, but it is rooted in the material interests of the great majority of the working class of the central capitalist countries. According to Emmanuel, indeed, in capitalist developed countries, the sum of total wages is greater than the total value created by the entire workforce, so that the central workers are net beneficiaries of exploitation because they directly appropriate part of the surplus-value extorted to [sic] peripheral workers. In other words, the central workers and capitalists of the whole world participate together to the exploitation of the peripheral workers, who then are the sole real producers of the worldwide surplus-value.[3] Emmanuel's po-

---

2 Emmanuel, Arghiri (1970) The Delusions of Internationalism. *Monthly Review,* Vol. 22, no.2. June 1970, pp. 13-19.

3 See Emmanuel, A. (1975). 'Unequal Exchange Revisited'. IDS Discussion Paper No. 77. Brighton: University of Sussex. p. 63: "Today, the vast majority of American workers, and even those in other large OECD countries, are no longer donors but receivers of surplus-value; and naturally this surplus can only come from the labour of workers of other nations, even though it is not directly extorted by those at the end of the line. [...] This is enough to make

> litical conclusion was that the international solidarity of the proletariat is a chimaera, because the central workers are fully aware of their privileges as net receivers of surplus-value, and for this reason, they give overall support to the imperialistic policy of the capitalist powers.[4]

Emmanuel made his position on the difference in class struggle in the center and periphery clear in a letter to Samir Amin:

> I agree with you that the bourgeoisie of the periphery is not exploited. How could it be? If I have somewhere implied such a thing, it is a serious mistake. I believe that the antagonism between the proletariat and the "national" bourgeoisie in the countries of the periphery is as irreducible as a class antagonism can be. This is not the case in the countries of the centre. There, in my opinion, there is a clear trend towards national integration. This does not mean that there are no more internal contradictions in the rich nations. There are some, and they can even sometimes take on extremely violent forms (see certain trade union struggles in the United States), but they are no longer irreducible. (I call an irreducible antagonism when the share of some can only improve in strict proportion to the deterioration of the share of others). They are constantly transcended by the national pact [...]
>
> The term "aristocratic nations" is literary, I grant you. It is true that there is a world bourgeoisie and a world proletariat. But there is also a world labor aristocracy. I didn't create this appellation. It was "created" by Engels a century ago, theorized by Lenin and Bukharin over half a century ago. There is nothing in this theory that allows us to set quantitative limits to the workers' aristocracy. Its limits are historical and contingent. There is nothing to exclude the fact that in this or that country at this or that time it encompasses the majority or even the entire working class of the nation, the concept of the world proletariat will not be altered by this. And we do not have the right to accept Lenin and Bukharin's theory of the workers' aristocracy for the period when it was of interest only to the minority of the working classes of certain nations, and to reject it when it happens to be of interest to the majority of these classes in another period and to disturb us terribly. But I do not think that our views differ fundamentally on this point.[5]

While the economic theory of unequal exchange was discussed and to some extent accepted in academic circles, the political consequences were dismissed. The "scandalous" idea that the workers of the rich countries benefited from the transfer of surplus value from the workers of the poor countries made Emmanuel few political friends in the "First World." However, the Indian Marxist historian Jairus Banaji states that: "Emmanuel's work is the closest Marxist counterpart I can think of to Fanon's *Wretched of the Earth* or to the films of Glauber

---

these sections, who know very well what they are doing, turn their faces resolutely against any kind of fraternal socialistic world."

4 Ricci, Andrea (2021) Value and unequal exchange in international trade: the geography of global capitalist exploitation. P. 41. New York: Routledge., 2021.

5 Emmanuel, Arghiri (1969) Letter to Samir Amin with remark to Samir Amin book *Accumulation on World Scale* p. 5. From the Emmanuel Archive. (Translated from French, my emphasis).

Rocha and Fernando Solanas."[6]

Emmanuel's standpoint was either heavily criticized, or the issues were treated as a taboo. It became difficult for Emmanuel to get published by traditional left-wing book publishers.[7] Other unequal exchange theorists, such as Samir Amin and Immanuel Wallerstein, were more reticent on the issue of the break in the global solidarity of the working class. Amin, however, stated that "In the centers, the popular classes benefited, during the postwar period, from an exceptional situation based on the historic compromise imposed on capital by the working classes."[8] Hickel, in his recent study, underlines that:

> It should be understood that unequal exchange is ultimately driven by the corporations and investors that control supply chains, and the states that determine the rules of international trade and finance, not by workers or consumers.[9]

In the mid-70s, as far as I know, very few organizations in the Global North supported Emmanuel's position on the split in the working class, except our group—the Communist Working Circle—with its theory of the Scandinavian countries as "parasite states." One of the few was the "Liberation Support Movement" founded in Vancouver in 1969 by Don Barnet, with branches in Oakland, California and New York City.[10] There were also some individuals, like Hodee W. Edwards (1914-2011) from Boston. She became a communist in the 1930s and, disillusioned by the anticommunism and racism of the '50s in the US, she and her family left for Ghana in 1961 to lend their support to the newly independent nation.[11] After the 1966 coup against Nkrumah, she moved to London. It was there that we got in contact with her, and she found a publisher of her important book, *Labor Aristocracy, Mass Base of Social Democracy.*[12]

So when we read Emmanuel's articles and his book, it's not surprising that

---

6 Banaji, Jairus (2019) 'Arghiri Emmanuel (1911–2001)', *Historical Materialism.*

7 It took Emmanuel ten years to find a publisher for the English edition of his book *Profit and Crises* despite the fact that *Unequal Exchange* had been a best seller. Correspondence with Wallerstein. (Emmanuel's Archive)

8 Amin, Samir (2003) World Poverty, Pauperization and Capital Accumulation, page 4. *Monthly Review.* Vol. 55, no. 5, pp. 1-9.

9 Hickel, Jason; Lemos, Morena Hanbury and Barbour, Felix: (2024) Unequal exchange of labour in the world economy. Page 8. *Nature Communications|* (2024) 15:6298, Springer Nature.

10 Liberations Support Movement, Liberation Support Movement Pamphlet Collection.

11 Edwards, Hodee Waldstein (1988) *Autobiography* 1988: H. W. Edwards. Estuary Press 2024

12 Edwards, Hodee Waldstein (1978) *Labor Aristocracy, Mass Base of Social Democracy.* Aurora Edition. Stockholm 1978. Republished by Estuary Press in 2024.

we were interested in getting in contact. In 1974, a member of our group who was visiting Paris went to Emmanuel's address to have a talk, but as Emmanuel was not at home, he slipped some of our pamphlets into the mailbox. A week later, he got a letter from Emmanuel, regretting that he was not at home and saying that he was interested in developing contact and exchanging materials:

> I have found your efforts to clarify your position very remarkable. What I admire in particular is your courage, morally and intellectually. I know from my own experience how difficult it is to resist conformism. There are very few passages in your text that I would not sign [...] What impressed me most [...] was the remarkable way in which you clarify that the Marxist notion of the labour aristocracy does not inevitably mean a minority. If Lenin generally (even if not always) wrote about the labour aristocracy as a minority, it simply reflected historical reality. But there is nothing in the theories of Marx, Engels, Lenin, or any other classical Marxist that limits the 'aristocratization' of the proletariat to a certain percentage or minimum of a specific nation. I have written about this previously myself, but I now see that you stated this before I did.[13]

Actually, this is not true. Emmanuel introduced the notion of unequal exchange in his article 'Échange inégal et politique de développement' [Unequal Exchange and Development Politics] written together with Charles Bettelheim in 1962. In it, they asked the question: "*Must we* [...] *enlarge Lenin's notion of the labour aristocracy, by saying that the working classes of today's advanced countries constitute the labour aristocracy of the Earth?*"[14]

The international solidarity of the proletariat has always been cherished as an important strategic position for communists, and it is indeed important. However, it is problematic to *not* face reality when this solidarity does not exist. In spite of Marx's and Engels's persistent call for international solidarity in the *Communist Manifesto*, they did not shy away from criticizing workers when this solidarity was lacking, as in the case of workers' support for European colonialism. Lenin fought against the pro-colonial policy of the European social democrats in the Second International, and the Third International, established in 1919, tried to make the communist parties in Western Europe prioritize anti-imperialism, but this proved to be in vain.[15] Emmanuel comments on this lack of anti-imperialism and international solidarity by the working class in the West:

> And yet the hopes that revolutionary Marxism based upon this solidarity have been so cruelly disappointed in recent years that perhaps the time has come to emancipate ourselves from this taboo [...] Marxism did not completely overlook the possibility of the

---

13 Private letter from Emmanuel in French dated 15.3. 1974. My translation

14 Emmanuel, Arghiri & Bettelheim, Charles (1962) *Échange inégal et politique de développement, Problèmes de planification*, No. 2, Sorbonne: Centre d'Étude de Planification Socialiste. Paris 1962

15 Lauesen, Torkil (2018) *The Global Perspective, Reflections on Imperialism and Resistance*, pp. 114-137. Montreal: Kersplebedeb, 2018.

class struggle becoming weakened through a certain margin of reforms that the advanced capitalist countries were able to provide by dipping into the super profits of international exploitation. But it linked this phenomenon with the imperialist phase and restricted its bearing to the upper stratum of the proletariat, so that it appeared to be transitory in character. This was approximately Lenin's position, and Bukharin could say at the Sixth Congress of the Comintern, in 1928 : ". . . we see certain countries which are, so to speak, 'aristocratic', countries, which (to use an expression that needs to be made more precise) possess a 'labor aristocracy', that is, a proletariat whose standard of living is higher than that of the average for the world proletariat."[16] Sometimes the narrow limits of the "labor aristocracy" were transcended, but never those, equally transitory, of imperialism and colonial profits. Thus, in some passages of Imperialism and World Economy (1917) Bukharin speaks, still with regard to the imperialist countries, of a relative and momentary solidarity of interest between capital and labor, coexisting with a deeper and more lasting antagonism between them, or of a momentary association of the interests of capital and labor on the basis of an increase in wages made possible by colonial superprofits, etc., without making any distinction between the privileged stratum of the "labor aristocracy" and the other strata of the proletariat. Sometimes he even uses terms that exclude this distinction: "The bill for this [colonial] policy is paid, not by the continental workers, and not by the workers of England. [...] The European workers, considered from the point of view of the moment are the winners [i.e., gainers—Trans.]."[17] When we read this passage and other, similar ones in the writings of Marxist authors, we ask ourselves whether this solidarity of interests between the capitalists and workers of the imperialist countries, however temporary and transitory it may be, has an objective basis or is merely the effect of a monstrous deception of the working class. This last phrase of Bukharin's gives one to suppose that objective conditions determine this situation. So far back as 1858, that is, in the midst of the free-trade epoch, Engels went further along this path: "The English proletariat is actually becoming more and more bourgeois, so that this most bourgeois of all nations is apparently aiming ultimately at the possession of a bourgeois aristocracy and a bourgeois proletariat as well as a bourgeoisie. For a nation which exploits the whole world this is of course to a certain extent justifiable."[18] But this was only one of those whimsical outbursts that were habitual with Engels, and, as such, need not be accorded any importance.

In the orthodox line of Marxism this "objective" basis has rather been regarded as illusory. Revolutionary Marxism chose to consider that what actually happened was an opportunist deception of the proletariat based on the increased employment that imperialist policies created in the metropolitan countries, together with what Bukharin called "the additional pennies received by the European workers from the colonial policy of imperialism."[19] Accordingly, over a long period revolutionary Marxism concentrated all its fire upon the instigators and beneficiaries of this deception, the Social Democratic leaders, in the vain hope of exposing them in the eyes of their supporters. After the

---

16 To have a standard of living higher than "the average for the world proletariat," it is today not necessary to belong to the "labor aristocracy" of the rich countries. It is enough to be the humblest of their street sweepers.

17 Nikolai Bukharin, *Imperialism and World Economy*. pp. 164-165. London, 1930,

18 Letter to Marx, October 7, 1858, Marx on Britain (Moscow, 1953), pp. 491-492. My emphasis, A. E.

19 Bukharin, *Imperialism and World Economy*, p. 167.

> bitter and repeated defeats suffered by this approach, after World War I, contrary to all expectations, had broken the unity of international organizations of the working class instead of drawing them closer together, and had opened a period of crisis in the socialist movement, and after the four Internationals had disappeared or declined (the second continuing its formal existence only at the price of abandoning any internationalist action, and the third being born only to be wound up after barely two decades), the experience and instinct of self-preservation of the first workers' state was still needed before it was realized that little was to be expected for the defence of this state from the solidarity of the working classes in the capitalist countries [...]
>
> To explain a historical fact that has endured for nearly a century by the corruption of the leaders and the deception of the masses is, to say the least, hardly in conformity with the method of historical materialism.[20]

The concept of false consciousness was introduced to explain why workers seemed more interested in the benefits of being citizens than in international class solidarity.[21] Propaganda has an effect, but it does not last for generations, and it does not work without some kind of material basis. The working class support the imperialist policy of their nation because they instinctively understand that they benefit *as a class* from the exploitation enabled by that policy. The working class are not innocent sheep. "Manufacturing consent,"[22] as Chomsky and Herman call it, plays a role, but it should not be exaggerated, as this obscures the material basis of the consent and that anti-communist and racist propaganda is consumed and functions as a license for part of the Western working class to support the policy of imperialism.[23]

Emmanuel continues:

> Political parties are not churches possessing eternal truth and renouncing on principle any interest in the present moment and the men of the moment. Political parties are "opportunist" by nature, since their business is the conquest of the masses and the seizure of power at a given historical moment and under given historical conditions. A political party anxious to preserve its identity may consent to make temporary retreats, refusing to bow to transitory objective conditions. But it cannot ignore structural objective conditions persisting for several generations, on the excuse of service to a transcendental truth. Itself an objective condition, the party as such can and must "make" history; it cannot do violence to history. When a deep-seated change has occurred in objective conditions, a class party, though it can still go on, through inertia, living outside the realities of its epoch, must eventually reach a moment when it has either to transform itself or

20 Emmanuel, A. (1972). *Unequal Exchange: A Study of the Imperialism of Trade*, pp. 177-179. New York: Monthly Review Press 1972.

21 Lukács, György (1920). *History and Class Consciousness: Studies in Marxist Dialectics*, London: Merlin Press, 1967.

22 Herman, Edward S.; Chomsky, Noam (1988) *Manufacturing Consent.* New York: Pantheon Books., 1988.

23 Day, Roderic (2022), 'Masses, Elites, and Rebels: The Theory of "Brainwashing"' (2022). RedSails.org

> to disappear. Due to this time lag between base and superstructure, however, when the objective antagonisms are intensified the masses are more revolutionary than their parties, but when the antagonisms soften the parties remain for a long time more radical than the masses. This is what has happened between the end of the nineteenth century and our time. It is not the conservatism of the leaders that has held back the revolutionary elan of the masses, as has been believed in the Marxist-Leninist camp; it is the slow but steady growth in awareness by the masses that they belong to privileged exploiting nations that has obliged the leaders of their parties to revise their ideologies so as not to lose their clientele.[24]

Julius K. Nyerere, at the time the president of Tanzania, compared the conditions of the nineteenth-century European working class with the labor force of the poor nations in 1973:

> The only difference between the two situations is that the beneficiaries in the international situation now are the national economies of the rich nations—which includes the working class of those nations. And the disagreements about division of the spoils, which used to exist between members of the capitalist class in the nineteenth century, are now represented by disagreement about the division of the spoils between workers and capitalists in the rich economies.[25]

The Imperial Mode of Living

Instead of using terms like treason, corruption, and bribery to explain the pro-imperialist attitude of the leaders of trade unions and political parties and the working class, Brand and Wissen have introduced the less "moralistic" concept of "the imperial mode of living."[26] This concept breaks the taboo around the existence of a bourgeois-minded working class in a nuanced way, by describing the evolution of consumption patterns that developed historically and are integrated and normalized in everyday life in the Global North. Brand and Wissen defined it thus:

> [...] the deeply rooted patterns of production and consumption, which predominate above all in the early industrialized capitalist societies [and] presuppose the disproportionate access to nature and labour power on a global scale. Developed capitalism is

24 Emmanuel, A. (1972). *Unequal Exchange: A Study of the Imperialism of Trade*, pp. 179-180. New York: Monthly Review Press 1972. It is impossible to refrain from quoting Eduard Bernstein: "The formula according to which the proletariat has no fatherland ceases to be true in proportion as the worker ceases to be a proletarian and becomes a bourgeois," *Revolutionary Socialism*, London, 1909.

25 Nyerere, Julius K. (1972) "A Call to European Socialists" (November 1972), here quoted from Nyerere, *Freedom and Development: A Selection from Writings and Speeches 1968-1973*, pp. 374-375. Dar es Salaam: Oxford University Press, 1973.

26 Brand, Ulrich & Wissen, Markus (2021), *The Imperial Mode of Living—Everyday Life and the Ecological Crises of Capitalism*. London: Verso, 2021.

> characterized by the fact that it requires a less developed or non-capitalist geographical and social 'outside', from which it obtains raw materials and intermediate products, to which it shifts social and ecological burdens, and in which it appropriates both paid labour and unpaid care services. It is exclusionary and exclusive and it presupposes an imperialist world order, which at the same time is normalized in countless acts of production and consumption so that its violent character is rendered invisible for those who benefit from it [...]
>
> We understand the imperial mode of living as a concept of hegemony theory in the tradition of Antonio Gramsci, which connects the everyday life of people with the social and international structures and thus reveals the prerequisites of capitalist patterns of production and consumption. As such, it also refers to the way of working and producing in capitalist societies. Exploitation of nature and labour power is not only a structural feature of the relationship between the Global North and the Global South. Instead, it takes place in the class, patriarchal and racialized societies of the Global North itself, where significant social and spatial inequalities exist and have increased in recent decades. What we want to emphasize however is that the exploitation of labour power in advanced capitalist countries is inherently linked to, and mediated by, exploitative structures elsewhere.[27]

What caught my interest was the very wording of the concept, "the imperial mode of living—living at the expense of others." A mode of living built on the empire. The concept of the imperial mode of living is broad and deep; it includes both consumption patterns and the role of the capitalist welfare state and unequal exchange in terms of ecology. Brand and Wissen point out that:

> Humankind has become a driving geophysical force: human beings have changed natural systems to such an extent that they can hardly be called 'natural' any more [...] One thing, however, is lost in this debate, namely that not just 'humankind' is at work here, human impact on the environment is always mediated socially through relation of power, class, gender and 'race'. And it is this mediation that counts; people in the capitalist societies of the Global North, and the upper classes of these societies in particular, consume, on average, considerably more resources than, for example, the members of (semi-) subsistent indigenous societies in the Global South.[28]

The concept of the imperial mode of living also incorporates a feminist perspective in terms of unpaid care and household work and an antiracist perspective in terms of the question of migrants and refugees.

One of the reasons for the patriarchal nuclear family model spreading into the working class was colonial profits. The gender roles championed by the workers' movement in the late nineteenth century corresponded to the development of the labor aristocracy. During the second half of the nineteenth century,

---

27 Brand, Ulrich & Wissen, Markus (2020) 'The imperial mode of living and the political ecology of labour', paper presented at the Conference on International Solidarity and Relational Inequality Amsterdam, September 13, 2020.

28 Brand, Ulrich & Wissen, Markus (2021), *The Imperial Mode of Living—Everyday Life and the Ecological Crises of Capitalism*, pp. 27-8. London: Verso, 2021.

the ratio of women to men in the industrial workforce fell by 0.7 percent a year on average. During the 1780s, for example, the percentage of married women in the small town of Cardington who worked for a wage was 67.5. In 1911, in all of England, it was 10 percent. This shift was due to factory legislation, the ten-hour workday, rising wages, and the spread of the bourgeois family model within the working class.[29] The male worker saw the woman as a competitor in the labor market. The demand was a wage that could sustain the family. Maria Mies described this process as follows:

> Without the ongoing exploitation of external colonies—formerly as direct colonies, today within the new international division of labour—the establishment of the 'internal colony,' that is, a nuclear family and a woman maintained by a male 'breadwinner,' would not have been possible.[30]

White men in Western Europe and North America ruled over their own "colonies" in the form of a nuclear family with a wife to take care of the household. This was one of the factors ensuring that the former members of the dangerous class would become loyal citizens.

The European workers' movement not only found it difficult to stand in solidarity with the women's movement, but it also showed an almost complete lack of sympathy for the struggles of indigenous and oppressed peoples in the colonies. This was particularly pronounced in the attitudes of the white US working class toward enslaved Africans. The attitudes of English workers toward Irish immigrants were similar: they were seen as competitors on the labor market and met with hostility. As a result of colonialism, racism and notions of European superiority emerged, and the mainstream workers' movement was far from immune to this. In *The Wretched of the Earth*, the psychiatrist and anticolonial militant Frantz Fanon wrote:

> Latin America, China, and Africa. From all these continents, under whose eyes Europe today raises up her tower of opulence, there has flowed out for centuries towards that same Europe diamonds and oil, silk and cotton, wood and exotic products. Europe is literally the creation of the Third World.[31]

When Fanon wrote that Europe is the creation of the Third World, he meant it literally. This was not limited to material or economic aspects; in colonial discourse, "European" came to mean "civilized", and other peoples were

---

29 Sara Horrell and Jane Humphries, "Women's Labour Force Participation and the Transition to the Male Breadwinner Family." *Economic History Review*, vol. 48, no. 1, p. 93. In: Foster, John Bellamy and Brett Clark (2018), "Women, Nature, and Capital in the Industrial Revolution." *Monthly Review*, vol. 68, no. 8 (January 2018).

30 Ibid., p. 110.

31 Fanon, Frantz (1961) *The Wretched of the Earth*. London: Penguin Books (1961), p. 81

"barbaric." Such claims were made despite the obvious barbarism of European civilization. Democracy and social justice might have been hot topics in Europe and North America in the 19th century, but that did little to stop European oppression, plunder, and exploitation around the world. The distinction between "us" and "them" was necessary to justify this brutality. Racism reflects the hierarchical division of humankind created by colonialism. The dehumanization of the colonies' indigenous and oppressed peoples was a prerequisite for presenting the Western world as the supposed cradle of civilization. This attitude lingers on in the present differences in how immigration laws treat non-Western "immigrants" and Western "expats."

Brand and Wissen continues:

> The imperial mode of living implies a hierarchy on a global scale: Since the onset of colonialism, the working and living conditions in the economies of the Global South, with their predominant forms of resource extraction, industrial or service production, have been largely geared to the economic needs of the capitalist centres. Domestic class, gender, and racialised relations are not exclusively, but essentially, oriented towards these needs. This is the core of the concept of the 'coloniality of power' developed by the Peruvian sociologist Aníbal Quijano (2000).
>
> The fact that Europe became the supposed centre of modernity is therefore due to a long historical process imbued with power that constituted certain forms of division and control of labour in the respective societies and on an international scale. In the course of colonisation, race became 'the fundamental criterion for the distribution of the world population into ranks, places and roles in the new society's structure of power' (ibid, p. 535) of the colonised countries [...][32]

Through the history of colonialism and the structures of imperialist exploitation, an imperial mode of living has developed in the imperialist center. The population in the Global North are born and socialized into this mode of living. Their actions and choices are made not just under conditions of their own choosing but also under conditions transmitted from the past. A person's place of birth seems more important than their class in terms of access to education, health system, and welfare in general. The imperial mode of living is normalized in daily acts of production and consumption so that its violent character and consequences are kept at a distance for those who benefit from it. Imperialism is just how the world works.

Brand and Wissen continue:

> In the Global North, the infrastructures of everyday life in areas such as food, transport, electricity, heat or telecommunication to a large extent rely on material flows from elsewhere, on the workers who extract the respective resources and on the ecological sinks on

32 Brand, Ulrich & Wissen, Markus (2020) 'The imperial mode of living and the political ecology of labour', paper presented at the Conference on International Solidarity and Relational Inequality Amsterdam, September 13, p. 5, 2020.

> a global scale that absorb emissions produced through the operation of infrastructural systems. Workers in the Global North draw on the latter not just because they consider them as components of a good life, but because they depend on them (cf. Lessenich 2019, 34). Mostly, it is not an individual choice that makes workers purchase cheap 'food from nowhere' (McMichael 2009), drive a car or light their homes with electricity that is generated by burning fossil fuels. Rather, they have to do so in order to nourish their families, to get to work or because the utility does not offer renewable alternatives. Thus, they are forced into the imperial mode of living simply because the latter is materialised and institutionalised in many of the life-sustaining systems of the Global North.[33]

The 'imperial mode of living' is described as consumption-patterns and institutions historically developed and integrated and normalized in everyday living. We are not born right-wing nationalists or social chauvinists. However, that we should be "forced into the imperial mode of living", as the quote says, is maybe too much. The working class has fought hard to improve their living standards. The reason that they succeeded in obtaining an imperial mode of living is, however, due to the fact that the struggle took place in the context of global capitalist accumulation (imperialism). The political result was a state based on power-sharing between capital and labor—through the parliamentary system—within the framework of the capitalist welfare state.

The improved living conditions and political influence of the working class were not the results of some shrewd capitalist plot or a payoff to keep workers submissive. They were a consequence of working-class struggles. And yet, they would not have been possible without imperialism. To speak of "bribes" for the working class is an oversimplification. But as a result of improving conditions for the European working classes, the reformist sections of the labor movement were certainly strengthened and the revolutionary ones weakened.

As Emmanuel writes:

> This does not mean that antagonisms have disappeared within the developed capitalist nations. Whether wages be high or low, whether the social product be large or small, the two shares, that of the working class and that of the receivers of surplus-value, continue to be magnitudes that are inversely proportional to each other, and so the antagonism continues. When, however, the relative importance of the national exploitation from which a working class suffers through belonging to the proletariat diminishes continually as compared with that from which it benefits through belonging to a privileged nation, a moment comes when the aim of increasing the national income in absolute terms prevails over that of improving the relative share of one part of the nation over the other. From that point onward the principle of national solidarity ceases to be challenged in principle, however violent and radical the struggle over the sharing of the cake may be. Thereafter a de facto united front of the workers and capitalists of the well-to-do countries, directed against the poor nations, coexists with an internal trade-union

33 Brand Ulrich and Wissen Marcus (2020): 'The imperial mode of living and the political ecology of labour', paper presented at the Conference on International Solidarity and Relational Inequality Amsterdam, September 13, 2020 pp. 4-5.

struggle over the sharing of the loot. Under these conditions this trade-union struggle necessarily becomes more and more a sort of settlement of accounts between partners, and it is no accident that in the richest countries, such as the United States—with similar tendencies already apparent in the other big capitalist countries—militant trade-union struggle is degenerating first into trade unionism of the classic British type, then into corporatism, and finally into racketeering. The workers in the most advanced capitalist countries now hold front line positions in the defense of the national interest. President Johnson had only to point out the harmful effects that it would have on the war in Vietnam to stop any strike by American dockers. He did not have the same success with some bourgeois elements, and still less with their sons and daughters in the universities. In former times dockers went on strike precisely in order to prevent imperialist interventions. Today they stop strikes they have begun for other reasons in order to avoid embarrassing these interventions in any way. They even go on strike rather than unload ships trading with Cuba, against the advice of their own government. (President Kennedy used to refer to the interviews he had with American trade-union leaders as "pressure from my Right.") The bloody struggle being waged by the blacks in the United States today shows, by its very violence and its style, that this is the revolt of a disappointed partner rather than a thoroughgoing challenge to America's Great Society and its overseas adventures. The strongest of the arguments formulated during this crisis is at bottom an argument of petty blackmail, namely, that the American blacks cannot fight in Asia for principles that the whites deny to them at home; this implies that if these principles were to be accorded to them and if one day they were to become fully privileged citizens of their country—something that is not materially impossible—they would then have no further objection to fighting the Vietnamese people. Oskar Lange's "people's imperialism" is today becoming a living reality in the big capitalist countries. Hardly thirty years ago the title of "social patriot" was regarded as a serious insult by any militant worker. Who would take offense at it today? "Popular movements," writes Myrdal, "which fifty years ago were imbued with internationalism have now become narrowly nationalistic." And speaking of Britain, the author adds: "Labour economists have usually carried out their practical studies under more narrow national premises than their colleagues to the right."[34] The same writer goes on: "There does not exist for mankind as a whole that psychological basis [...] of mutual human solidarity."[35] [36]

Band and Wissen state that:

The concept of the imperial mode of living—which, thanks to the adjective 'imperial', joins a strongly political semantic—the finger of moral disapprobation is not to be pointed at people who have and drive a car, or at those who, without questioning it, take flights over short distances despite the availability of alternative transport, or at those who eat industrially produced meat. These behaviors should be criticized and changed—through individual behavior, legal restraints or even prohibition, while alternatives are also made possible on a societal level. [...] In this sense, the core starting point for social change is not 'taking personal responsibility' and making an individual choice 'between moral and immoral behavior'. Rather, it is primarily a question of

34 Gunnar Myrdal, *An International Economy* (London, 1956), pp. 36-37.

35 Gunnar Myrdal, *Economic Theory and Underdeveloped Regions* (London, 1963), p. 63.

36 Emmanuel, A. (1972). *Unequal Exchange: A Study of the Imperialism of Trade*, New York: Monthly Review Press, 1972, pp. 180-181.

pointing out the social structures and patterns of inequality that reproduce the imperial mode of living.[37]

However, I would like to add that there is a relation between being and consciousness. The imperial mode of living has political consequences; it creates an interest in the defence of the imperial structures. The social democrats of the Second International defended colonialism and were loyal towards their respective national states in the inter-imperialist World Wars.

The History of the Imperial Mode of Living

The imperial mode of living came to exist gradually through the history of colonialism. By the end of the nineteenth century, the Northwestern European population had become users of several goods imported from the colonies for mass consumption, especially sugar, rice, tea, coffee, and tobacco. For capital, the most important raw material in the first phase of the industrial revolution was cotton. It was imported from the slave plantations in the US before the American Civil War and from India and Egypt afterward. In 1850, the amount of sugar imported from the colonies was only surpassed by that of cotton. Even the poorest classes spent 6-7% of their income on colonial imports.[38] Between 1850 and 1875, the per capita consumption of these goods increased even more: tea by 60%, sugar by 75%, tobacco by 18%, liquor by 33%, and wine by 66%.[39] People were having tea with sugar, as well as bread and jam for breakfast, instead of porridge, which had been the staple food of the poor for centuries. While the British consumed sugar mainly in tea, the French had it in coffee with milk. As early as 1800, more than six hundred coffee shops in Paris served *café au lait*.[40]

The discussion of the relationship between imperialism and the change in living conditions in the imperial center is not new. It was already raised by J. A. Hobson (1858–1940), who was an English left-leaning social liberal economist and was critical toward imperialism. In his book *Imperialism: A*

---

37 Brand Ulrich and Wissen Marcus (2021) *The Imperial Mode of Living—Everyday Life and the Ecological Crisis of Capitalism*, p.77. London: Verson, 2021.

38 Jonathan Hersh and Hans-Joachim Voth, "Sweet Diversity: Colonial Goods and the Rise of European Living Standards after 1492." Economics Working Papers, no. 1163. Universitat Pompeu Fabra, p. 11.

39 G.D.H. Cole and Raymond Postgate, *The Common People, 1746–1946*. London: Methuen and Co. (1949), p. 351.

40 Jonathan Hersh and Hans-Joachim Voth, "Sweet Diversity: Colonial Goods and the Rise of European Living Standards after 1492." Economics Working Papers, no. 1163. Universitat Pompeu Fabra, p. 11.

Study, published in 1902, he provided an economic study of the imperialist system, in which he explained why capital needs colonial markets and relies on the exploitation of foreign territories.[41] Rosa Luxemburg picked up this idea,[42] which is also central to Brand and Wissen's concept of the imperial mode of living. Capitalism needs external areas both to exploit and also as a place to dump its ecological and social problems.

However, Hobson not only coined and popularized the term "imperialism" but was also the first to speak of the colonizing power as a "parasite" on the colony. He expected the future rulers of European countries to consist of a wealthy elite, working mainly in finance. They would keep the masses content by paying them relatively high wages for service-oriented jobs. This idea is similar to "living on another's expense" in the discourse of the "imperial mode of living."

In the racist language of his time, Hobson anticipates the following result of the colonial intervention in China:

> In a word, the investors and business managers of the West appear to have struck in China a mine of labor-power richer by far than any of the gold and other mineral deposits which have directed imperial enterprise in Africa and elsewhere; it seems so enormous and so expansible as to open up the possibility of raising whole white populations of the West to the position of "independent gentlemen", living, as do the small white settlements in India or South Africa, upon the manual toil of these laborious inferiors. [...] such an experiment may revolutionize the methods of Imperialism; the pressure of working-class movements in politics and industry in the West can be met by a flood of China goods, so as to keep down wages and compel industry [of Western workers].[43]

This is more or less a description of how the world economy looks during neoliberal globalization. Hobson suggested that capitalists might buy the docility of Western working classes by sharing the profits obtained by the exploitation of low-wage Chinese labor. China has indeed become the productive industrial center of the world, while the countries of Western Europe and North America have primarily turned into consumer and service societies, as Hobson states:

> We have foreshadowed the possibility of an even larger alliance of Western States, a European federation of great Powers which, so far from forwarding the cause of world civilization, might introduce the gigantic peril of a Western parasitism, a group of advanced industrial nations, whose upper classes drew vast tribute from Asia and Africa, with which they supported great tame masses of retainers, no longer engaged in the sta-

---

41 Hobson, John (1902), *Imperialism: A Study*. London: Allen and Unwin, 1948.

42 Luxemburg, Rosa. 'The Accumulation of Capital: A Contribution to the Economic Theory of Imperialism', *The Complete Works of Rosa Luxemburg*, Vol. 2, p. 748. London: Verso, 2015.

43 Hobson, John (1902), *Imperialism: A Study*. Ch. V, Part II, p. 314. London: Allen and Unwin, 1948.

> ple industries of agriculture and manufacture, but kept in the performance of personal or minor industrial services under the control of a new financial aristocracy.[44]

This parasitism brings to mind the imperial mode of living in significant parts of Europe and North America. Lenin adopted Hobson's terms imperialism and parasitism but extended the analysis. Lenin (1917) summarized the creation of parasite states thus:

> The export of capital, one of the most essential economic bases of imperialism, still more completely isolates the rentiers from production and sets the seal of parasitism on the whole country that lives by exploiting the labor of several overseas countries and colonies.[45]

When Lenin wrote a preface for the 1920 edition of *Imperialism, the Highest Stage of Capitalism* in German and French, he emphasized the system's parasitic element:

> A few words must be said about Chapter VIII, "Parasitism and Decay of Capitalism."As already pointed out in the text, Hilferding, ex-"Marxist," and now a comrade-in-arms of Kautsky and one of the chief exponents of bourgeois, reformist policy in the Independent Social-Democratic Party of Germany, has taken a step backward on this question compared with the frankly pacifist and reformist Englishman, Hobson. The international split of the entire working-class movement is now quite evident (the Second and the Third Internationals). The fact that armed struggle and civil war is now raging between the two trends is also evident—the support given to Kolchak and Denikin in Russia by the Mencheviks and Socialist-Revolutionaries against the Bolsheviks; the fight the Scheidemanns and Noskes have conducted in conjunction with the bourgeoisie against the Spartacists in Germany; the same thing in Finland, Poland, Hungary, etc. What is the economic basis of this world historical phenomenon? It is precisely the parasitism and decay of capitalism, characteristic of its highest historical stage of development, i.e., imperialism. As this pamphlet shows, capitalism has now singled out a handful (less than one-tenth of the inhabitants of the globe; less than one fifth at a most "generous" and liberal calculation) of exceptionally rich and powerful states which plunder the whole world simply by "clipping coupons." Capital exports yield an income of eight to ten thousand million francs per annum, at pre-war prices and according to pre-war bourgeois statistics. Now, of course, they yield much more. Obviously, out of such enormous superprofits (as they are obtained over and above the profits which capitalists squeeze out of the workers of their "own" country) it is possible to bribe the labor leaders and the upper stratum of the labor aristocracy. And that is just what the capitalists of the "advanced" countries are doing: they are bribing them in a thousand different ways, direct and indirect, overt and covert. This stratum of workers-turned-bourgeois, or the labor aristocracy, who are quite philistine in their mode of life, in the size of their earnings and in their entire outlook, in the principal prop of the Second International, and in our days, the principal social (not military) prop of the bourgeoisie. For they are the real agents of the bourgeoisie in the working-class movement, the labor lieutenants of the capitalist class, real vehicles of reformism and chauvinism. In the civil war be-

---

44 Ibid., Ch. VII, part II, p. 364.

45 Lenin, V.I. (1916), "Imperialism, the Highest Stage of Capitalism. VIII." In: Lenin (1971), *Collected Works,* Vol. 22. Moscow: Progress Publishers, 1972.

> tween the proletariat and the bourgeoisie they inevitably, and in no small numbers, take the side of the bourgeoisie, the "Versaillais" against the "Communards." Unless the economic roots of this phenomenon are understood and its political and social significance is appreciated, not a step can be taken toward the solution of the practical problems of the communist movement and of the impending social revolution.[46]

Lenin develops Hobson's theory of the parasite state by including the concept of "labor aristocracy" and its political representatives—the social democrats—in the parasitism. He thereby also highlights the power-sharing between labor and capital in the management of the parasite state in the form of parliamentarism. Brand and Wissen quote a Gramsci statement that also points in that direction:

> Obviously, the fact of hegemony presupposes that the interests and tendencies of those groups over whom hegemony is exercised have been taken into account and that a certain equilibrium is established.[47]

The parasite state is undoubtedly still a capitalist state. It is based on the accumulation of capital, and private property is protected by law. However, the parasite state is a special form of the capitalist state. Its political form is a parliamentary democracy. There is universal suffrage and welfare for the majority of the working class. Even though the welfare state has come under pressure by neoliberal policies, politicians of all stripes remain committed to its most basic framework. The parasite state is certainly not a dictatorship of the bourgeoisie. But who then has the power in the parasite state? Moreover, what is the nature of its class struggle?

The form a particular state takes depends on the class struggle that shapes it. The parasite state needs to protect the capitalist mode of production. However, as a parliamentary democracy, it also needs to consider the balance of power between the classes that uphold it. Hence, the parasite state is based upon the imperial mode of living.

There is nothing new in power sharing between classes in the ruling of the state. The absolutist state of the seventeenth century stood for a power-sharing agreement between the feudal aristocracy and the emerging bourgeoisie. The modern democratic parasite state represents a power-sharing between capitalists and the working class. Its government does not represent the sole interests of capitalists or the working class; it represents the interests of a particular mode of

---

46 Lenin, V.I. (1920), "Imperialism, the Highest Stage of Capitalism. Preface " In: Lenin (1971), *Collected Works, Volume 22*. pp. 193–194. Moscow: Progress Publishers, 1972.

47 Brand, Ulrich & Wissen, Markus (2021), *The Imperial Mode of Living—Everyday Life and the Ecological Crises of Capitalism*. p. 39. London: Verso, 2021. Gramsci, Antonio (1929-35) *Prison Notebooks*, Vol. 2, Notebook 4, page 183. New York: Columbia University Press, 1996.

production: global capitalism. The modern democratic state is a compromise that has allowed the easing of the working class's misery in the Global North, within the capitalist order, and on the back of the countries of the Global South.

There are no references to Hobson's or Lenin's texts on "parasite states" in Brand and Wissen's development of the concept of the imperial mode of living. There are also very few references to the theory of the political economy of imperialism in general.[48] Their argument refers more to sociology, critique of ideology, and state theory. However, such a difference in theoretical perspectives can be fruitful if the ideas are combined. The imperial mode of living has the strength of describing the class, gender, race, and ecological effects of imperialism on society. It describes how economics works at the micro-level, in shaping identities and political attitudes.

Brand and Wissen describe how the automobile industry, state, infrastructure, fossil energy companies, private consumption, and branding fuse into "imperial automobility."[49] The car advertisements connect driving with the freedom to move wherever you like, whenever you like, and the freedom to choose the car which matches your identity or who you want to be. The imperial mode of living promises individuality:

> [...] the imperial mode of living goes hand in hand with material well-being for many people [...] its attractiveness lies in enabling—or at least promising— [...] individuality and autonomy in one's own conduct of life. At the same time, the imperial mode of living breaks with the universal norms of equality based on human rights and stands for individual liberty, to remain unmolested in one's own conduct of life and consumption.[50]

The commercials don't only present the properties of a specific product but also visualize the lifestyle we can become part of by consuming the product. We choose products depending on who we are or the identity we want. According to liberalism, "free" choice in consumption makes us "free" individuals. A free market equals free people. We interpret our past and imagine our future as the result of the choices that have been made and the choices that need to be made. These choices are, in turn, seen as the realization of the personality of individuals. A competent human being is an individual who is able to realize themself through the exercise of a constant series of free choices. According to neoliberalism, the fate of individuals is no longer determined by social circumstances, such as class or status, but by the ability to acquire the skills needed to make the right

---

48 Brand and Wissen have one reference to Andre Gunder Frank, on p. 76.

49 Brand, Ulrich & Wissen, Markus (2021), *The Imperial Mode of Living—Everyday Life and the Ecological Crises of Capitalism*. pp. XXIV and 135-160 London: Verso, 2021.

50 Ibid., p. XXIV.

choices to realize one's dreams. Through these management technologies, the imperial mode of living is internalized—neoliberalism runs through our veins.

More Than Our Chains to Lose

I would like to draw attention to other sides of the imperial mode of living, not mentioned by Brand and Wissen. As neoliberalism introduced more privatized and individualized patterns of consumption and finance capital penetrated the everyday lifestyle of the middle class and large sections of the working class, it became common to invest a large part of income in real estate. Former tenants became real estate owners. In the US, around 65% own their home. In Western Europe, it ranges between 50% and 85 %.[51] It is not the ownership of a home itself which is the problem. To own your home as "use-value"—a roof over your head, so to speak—is widespread all over the world, even among poor people. The problem arises when ownership turns into finalization and speculation and becomes an important source of income. Since the 1970s, there has been a huge increase in the price of real estate, especially in the major cities. A *yearly* increase in prices of 10-15% is not unusual. Common wage earners developed interests in the real estate market and the taxation of property. There is a real estate agent on every corner. Political parties are very hesitant to tax gains on real estate because they know they will lose votes if they do. By making the right decisions in selling and buying houses or flats, ordinary people could make more money on the real estate market than they could on the job, using the rise in the equity of their property to renew the bathroom or kitchen or for consumption. Just as you can have a career in the labor market, many have a career in the real estate market, increasing the square meters and location of properties. Financial speculation made its way into our daily life.

Another link which chains the working class in the Global North to the wellbeing of global capitalism is the spread and extension of the pension system since the 1980s. Historically, only state employees from whom special loyalty was required, such as the police, army officers, railroad, and the postal staff, received an occupational pension. However, today, an occupational pension is an essential part of collective bargaining in both the public and private labor markets in the Global North.

An occupational pension is generated by payments of a certain percentage of the wage into an individual account of each employee, in a pension fund. The percentage varies from country to country and by labor agreement, but it's typ-

---

51 *Wikipedia*, 'List of countries by home ownership rate'.

ically between 10 and 20%. The pension fund invests this capital as ordinary capital, in the markets of shares, equities, or bonds, or it invests in real estate to get the highest profit for the individual wage earner accounts. Occupational pension funds thus form part of the accumulation process, like all other capital. The funds create profits for capital and interest for the wage earner and thus social security for old age, if capitalism is doing well. The workforce in the Global North has become structurally integrated into the global financial circuits. As Peter Gowan writes:

> Yet another explanation [for the lack of regulation of highly speculative financial transactions in the US economy] might be that all the strategic social groups within American society have themselves been captured by the institutional dynamics of the financial markets. The income and wealth of the managements of the big corporations have become tied to future prices on the stock and bond markets, they have invested their savings in the investment banks, mutual and hedge funds and have been restructuring their own corporations to make the augmentation of 'share-holder value' their governing goal. And American workers also have come to rely upon the securities markets for their pensions, health care and even their wages, which have been increasingly combining cash with securities. Any regulatory drive would inevitably have a depressive effect on current activities and would therefore cut off the politicians involved in pushing for the regulation from important and broadly based political constituencies. This political barrier is then powerfully buttressed by the rentier ideology of laissez-faire and free markets. But the power of ideology should not be exaggerated. The lives of workers in modern capitalism are tied to capital not only through the wage relation, but also through the savings relation. If the savings relation is mediated through the state, as in Western Europe, workers' security is less tied to market developments and rentier interests. But if the savings relation is in the direct control of private financial markets, then workers themselves acquire a rentier interest.[52]

In Sweden and Denmark, more than 90% of wage earners have an occupational pension. The total size of Danish occupational pensions is growing so fast that by 2030 they will exceed the value of the public old-age pension. Already today, the size of the assets of the pension funds is 1.5 times Denmark's gross domestic product.[53] Employers, employees, and representatives of the state usually manage the pension funds jointly. They manage huge sums of money. In North America, approximately 30% of the financial capital comes from pension funds. In Western Europe, it is around 40%.[54]

The size of pension funds is far from marginal. Total private pension assets in the 36 countries in the OECD amounted to 42.5 trillion USD at the end

---

52 Gowan, Peter (1999) *The Global Gamble: Washington's Faustian Bid for World Dominance*, p. 56. London:Verso, 1999.

53 Lauesen, Torkil (2018) *The Global Perspective*, pp. 296-98.

54 Allianz (2014), *Allianz Wealth Report*. Nationale Zentralbanken und Statistikämter, Allianz SE.

of 2018. By contrast, 52 non-OECD countries, where more than two-thirds of the global population live, held approximately $1.9 trillion in pension fund assets.[55] In other words, around 75 times more wealth per head is invested in pension funds in OECD countries than in the rest of the world. OECD countries have the highest pension coverage in the world. In most cases, coverage is estimated to be more than 90% of wage earners. South Asia and sub-Saharan Africa have the lowest coverage, with less than 10% of working-age people.[56] The fact that large parts of the working class have invested in real estate and shares binds them to a desire for the wellbeing of capitalism and the defence of imperialism. Large parts of the working population of the Global North countries live or will live as rentiers on their pension capital.

The benefits from first colonialism and then imperialism changed the political dimensions of class struggle in the center. It strengthened the workers' belief in reformism. For the employers, accepting certain reforms was far less risky than provoking revolutionary uprisings. This was not some shrewd capitalist plot or a payoff to keep workers submissive. It was a consequence of an effective trade union struggle by the working-class. On the national level, the working class struggles to get its share of the social product; however when it comes to the international dimension of class struggle, then the former "dangerous classes" have turned into citizens, identifying themselves with the interest of their imperialist national state.

As Emmanuel writes:

> To an increasing extent the attitude of the working class in the advanced capitalist countries as a whole in relation to the Third World is becoming like that of the British working class toward the rest of the world all through the nineteenth century: struggles for wage-and-hour demands, sometimes very violent and very effective, inside the country; a united national front against the outside world, with the working class sometimes taking up vanguard positions. This is what Joseph Chamberlain expressed in his equation: democracy means imperialism plus social reforms. The socialist, Marxist, and Darwinist Karl Pearson did not shrink from writing in 1894: "No thoughtful socialist, so far as I am aware, would object to cultivate Uganda at the expense of its present occupiers if Lancashire were starving."[57]
>
> Marx and Engels cherished no illusions about the sentiments of the British workers at the time when they alone constituted the labor aristocracy of the whole world. Speaking of the underpaid Irish workers, they observed: "Every industrial and commercial center in England now possesses a working class divided into two hostile camps, English

55 OECD (2019), Pension Markets In Focus 2019, Table A B.2.

56 Romero-Robayo, Palacios; Pallares-Miralles and Whitehouse (2012), *World Bank Pension Indicators and Database. Social Protection and Labor*, page 81. Human Development Network, World Bank, Washington, D.C. 2012.

57 Quoted by B. Semmel, *Imperialism and Social Reform* (London, 1960), p. 42.

> proletarians and Irish proletarians. The ordinary English worker hates the Irish worker as a competitor who lowers his standard of life. [...] He cherishes religious, social and national prejudices against the Irish worker. His attitude toward him is much the same as that of the 'poor whites' to the 'Negroes' in the former slave states of the U.S.A."[58] As we see, Marx and Engels did not hesitate to speak of the deep feelings of "the ordinary English worker" in general and did not put the blame for them on the opportunism and treachery of their leaders. Today everything suggests that there is more socialism and internationalism in the brains of the intellectuals of the Labor party, and perhaps more still in those of some bourgeois liberals, than in the feelings and reactions of the British working class. At each of the recent British general elections [i.e., 1951, 1955, 1959—Trans.] it was enough for the Conservatives to claim that the Labor party was planning to carry out fresh nationalizations for that party's chances to be gravely jeopardized. Naturally, the Laborites hasten each time to deny with vigor this frightful "slander." A charge to which the British workers would have been even more sensitive would have been lack of loyalty to British imperial interests. On that point, however, the Labor party has given such guarantees in the past that nobody would have taken such a charge seriously. In France, Cartierism, the supreme expression of national egoism, addressed itself neither to the capitalists nor to the intellectual elite but to the "little people" of town and country, whose language it spoke.
>
> On their part the representatives of the Third World have not been deceived. Sometimes using in their analyses, more correctly than some Western Marxists, the method of historical materialism, they have arrived at conclusions that are extremely realistic and disillusioned. "In contrast to what for a long time I used to believe," wrote Ferhat Abbas, "the existence of a revolutionary proletariat and of liberals in France made no difference to the fundamental facts of the Algerian problem."[59][60]

If this division of the global working class created by imperialism is a fact, we have to deal with it among the left in the West. It seems to be taboo and provocative to mention the fact that large sections of the population living in the Global North benefit from how global capitalism works, and that our imperial way of living is based on this relation and this is reflected in the political choices we make. The reason why I insist on breaking this taboo is the need to face reality if we are to develop a realistic and effective strategy for another world order. Marx and Engels did not pull any punches in their description of the connection between colonialism and national chauvinism, racism, and reformism in the English working class. Lenin portrayed rather bluntly the connection between imperialism and opportunism in the European working class in the years

---

58 Marx and Engels, *On Colonialism* (Moscow, 1960), p. 301: Marx to S. Meyer and A. Vogt, April 9, 1870.

59 Ferhat Abbas, "La nuit coloniale," Presence africaine, 4th quarter (1962), p. 198. (The reference to "Cartierism" in the previous paragraph relates to a series of articles in *Paris-Match* by Raymond Cartier, urging that the French government stop all aid to France's ex-colonies, on the ground that their peoples and governments are idle and corrupt.—Trans.)

60 Emmanuel, A. (1972). *Unequal Exchange: A Study of the Imperialism of Trade*. Page 181-182. New York: Monthly Review Press, 1972.

leading up to the First World War. He did so because an assessment of class interests was crucial for choosing the right partners in the struggle for socialism. In his polemic with Bettelheim, Emmanuel writes:

> Finally, I should like to answer another reproach made by Bettelheim, namely, that my theory is politically dangerous. Sixty-one years ago, Lenin wrote:
>
> "Marx frequently quoted a very significant saying of Sismondi's. The proletarians of the ancient world, this saying runs, lived at the expense of society; modern society lives at the expense of the proletarians. [...] Only the proletarian class, which maintains the whole of society, can bring about the social revolution. However, as a result of the extensive colonial policy, the European proletarian partly finds himself in a position where it is not his labor, but the labor of the practically enslaved natives in the colonies, that maintains the whole of society. The British bourgeoisie, for example, derives more profit from the many millions of the population of India and other colonies than from the British workers. In certain countries this provides the material and economic basis for infecting the proletariat with colonial chauvinism. Of course, this may be only a temporary phenomenon, but the evil must nonetheless be clearly realized and its causes understood in order to be able to rally the proletariat of all countries for the struggle against such opportunism. This struggle is bound to be victorious, since the "privileged" nations are a diminishing fraction of the capitalist nations."[61]
>
> What is characteristic in this passage is that Lenin did not see the certainty of victory in the prospect of the "illusions" of the workers in the privileged nations themselves becoming dispersed, but in the fact that these nations were in the minority. In other words, he did not say that the revolution would take place in opportunist Britain, after all, but that it would take place without Britain.
>
> I can easily see that it is harder to accept such a view today, when the place of "Britain" is held by all the industrialized countries, than it was in 1907, when "Britain" meant only a few countries. Nevertheless, the "Britains" are still only a minority in the world. Let us therefore, if we are concerned about dangers, take care not to incur this one: the danger that, by concentrating our revolutionary ardour inside this minority group of countries, we may find ourselves, in tomorrow's tempest, on the side of the minority. It will not be the first time in history that Rome will have fallen, not under the blows of the Romans but under those of the "barbarians."[62]

While the above was written in 1969, the Italian Marxist Leonardo Bargigli puts it in the context of the current situation:

> As uncomfortable as his conclusions were, Emmanuel's method was purely Marxist. Since the superstructure is ultimately determined by structure, if we observe that the majority of the working class is ready to follow the policy of its bourgeoisie, it is a consistently Marxist conclusion to deduce from this that the working class has economic interests in common with it [...] Thus we return to Emmanuel's uncomfortable truth, which is more important than ever to keep in mind today, because we are part of a West that is experiencing a very deep crisis of perspectives. The heated political competition

---

61 Lenin, "The International Socialist Congress in Stuttgart" (August 1907), in *Collected Works*, 4th ed. 13: p. 77.

62 Emmanuel, A. (1972). *Unequal Exchange: A Study of the Imperialism of Trade*, pp. 339-340. New York: Monthly Review Press 1972. Original emphasis.

between a declining liberal-liberal camp and a rising populist-reactionary camp is the mirror of a bourgeoisie divided as never before between openness and isolation, dragging the Western working class into the vortex of its own contradictions.

Paradoxically, the contestation of globalization today does not come from the Global South, but from the West itself. While multipolarity aims to put international economic relations on a new footing, the West acts destructively because it fears losing its hegemony.

The neoliberal strategy was based on the idea that convergence towards its own economic and cultural model would allow the West to reshape global political systems, definitively archiving the political experiences born of revolutionary and decolonization processes and replacing them with complacent regimes.

In this strategy, the main role is played by soft power, which exports the West as a space of freedom, opportunity and rights for all, using its vehicles of influence for this purpose.

The latter are used first to create and then to put their internal referents in power. When this program meets resistance, internal subversion, coups d'état, "color revolutions" are resorted to. If this is still not enough, the card of military aggression conducted unilaterally or through NATO is being played.

In the neoliberal framework, the push towards integration prevails on the external level, thanks to a highly asymmetrical economic situation, which brings enormous benefits to Western capital. Domestically, the rhetoric of integration prevails to assimilate the migrant components. In exchange for a promise of well-being, they are required to accept the erasure of their identity and the unconditional assimilation of so-called Western values.

The construction of consensus for the populist-reactionary option passes through the appeal to defend the immediate interests of the white proletariat as opposed to those of the multinational proletariat. External competition, whether it is immigration or Chinese goods, is to blame for the economic difficulties.

The suggestions of protectionism and a welfare redefined on a racial basis are proposed to the most impoverished components of the white population, as well as to the most integrated components of the working class, as responses capable of preserving the well-being that the system can no longer ensure.

It should not surprise us that these suggestions are supported by broad sections of the population. This confirms once again Emmanuel's inconvenient truth, namely that an important part of the proletariat is willing to follow its bourgeoisie, as yesterday on the level of social-democratic compatibility, so today on the populist-reactionary level.

This component forms the mass of manoeuvre necessary to discipline the multinational proletariat on the home front, as well as to push society down the slope of war. For both tasks, the revival of a racial hierarchy based on white supremacism, which is taking hold in increasingly explicit terms, is functional. [...] we should not be surprised that sections of the Western working classes are mobilising in a reactionary direction, given the structural and superstructural factors at work in imperialist societies. [...]

The neoliberal left cannot oppose the right because it shares its basic objectives. But the radical left cannot oppose the neoliberal left if it accepts the same compatibilities and follows the same logic in foreign policy. International solidarity is the best antidote to instrumentalization, because the liberation struggle of oppressed peoples is not compatible with either racism or neoliberal cosmopolitanism.

> In the same way, we should be clear that the struggle for peace, freedom and the equal dignity of all peoples is as incompatible with nationalism and protectionism as it is with militarism. It is a question of putting globalization on a new basis to proceed on the path of international solidarity and socialism, not of returning to a past that has nothing positive to offer.[63]

There Will Come a Day...

In the description of unequal exchange's political consequences in the form of the development of the labor aristocracy, the parasite state, and the imperial mode of living, it is important to keep in mind that these phenomena and processes are historical. Just as unequal exchange can explain the emergence of these political trends, future changes in the balance between appropriation of value through consumption and exploitation by wage labor in a national context will have political consequences.

There is, of course, no one-to-one relationship between the above-mentioned economic balance and the revolutionary potential of a given working class. Want and misery do not necessarily lead to revolution; they can even sometimes be an obstacle, and there are many other factors involved in the development of a revolutionary process. A revolutionary situation requires both that the ruling class can no longer rule in the old way and that the oppressed will no longer accept being ruled in the old way.[64] The ruling class is certainly facing problems, but what about the working class?

The "parasite state" theory of the Communist Working Circle did not *only* state that the working-class gains from imperialism.[65] The bourgeoisification was a historical phenomenon created by very specific historical, economic, and political developments in capitalism, and since it is a historical explanation, it opens up the possibility of change in the position of the class.

The "parasite state" theory states that the working class in Western Europe and North America occupy a dual position. They are an object of exploitation as they perform wage labor which creates surplus value and thus profit for capital. However, by virtue of their relatively high wage level, they are also able to

---

63 Bargigli, Leonardo (2024) 'An Inconvenient Truth About the Working Class in the West', *Contropiano* 25 August 2024. 'Una scomoda verità sulla classe operaia in Occidente'—*Contropiano.*

64 Lenin. V. I (1915) 'The Collapse of the Second International', Part II, pp. 205-259, *Collected Works*, Volume 21, Progress Publishers Moscow 1974.

65 Lauesen, Torkil (2018) 'The Parasite State in Theory and Practice', pp. 285–300. *Journal of Labor and Society*, Vo. 21. Issue 3.

acquire value through their consumption of goods produced by low-wage labor in the Global South. Whether they are exploited or are exploiters—from a global perspective—is a matter of a balance between the acquisition of value through consumption and exploitation through their contribution of surplus value to capital.

Without this double perspective on the position of the working class, the "parasite state" theory becomes static and loses its revolutionary content. Via this double perspective on the relation between exploitation in the national framework and international exploitation, the theory can explain both the historical process of bourgeoisification and the working class's support for colonialism and imperialism up through the 20th century, but at the same time maintain a future possibility of the class as gravediggers of capitalism.

If one denies the significance and consequences of imperialism's transfusion of value to the working class in the Global North, one falls into the fog of seeing every economic struggle as a revolutionary struggle on the road to socialism. If one denies that the highly paid workers in the imperialist countries produce value, surplus value, and so profit, then one rejects the possibility that the working class in the imperialist center can ever play a role in the struggle against capitalism. Moreover, one loses sight of political activity in the Global North and gives up the task set by Lenin:

> To be able to seek, find and correctly determine the specific path or the particular turn of events that will lead the masses to the real, decisive and final revolutionary struggle—such is the main objective of communism in Western Europe and America today.[66]

The rise of China, breaking two hundred years of polarizing the world-system, has changed the ballgame. The US can no longer dominate the world through economic and technological superiority, and so it is destroying the neoliberal world market, which served it so well in the past, by economic, political, and military warfare. Trade patterns are shifting from South-North to South-South, which is less unequal because the wage differences between the trading partners are less. Alternative financial institutions to the ones dominated by the West are being developed. The position of the dollar as world money is challenged. The EU, clinging to the US, is being dragged down along with declining US hegemony. The economic and political crises resulting from these changes in the world-system—not seen in a hundred years[67]—can change the balance

---

66 Lenin, V. I (1920) "Left-Wing" Communism: An Infantile Disorder. In Collected Works, Volume 31, pp. 112. Progress Publishers, USSR, 1964.

67 **Ed. Note:** In March 2023, during a meeting between Chinese President Xi Jinping and Russian President Vladimir Putin, Xi Jinping was recorded as remarking "Right now there are changes – the likes of which we haven't seen for 100 years – and we are the ones driving these

between the appropriation of value and exploitation of the working class in the Global North. If so, what will the political consequences be? Will the working class still support imperialism in order to regain their position, or will they join forces with the Global South? The hallmark of a Marxist is to have an analysis, strategy, and praxis in the vortex.

As stated, the working class is not an innocent sheep, nor is it an easy victim of propaganda. Classes act out of interest. We must present a political strategy that demonstrates why the working will benefit from abandoning their support of the US and EU against the emerging multipolar world-system—not as some long-term promise of utopian socialism after the revolution, but to secure their wellbeing and peace in the near future. We must present a realistic alternative to being dragged down by declining US hegemony into a deep economic crisis, and an. An alternative to the waste of resources in senseless military build-up, and the threat of major wars, not to speak of a nuclear war. An alternative to the recurring floods, droughts, storms, and fires induced by capitalism's destruction of planet Earth's ecosystems. To develop such a strategy requires a detailed class analysis of the center and its interactions with global class forces.

---

changes together."

5

Profit and Crisis

EMMANUEL IS BEST KNOWN for his seminal work on the theory of unequal exchange. However, his research also extensively examined other elements of political economy and global politics: the fundamental contradictions in the capitalist mode of production, development and underdevelopment, the role of technology in the development of the productive forces, and the transition towards socialism. Living in the Congo for more than twenty years, Emmanuel also had a keen interest in the topic of settler colonialism. Not surprisingly, his work displays a distinctive coherence on each of these questions.

In the beginning of the 1970s, capitalism encountered its first major economic crisis since the end of the Second World War, triggered by the increase of the oil price by OPEC, which led to economic stagnation combined with inflation—"stagflation." Emmanuel wrote several articles on the subject, and in 1974 he published his second major contribution in political economy, *Le profit et les crises*, with Éditions Maspero in Paris. The book was soon published in Spanish and Italian. However, Emmanuel had difficulties in securing an English language left-wing publisher for the book. The political implications presented by Emmanuel in *Unequal Exchange* about the working class in the imperialist center did not make him many political friends in North America and Western Europe. In a letter to Immanuel Wallerstein in 1976, Emmanuel reflected on the problem of finding a publisher for *Profit and Crises*:

> The paradox is, that contrary to *Unequal Exchange*, which stirred up worldwide hostility, this time reviews are almost 100% favourable? That seems a sufficient reason for people not to get excited over it.[1]

Finding a willing English-language publisher for *Profit and Crises* took ten

1 Emmanuel, Arghiri (1976) *Letter to Immanuel Wallerstein*, 25.10 1975, From Emmanuel's personal archive.

years, with Heinemann finally publishing the work in 1984.[2]

Profit and Crises addresses the fundamental contradiction in the capitalist mode of production, the contradiction between production and consumption, which creates recurrent crises. To maximize profits, capital needs to expand production and thereby provide the market with an ever-increasing quantity of goods. However, the consumption power of the market, which is created by this production, cannot absorb these goods. The result is recurring overproduction that produces a crisis of capital. As Marx wrote:

> Overproduction is specifically conditioned by the general law of the production of capital: to produce to the limit set by the productive forces, that is to say, to exploit the maximum amount of labour with the given amount of capital, without any consideration for the actual limits of the market or the needs backed by the ability to pay.[3]

The purchasing power of the market is limited by the exploitation necessary for capitalist accumulation. On the one hand, the capitalist needs to keep wages as low as possible to make the biggest profits possible. On the other hand, wages make up a significant part of the purchasing power that is required to realize a profit through sale. In other words, the capitalist form of accumulation tends to destroy its market. If capitalists increase wages, their profits decrease; if they decrease wages, their markets decrease. In both cases, capitalists become hesitant to invest, not because they can't produce, but because they don't know if what they produce can be sold.[4] Emmanuel explains it in this way:

> In all other systems, the remuneration of the direct producers constitutes an income and nothing but that. In the system of wage-labour, this remuneration, besides being an income for the wage-earners, is a cost for the employers, who happen also to be the only decision-makers where allocation of the factors is concerned. In order to maximise their profits, the employers have to minimise their costs, which means keeping wages at the lowest level possible. But profits are proportional to sales, and sales proportional to social incomes. Since wages are certainly a social income (and even the biggest) the ex-ante [before] efforts of the entrepreneurs to maximise their profits through reduction or stagnation of wages lead ex post [after] to the minimising, of both sales and profits.
>
> Of course, consumer goods are not the exclusive objects of profitable sales. Means of production can play that role just as well. The problem is, and this is crucial, that in the capitalist system sales of means of production cannot serve as a substitute for sales of consumer goods. They are an increasing function of the latter.[5]

---

2 Emmanuel, Arghiri, (1984) *Profit and Crises.* London: Heinemann, 1984.

3 Marx, Karl (1861) Economic Manuscripts, 1861–63, Theories of Surplus Value. In: *Karl Marx & Friedrich Engels: Collected Works,* Vol. 32, p. 80. Moscow: Progress Publishers, 1975.

4 Emmanuel, Arghiri (1984) *Profit and Crises*, pp. 217–218. London: Heinemann, 1984.

5 Emmanuel, Arghiri (1984) *The Economic Crisis and the Ways to Get Out of It.*

In volume three of *Capital*, Marx emphases this fundamental contradiction of the capitalist mode of production:

> The ultimate reason for all real crises always remains the poverty and restricted consumption of the masses as opposed to the drive of capitalist production to develop the productive forces as though only the absolute consuming power of society constituted their limit.[6]

As in *Unequal Exchange*, Emmanuel's method in *Profit and Crises* is a critique of the classic economists, this time, the French J.B. Say (1767-1832). Say argued that production creates its own market, keeping the system in a natural balance.[7]

However, historical experience has indicated that capitalism does not have a problem in producing commodities; it has a problem selling them. Even if capitalists were able to predict the exact amount and quality of commodities that consumers want (which they can't), the consumption power generated by production is not enough to buy all the products, realize profit, and continue accumulation.

At first glance, Say's thesis seems logical. The share of the price the producer has spent on raw materials, auxiliary materials, machines, factories, etc., can secure their part of the purchasing power for the commodities, even before they are even finished. Wages paid and profits made by subcontractors create their part of demand. The workers producing the commodities can buy their share of the finished product, and the profit can buy the rest. All this does indeed seem to guarantee a balance between production and purchasing power.

However, Emmanuel insisted on a structural imbalance between production and purchasing power. The wage component was not a problem. It turns into consumption power as soon as it is paid out. It was the other component, on the consumption side of the balance—the capitalist profit—which constituted the problem. The profits are not available until all commodities are sold, and all commodities are not sold because the profit is missing on the consumption side of the balance between production and consumption. Purchasing power is therefore always a step behind supply. This is confirmed by the simple fact that you can always get commodities for your money, but not always money for your commodities.

"Real existing" capitalism is a combination of economic laws to which the

---

6 Marx, Karl (1863-83) *Capital*, Vol. III, Part V, Ch. 30. 'Money-Capital and Real Capital', pp. 483-4 Moscow: Progress Publishers, 1962.

7 Say, Jean-Baptiste (1803) *A Treatise on Political Economy*. P. 138. Philadelphia: Lippincott, Grambo & Co., 1855.

system must adhere to function—basically, it must generate profit—and historical development which makes this possible. The development of unequal exchange was the historical solution to mediate the contradiction between capitalism's need to expand production, on one hand, and the ability of consumption power to absorb the produced commodities, on the other hand. The form that allowed this contradiction to exist without blocking the system was imperialism—the transfer of value to the center by unequal exchange. To be more specific: the development of colonialism using super-exploitation in the periphery generated the value transfer needed to raise the wage-level in the center, which was necessary to provide sufficient consumption power to meet the growing level of production and thereby realize the profit by the sale. Emmanuel writes, "Overproduction [...] is always latent in capitalism and it does become manifest under certain conditions [...] After 1870, the trade-union struggle and the rise in salaries helped advanced capitalism out of this dilemma, at any rate to a certain extent."[8]

In this specific way, "history" found a way in which the contradiction in the capitalist mode of production could move ahead and continue the development of the productive forces. It created a dynamic economic development in the center and a permanent crisis in the periphery, where the value transfer decreased consumption power, blocking capitalist development.[9]

The Political Economy of Trade Balance

Value transfer by unequal exchange is not the only method to mobilize extra consumption power in order to get the expanded accumulation process running. Another method is to get access to *other* countries' markets (consumption power). With an export surplus, you get rid of surplus production in exchange for foreign currency, which can be exchanged to local currency in the national bank, turning it into consumption power in the home market. In addition to the extra consumption power acquired from foreign markets, this keeps the employment rate at home high, which also adds to an affluent home market. This is the reason for the obsession of economic experts and ministers, regardless of their purported political view, with having a permanent export surplus (also known as a positive trade balance).[10]

---

8 Emmanuel, Arghiri (1972) 'White Settler Colonialism and the Myth of Investment Imperialism', *New Left Review*, no. 73, p. 56.

9 Emmanuel, Arghiri (1976) 'The Multinational Corporations and Inequality of Development'. *International Social Science Journal*, vol. 28, no. 4, pp. 761–762.

The aspiration, found across the political spectrum, to have a positive trade balance reflects the contradiction in the capitalist mode of production. To export is equivalent to goods leaving the country, and to import is equivalent to receiving goods. To give more than you receive is, at first sight, a very foreign thought in capitalism, but when it comes to the national economy, it is different. If, by this drain of goods to foreign markets, an overproduction crisis which blocks internal reproduction can be avoided, and instead these exports lead to increased production and employment, then this drain will be amply compensated by a higher rate of accumulation in the longer run.

On the global level, overall trade is always in balance. What gives a country with a positive trade balance dynamic development generates a deficit and problems for others. The competition to get a trade surplus is a zero-sum game. It does not solve the contradiction between the need to expand production and the consumption power on the global level; it just moves it around geographically.

The consequence of individual countries' attempts to improve their own competitiveness by holding back wage levels, cutting the state budget, protectionism, tariffs, and so on is that the total level of world production and trade diminishes. One country's home market is another country's export market. This is what the US is doing at the moment. The blockade, sanctions, and tariffs imposed by the US in the past decade are disrupting the neoliberal world market which served the US so well for half a century. By the end of the Second World War, the US had become the dominant global industrial power. The US preached "free trade" because it had a large surplus production and insufficient domestic demand. By imposing "free enterprise"—often forcibly—it could open new markets for its exports, in Europe and in the former European colonies worldwide. Up until 1976, the US had a positive trade balance. Since then, the US trade balance has been negative, without exception, running the largest account deficit seen in history. As an exception, this has only been possible due to the fact that the US can print dollars without any backing in produced goods, because the dollar is the global reserve currency. Billions and billions of dollars are circling around the world, used as payment in trade transactions—dollars which never return to the US to claim US goods.

The constant pursuit of a permanent surplus in the trade balance of a country is an expression of the imbalance, at the national level, between the size of production and the consumption power generated by this production. The wish to maximize profit drives capitalists to produce more, more effectively and at a reduced cost, including reducing wages. The fact that it is those wages which, used

10 Lauesen, Torkil (1986) Handelsbalansens Politiske Ekonomi. *Häften för Kritiska Studier.* Vol. 19, No. 3, pp. 41-49. Göteborg, 1986.

for consumption on the market, will realize the wish for yet more profit is a weak point in the system. To produce is not the problem; it is the market—the ability to sell—which is the limiting factor in capitalism.

The relationship between production and consumption is turned upside down. The size of production, and the types of goods, are decided by market forces. Human needs are only valid if they are backed up by purchasing power. Nothing is produced without an expectation of selling it, and anything will be produced if it can be sold. There may be idle hands and underutilized resources, on the one hand, and an urgent need for food, clothing, and shelter, on the other, and yet there will exist no possibility of these needs ever being met if they are not backed by the promise of cash. In capitalism, purchasing power is not just a matter of the distribution of the product: it is the very condition of the scale and nature of production. It is a common experience that you can get the goods you want if you have money. But you cannot always get money for the goods you have. Capitalism is driven by the market, and one of the ways in which a capitalist country can solve the problem of overproduction is to sell as much as possible on the world market. Marx observed:

> [...] the more capitalistic production develops, the more it is forced to produce on a scale which has nothing to do with the immediate demand but depends on the constant expansion of the world market.[11]

Capitalism is a buyers' market. There is a struggle between capitalist countries to conquer the world market.

So, a deficit in trade balance, *measured in world market prices*, does not necessarily mean a negative balance in terms of consuming use-values, because it accelerates growth, and thereby employment and consuming power in the center. In addition, this deficit in terms of the price of goods is balanced out by a "drain" of value in terms of labor time, concealed in the price structure.

Debt—Pushing the Problem into the Future

A third way of getting the much-needed extra consumption power, in order to balance expanded accumulation, is to postpone the problem into the future by creating debt. The amount of public and private debt has consistently grown through the 20th and 21st centuries, amounting to 250 trillion USD in 2023. That is 237% of the global GDP that year. The private part of the debt is around

11 Marx, Karl (1861) 'Economic Manuscripts, 1861–63, Theories of Surplus Value'. In: *Karl Marx & Friedrich Engels: Collected Works, Volume 32.* Moscow: Progress Publishers (1975), p. 101.

150 trillion, the public part around 100 trillion.[12]

Cash flow is created by letting the banknote press run and issuing government bonds. A government bond is a loan certificate which the government guarantees to repay with interest after a certain number of years—for example, ten years. These government bonds are an investment opportunity for "excess" capital, as the investor does not expect governments to go bankrupt. US government bonds are considered a "safe haven," as it is the world hegemonic power. The US has thus been able to increase its government debt to a new height of 33.17 trillion in 2023. Add to this private debt at around 60 trillion. Total US debt was 722% of the country's GDP in 2024 and around 40% of the global debt. Looking ahead, debt levels are projected to increase even faster as geopolitical tensions lead to massive spending on arms, adding strain to government budgets.

Governments around the world continue to pump huge sums of paper money into circulation to keep the wheels turning. This money has no backing in the production of goods or services, but is based on loans, government bonds, or simply the printing of more notes. These mountains of debt create bubbles of financial capital, bubbles that risk bursting in an explosion that will paralyze the world economy. The problem is that the strength of the bubble rests on *trust* that the debt will be paid or can be postponed once more into the distant future. If not, the debt bubble will burst. When it comes down to it, banknotes and bonds are just pieces of paper or numbers in accounts. Their value relies on the trust that they can be turned into goods that possess some kind of use-value.

The trust in US bonds and the dollar in general is linked to the trust in the US economy and its political status in general. This status was consolidated in the era following the end of the Second World War by the Bretton Woods agreement and the establishment of institutions as the International Monetary Fund (IMF) and the World Bank. This dominating status has been upheld ever since by the economic, political, and military power of the US, but is it being challenged by the emerging multipolar world order. The threats by Trump, of tariffs on all countries which avoid using the dollars in their trade transactions, indicate the seriousness of that challenge.

The change in global trade patterns towards more South-South trade and less South-North trade, the fragmentation of the former neoliberal world market by tariffs and sanctions, the threat of bursting financial bubbles, and the declining role of the dollar as world money—all these trends in the world economy herald a major economic crisis in capitalism in the coming decades.

---

12 IMF, 2024 Global Debt Monitor.

6

Over- and Under-development in Capitalism

THE CENTER-PERIPHERY STRUCTURE created by European colonialism released the forces of production—this led to the breakthrough of modernity in Western Europe. In a dialectical way, Marx on the one hand affirms the positive, progressive features of capitalism: new technology and the development of science, industrialization, urbanization, mass literacy, and so on. On the other hand, he denounces the exploitation, the human alienation, the commodification of social relations, the false ideology, colonialism and its connected mass extermination, all of which were inherent in this modernization process.

This dialectical conception of capitalism permeated Marx's writings. In *The Communist Manifesto,* Marx describes the rise of capitalism as a progressive stage of historical development. In the first pages he describes "modern industry," "modern bourgeois society," "modern workers," "modern state power," "modern productive forces," and "modern relations of production."[1] In the preface to *Capital*, Marx writes that the "purpose" of the book is to "disclose the economic law of motion of modern society."[2] Marx defended modernity because it prepared the way to a more fully developed modernity—socialism.[3] In 1847, Friedrich Engels wrote about the progressive role of capitalism, paving the way for socialism:

---

1 Marx, Karl and Engels, Friedrich (1848) 'The Communist Manifesto'. In *Marx/Engels Selected Works, Vol. I.* Moscow: Progress Publishers (1969), pp. 12–13.

2 Marx, Karl (1867) *Capital,* Vol. I. Preface to the First German Edition. Moscow: Progress Publishers, 1962.

3 Therborn, Göran (1996) 'Dialectics of Modernity: On Critical Theory and the Legacy of Twentieth Century Marxism.' *New Left Review,* I/215 Jan/Feb. 1996.

> Even in quite barbarous lands the bourgeoisie is advancing [...] What of all the glorious advances of "civilisation" in such lands as Turkey, Egypt, Tunis, Persia, and other barbarous countries? They are nothing else but a preparation for the advent of a future bourgeoisie [...] Wherever we look, the bourgeoisie are making stupendous progress. They are holding their heads high, and haughtily challenge their enemies. They expect a decisive victory, and their hopes will not be disappointed. They intend to shape the whole world according to their standard; and, on a considerable portion of the earth's surface, they will succeed. We are no friends of the bourgeoisie. That is common knowledge [...] We cannot forbear an ironic smile when we observe the terrible earnestness, the pathetic enthusiasm with which the bourgeois strive to achieve their aims. They really believe that they are working on their own behalf! They are so short-sighted as to fancy that through their triumph the world will assume its final configuration. Yet nothing is clearer than that they are everywhere preparing the way for us, for the democrats and the Communists; than that they will at most win a few years of troubled enjoyment, only to be then immediately overthrown. Behind them stands everywhere the proletariat, sometimes participating in their endeavours and partly in their illusions, as in Italy and Switzerland, sometimes silent and reserved, but secretly preparing the overthrow of the bourgeoisie, as in France and Germany; finally, in Britain and America, in open rebellion against the ruling bourgeoisie [...] So just fight bravely on, most gracious masters of capital! We need you for the present; here and there we even need you as rulers. You have to clear the vestiges of the Middle Ages and of absolute monarchy out of our path; you have to annihilate patriarchalism; you have to carry out centralisation; you have to convert the more or less propertyless classes into genuine proletarians, into recruits for us; by your factories and your commercial relationships you must create for us the basis of the material means which the proletariat needs for the attainment of freedom. In recompense whereof you shall be allowed to rule for a short time. You shall be allowed to dictate your laws, to bask in the rays of the majesty you have created, to spread your banquets in the halls of kings, and to take the beautiful princess to wife—but do not forget that 'The hangman stands at the door!' (Heinrich Heine, 'Ritter Olaf').[4]

As we know, the hangman's face remains well hidden. At the time of *The Communist Manifesto*, Marx and Engels believed that capitalism would be a rather short affair of decades rather than centuries. However, the contradiction in the capitalist mode of production between expansion of production and consumption power was addressed through globalization. In *The Communist Manifesto*, Marx describes the early tendency towards globalization:

> The need for a constantly expanding market for its products chases the bourgeoisie over the whole surface of the globe. It must nestle everywhere, settle everywhere, establish connexions everywhere [...] The bourgeoisie, by the rapid improvement of all instruments of production, by the immensely facilitated means of communication, draws all, even the most barbarian nations into civilisation. The cheap prices of its commodities are the heavy artillery with which it batters down all Chinese walls, with which it forces the barbarians' intensely obstinate hatred of foreigners to capitulate. It compels all nations, on pain of extinction, to adopt the bourgeois mode of production; it compels them to introduce what it calls civilisation into their midst, i.e., to become bourgeois themselves. In one word, it creates a world after its own image.[5]

---

4 Engels, Freidrich (1847) 'The Movements of 1847'. In: *Marx & Engels Collected Works, Volume 6.* New York: International Publishers (1975), p. 520.

It was not just a question of new markets; Marx saw capitalism's development as a centrifugal process that would spread quickly across the globe. English capital would venture far and wide and turn the rest of the world into a mirror image of England. In *Capital*, he wrote: "The country that is more developed industrially only shows to the less developed, the image of its own future." [6]

The first phase of industrialization ended in England around 1830, when industrialization had barely started in the countries of continental Europe and in the US. The European countries and the US, however, never turned into a periphery. English capital helped them to become developed capitalist countries themselves. So far, Marx's predictions were correct. By about 1880, the industrial development of both Germany and the USA had surpassed that of England. Marx believed that a similar process was awaiting the colonies of Asia and Africa. Once England had erased the traditional social structures and introduced capitalism, the colonies would undergo rapid development, echoing the modernization of the motherland. About England's role in India, Marx wrote:

> England has to fulfil a double mission in India: one destructive, the other regenerating—the annihilation of old Asiatic society, and the laying of the material foundations of Western society in Asia [...] I know that the English millocracy intend to endow India with railways with the exclusive view of extracting at diminished expenses the cotton and other raw materials for their manufactures. But when you have once introduced machinery into the locomotion of a country, which possesses iron and coals, you are unable to withhold it from its fabrication. You cannot maintain a net of railways over an immense country without introducing all those industrial processes necessary to meet the immediate and current wants of railway locomotion, and out of which there must grow the application of machinery to those branches of industry not immediately connected with railways. The railway-system will therefore become, in India, truly the forerunner of modern industry.[7]

According to this view, the opening of new markets in Africa and Asia, and the export of capital to the Americas, promised to temporarily postpone capitalism's collapse.

In 1916, Lenin still seemed to believe in this centrifugal power of capitalism, as it is evident in *Imperialism, the Highest Stage of Capitalism*. He writes:

> The export of capital influences and greatly accelerates the development of capitalism in

---

5 Marx, Karl (1848) 'The Communist Manifesto', Ch. IV. Position of the Communists in Relation to the Various Existing Opposition Parties. In: *Marx/Engels Selected Works,* Vol. I. Moscow: Progress Publishers (1969), pp. 12–13.

6 Marx, Karl (1867) *Capital,* Vol. I. Preface to the First German Edition. Moscow: Progress Publishers, 1962.

7 Marx, Karl (1853) 'The Future Results of British Rule in India'. In the *New York Daily Tribune*, August 8, 1853. In: *Karl Marx & Friedrich Engels: Collected Works,* Vol. *12*. p. 217.: Moscow: Progress Publishers, 1975.

> those countries to which it is exported. While, therefore, the export of capital may tend to a certain extent to arrest development in the capital-exporting countries, it can only do so by expanding and deepening the further development of capitalism throughout the world.[8]

This effect was an age-old historical reality. The excess capital of the cities of Northern Italy went to finance the development of Holland, and Dutch capital contributed to the take-off of industrial capitalism in England; English capital in turn developed North America and Oceania.

According to the dominant Marxism at the time, the difference in degree of development was only a matter of time-lag. The deadlock that was threatening capitalist accumulation was located in the center, the region with too much capital and too many commodities. The center needed a periphery; however, not primarily as a resource for value intake but as an outlet of capital and commodities—that is, as a market.[9]

Yet in the eyes of revolutionary Marxism at the time—for instance, Rosa Luxembourg—this was only putting things off,[10] for the peripheries of this world are not infinite. When it had become a mirror of England, the system would have exhausted the margins of development of the productive forces that it was large enough to contain. The relief wouldn't last long. As a result, the expansion of capitalism would only be more accumulation and a new, even worse, crisis of overproduction. This centrifugal perception of capitalist global development and line of argument by both Marxist and mainstream economics raises several questions. Emmanuel formulates them in this way:

> The first question is what, during this first phase in the career of the capitalist system (1850-1900), was it that caused the country at the head of the pack (England) to get so quickly out of breath and put its excess capital and technology into those behind it (continental Europe and North America). The second question is why, starting from a certain moment which seems to be around the end of the 19th century, this classic Marxist scheme stopped reflecting reality. In other words, what provoked this unforeseen reversal of the conditions of accumulation in the international sphere so that the former centrifugal forces of diffusion of progress gave way to the present-day centripetal forces of the "siphoning" of resources.[11]

---

8 Lenin, V.I. (1916) 'Imperialism, the Highest Stage of Capitalism'. In *Selected Works* Vol. I, pp. 667-766. Moscow: Progress Publishers, 1963.

9 Emmanuel Arghiri (1976) Europe-Asia Colloquium. For the use by the Commission on International Relations. Some guidelines for the "problematique" of the world Economy. IEDES Dated 6.10.76 Manuscript found in Emmanuel's archive. Green portfolio marked "Imperialism", p. 6.

10 Luxembourg, Rosa (1913) *The Accumulation of Capital*. London: Routledge and Kegan Paul Ltd., 1951.

11 Emmanuel Arghiri (1976) Europe-Asia Colloquium. For the use by the Commission on In-

Why was it that continental Europe, North America, and Oceania seemed to confirm the rule of centrifugal development of the productive forces, becoming a mirror of England, but not India, where the development of the productive forces became blocked? What changed the centrifugal process to a polarizing process?

The answer to these questions is decisive for an understanding of imperialism—the exploitation of one nation by the another—and to understand what the motive force behind the development of the productive forces is, which results in development and underdevelopment in the world-system.

First, one must grasp the mechanism by which material resources are transferred from the periphery to the center. This transfer will, on one side, permit the center to exceed the limits set by the lack of sufficient consumption power (cheap colonial products bought with a relatively high wage level) and, on the other side, block development in the periphery by low wage super-exploitation.

In this analysis, it is important to distinguish the size, functioning, and consequences of financial imperialism (investment and repatriation of profits) and trade imperialism (unequal exchange, based on differences in wage levels). On this, Emmanuel writes:

> In the final analysis, no economic relation between nations and, more so, no relation of exploitation can materialize, indeed have any meaning, outside of the circulations of merchandise—material goods or service. Nonetheless, directly and primarily, it is necessary to see what are the vectors of these relationships (financial and trade imperialism) and what are their relative dimensions.[12]

This is what we, in the Communist Working Circle, did in the late '70s, when we updated Lenin's data from 1914 in his book *Imperialism, the Highest Stage of Capitalism*, and in particular, his concept of "superprofits"—extraordinarily high profits from colonial investments—an exercise that had already been done by Varga and Mendelsohn in 1938.[13] We collected current data and processed them into categories similar to Lenin's. We concluded that the profits from investments in the Third World were not of a size that could explain the difference in living standards between the imperialist countries and the Third World. However, our empirical studies also revealed that the differences in wage levels between the imperialist center and former colonies had expanded from

---

ternational Relations. Some guidelines for the "problematique" of world economy. IEDES Dated 6.10.76 Manuscript found in Emmanuel's archive. Green portfolio marked "Imperialism", p. 6. (The parentheses are mine).

12 Ibid., p. 8. (The parentheses are mine).

13 Varga, E and Medelsohn, L (1938) *New Facts for V.I. Lenin's Imperialism, the Highest Stage of Capitalism*. Moscow: Foreign Languages Publishing House, 1939.

five to one before the Second World War to fifteen to one at the beginning of the 1970s. We also noted a substantial increase in international trade based on an international division of labour exchanging raw materials and agricultural products from the Third World for industrial goods produced in the imperialist countries. We calculated that the unequal exchange amounted to more than 300 billion dollars yearly in the late 1970s. Samir Amin reached the same figures, and Emmanuel writes in 1976:

> Needless to recall that, outside of any other considerations, the quantitative dimension of the terms of trade are of a size incomparable with that of capital flows. Sufficiently illustrating this is the ever so present fact of petroleum, of which the rectification of the prices of just one primary product cost the "centre" a yearly surcharge of approximately 70 billion dollars. In contrast, the total profit of the centre in the periphery, repatriated or otherwise, resulting from direct investment, multinational or otherwise, are by the most liberal estimates no higher than 8 billion per year.[14]

Capital investment is the generator of the development of the productive forces, and hence the production of commodities. However, the profit from these investments is not the primary vehicle of international value transfer; when these commodities are traded internationally, it is the price structure of the commodities, based on the wage differences, which carry the value from the Global South to the North.

Polarized Development

The origins of unequal exchange and the polarized development of the productive forces between center and periphery in the past two centuries are the same—the development of different wage levels. Emmanuel, for his part, describes the rise of the wage level in the center by trade union struggle. Marini, on the other side of the Atlantic, describes in *The Dialectics of Dependency*, how the flow of first gold and silver, then raw materials and agricultural products, from Latin America in exchange for manufactured goods linked its economic development to Europe at the latter's requirements. Marini writes:

> It is from this moment on that Latin America's relations with the European capitalist centers are inserted into a defined structure: the international division of labor, which will determine the course of the region's subsequent development. In other words, it is from then on that dependence takes shape, understood as a relationship of subordination between formally independent nations, in the framework of which the relations of production of the subordinate nations are modified or recreated to ensure the expanded

14 Emmanuel Arghiri (1976) Europe-Asia Colloquium. For the use by the Commission on International Relations. Some guidelines for the "problematique" of world Economy. IEDES Dated 6.10.76 Manuscript found in Emmanuel's archive. Green portfolio marked "Imperialism", p. 9.

> reproduction of dependence [...] Andre Gunder Frank's well-known formula on the "development of underdevelopment" is impeccable, as are the political conclusions to which it leads.[15]

The international division of labor made by colonialism created one circle of capital accumulation in Latin America and another in Europe. However, the two forms were linked together in the expanded reproduction on a world scale of the capitalist mode of production. As an exporter of raw materials and food products, the internal circle of capital accumulation in Latin America was tied to the world economy. The economies in Latin America developed to meet the demands of capitalist circulation in industrial countries in Europe and North America.

In the dependent accumulation, the two fundamental moments of the cycle of capital—production and consumption of merchandise—are separated geographically into two spheres. Productions take place in the dependent country; consumption takes place in the imperialist center. Being export-orientated, Latin American capital circulation does not depend on the domestic capacity for consumption. The contradiction between capital's need for, on the one hand, expanded production and, on the other hand, for consumption to complete the circle of accumulation, and thereby realize profit, is solved by European and North American consumption. This contradiction is also expressed in the relation between capital and the worker, as a seller of labor-power and buyer of merchandise. As Marx noted:

> "Contradiction in the capitalist mode of production: the labourers as buyers of commodities are important for the market. But as sellers of their own commodity—labour-power—capitalist society tends to keep them down to the minimum price."[16]

In other words, the capitalist form of accumulation has a tendency to destroy its own market, as the wage represents a significant part of the consumption power needed to realize the profit by the sale of the produced commodities. Marini put it this way: "The individual consumption of the workers thus represents a decisive element in the creation of demand for the commodities produced, being one of the conditions for the flow of production to be adequately resolved in the flow of circulation."[17]

This is not just an abstract contradiction in capitalism. These struc-

15 Marini, Ruy Mauro (1973) *The Dialectics of Dependency*, ed. Amanda Latimer and Jaime Osorio, p. 117. New York: Monthly Review Press: 2022.

16 Marx, Karl (1859) *Capital*, Vol. 2; (Ed. Frederics Engels in 1884) Ch. 16, p. 391 note 1, London: Penguin Books, 1978.

17 Marini, Ruy Mauro (1973) *The Dialectics of Dependency*, ed. Amanda Latimer and Jaime Osorio, p. 138. New York: Monthly Review Press: 2022.

tural problems came to the surface in England during the first half of the nineteenth century. Capitalists could not meet workers' demands for higher wages if they wanted to keep their profit rates intact; it would have threatened capitalism's entire existence at the time. This is why Marx opened *The Communist Manifesto* in 1848 with "A spectre is haunting Europe—the spectre of communism."[18]

Due to the industrial revolution in the first decades of the nineteenth century, the productive forces underwent a revolution with the introduction of spinning and weaving machines, the steam engine, and railways. Productivity increased severalfold. However, this did not bring better conditions for the working class. On the contrary, the 1840s became known as the "hungry forties," as millions suffered from starvation all across Europe. During the Great Famine in Ireland, which lasted from 1845 to 1852, roughly one million people died of hunger and related diseases. During the famine, Ireland was exporting enough corn, wheat, barley, and oats to England to feed about two million people there. It is simply that Ireland was a food-producing colony, like India and the sugar islands of the Caribbean and Latin America, and its population had to suffer the consequences.[19]

The misery was not limited to the colonies. In his 1845 book *The Condition of the Working Class in England*, Freidrich Engels described the terrible conditions in industrial towns.[20] Many English proletarians emigrated to North America, Australia, New Zealand, or one of the other English colonies. So, too, did the proletarians of Ireland—over one million left during the Great Famine alone. The same scenario played out in Sweden. Around 70 million Europeans emigrated from the continent between 1848 and 1914. In their voyage over the ocean, they became settlers in the "new world," creating a copy of the center and climbing up the hierarchy of labor, on top of the enslaved, the original populations, and immigrants from Asia and Latin America. At the same time, mass emigration reduced the reserve army of labor back in Europe, creating better conditions for the rising trade union struggles.

In the first half of the nineteenth century, workers' wages in England, as in Latin America, covered the bare essentials necessary for survival.[21] This weak-

18 Marx, Karl, Engels, Freidrich (1848) *The Communist Manifesto.* Ch. 4,'"Position of the Communists in Relation to the Various Existing Opposition Parties', in Marx/Engels *Selected Works*, Vol. 1, p. 98. Moscow: Progress Publishers: 1969.

19 Vernon, James (2007) *Hunger: A Modern History*, Ch. 1–3. Cambridge: Belknap Press, 2007.

20 Engels, Freidrich (1845) *The Condition of the Working Class in England,* New York: Panther Books, 1969.

ened the domestic market, and the recurring problem of stagnant consumption vis-à-vis ever-expanding production caused the profit rates of English industrialists to fall.

One of the ways in which a capitalist country can solve the problem of overproduction is to sell as much as possible on the world market. The export surplus provides the purchasing power needed to keep domestic supply and demand in balance. English capital set out to find new markets and possibilities for foreign investment.

As stated above, Marx saw capitalism's development as a centrifugal process. The lower the possibilities for profitable investment in the most developed capitalist countries, the more important profitable investments in the colonies and the less developed capitalist countries became. Marx predicted that capitalism would spread quickly across the globe. According to this view, the opening of new markets in Africa and Asia, and the export of capital to the Americas, promised to temporarily postpone capitalism's imminent collapse, but not to solve the problem. Capitalism was wracked by regular crises in the middle of the nineteenth century. At the same time, the strength and resistance of the proletariat grew. The "spectre of communism" materialized with the Paris Commune in 1871. The bourgeoisie was terribly afraid of widespread revolution. What Marx and Engels did not foresee was that the proletariat's struggle for better living conditions would initiate new forms of imperialist accumulation that would in turn revitalize global capitalism. Colonialism was not just a centrifugal phenomenon; it was also a polarizing one. The division of the world into rich and poor countries, into center and periphery, lay the basis for capitalism's growth and extended longevity.

Around 1850, the living conditions of the English proletariat slowly began to improve. For the first time, capitalists were paying wages above the subsistence level. This was not yet a result of the proletarian struggle. The workers' movement was still weak, not least due to fragmentation and corruption. Instead, the rise in wages was due to contradictions within the ruling class itself. English landowners had great influence in the British parliament. In 1804, they passed a prohibition against the import of grains and other agricultural products into England. This explains why prices for foodstuffs remained high throughout the first half of the nineteenth century, which impacted the subsistence wages the industrialists had to pay. In essence, the landowners took a significant chunk out of the extra profits made by the monopolies of the English industry. In the 1840s, the industrialists campaigned to lift the import prohibition. Supported

21 Hobsbawm, Eric J. (1957) 'The British Standard of Living 1790–1850', *Economic History Review* 10, No. 1: pp. 46-68.

by the working class, they succeeded in 1846. By 1872, wheat imports had doubled and those of meat had increased eightfold, and the same was true for sugar and other agricultural products from Latin America. Food became significantly cheaper.

As the prices for foodstuffs, and therefore the subsistence level, were falling in England, the industrialists wanted to decrease wages. Now, however, this was prevented by the fledgling workers' movement, which was helped by the decrease in the reserve army of labor due to emigration from Europe in the late nineteenth century. The consequence was a significant increase in real wages.

The class struggle provided the economic laws with a concrete historical framework. The forms which these frameworks take are determined by the structural possibilities and limitations created by history.

Class struggle in Europe during the second half of the nineteenth century—colonialism's heyday—provided capitalism with a new framework. The global market was expanding. Cheap imports of raw materials and food enabled high-profit rates and secured ongoing accumulation. None of this was the result of any master plan but of the struggle between those trying to maximize profits and those trying to receive the highest possible wages.

In the periphery of the capitalist world-system, the contradiction between production and consumption found a quite different solution. As Marini explained:

> In the Latin American export economy, things are different. Since circulation is separated from production and takes place basically in the sphere of the external market, the individual consumption of the worker does not interfere in the realization of the product, although it does determine the share of surplus-value. Consequently, the natural tendency of the system will be to exploit to the maximum the labor force of the worker, without worrying about creating the conditions for him to replace it, as long as he can be replaced by incorporating new arms to the productive process.[22]

The existence of a reserve army of labor allowed for a constant increase in the mass of workers, compressing the individual consumption of the worker and thereby increasing the profit rate. This develops a certain form of capitalism in the periphery:

> The export economy is, then, something more than the product of an international economy founded on productive specialization: it is a social formation based on the capitalist mode of production, which accentuates to the limit the contradictions inherent to it. In doing so, it configures in a specific way the relations of exploitation on which it is based, and creates a cycle of capital that tends to reproduce on an enlarged scale the dependence in which it finds itself vis-à-vis the international economy.[23]

---

22 Marini, Ruy Mauro (1973), *The Dialectics of Dependency*, ed. Amanda Latimer and Jaime Osorio, p. 139. New York: Monthly Review Press: 2022.

Worker consumption is depressed to raise profits in the export industry, and the capitalist consumption of luxury products is fulfilled by imports from the center.[24]

Thus, the sacrifice of workers' individual consumption for the sake of exporting to the world market depresses the levels of domestic demand and makes the world market the only outlet for production. At the same time, the resulting increase in profits puts the capitalist in a position to develop consumption expectations without a counterpart in domestic production (oriented towards the world market), expectations that have to be satisfied through imports. The separation between individual consumption based on wages and individual consumption generated by unaccumulated surplus value thus gives rise to a stratification of the internal market, which is also a differentiation of spheres of circulation: while the "low" sphere, in which workers participate—which the system strives to restrict—is based on internal production, the "high" sphere of circulation, proper to non-workers—which is what the system tends to widen—is linked to external production, through the import trade.

The relationship between production and consumption develops differently from the imperialist core, where there is a correspondence between the growth of production and the expansion of the home market. The possibility for the industrial capitalist to obtain abroad the food necessary for the worker at a low price did not entail a fall in wage level but made space for the consumption of other manufactured goods by the working class. In the imperialist core countries, industrial production became centered on goods for popular consumption. As the wage level increased, capital was oriented toward increasing the productivity of labor by introducing new technology and effective organization of the labor process. The way to increase profit was to produce more goods with less labor.

Marini draws the conclusion that the super-exploitation of labor-power in the periphery has an impact on the pattern of extraction of surplus value in the core of the imperialist system, shifting it from being dependent on absolute surplus value (longer and more intensified labor) to relative surplus value (greater productivity) due to the dynamic development of industrial capitalism in the second half of nineteenth century.

Super-exploitation is the basis of unequal exchange from the Latin American side, as it became the key mechanism for periphery capital to increase its profit. However, this form of exploitation curbs the development of the pro-

---

23 Ibid.

24 Ibid., p. 140.

ductive forces, as it prefers absolute surplus value to relative surplus value. The capacity to compete in the world market rests on the low wage level. The super-exploited workers are necessary as producers but are irrelevant as consumers. Emmanuel formulates it in this way:

> As I said so far back as 1962, "it is the capacity of the underdeveloped sections of mankind to wield the tools of our epoch while they are still a long way from possessing the needs of our epoch that in the last analysis gives rise to the superprofit of unequal exchange."[25]

The value transfer by unequal exchange from the periphery, in the form of cheap food and raw materials, created the economic basis for the successful struggle of the working class in the imperialist center for a higher wage. This, in turn solved the problem of a lack of consumption inherent in capitalism and gave rise to accelerated accumulation. The increase in wage level was also an incentive to increase the relative surplus value, that is, to raise productivity with new technology and management systems in order to produce more goods with less labor. This then meant the cheapening of the commodities that make up the worker's individual consumption.

Not only does the difference in wage levels between the center and periphery create a value transfer in the form of unequal exchange, but the difference in consumption power also creates two types of interlinked forms of capitalist accumulation. This difference polarized the capitalist world-system up through the twentieth century. Development and underdevelopment are two sides of the same process. It is by considering the unity of the different forms that capitalism takes that it becomes possible to understand and explain the dependent capitalism in the Third World and the rise of welfare capitalism in Northwestern Europe and parts of North America as part of the same system.

According to Marini, capitalist exploitation in the dependent countries was based on absolute surplus value (long working time with high intensity—blood, sweat, and tears). With the change in the international division of labor created by the neoliberal industrialization of the Global South in the last quarter of the twentieth century, relative surplus value (new technology and organizational structures of work) was added to methods of exploitation. However, absolute surplus value continued to play a significant role, as industrialization was based on exports to the imperialist center. As the consumption power which is needed to realize profit was located in the Global North, there was no need for the de-

---

25 Emmanuel, Arghiri (1962) Lecture at the Sorbonne, 6 Section, Ecole Pratique des Hautes Etudes, December 18, 1962, published in Problemes de planification, no. 2. Here from: Emmanuel, A. (1972). *Unequal Exchange: A Study of the Imperialism of Trade*. p.70. New York: Monthly Review Press, 1972.

velopment of a domestic market to secure capital accumulation.

So, contrary to Marx's prediction, India never became the modernized mirror image of England. Later in life, Marx acknowledged this. He realized that there was instead a process of polarization. In a letter to N.F. Danielson, dated February 19, 1881, he wrote:

> In India serious complications, if not a general outbreak, is in store for the British government. What the English take from them annually in the form of rent, dividends for railways useless to the Hindus; pensions for military and civil service men, for Afghanistan and other wars, etc., etc.—what they take from them without any equivalent and quite apart from what they appropriate to themselves annually within India, speaking only of the value of the commodities the Indians have gratuitously and annually to send over to England—it amounts to more than the total sum of income of the sixty millions of agricultural and industrial labourers of India! This is a bleeding process, with a vengeance! The famine years are pressing each other and in dimensions till now not yet suspected in Europe![26]

Meanwhile Western Europe, as well as of the settler states of the US, Canada, Australia, and New Zealand, became clones of England. The settler states were populated by emigrants who, as they exterminated the original population, demanded wages similar to their ancestors in Europe. This was made possible as they developed their own periphery to exploit in Latin America, Asia—and, in the case of the US, also by extensive slavery.

In contrast to this dynamic, the development of Latin America, Asia, and Africa was blocked. Their exploitation and underdevelopment were required for European and European settler states' modernity. Colonialism was a catastrophe for the world outside of Europe. From 1500 to 1900, the non-European share of the world population dropped from 83 to 62 percent.[27]

Over- and Under-development

The relatively high wages in the center created a growing market, which brought about investment in expanded production. The high wages also encouraged investments in new technology to save labour and raise productivity. This took place within an international division of labour in which the periphery exported raw material and agricultural products and imported industrial goods from the center.

26 Marx, Karl (1881) "Letter to N.F. Danielson, dated February 19, 1881". *Marx and Engels Correspondence*. Moscow: International Publishers, 1968.

27 Amin, Samir (2017) The Sovereign Popular Project: The Alternative to Liberal Globalization. *Journal of Labor and Society*, vol. 20, no. 1, , p. 11, March 2017.

It was the opposite in the periphery. The relatively small market did not give rise to investment in local industrial production. The low price of labour made it more profitable to expand the super-exploitation of labour instead of investing in new technology to replace labor in the raw material extraction and agricultural export sectors.

These differences polarized the capitalist world-system from the latter part of the 19th century and up through the 20th century. Development and under-development were two sides of the same process. Emmanuel stated in 1976:

> The centre finds itself today overdeveloped to the very extent that the periphery is un-derdeveloped.
>
> [...] a country is over or underdeveloped in relation to the general level of development of the productive forces that the existing system of market economy is, in the given his-torical conditions, capable of securing on a world scale.
>
> This would denote that the United States is able to be the United States or Sweden, Sweden, only because the others, that is to say the two billion people, are neither the one nor the other.
>
> This would denote as well, that equalization at the highest level is materially excluded, at least with regards to the overall national averages (the world "materially" referring to the dual limitation on the pool of basic resources on the one hand, the ecological balance on the other).
>
> [...] One can thus ask oneself if this is not sufficient reason for these working classes (in the overdeveloped countries) to dismiss such a communal and fraternal system and express this opposition either through openly integrating themselves in the existing sys-tem, as in the USA or West Germany or by advocating a national path to socialism as in France and Italy [...]
>
> Thus then, must we say that the impossibility of quantitative equalization does not bar the integration of mankind provided that this is based on a qualitative-type change of consumption and lifestyle? One thing is clear, this is the only conceivable solution. Without a qualitative change in the pattern of consumption itself, an egalitarian hu-manity could neither come about nor survive.[28]

The polarization of the world-system in terms of the disparity in the stan-dards of living and the development of the productive forces remained in place through the 20th century, first within the framework of colonialism and then through neo-colonialism. When Emmanuel formulated his thesis in *Unequal Exchange,* raw materials and agricultural products were produced in the "Third World" countries on the global periphery, and advanced industrial production dominated countries of the imperialist core.

---

28 Emmanuel Arghiri (1976) Europe-Asia Colloquium. For the use by the Commission on In-ternational Relations. Some guidelines for the "problematique" of world economy. IEDES Dated 6.10.76 Manuscript found in Emmanuel's archive. Green portfolio marked "Imperial-ism", pp. 1-3.

Industrial production was not yet outsourced on a large scale because transport costs and communications posed much bigger obstacles to controlling production at a distance than they do today, with computers, the internet, cell phones, the standardized container, and "just in time" management. The trade unions in the Global North also still had the strength in the '70s to resist outsourcing. In addition, the social democrat-led states of the time had the ambition to control the multinational companies through the regulation of investment and trade. All this, however, would change with neoliberalism.

Capitalism was still a dynamic system. It had an ace to play. Its need to expand and its hunger for profit led it to outsource industrial production *én masse* to the Global South. The control of globalized production chains was made possible by new technologies of communication and transport. Geographic distance did not seem to matter anymore.

Emmanuel somehow anticipated this development in 1976:

> Another specific feature of the multinational company (MNC) which is vaguely considered to generate prejudice but which, if it really exists, is eminently advantageous, is its independence of the domestic market of the receiving country. Since the main problem of capitalism is not to produce but to sell, less traditional capital was attracted by the low wage rates of certain countries than was discouraged by the narrowness of the local market associated with such wages. This lack of capital in turn prevented growth and hence wage increases. The result was deadlock. In theory the solution was production for exports alone. But except for standardized primary products, such an operation appeared to transcend the fief of the traditional capitalist. In any case, it has never occurred.
>
> The MNC, with its own sales network abroad and, even more, its own consumption in the case of a conglomerate, would not be put off by the lack of 'pre-existing' local outlets. It would take advantage of both the low wages of the periphery and the high wages of the centre. I have no idea of the relative importance of the phenomenon. Here, as elsewhere, statistical information is lacking. Albert Michalet considers that it is very extensive in quantity and very important from the point of view of quality. All I can say is that, if this is so, this gives us for the first time the possibility of breaking the most pernicious, vicious circle which was holding up the development of the Third World. It is rather a matter for rejoicing.[29]

This was exactly what happened. Emmanuel was aware of the role that the transnational companies had in the Third World, both in terms of value transfer by unequal exchange towards the center and in terms of developing the productive forces and technology transfer in the periphery. We have to differentiate between development *within* the capitalist mode of production and the *change* of the mode of production. Emmanuel did not like multinational companies, but he shared Marx's dialectical approach concerning the development of capi-

29 Emmanuel, Arghiri (1976) 'The Multinational Corporations and Inequality of Development', *International Social Science Journal*, vol. 28, no. 4, pp. 766-67.

talism, the need for development of the productive forces, because it prepared the way to a more fully developed modernity—the next step, socialism.

Transnational capital established production in China for export to the consumer markets in the Global North; however, at the same time, it developed the productive forces in China to the extent that China could break the century-old polarizing dynamic in world capitalism between an overdeveloped North and underdeveloped South. This will be discussed at greater length in following chapters.

Appropriate or Underdeveloped Technology?

Capitalism solved its economic and political crises in the "long sixties" through the neoliberal counteroffensive against the "social state" in the Global North and anti-imperialist socialist forces in the Global South. Eventually, it even managed to dissolve the transitional states in the Soviet Union and Eastern Europe, and block continuing sovereign development in the nominally independent, formerly colonized states. Deregulation of global capital movement and trade paved the way for a new international division of labor. It was no longer just raw materials, agricultural products, and labor-intensive industrial products from the Third World against high-tech industrial products from the imperialist center, as it had been in the post-war period. From the 1980s onward, industrial production was outsourced on a mass scale from high-wage countries in the North to low-wage countries in the South. Millions of new industrial workers were recruited, most prominently in China, while the Global North was deindustrialized to a certain extent. China became the largest producer of industrial commodities in the world. Not only were investment and trade globalized, but production itself also became transnational, in the form of production chains stretching from the Global North to the South and back again. This development caught Emmanuel's attention at a very early stage, and in 1982 he published the book *Appropriate or Underdeveloped Technology?*.[30]

In the 1970s, dependency theorists thought that it would be impossible for the Third World to industrialize within the imperialist system. They believed that Third World countries would continue to supply raw materials, tropical agricultural products, and simple, labor-intensive industrial commodities. Their economies would remain dependent, and they would continue to constitute the periphery of the capitalist world-system. The only way out of this situ-

30 Emmanuel, Arghiri (1982) *Appropriate or Underdeveloped Technology?*, London: John Wiley & Sons, 1982.

ation was a socialist revolution and delinking, as recommended by Samir Amin. This might have seemed like an option from 1965 to 1975. However, after this period it no longer seemed possible, not in the era of neoliberal globalization under US hegemony.

Dependency theory did not foresee the massive industrialization of the periphery in the past forty years, because it assumed that a domestic market had to be developed before industrialization could become possible. It underestimated the development and the power of the capitalist productive forces that led to the globalization of the production process itself.

Few at the time could imagine the collapse of the Soviet Union and the integration of China into the world market. It seemed unthinkable that only a few decades later, 80% of the world's industrial proletariat would live and work in the Global South, and the Global North would be rapidly deindustrialized.

The export-oriented industrialization of the Global South, and the creation of global chains of production, increased the transfer of value from low-wage workers in the South to corporations and consumers in the North, hidden through the distortion of prices on a massive scale. The "happy smiley" curve of prices against the "sour[-faced] smiley of labor time."[31]

But the question of unequal exchange was not the only issue at stake in the outsourcing of industrial production to the Global South. The discussion of advanced capitalism's role in the development of the productive forces in the periphery had been raised by Emmanuel in 1982, in *Appropriate or Underdeveloped Technology?*. The value-transfer had in the past entailed a dynamic development of the productive forces in the center but blocked the development in the periphery. Neoliberal globalization changed that. As an unintended side effect of the exploitation of the proletariat of the Global South, it began to develop their productive forces. In this book, Emmanuel claims that multinational companies' investments and the implicit transfer of appropriate technology were better for accumulation than the use of the underdeveloped technology at the disposal of Third World countries. Capitalism is bad, but underdeveloped capitalism is worse.

Arghiri Emmanuel says that we should not:

> [...] *slide from the criticism of capitalism in general to the denial of development within capitalism. In other words, this trend forgets that if capitalism is hell there exists a still more frightful hell: that is less developed capitalism. This is because, if capitalism has not got a historical "mission", it nonetheless has a place in human history; it is not a bad dream. By its very nature, it develops the productive forces, and if this development does not ipso*

31 **Ed. Note:** Refer back to page 72 of this book.

> *facto lead to the satisfactions of "social needs it nonetheless constitutes* [...] *a much more favourable framework for a certain satisfaction of these needs than those of the past class regimes."*[32] *Appropriate or underdeveloped Technology?, p. 105. New York: John Wiley & Sons, 1982.*

This was a provocative stand, as multinational capital was the face of the enemy—capitalism. However, Emmanuel's point of view was not new but in tune with the progressive role of capitalism in developing the productive forces, mentioned in the quotes from *The Communist Manifesto* above.

The encounter with neoliberalism was different from place to place. In the Soviet Union and Eastern Europe, neoliberal "shock therapy" broke down the national project of "real existing socialism." In Africa and Latin America, where transnational capital was in command of the process, "structural adjustments" led to brutal exploitation and national economies in deep debt crises. Neoliberalism also penetrated deep into the Chinese economy in the 1990s. However, the Communist Party of China was able to keep its national project intact.

The rise of China as an economic world power in recent decades proved Emmanuel right. In a world-system where capitalism is still the main driver of the development of the productive forces, a poor country, trying to develop socialism, cannot—and should not—avoid interactions with the most advanced parts of capitalism, because their investment entails the transfer of advanced technology. However, it is a complicated and dangerous game, in which a successful outcome is dependent on the poor state's ability to uphold and defend a national project for the benefit of its working classes. Hence the difference in the encounter with neoliberalism in China and most of the Global South. Emmanuel discussed this problem in several articles, including "The State in the Transitional Period."[33]

The State in the Transition Period

The question of developing the productive forces is not just an academic debate but also a practical question for transitional states—that is, those trying to develop socialism in a world-system dominated by the capitalist mode of production. They have to adopt the same dialectic between the progressive role of capitalism and the agony it produces. Marx writes in *The Critique of Political*

32 Emmanuel, Arghiri (1982)

33 Emmanuel, A. (1979) The State in the Transitional Period. *New Left Review*, No. 113-114, January-April 1979, pp. 110-131. London 1979. Also published under the title as 'The State and the Transition to Socialism'.

Economy:

> No social order is ever destroyed before all the productive forces for which it is sufficient have been developed, and new superior relations of production never replace older ones before the material conditions for their existence have matured within the framework of the old society. [34]

Why is this so? As long as the capitalist mode of production is dynamic, generating profit, expanding accumulation, it will strengthen the power of the ruling class and the hegemonic state in the world-system. However, when the mode of production becomes dysfunctional, when the development of the productive forces is blocked, the global system will face a threat of crisis.

Imperialist value-transfer entailed a dynamic development of the productive forces in the center and at the same time blocked development in the periphery. As a consequence, there was no "need" for—and no successful—revolutions in the center; capitalism had not played out its role. In the periphery, on the other hand, capitalism eroded feudal and other precapitalist modes of production, while development of the productive forces was blocked by super-exploitation.

All this happened within a world-system in which the capitalist mode of production as a whole is dominant in technology, finance, and political and military power. In the periphery only a revolutionary process, led by communist parties, could unblock the development of the productive forces and get the wheels of the economy running again by initiating the development of a "transitionary" mode of production, to develop the preconditions to move towards socialism at a later stage. The transitional state has two main tasks: to defend the power of the pro-people government and to develop the productive forces to satisfy the needs of the people. To accomplish these tasks, the transitional states have pursued a multiplicity of strategies, at times interacting with the dominant capitalist system, and at other times pursuing a strategy for a world revolution. This is the history of the Soviet and Chinese revolutions, and their efforts to move towards socialism in the 20th century.[35]

---

34 Marx, Karl (1859) *Contribution to the Critique of Political Economy. Part One Preface.* In: *Collected Works.* Vol. 29, p. 263. Moscow: Progress Publishers, 1977.

35 Ed. Note: For an extended assessment of the role of transitional states in history and their economic implications see Lauesen, Torkil (2024), *The Long Transition Towards Socialism and the End of Capitalism*, Washington: Iskra Books, 2024.

Lenin and the New Economic Policy

Vladimir Lenin did not believe that socialism was equivalent to the generalization of poverty. To overcome mass poverty, the Soviet Union was compelled to regenerate its economy and develop its productive forces. He believed that the Soviet Union had not reached the level of development necessary to make socialism possible. For Lenin, the 'New Economic Policy' (NEP), instituted a few years after the revolution and shortly following the conclusion of the anti-communist "Civil War", was a necessary step backward in the transition to socialism in order to solve this problem.

The Bolsheviks required investment and new technology. On November 23, 1920, Lenin had already introduced a law on concessions that gave advantages to foreign investors. In 1921, the NEP was formally adopted, substituting militarized production, strict state distribution, and the compulsory appropriation of grain with market conditions. The Soviet state gave preferential treatment to organized large-scale capital. The Bolsheviks used the technology and management associated with capitalism to boost production. However, the "commanding heights" of the economy—finance, infrastructure, large industry, and mining—remained in the hands of the state.[36]

Lenin called the newly emerged trusts of his time "progressive phenomena" despite the suffering they caused. Trusts were a new form of capital concentration, where different capitalists linked their capital and businesses together to achieve a monopoly position. He knew that one does not struggle for socialism by defending and going back to previous stages of capitalism.

According to Lenin, Kautsky's critique of monopoly capitalism was a result of a "petty bourgeois opposition to imperialism, caused by the general reactionary tendency in society."[37] At the present time, we are experiencing the same opposition in the general reaction to transnational globalization, both in the form of right-wing national conservatism and in left wing populism longing for the "Paradise Lost" of small-scale national capitalism. Lenin approvingly quotes Hilferding, who says from a historical materialist point of view: "The reply of the proletariat to the economic policy of finance capital and to imperialism cannot be free trade, but socialism."[38]

36 Lenin, V. I. (1922) 'The role and functions of the trade unions under the new economic policy', Lenin *Collected Works*, Vol. 33, p. 188. Moscow: Progress Publishers, 1965.

37 Lenin, V.I (1916) Imperialism, the Highest Stage of Capitalism, IX, In, Lenin *Collected Works* vol. 22, p. 287. Moscow: Progress Publishers, 1965.

The answer to the new phase of imperialism cannot be a struggle to maintain the old form of more nationally based capitalist economics; it should be a struggle for a more social treatment of the productive forces, a more social version of globalization, necessary for creating a more equal world-system. As Lenin said:

> The questions as to whether it is possible to reform the basis of imperialism, whether to go forward to the further intensification and deepening of the antagonisms which it engenders, or backward, towards allaying these antagonisms, are fundamental questions in the critique of imperialism.[39]

Mao, Deng, and Neoliberal Globalization

In 1949, China was in the same circumstances as Russia in 1917. Both could not just collectivize property but had to develop their productive forces to move towards socialism. China's existing level of productive forces and technology in 1949 was among the lowest in the world. Emmanuel writes:

> In order to support the 'appropriate' technology argument (which basically is just a euphemism for 'intermediate' technology), reference is sometimes made to Chinese practice. But, in fact, the basic Chinese principle is the plurality of technologies which is just about the opposite of the 'intermediate' technology suggested by critics, such as E. F. Schumacher. The latter dilutes the available capital among all the production units involved. The former introduces straight away the pioneer technology entailing the highest organic composition in as many units as possible, regardless of the fact that the shortage of capital prevents its immediate spread over the rest of the branch. Macroeconomic calculations show that this is the method giving maximum long-term output. However, it is an impossible method in a market economy where competition forbids any disparity between the conditions of production in different undertakings. It is only possible in a planned economy.[40]
>
> The following passage from a text by Mao is very explicit on this point:
>
>> The fact that we are developing small and medium-size industries on a large scale, although accepting that the large undertakings constitute the guiding force, and that we are using traditional technologies everywhere, although accepting that foreign technologies constitute the guiding power, is essentially due to our desire to achieve rapid industrialization.[41]
>
> It appears to me that the 'appropriate' technology is the very thing to be outlawed. An appropriate technology for poor countries can only be a poor technology; an

38 Ibid., p. 289.

39 Ibid., p. 287.

40 Bettelheim, Charles (1952) *Le Problème de l'Emploi*, p. 106, Paris, 1952.

41 Chi-Hsi, Hu(1975) *Mao-Tse-Tung et al Construction du Socialisme*, p. 85, Paris, Le Seuil, 1975.

> appropriate technology made to measure for underdeveloped countries can only be an anti-development technology. ("There cannot be," says Boumediène, "one industry for the under-developed and another industry for the developed.") Rehabilitating the neo-classical theory which had been previously pilloried, certain people complain that the technology introduced into developing countries by the MNCs does not correspond to the resources available there. Nor should it. If it did, the mix of factors would be frozen, and the deficiencies reproduced ad infinitum. If 'transfer' is viewed as a vehicle of domination we must not forget that if there were no transfer at all, the technological domination of the centre would be even more decisive.[42]

In 1949, China was completely isolated and could not import technology. However, the Soviet Union came to its rescue in 1950 and provided China with blueprints, technical assistance, and turnkey ready factories on a massive scale. "The most extensive transfer of techniques in the whole history of humanity," wrote Leo Orléans in an OECD report.[43] It was not the most advanced technological equipment, as the transitional state of the Soviet Union was itself lacking behind the West. Nevertheless, it was of huge importance for building the industrial base in China. However, due to political disagreements, the transfer of Soviet technology was cut off in the late 1950s.

Technology transfer can take two forms: a direct form and an indirect form. In the direct form, the developing country buys turnkey advanced factories with the knowledge to operate them. The second indirect form compels the developing country to open up to transnational companies to invest, and by so doing, obtain a transfer of innovative technology. It is a mistake to think that the quest for advanced technology is a feature of the post-Mao era. After the break with the Soviet Union, China imported machines and turnkey factories from the West. Deng Xiaoping just opened up a second form of technology transfer—investments from transnational capital.

In a conversation on October 10, 1978, Deng maintained that the technological gap with advanced countries was growing.[44] He criticized the model of political mass mobilization, because the recent practice demonstrated that the country was incapable of developing the productive forces and therefore could not genuinely satisfy the economic needs of China.[45]

---

42 Emmanuel, Arghiri (1976) "The Multinational Corporations and Inequality of Development". *International Social Science Journal*, vol. 28, no. 4, p 764.

43 Orléans, Leo (1977). *La Science et la Technologie en République Populaire de Chine*, page. 106. OECD 1977.

44 Xiaoping, Deng (1978) 'Carry Out the Policy of Opening to the Outside World and Learn Advanced Science and Technology From Other Countries.' In: Xiaoping, Deng, *Selected Works*. Vol. 2, p. 143. Beijing: Foreign Languages Press: 1992.

45 Xiaoping, Deng (1985) 'We Shall Expand Political Democracy and Carry Out Economic Re-

Deng drew on ideas from Lenin's NEP in his reforms. During his stay in the Soviet Union in 1926, Deng became acquainted with NEP (1923-28), an experience that he tried to apply first between 1949 and 1952, when he led the Regional Committee of the CPC in southeastern China, and again when he recommended it in the aftermath of "The Great Leap Forward." In 1978, in control of the CPC, he finally had the chance to implement his policy on a national scale.

Global capitalism was still characterized by its significant advancement of productive forces, with an extensive division of labour accompanied by an increasing concentration of capital in multinational corporations. Neoliberal globalization marked a further step along this road. The new technological revolutions in computers and communication, new logistics and management systems, and the new, large-scale transnational operations in finance, production, and trade demanded to be treated as transnationally political. Neoliberalism eroded the individual national state's ability to control transnational finance and trade and required them to instead build international institutions like the WTO to be the new political framework of global capitalism. This new setup gave global capitalism 40 golden years. The global production chains expanded the transfer of value by unequal exchange, securing cheap products for Northern consumers and high profits for capital.

Deng's reform strategy does not stem from a neoliberal perspective. Deng advocated for the acceleration of foreign investment capital in a planned way, believing that planning and markets could be applied to serve the development of a socialist system. Nor did Deng introduce economic shock therapy, as Yeltsin did in the post-Soviet era. Rather, elements of capitalism were introduced gradually. "Crossing the river by feeling for the stones" became a popular slogan.[46] Referencing the NEP in the Soviet Union, Deng said that "socialism does not mean shared poverty." In an interview with CBS in 1986, he explained his approach:

> During the "Cultural Revolution" there was a view that poor communism was preferable to rich capitalism [...] According to Marxism, communist society is based on material abundance. Only when there is material abundance can the principle of a communist society—that is, "from each according to his ability, to each according to his needs"— be applied [...] There can be no communism with pauperism, or socialism with pauperism. So to get rich is no sin. However, what we mean by getting rich is different from what you mean. Wealth in a socialist society belongs to the people. To get rich in a socialist society means prosperity for the entire people. The principles of socialism are first, development of production, and second, common prosperity. We permit

form'. In: Xiaoping, Deng, *Selected Works* Vol. 3, p. 122. Beijing: Foreign Languages Press 1992.

46 Naughton, B. (2008). 'A political economy of China's economic transition'. In. Brandt. L & Rawski, T. G. (Eds.), *China's Great Economic Transformation*, p. 98. Cambridge: Cambridge University Press, 2008.

> some people and some regions to become prosperous first, for the purpose of achieving common prosperity faster. That is why our policy will not lead to polarization, to a situation where the rich get richer while the poor get poorer. To be frank, we shall not permit the emergence of a new bourgeoisie.[47]

Transnational capitalism required low-wage labor power to continue its expansion, and China possessed a huge proletariat and developed infrastructure that was ready to connect to global capitalism. In its effort to maximize profit by outsourcing as much production as possible to low wage countries, transnational capitalism developed the productive forces in the periphery and semi-periphery of the world-system, in terms of both quantity and quality. Transnational capital could not just demand "structural adjustment" to gain access to China, as in the rest of the Third World. China's encounter with neoliberalism was different from the rest of the world. Isabella Weber writes:

> China was keen on avoiding unconditional integration into global capitalism. The government defended its sovereign economic planning and forced global capital entering the country to adapt to it, not vice versa. [48]

It was crucial for the Chinese government to control private capital within the framework of a planned economy with an objective to develop a diverse industrial sector based on joint ventures with transnational corporations according to a strategic plan.

Under pressure from neoliberal globalization, China had no choice but to build its peculiar form of state capitalism and market socialism to maintain its national project. China chose to open up to the force of neoliberal globalisation using a "kung fu" strategy: absorbing the neoliberal thrust and bending like a bamboo branch, without breaking the power of the Communist Party, as happened in the case of the Soviet Union. By keeping control over the central features of the economy, the party aims to eventually turn the power of the productive forces, which neoliberalism had helped to develop, against the capitalist center.

Through this strategy, the transitional state of the People's Republic of China survived the offensive from global capitalism. After the financial crisis of 2007/8, China began to shift the cycle of capital accumulation from being focused on export to the world markets towards domestic circulation. By tripling the wage level and through massive state programs for internal investment that have pulled hundreds of millions out of poverty, China has reduced unequal ex-

---

47 Xiaoping, Deng. (1986). Interview with Mike Wallace of CBS 60 Minutes. CBS, September 2, 1986. Here from: *All Asia Times*, December 13, 2006.

48 Weber, Isabella M. (2021) *How China Escaped Shock Therapy: The Market Reform Debate*, p. 21, New York: Routledge, 2021.

change and broken the polarizing tendency that has ruled capitalism for more than 150 years.

The competition between the West and the Soviet Union in the former Cold War, and between the US and China in the current Cold War, was not and is not between capitalism and socialism. It is between capitalism and a transitional mode of production—transitional because it cannot develop into a socialist mode of production as long as the capitalist mode and its political superstructure rule the world. What is different between the old Cold War and the contemporary one is that the transitional mode of production is becoming more effective in terms of developing the production forces, both in quantitative and qualitative terms. Between 2003 and 2007, the United States led in sixty of sixty-four critical technologies, while China led in only three of them. Recent studies have shown China to now be at the forefront in many critical technologies, in which regions, even as recently as the beginning of the century, they were trailing far behind. China leads in areas as diverse as advanced integrated circuit design and fabrication, high-performance computing, quantum sensors, AI, and solar energy.

The English magazine *The Economist*, hardly a pro-Chinese journal, wrote in January 2025:

> The goal was to turn China into a green and innovative "manufacturing power", one that relied less on labour and Western supply chains, and more on automation and new home-grown technologies. This was Xi Jinping's vision for the Chinese economy [...] It has, for the most part, been a resounding success. Aided by the government, Chinese firms have risen to the very top of some industries. They have grown more automated and sophisticated.
>
> [...] In the area of clean energy [...] the gains of Chinese companies are unambiguous. Whereas in 2015 they produced 65% of the world's solar panels and 47% of its batteries, today they are responsible for around 90% and 70% [...] In much of the world, the green transition is powered by kit made in China. [...] Chinese manufacturers are making more stuff, but the government also wanted them to make more innovative stuff [...] A related aim, for firms to file more patents, has also been surpassed. China's manufacturing workforce was over 123m people in 2023. These labourers have become more productive: output per worker has increased by roughly 6% a year on average from 2014 to 2023.[49]

We have reached the point where the "pure" capitalist mode of production has lost its position as leading the development of the forces of production. This opens the door for taking the next steps towards a developed socialist mode of production.

---

49 *The Economist* (2025) The Consequences of Success, January 18, 2025.

The Need to Continue the Development of the Productive Forces

Socialism is not only about eliminating poverty within the national framework, but also about the creation of a more equal world. As mentioned above, it is not possible to raise the living standards of billions of poor people in the Global South to the level of the US or Germany within the capitalist mode of production, due to the simple lack of natural resources and other ecological restrictions.

However, it is not only a change in the mode of production and patterns of consumption which is needed to develop socialism on a global scale, meaning an equal world—it is also a continued development of the productive forces and the implementation of the most advanced technology on a massive scale. It is important to differentiate between capitalist growth and development of the productive forces. On this Emmanuel writes:

> The "Quality of Life"
>
> Another tactic in the face of certain embarrassing phenomena today is to [advise] the underdeveloped countries against the abominations of the "consumer society" into which the developed countries have been led by a quantitative growth which has become an end in itself.
>
> What is in question here?
>
> As we have already had occasion to point out, the developed countries consume enormously more than their share of the world's raw materials. But in the midst of this extraordinary abundance, people are bored—among other things by the monotonous routine of their working lives. (What the French call "metro-boulot-dodo"—travel-work-sleep). We find that our affective life is impoverished instead of enriched, that human relations become impersonal, that our cities are polluted and our motorways inhuman.
>
> So people advise the poor countries to look for other ways of development, without, of course, saying which these are. Height of the paradox: the fact that we previously proposed our quantitative growth model to the underdeveloped countries is called "Eurocentricity". It is not difficult to see what is particularly European (indecent into the bargain) about making the boredom of the dyspeptic rich into the main problem of a world where hundreds of millions of men are hungry, deprived of medical care, unable to read and write, and with only an average life expectancy at birth of 40 years. Surely it is completely ridiculous to condemn technical progress and "productivism" on the pretext that one risking one's soul to the private car and the washing machine, in a world where two thirds of the population go barefoot and are underfed.
>
> The development of the productive forces **inside the capitalist system** is a "for-better-and-for-worse" commitment. It makes for man's transformation into a consumer of gadgets, but also for his general education; for pollution as well as for abundant and efficient medical services; for the greatest possible exploitation as well as for proteins for adults and milk for children; for the alienation and desocialization of man and the

> desiccation of his affective life as well as for a certain material comfort, for children's nurseries and a considerable lengthening of the expectation of life at birth.
>
> If one is obliged to dispute the ends one cannot simply ignore the problem of the creation of the means.
>
> It is quite true that a social revolution would not only radically change our choices and our ends but would also rationalize and speed up the creation of the means themselves. It still remains, though, that considerable means are already being created before the advent of the socialist revolution and this creation itself constitutes a very important problem, not only because while capitalism still exists and in spite of all the "negative fall-out" affecting social conditions it is raising the material standard of the masses, but also because to a certain extent it conditions the advent of the socialist revolution itself.
>
> What is more important though is that these same means are necessary, at least in part, for the various ends that will still persist uncontested. For it is all too often forgotten that steel, cement, copper, tin, oil and plastics not only serve to produce private cars and gadgets but also, for instance, doctors—a lot of steel and cement and all kinds of materials are needed to make a good modern doctor—healthy leisure, concerts, books and so on.
>
> If "the quality of life" has any meaning at all, which I am not very knowledgeable about, it ought to mean, among other things and perhaps most of all, replacing individual consumption by community consumption. But the materials like those just mentioned are needed just as much for one type of consumption as for the other; and the needs of this second kind, though they may be healthier and more suited to man's nature, are just as limitless.
>
> So first and foremost, we must produce these materials; and for this we must improve technology, accumulate the product of past work, and increase the productivity of living labour. In other words, we need growth and never mind the type of production and consumption.
>
> And even if the social system that replaces the so-called consumer society opts for more leisure time instead of greater consumption, an increase in the productivity of labour will still be necessary to produce what is essential in a shortened working period. More and yet more growth will be needed, if not that of product per inhabitant, at least of product per unit of active work. Whatever happens, economic problems are by their very nature quantitative ones.[50]

For sure we need other ways to produce and consume in order to live in balance with nature; however, the majority of the world's population has urgent basic needs. To fulfil these needs, they need more use-values. To produce these goods sustainably, the innovation of new technology is an imperative, and we need to change our "imperial mode of living" to a new quality of life. On this issue Emmanuel writes:

> While no one up to now has laid out the model of this "anti-consumption" society, there exists at least one point on which everyone is in agreement. That is the absolute priority of the maximization of available leisure, time being the prerequisite for the quality of

50 Emmanuel, Arghiri (1975) 'Unequal Exchange Revisited', pp. 85-87. IDS Discussion Paper No. 77 Institute of Development Studies, Sussex University, Brighton, UK.

life. How then can we rid ourselves of "productivism" since for any given physical consumption, whatever its volume, leisure time is an increasing function of the return on time passed at work?

Naturally, if it is shown that the "consumer society" is in any case a material impossibility on a world scale, the question of choice no longer presents itself for four-fifths of humanity. However, the idea that the remaining one fifth, which has the privilege of this type of society would profit from the change, is not a statement so obvious that one could excuse oneself from demonstrating.[51]

---

51 Emmanuel Arghiri (1976) 'Europe-Asia Colloquium. For the use by the Commission on International Relations. Some Guide-lines for the "problematique" of World Economy'. IEDES Dated 6.10.76. Manuscript found in Emmanuel's archive. Green portfolio marked "Imperialism.", pp. 3-4.

7

Ecology and Unequal Exchange

ABOVE THE ECONOMIC AND POLITICAL STRUCTURAL CRISES is the deepening contradiction between the capitalist mode of production and planet Earth's ecosystem. In the seventeenth century, Thomas Hobbes argued that it was humankind's destiny to conquer, domesticate, and control nature in order to ensure its own survival. Capitalism is an extension of this logic: it positions humankind against nature and makes sure that the former dominates and exploits the latter. Five hundred years of capitalism have put so much pressure on non-renewable resources and natural habitats that we are now facing the consequences in the form of climate change and the pollution of land, air, and water. Marx and Engels were well aware of this problem, with the latter writing:

> Let us not, however, flatter ourselves overmuch on account of our human victories over nature. For each such victory nature takes its revenge on us. Each victory, it is true, in the first place brings about the results we expected, but in the second and third places it has quite different, unforeseen effects which only too often cancel out the first [...] Thus at every step we are reminded that we by no means rule over nature like a conqueror over a foreign people, like someone standing outside nature—but that we, with flesh, blood, and brain, belong to nature, and exist in its midst, and that all our mastery of it consists in the fact that we have the advantage over all other creatures of being able to learn its laws and apply them correctly.[1]

The exploitation of raw materials, the depletion of the soil, and the burning of fossil fuels—all to satisfy capitalism's need for growing production, consumption, and capital accumulation—steadily sharpened this contradiction throughout the twentieth century and until the present day. In the 1950s, the contradiction took on a new quality, entering a "period of Earth's history during which

---

1 Engels, Freidrich (1884) 'The Dialectics of Nature', Chapter IX: The Part Played by Labour in the Transition from Ape to Man. In: *Marx & Engels Collected Works, Vol. 25*, pp. 460–61 New York: International Publishers, 1975.

humans have a decisive influence on the state, dynamics, and future of the Earth System." [2]

The rise of the "consumer societies" in North America, Western Europe, Japan, and Australia/New Zealand after the Second World War resulted in a dramatic rise in the consumption of oil and other raw materials and, in turn, in carbon emissions. Land, water, and air pollution have since become serious problems.

So far, the US, Canada, Europe, Japan, and Australia/New Zealand have contributed a total of 61% of global carbon emissions; China and India combined account for 13%; Russia is responsible for 7%, and the rest of the world for 15%. International shipping and air travel account for the remaining 4%. The obvious global inequality becomes even more pronounced if we calculate emissions based on consumption rather than production.[3]

The logic of the capitalist mode of production, the unremitting need for expansion, and the competition between nations for resources and markets make it difficult to solve, or even diminish, the climate problems through negotiation in an international framework. It seems that the discourse is moving from trying to achieve sustainability towards gaining resilience to nature's "revenge on us." It is the old battle of trying to dominate nature.

Emmanuel's Contribution

Ecological sustainability was more or less absent from theories of imperialism in the 1970s. Emmanuel, however, was aware of it. The periphery was not just under-developed; the center was *over*-developed. In 1975, he wrote:

> **And in Real Terms,**
>
> Americans consume nearly 700 kilos of steel per head per year. If the whole world started to consume as much, all known reserves of iron ore would be completely exhausted in 40 years—provided the world's population ceased to increase, otherwise depletion would come even sooner.
>
> The same equalisation of world consumption from above, still with a stable population, would exhaust the known reserves of copper in 8 years, tin in 6 years, etc.
>
> But where the deadlock is total is once again oil. At the level of North American consumption, the world needs some 14-15 billion tons a year. But known world resources only amount to about 80 billion tons, which, with a stable population and economy,

2 Anthropocene Working Group (2019) 'Results of Binding Vote by AWG', May 21, 2019.

3 Peters, Glenn P. (2008) From Production-Based to Consumption-Based National Emission Inventories, in *Ecological Economics* 65, no. 1 (2008): pp. 13–23; World Resources Institute.

would be enough for 5 & 1/2 years.

If we add reserves yet to be discovered or those which might be exploited with new technological inventions, we could, according to OECD experts, count on twice that amount, or about 160 billion tons. In other words, and assuming the same stable situation, there would be enough to last 11 years. Finally, taking into account the marine subsoil of the whole planet, we arrive, according to certain experts, at a total of 320 billion tons, i.e. 22 years' consumption at the American rate.

Ecological Constraints

But exhaustion of present and future resources is not the only factor preventing world equalisation from above. Ecological limits constitute another factor.

If the present developed countries can still get rid of their waste products by dumping them in the sea or expelling them into the air, it is because they are the only ones doing it.

Just as their inhabitants can still travel by air and fly the world's skies only because the rest of the world does not have the means to fly and leaves the world's air routes to them alone. And so on...

International Solidarity

In all these calculations it is not a matter of abstract concepts like surplus-value, capital, etc., or book-keeping categories like profit, interest rates etc., but of the consumption of real substances. So it is the vast mass of the population and the wage-earners themselves who are implicated. Similarly, leaving aside all other considerations and all other antagonisms, and given the objective natural and technological conditions of today and the foreseeable future, the rich countries can only consume all the commodities that make up their material welfare, which they seem keen to preserve, because the others consume very little or nothing at all.

They can only abstain from recycling their waste products because the others do not have much to recycle; otherwise the ecological balance of the world would be irrevocably disturbed. This is what destroys working-class solidarity between the rich and the poor countries.

Everything happens today as though certain nations had been able to fuse into a sort of class-nation, while others remained merely nations divided into classes. This means that in the first type of country a true political struggle becomes more and more impossible: there can only be a strictly economic struggle, as there has always been inside any class. This also means, in a sense, that the countries on the periphery are henceforth not the weakest link in the chain but the only true revolutionary area. Their local conservative forces are allied, not with certain classes in other countries, but with certain nations belonging to the same class. At any rate, the physical terms of the problem as set out above show clearly that its solution has as its framework and parameters mankind as a whole. Any class contradictions that may remain in the developed countries become secondary. The main contradiction—the motive force of change—is henceforth to be found in international economic relations.[4]

The over- and under-development dichotomy also has an ecological mean-

4 Emmanuel, Arghiri (1975) 'Unequal Exchange Revisited', pp. 65-67. *IDS Discussion Paper*, no. 77, University of Sussex. Brighton, U.K 1975.

ing.

Ecological Unequal Exchange

On the basis of Emmanuel's economic model of "unequal exchange," a whole school of theorists has related the notion of "unequal exchange" to ecological devastation. Instead of focusing on trade of commodities, they are looking at global flows of materials and the disposal of waste. One of the pioneers of Ecological Unequal Exchange was Stephen G. Bunker. In an article from 1984, he compared a "mode of extraction" to a "mode of production" and reached the conclusion that:

> [...] *the unbalanced flows of energy and matter from extractive peripheries to the productive core provide better measures of unequal exchange in a world economic system than do flows of commodities measured in labor or prices.* [...] *the fundamental values in lumber, in minerals, oil, fish, and so forth, are predominantly in the good itself rather than in the labor incorporated in it.*[5]

Bunker is of the opinion that the extraction of natural resources, whether by mining, drilling, harvesting, or cutting trees, is a crucial factor for understanding unequal exchange, since energy and matter are contained in all commodities. However, while the difference in the usage of biomass is a material expression of the difference between rich and poor, it does not explain the mechanisms that create that difference. Wages do. For the German economist Jürgen Lipke, the ecological aspects of unequal exchange are better understood as a complement to the economic ones. Unequal exchange creates patterns of consumption that have ecological consequences,[6] much like Brand and Wissen's concept of the imperial mode of living.[7]

Environmentalists use the concept "natural capital" to refer to a region's capacity to sustain economic activity. To be sustainable, a society cannot exhaust its natural capital but must live off its interest, so to speak. In simple terms, people must leave resources behind just as they receive them. Analysts have mea-

---

5 Bunker, Stephen G. (1984) 'Modes of Extraction, Unequal Exchange, and the Progressive Underdevelopment of an Extreme Periphery: The Brazilian Amazon 1600–1980', *American Journal of Sociology*, Vol. 89, No. 5 (1984), pp. 1018, 1054.

6 Lipke, Juergen (2002) 'Unequal Exchange and Ecological Consumption—a Quantitative Study of Dependency Structures in the world-system' (2002), p. 1.The article is his thesis (Staatsexamensarbeit) at the *Zentrum furEntwicklungslunderforschung* (Geographisches Institut, Freie Universitet Berlin).

7 Brand, Ulrich & Wissen, Markus (2021), *The Imperial Mode of Living—Everyday Life and the Ecological Crises of Capitalism.* London: Verso, 2021.

sured the "natural capital" we are using by calculating the area necessary to sustain one human life. The world average is 2.85 hectares per person. This is 30 percent higher than what is considered sustainable, namely 2.18 hectares per person. Residents of OECD countries require 7.22 hectares on average, which is four times as much as what residents of non-OECD countries require. The bottom line is that citizens of the Global North are wearing out the planet.[8]

On the basis of Emmanuel's economic model of "unequal exchange," Alejandro Pedregal and Nemanja Lukić conclude that:

> The extension of the analysis of unequal exchange to the ecological field has incorporated the role of consumption and externalization in the environmental burden of the ecological footprint and other global and local ecosocial imbalances into the study of trade and labor. This has served to enrich research on the impact of these imbalances between the valorization of natural goods and manufacturing on all types of ecosystems and societies.[9]

John Bellamy Foster and Brett Clark emphasize:

> [...] transfers of economic values are accompanied in complex ways by real "material-ecological" flows that transform relations between city and country, and between global metropolis and periphery.[10]

Unequal exchange combined with political and military power allow the Global North to import and consume natural capital far beyond its own. The capitalist market obliges the poor countries to surrender their natural capital and pursue non-sustainable economic development. The consequence is that we are not only confronted with an increasing divide between rich and poor but also with a dying planet.

What makes the ecological dimension of unequal exchange different from the economic one is that the borders between the countries that benefit and those that suffer can't be drawn as clearly. Most environmental problems are global problems; they aren't confined to individual countries, and they cannot be solved by them. Pollution in China can already be detected on the west coast of the United States. Neither the pollution of our air and our oceans nor climate change respects national borders.

There is a need and possibility to build a bridge between the political econ-

---

8 Lipke, Juergen (2002) 'Unequal Exchange and Ecological Consumption—a Quantitative Study of Dependency Structures in the World-system', p. 9.

9 Pedregal, Alejandro and Lukic, Nemanja (2024) 'Imperialism, Ecological Imperialism, and Green Imperialism: An Overview', p.117. *Journal of Labor and Society*, vol 27, no. 1, 2024, pp. 105–138.

10 Foster, J. B. and B. Clark (2204) 'Ecological Imperialism: The Curse of Capitalism', p. 187. *Socialist Register 40.* 2004, pp. 186–201.

omy of unequal exchange and political ecology. Pedregal and Lukic write:

> Combined, they can offer a totalizing ecological view on the integration of our economies within global capitalism, providing us with a systemic perspective on the hierarchization of the distribution of ecosocial burdens across the planet, as well as the tools to overcome those hierarchies.[11]

Globalization has eradicated any natural limits on the exploitation of resources, since the people responsible won't suffer the consequences (at least not right away). Not only do we receive cheap commodities from the Global South, but we are also destroying their environment.

Overconsumption and the destruction of the planet lead to increased economic, political, and military competition over natural resources. The global market obliges the poor countries to surrender their natural capital and pursue non-sustainable economic development in order to satisfy the demands of consumers in the Global North.

The exponential growth that characterizes capitalism resembles cancer. Sustainability is impossible within a capitalist framework. Competition between countries hoping to attract foreign investment means ecological concerns are pushed to the side. Capital has always looked to externalize the costs of pollution; paying for them would threaten profits and accumulation. In the coming decades, the lack of raw materials and clean water and other ecological shortages will have enormous consequences for our societies, yet hardly anything is being done politically to prevent this. If anything, politicians do their utmost to sabotage such efforts. The notion of *resilience* has replaced that of sustainability. In this context, "resilience" simply means being able to make it through catastrophes, not averting them. But it is a losing game. Our survival depends on entirely new approaches to growth, consumption, and the relationship between humankind and nature.

The current geopolitical struggle has diminished the possibility of solving the climate problems within the current world order. The rapidly growing arms industry is difficult to greenwash, and there are no ecological wars. The ruling class and hegemonic powers, have no realistic plan to solve the climate crises, just empty words. Appeals to capitalist-based government are in vain. The ecological crises of the planet cannot be solved within the capitalist mode of production.

Jason Hickel writes:

> The past half-century is littered with milestones of inaction. A scientific consensus on

---

11 Pedregal, Alejandro and Lukic, Nemanja (2024) 'Imperialism, Ecological Imperialism, and Green Imperialism: An Overview', p.129. *Journal of Labor and Society*, vol 27. No.1 2024, pp. 105–138.

> anthropogenic climate change first began to form in the mid-1970s [...] The UN Framework Convention on Climate Change (UNFCCC) was adopted in 1992 to set non-binding limits on greenhouse gas emissions. International climate summits—the UN Congress of Parties—have been held annually since 1995 to negotiate plans for emissions reductions. The UN framework has been extended three times, with the Kyoto Protocol in 1997, the Copenhagen Accord in 2009, and the Paris Agreement in 2015. And yet global CO2 emissions continue to rise year after year, while ecosystems unravel at a deadly pace.[12]

We do not yet have another mode of production —but there are possibilities to develop it, and it has to be done within this century if we are to avoid a major collapse of Earth's ecosystem. We are working under pressure. We need to reach the stage where the capitalist mode of production is in decline and new forms of production and consumption are on the rise, by 2050. China, with its transitional mode of production, has presented a vision of an "ecological civilisation." It is not just a mirage. Despite China still having a significant capitalist sector, the transitional state has the advantage that politics is in command of the economy, and is increasingly oriented towards sustaining their ecology. Ecology has become integrated into all levels of policy-making and economic planning. China' s investments in these projects have largely been made by state banks, and key projects are carried out by state-owned companies, according to plans laid out by the government.

In this way, China has become the global leader in renewable energy and electric transport. Over the past decade, this strategy has led to the costs of solar and wind power falling by 90%, and batteries by more than 90%. With China now building two thirds[13] of the world's wind and solar projects, these sources of energy represented 39% of China's total energy production at the end of 2024.[14] Chinese manufacturers dominate the solar panel industry, accounting for over 70% of global production. Cheap solar energy is very important for the Global South as they try to get rid of fossil energy production.

China's development of "ecological civilisation" gets swept under the table of even mainstream left discourse in the West, where it is labelled as the propaganda of an authoritarian "hyper-industrial" regime.[15] In terms of contemporary annual carbon emissions, China is the world's largest polluter. However,

---

12 Hickel, J. (2020) *Less is More: How Degrowth Will Save the World*, p. 20. United Kingdom: Random House, 2020.

13 Hawkins, Amy (2024) 'China building two-thirds of world's wind and solar projects', *The Guardian*, 11.7. 2024.

14 ESG News (2024) 'China Dominates Global Wind and Solar Energy Construction', *ESG News*, July 12, 2024. China Dominates Global Wind and Solar Energy Construction—ESG News.

China's historic carbon emissions are still far exceeded by those of the United States and Europe, and the US is responsible for seven times as much per capita of the carbon dioxide concentrated in the atmosphere as China. In terms of per capita carbon dioxide emissions, China's emissions today are less than half those of the US level.[16]

John Bellamy Foster, in an article on China's vision of an "ecological civilisation," writes:

> *There is no doubt that China's struggles to create an ecological civilization are revolutionary when placed against the efforts of other countries. This is largely due to its role as a post-revolutionary, socialist-oriented social formation that retains a large element of economic planning capability, state direction, and collective values, invigorated by continual popular mobilization in both rural and urban areas.[17] Monthly Review vol. 74, no. 5, October 2022.*

This environmental focus can be seen in the radical transformations that China has been introducing in areas such as pollution reduction, reforestation and afforestation, development of alternative energy sources, restrictions in sensitive river areas, rural revitalization, food self-sufficiency through collective means, and many others.[18]

John Bellemy Foster continues:

> Rather, the fundamental division is between a post-revolutionary society that has adopted Marxism with Chinese characteristics—embracing the ecological critique emanating from classical historical materialism and treating it as central to the entire long revolution of socialism—and an unalloyed capitalist order in which the sole mantra is "Accumulate, accumulate! [...]"[19]

This development shows that the transitional mode of production is already superior to capitalism. As the global economic and political crises exacerbate, the transitional mode of production can move from its current defensive position, out of the shadow of capitalist dominance, into forms of production and consumption in balance with the global ecosystem.

---

15 Lent, Jeremy (2018) What Does China's 'Ecological Civilization' Mean for Humanity's Future?, *Ecowatch*, February 9, 2018, ecowatch.com.

16 Union of Concerned Scientists (2023), 'Each Country's Share of CO2 Emissions', https://www.ucs.org/resources/each-countrys-share-co2-emissions.

17 Foster, John Bellamy (2022) "Ecological Civilization, Ecological Revolution: An Ecological Marxist Perspective."

18 See Joe Scholten, 'How China Strengthened Food Security and Fought Poverty with State-Funded Cooperatives', *Multipolarista*, May 31, 2022.

19 Foster, John Bellamy (2022) 'Ecological Civilization, Ecological Revolution: An Ecological Marxist Perspective', *Monthly Review* vol. 74, no. 5, October 2022.

8

Resisting Unequal Exchange

THE ECONOMIC AND POLITICAL DEVELOPMENTS of the past two decades, since Emmanuel passed away in 2001, show that his ideas are still relevant for understanding global value transfer, the structural crises of capitalism, and the ecological mess we've gotten ourselves into. Imperialism is not just a feature of capitalism. Colonialism was the midwife, and imperialism was the driver of the development of the capitalist world-system into the center-periphery structure. By boosting consumption power in the center, unequal exchange became the solution to the contradiction, within the capitalist mode of production, between expanded accumulation and the lack of market.

The value-transfer by unequal exchange took off in the second part of the 19th century, when wages in Western Europe and North America began to rise compared to the wage level in the periphery, moving from 3:1 around 1850 to 6:1 around 1875.[1] The size of the unequal exchange accelerated after the Second World War, with the change from colonialism to neocolonialism and the breakthrough of the consumer society in the center. Around 1970, the scale of the wage gap between the center and the periphery was around 15:1. During neoliberal globalization, from 1980 until the financial crisis of 2007/8, the wage gap declined to around 10:1; however, the massive outsourcing of industry to the periphery, caused the volume of low-wage produced goods, consumed by high wage laborers in the center, to increase on a massive scale, and thus so did the size of unequal exchange.[2]

---

1 Allan, Roberts C (2009) 'The British Industrial Revolution in Global Perspective', p. 40. Cambridge: Cambridge University Press, 2009. Allan, Roberts C (2015) 'The High Wage Economy and the Industrial Revolution: A Restatement'. *Economic History Review,* Vol 68, No.1 pp. 1-22, 2015.

2 See chapter 5: Hickel, Jason; Lemos, Morena Hanbury and Barbour, Felix: (2024) Unequal

The imperialism of unequal exchange is still a pillar upholding the current capitalist world-system, and hence an important factor in the major contradictions of the current global capitalist system: the geopolitical struggle between the decline of US hegemony and the rise of the Global South, the class struggle in each capitalist society over wages, and the contradiction between the capitalist mode of production versus planet Earth's ecological systems.

An analysis of how the system works is a necessary foundation and starting point for developing a strategy and praxis. The struggle against the imperialism of unequal exchange offers possibilities for uniting forces against the current world order, ruled by the West, and there is a clear opportunity to build an alternative economic and political multipolar world-system, which itself opens up pathways for a transition towards a socialist mode of production. The Global South is breaking centuries of polarization of the world-system into rich and poor countries. They are increasing South-South trade and developing alternative financial institutions to the US-dominated World Bank and IMF. There are new possibilities to unite the anti-imperialist struggle and the ecological movements around a common agenda, as the need for global social justice and the need for a sustainable global environment both require the end of capitalism.

So, the objective conditions for change are favourable: capitalism is no longer progressive but seems irrational and destructive. The hegemonic power cannot rule in the old anymore. After half a century of neoliberalism globalisation, it has lost its economic superiority, and the capitalists are desperately searching for new ways to uphold its power.

What about the subjective forces of change? The victims of unequal exchange in the Global South will be the driver in the transformation process. Despite differences in political outlook, there are interests that bind them together. They are fed up with the dominance of the West. However, in order to be able to move from resistance to the existing world order towards building a socialist mode of production, the subjective forces have to be developed significantly. A multipolar world-system can provide the space for this process. In the Global North, the economic crises caused by declining unequal exchange and Western political hegemony can, in the long run, also open up fertile ground for changing the mindset of the population, from the current support of imperialism to a united struggle with the Global South for socialism based on class solidarity.

Let's take a more detailed look at the development and possibilities for resisting unequal exchange.

---

exchange of labour in the world economy. *Nature Communications*| (2024) 15:6298, Springer Nature.

The History of Resistance

The development of unequal exchange has not been without resistance from the exploited nations. Dadabhai Naoroji (1825-1917), the Indian independence activist and founding member of the Indian National Congress, was convinced that the main reason behind poverty was the colonial drain of wealth.[3] In general, colonial plunder blocked the development of the productive forces in the periphery, creating economic and political crises and recurring revolutionary uprisings, exemplified by the Russian Revolution (1917), the Mexican revolution (1910-20), and the Chinese rebellion and revolution (1900 and 1911).

Based on the superiority of its industrial production, Britain built an empire "on which the sun never set." However, Britain was already challenged economically and politically in the late nineteenth century by continental powers such as Germany and France and by the US. In the 1890s, the US overtook England as the world leader in industrial production.

However, in 1929, the Great Depression came with the Wall Street stock market crash. The US experienced what England had experienced the century before: a crisis of overproduction. The US had enjoyed the "Golden Twenties," but the market could not keep up with the acceleration of production. This ended in a financial crisis that spread like wildfire to the rest of the world.

Jawaharlal Nehru, India's first prime minister, wrote in 1934 in *Glimpses of World History*, which had originally been written to his young daughter:

> Marx said that capitalism would have to face difficulty after difficulty, crisis after crisis, till it toppled over because of its inherent want of equilibrium. It is more than sixty years since Marx wrote, and capitalism has had many crises since then. But far from ending, it has survived them and has grown more powerful, except in Russia where it exists no longer. But now, as I write, it seems to be grievously sick all over the world, and doctors shake their heads about its chances of recovery.
>
> It is said that capitalism managed to prolong its life to our day because of a factor which perhaps Marx did not fully consider. This was the exploitation of colonial empires by the industrial countries of the West. This gave fresh life and prosperity to it, at the expense, of course, of the poor countries so exploited.[4]

Following the economic policy of British economist John Maynard Keynes, the governments of the industrialized capitalist nations initiated state-sponsored

---

3 Visana, Vikram (2022) *Uncivil Liberalism: Labour, Capital and Commercial Society in Dadabhai Naoroji's Political Thought*, United Kingdom: Cambridge University Press, 2022.

4 Nehru, Jawaharlal (1934) *Glimpses of World History*, p. 548. Delhi: Oxford University Press, 1982.

infrastructure programs that increased employment and thereby buying power. Keynes saw the reason for capitalism's crisis in that demand became too low to secure full capacity utilization and employment. According to Keynes, production did not create an adequate market by itself, contrary to what Say had claimed. It was the opposite: demand determined adequate production.[5] In the US, these reforms were exemplified by President Franklin D. Roosevelt's "New Deal" of the 1930s. Similar programs were introduced in Western Europe, where social-democratic parties had risen to power. They invested in transport, housing, and social welfare, which created jobs and strengthened domestic markets. These were the first steps toward the capitalist welfare state. Keynesian policy helped solve the worst problems, but imperialism had to be updated in terms of political management and a new international division of labour in order to sustain and revitalize capitalist development.

In the mid-1930s, the inter-imperialist rivalry again became the principal contradiction in the world-system. The US economy was as big as that of Britain, Germany, France, Italy, Belgium, Russia, and Japan combined. This dominant position created contradictions for both allies and enemies. European colonialism still stood in the way of the US's global ambitions. Japan was a serious contender for the control of Southeast Asia and the Pacific region.

Germany, on its side, sought once more to become a major global power based on the strength of its industrial production. The principal contradiction during the Second World War was expressed in the "Axis Powers" (led by Germany, Japan, and Italy) fighting the "Allies" (led by the US, Britain, and the Soviet Union). This conflict affected all other contradictions worldwide. Germany intended to become Europe's strongest power and break the old colonial powers' grip on Africa and Asia. Japan intended to turn all of China, and much of the rest of the Western Pacific, into a Japanese colony. Like the First World War, the Second was a fight over control of the world's territories. As in the First World War, the fate of the colonized peoples in the Second World War was entirely in the hands of the imperialist powers. But compared to the First World War, there was much more fighting in the colonies. This played a role in the era of decolonization that followed.

As we know, Germany, Italy, and Japan lost the war. The empires of Britain, France, and the Netherlands were weakened. After two major inter-imperialist wars, the US finally managed to succeed Britain as the new hegemonic power in the world-system. The Soviet Union, however, was also a winner. The military strength it had built since the Russian Revolution proved powerful enough to

5 Keynes, John Maynard (1936) *The General Theory of Employment, Interest and Money*, Cambridge: MacMillan University Press, pp. 18–34.

overcome the German war machine. Despite the war's immense human and material costs, the Soviet Union had established itself as an important political player in the world-system.

The American World Order

With the US's hegemonic role in the world economy, the tendency towards globalization, which was already evident during the formation of the British Empire, returned with a vengeance. Capital became significantly more transnational. Following the end of the Second World War, international treaties were signed and the relevant economic, political, and military institutions were founded. Their purpose was to administer this increasingly global capitalism. The United Nations, with its Security Council and numerous subsidiaries for everything from development and culture to labor and health, was the most important. The international finance and banking system was reorganized under the Bretton Woods Agreement, which made the US dollar the "world currency" and solidified the US's leading global position. The US also established a global network of around 800 navy and air force bases in 177 countries. These allow the US government to intervene militarily almost anywhere in the world at the drop of a hat. At the end of the war, the US had demonstrated the power of its nuclear weapons in Hiroshima and Nagasaki. After the war, the US led the world's most powerful military alliance, NATO, founded in Washington, DC, in 1949. US capital demanded "free enterprise" and put pressure on the European colonial powers to give up their colonies in Asia and Africa and open them up for US capital investment. Latin America had already been treated as the US's exclusive backyard since the Monroe Doctrine in 1823. In short, from the 1950s to the 1970s, the US was the unquestioned leader of an increasingly globalized capitalism, while Canada, Western Europe, Australia/New Zealand, and Japan acted as junior partners, subject to US interests.

The contradiction between the US and the socialist bloc led by the Soviet Union increased after the Second World War. In 1949, Mao proclaimed The People's Republic of China, led by the Communist Party. That same year, the Soviet Union conducted its first nuclear tests, which strengthened the socialist bloc's geopolitical position. Essentially, the socialist bloc barred Western capitalism from roughly a third of the globe. The contradiction between the imperialist countries and the socialist bloc was also expressed in the division of Europe, the Berlin Wall, the establishment of the NATO and Warsaw Pact military alliances, the Korean War, and the so-called Cold War, with its nuclear arms race.

Finally, the contradiction between the US and the Third World increased.

This contradiction wasn't new. The US had long played an imperialist role in Central and South America, the Caribbean, and the Philippines. But with decolonization and neocolonialism, this contradiction became more pronounced. The global network of US navy and air force bases was established not only to combat communism but also to increase US influence in the Third World. However, the power shift from British to US hegemony, in combination with the change from direct colonialism to neocolonialism and the emergence of the Soviet Union as a balancing factor, opened up a window of opportunity for resistance in the periphery. Some movements were led by a national bourgeoisie, others by the petit-bourgeoisie, and some by communists representing the exploited peasants and workers. However, they were united in their demands for national sovereignty and economic development.

Iran nationalized its oil industry in 1951; Egypt took control of the Suez Canal in 1956; Iraq experienced a nationalist revolution and the nationalization of its oil industry in 1958. From Vietnam, Thailand, and the Philippines to Angola, Cuba, and Guatemala, anti-imperialist liberation movements were on the offensive. Had they been victorious, imperialism's reach would have shrunk even further than the third of the globe already lost to the socialist bloc. In other words, they had to be fought.

The Rise of the Third World

Kwame Nkrumah (1909–1972), the Ghanaian revolutionary, pan-Africanist and the first prime minister and then president of Ghana from 1957–1966, described in 1965 the political economy of neocolonialism in this way:

> The general objective [of neo-colonialism] has been mentioned: to achieve colonialism in fact while preaching independence. On the economic front, a strong factor favoring Western monopolies and acting against the developing world is inter-national capital's control of the world market, as well as of the prices of commodities bought and sold there. From 1951 to 1961, without taking oil into consideration, the general level of prices for primary products fell by 33.1 per cent, while prices of manufactured goods rose 3.5 per cent (within which, machinery and equipment prices rose 31.3 per cent). In that same decade this caused a loss to the Asian, African and Latin American countries, using 1951 prices as a basis, of some $41,400 million. In the same period, while the volume of exports from these countries rose, their earnings in foreign exchange from such exports decreased.[6]

Through the 1960s and the beginning of the 1970s, with its climax in the 1968 uprisings, a revolutionary wave washed over the world. Inspired by the

6 Nkrumah, Kwame (1965) *Neo-Colonialism, the Last Stage of Imperialism*, 'The mechanisms of neo-colonialism', pp. 187-188. London: Thomas Nelson & Sons, Ltd., 1965.

anti-imperialist victories in China, Cuba, and Algeria, and the successful resistance in Vietnam, revolutionary movements appeared in numerous countries: Laos, Cambodia, India, Nepal, Indonesia, Thailand, the Philippines, Palestine, Lebanon, South Yemen, Oman, Angola, Mozambique, Guinea-Bissau, Zimbabwe, South Africa, Namibia, Guatemala, El Salvador, Nicaragua, Brazil, Chile, Uruguay, and Mexico. In some of these countries, socialist movements came to power. In the decade from 1965-75, the principal contradiction on the world level was between imperialism, now led by the U.S., and the numerous anti-imperialist movements and progressive Third World states, which tried to build socialism.

The resistance from the periphery was also manifested in the formation of new international organizations and important gatherings. In 1955, the Indonesian city Bandung hosted the first Afro–Asian conference. Twenty-nine countries representing a total population of 1.5 billion people, 54% of the world's population, participated. China was a key organizer of the conference, which issued a declaration that opposed colonialism and neocolonialism and promoted Afro-Asian cooperation.

In 1961, drawing on the principles of the Bandung conference, the Non-Aligned Movement was formed.

The initiative came from the Yugoslav President Tito, Indian Prime Minister Jawaharlal Nehru, Ghanaian President Kwame Nkrumah, Indonesian President Sukarno, and President of the United Arab Republic Gamal Abdel Nasser. It consisted of 120 countries not aligned with either NATO or the Warsaw Pact. The purpose was summarized by Fidel Castro in 1979, then chairperson of the organization:

> As to ensure... the national independence, sovereignty, territorial integrity and security of non-aligned countries in their struggle against imperialism, colonialism, neo-colonialism racism and all forms of foreign aggression, occupation, domination, interference or hegemony as well as against great power and bloc politics.[7]

In the context of the United Nations, the Third World countries, via the General Assembly, managed to establish the United Nations Conference on Trade and Development (UNCTAD), which held its first congress in March 1964. The purpose was to promote the interests of the so-called developing countries in world trade.[8] At the conference, Che Guevara, then Minister of

7 Castro, Fidel (1979b): "Fidel Castro speech to the UN in his position as chairman of the non-aligned countries movement 12 October 1979". https://web.archive.org/web/20110611014358/http:/lanic.utexas.edu/la/cb/cuba/castro/1979/19791012.

8 UNCTAD: The organizations website is a resource of report and statistics dealing with international trade. Home|UN Trade and Development (UNCTAD)—https://unctad.org/.

Industry for Cuba, speaking on behalf of his adopted country, raised the problem of unequal exchange:

> Since the end of the last century this aggressive expansionist trend has been manifested in countless attacks on various countries on the more underdeveloped continents. Today, however, it mainly takes the form of control exercised by the developed powers over the production of and trade in raw materials in the dependent countries. In general, it is shown by the dependence of a given country on a single primary commodity, which sells only in a specific market in quantities restricted to the needs of that market. [...]
>
> These phenomena, which we have analysed in relation to Latin America, but which are valid for the whole of the dependent world, have the effect of enabling the developed powers to maintain trade conditions that lead to a deterioration in the terms of trade between the dependent countries and the developed countries.
>
> This aspect—one of the more obvious ones, which the capitalist propaganda machinery has been unable to conceal—is another of the factors that have led to the convening of this conference.
>
> The deterioration in the terms of trade is quite simple in its practical effect: the underdeveloped countries must export raw materials and primary commodities in order to import the same amount of industrial goods. The problem is particularly serious in the case of the machinery and equipment which are essential to agricultural and industrial development.
>
> We submit a short tabulation, indicating, in physical terms, the amount of primary commodities needed to import a thirty to thirty-nine horsepower tractor in the years 1955 and 1962. These figures are given merely to illustrate the problem we are considering. Obviously, there are some primary commodities for which prices have not fallen and may indeed have risen somewhat during the same period, and there may be some machinery and equipment which have not risen in relative cost as substantially as that in our example. What we give here is the general trend.
>
> We have taken several representative countries as producers of the raw materials or primary commodities mentioned. This does not mean, however, that they are the only producers of the item or that they produce nothing else.
>
> Many underdeveloped countries, on analyzing their troubles, arrive at what seems a logical conclusion. They say that the deterioration in the terms of trade is an objective fact and the underlying cause of most of their problems and is attributable to the fall in the prices of the raw materials which they export and the rise in the prices of manufactures which they import—I refer here to world market prices. [...]
>
> Treatment must be equitable, and equity, in this context, is not equality; equity is the inequality needed to enable the exploited peoples to attain an acceptable standard of living. Our task here is to lay a foundation on which a new international division of labor can be instituted by making full use of a country's entire natural resources and by raising the degree of processing of those resources until the most complex forms of manufacture can be undertaken. [...]
>
> It is inconceivable that the underdeveloped countries, which are sustaining the vast losses inflicted by the deterioration in the terms of trade and which, through the steady drain of interest payments, have richly repaid the imperialist powers for the value of their investments, should have to bear the growing burden of indebtedness and repayment, while even more rightful demands go unheeded. The Cuban delegation

> proposes that, until such time as the prices for the underdeveloped countries' exports reach a level which will reimburse them for the losses sustained over the past decade, all payments of dividends, interest, and amortization should be suspended.
>
> And the imperialists? Will they sit with their arms crossed? No!...
>
> They will try to show that the existing international division of labor is beneficial to all, and will refer to industrialization as a dangerous and excessive ambition.
>
> Lastly, they will allege that the blame for underdevelopment rests with the underdeveloped.
>
> To this we can reply that to a certain extent they are right, and they will be all the more so if we show ourselves incapable of joining together, in wholehearted determination, in a united front of victims of discrimination and exploitation.
>
> The questions we wish to ask this assembly are these: Shall we be able to carry out the task history demands of us?...
>
> The feeling of revolt will grow stronger every day among the peoples subjected to various degrees of exploitation, and they will take up arms to gain by force the rights which reason alone has not won them.
>
> This is happening today among the peoples of so-called Portuguese Guinea and Angola, who are fighting to free themselves from the colonial yoke, and with the people of South Vietnam who, weapons in hand, stand ready to shake off the yoke of imperialism and its puppets. [...]
>
> Let it be known that Cuba supports and applauds those people who, having exhausted all possibilities of a peaceful solution, have called a halt to exploitation, and that their magnificent defiance has won our militant solidarity. [9]

At the 19th General Assembly of the United Nations in New York in December 1964, Che Guevara, used the term "unequal exchange" explicitly. Maybe he had read Arghiri Emmanuel's article 'El Intercambio Desigual' introducing the concept in the Cuban journal *Revue Economica*, published in Havana in February 1964.[10]

> Furthermore, we state once more that the scars left by colonialism that impede the development of the peoples are expressed not only in political relations. The so-called deterioration of the terms of trade is nothing but the result of the unequal exchange between countries producing raw materials and industrial countries, which dominate markets and impose the illusory justice of equal exchange of values.
>
> So long as the economically dependent people do not free themselves from the capitalist markets and, in a firm bloc with the socialist countries, impose new relations between the exploited and the exploiters, there will be no solid economic development. In certain cases, there will be retrogression, in which the weak countries will fall under the political domination of the imperialists and colonialists.[11]

---

9 Guevara, Che (1964) Speech delivered March 25, 1964 at the plenary session of the United Nations Conference on Trade and Development (UNCTAD).

10 Emmanuel, Arghiri (1964) El Intercambio Desigual, in *Revue Economica*, Havana, February, 1964.

The Tricontinental Conference

On the more radical political front, the revolutionary first president of Algeria, Ahmed Ben Bella, planned to hold an Afro-Asian solidarity conference in Algiers in 1965. This, however, was prevented due to his overthrow and the bombing of the meeting hall. But this did not stop the effort to hold the meeting. Mehdi Ben Barka, an exiled Moroccan opposition leader, instead took charge of organizing the event and inviting guests. He first chose to host the conference in Geneva. However, while organizing, Ben Barka was abducted in October 1965 in Paris by French intelligence services, who handed him over to the Moroccan intelligence services, and no one has seen him since.[12] Following Ben Barka's abduction, the location of the conference was moved to Cuba.[13]

The conference was held on January 3-16, 1966, in Havana, and was attended by roughly 500 delegates from 82 countries. At the conference, the Organization of Solidarity with the People of Asia, Africa and Latin America (OSPAAAL) was founded.[14] Among the attendees were Amilcar Cabral, who from 1963 until his assassination in 1973 led the guerrilla struggle of The African Party for the Independence of Guinea and Cape Verde (PAIGC) against Portuguese colonialism in Guinea-Bissau; Nguyen Van Tien, the representative of the National Liberation Front of South Vietnam; Salvador Allende, later president of Chile; and Fidel Castro, the Prime Minister of Cuba. Che Guevara was absent, fighting in Bolivia at the time, but he sent a "Message to the Tricontinental," which he wrote just before leaving for Bolivia:

> "Create two, three [...] many Vietnams," that is the watchword: In Asia, as we have seen, the situation is explosive, and Vietnam and Laos, where the struggle is now going on, are not the only points of friction. The same holds true for Cambodia, where at any moment the United States might launch a direct attack. We should add Thailand, Malaysia, and, of course, Indonesia, where we cannot believe that the final word has been spoken despite the annihilation of the Communist Party of that country after the reactionaries took power. And, of course, the Middle East.
>
> In Latin America, the struggle is going on arms in hand in Guatemala, Colombia, Venezuela, and Bolivia, and the first outbreaks are already beginning in Brazil. Other centers of resistance have appeared and been extinguished. But almost all the countries

---

11 Guevara, Che (1964) Speech at 19th General Assembly of the United Nations in New York, December 11, 1964, in *The Che Reader*, Ocean Press, New York 2005.

12 "The Tri-Continental Conference and the Ben Barka Affair". *NACLA*.

13 Young, Robert J.C. (2018). *Disseminating the Tricontinental*, pp. 517–547. London: Routledge, 2018.

14 Ibid.

of this continent are ripe for a struggle of the kind that, to be triumphant, cannot settle for anything less than the establishment of a government of a socialist nature [...][15]

In addition to national liberation, the delegates also debated models of economic development and discussed how to delink from the economic exploitation by the rich countries in order to build socialism. The conference envisioned a new economic policy that saw the Third World as one entity characterized by cooperation and solidarity in that task.

Cuba stands out as an example of the spirit of the Tricontinental Conference, not only in words—but more importantly, in praxis. Having just carried out a successful revolutionary struggle in 1959, Cuba supported the anti-imperialist struggles in Algeria, the Congo, and Bolivia through the participation of its best cadres in the direct struggle, as part of the *"Create two, three* [...] *many Vietnams"* strategy. Cuba was true to this political line, even in hard times, and Cuba's efforts made a difference. It was the Cuban military assistance to Angola, beginning in 1976, which pushed back South African invasions of Angola, helping secure Namibia's independence. It was the defeat of the South African army by Cuban and Angolan forces at Cuito Cuanavale in Southern Angola, in 1988, which led to the end of the Apartheid regime.

Demand for a New International Economic World Order

The idea of a New International Economic World Order (NIEO) was proposed at the Tricontinental Conference. A central point was the demand for higher prices for raw materials and other goods exported from the Third World.[16] In the 1970s and 1980s, UNCTAD, the Group of 77, and the Non-Aligned Movement built on the values and priorities established during the Tricontinental Conference and promoted by Cuba. In 1973, Fidel Castro said in a speech:

> Another very serious problem confronted by underdeveloped countries is the problem of unequal trade. This is based on the fact that the products of the industrialized world are increasingly more expensive [...] Any of those things cost double what they did 10 years ago—above all, the equipment and plants. Yet the products of the underdeveloped world, generally raw materials, or some farm products are worth less and less every year. [...]
>
> This is brought up in all international conferences, in all the UN organizations [...] Thus the world faces the problem of ever-larger indebtedness, pressing conditions, develop-

---

15 Guevara, Che (1966) 'Message to the Tricontinental', in: Ernesto 'Che' Guevara: *On Socialism and Internationalism*, page 39. New Delhi: Left Word Books, 2020.

16 Stanley, Issac (2019) *Dreaming Revolution: Tricontinentalism, Anti-Imperialism and Third World Rebellion*, p. 163. London: Routledge, 2019.

> ment credits with short-terms, high interests, and harsh conditions, and finally, unequal trading. This means a higher cost for products of industrialized countries, and lower cost for products of underdeveloped countries.[17]

On October 12, 1979, Fidel Castro addressed the 34th UN General Assembly as the chairperson of the Non-Aligned countries:

> We have expressed our grave concern over the insignificant progress of the negotiations dealing with the implementation of the declaration and the action program on the establishment of an international economic order. We pointed out that this was due to the lack of political desire by most of the developed countries, and we expressly censured the delaying diversionist and divisive tactics adopted by those countries. The failure of the Fifth UNCTAD session demonstrated this situation.
>
> We confirm that unequal trade in international economic relations, denounced as an essential characteristic of the system, has become even more unequal. While the prices of manufactured goods, capital goods, food products and services which we import from the developed countries constantly increase, the prices of the raw materials which we export are stagnant and are subject to constant fluctuations. Trade relations have worsened.[18]

In spite of all these efforts, the demand for a "New World Order" was in vain. National liberation proved much easier to obtain than ending imperialist exploitation. Delinking from the exploitation of global capitalism is a difficult and complex process.

The anti-colonial movements were well aware that the struggle to develop the forces of production was a necessary continuation of national liberation towards socialism. Following the Algerian revolution's military victory, the key question became the production front. In a speech on December 23, 1964, in Algeria, Che Guevara said:

> This is a time for construction, something much more difficult, and seemingly less heroic, but demanding all the nation's forces [...] It is necessary to work, because at times like these that is the best way of struggling [...] Fatherland or death[19]

Echoing Che in 2006, the Vice President of Bolivia, Garcia Linera, launched the slogan "industrialization or death."[20] While the Cuban "fatherland or death" expresses the identity, in specific circumstances, of the class and

---

17 Castro, Fidel (1973) Speech by Fidel Castro, 4th of January 1973. Latin American Network Information Center.

18 Castro, Fidel (1979a) Speech delivered at the 34th Session of the United Nations General Assembly, in New York City, 12, October 1979.

19 Guevara, Che (1964). Remarks in Algeria to Jeunesse, December 23, 1964, Published in *Revolución*, December 26, 1964. Here from, Losurdo, Domenico (2016) *Class Struggle. A Political and Philosophical History*, p. 188. New York: Palgrave Macmillan, 2016.

20 Stefanoni, Pablo (2006). 'Bolivia a due dimensioni', *Il Manifesto*, 22 July 2006.

national struggle, "industrialization or death" expresses the idea that political independence proves illusory if not sustained by economic independence, by the development of the productive forces.[21]

The conditions for moving from national liberation towards economic liberation were even more difficult for the relatively small Third World countries than for huge countries like Russia and China. They had only been semi-colonialized and had more diverse economic foundations, and land reforms and a planned economy made it possible to create more viable transitional economies and mount a defence against hostile imperialist encirclement.

However, the most important barrier to a transition towards socialism was the century old polarizing dynamic caused by the unequal exchange on the world market. Raw materials and agricultural products, produced by low-wage labor in the Third World, were exchanged for industrial products produced by relatively high wage labor in the imperialist center. The newborn Third World states did not have the power to change this dynamic. They could not simply increase wages, and thereby the prices of the raw materials and agricultural products they supplied to the world market, which was dominated by Western monopolies. Without the essential development and diversity of the productive forces to allow delinking from the world market and production mainly for the domestic market in the interest of the workers and peasants, Third World states risked throwing their economies into ruin. They had inherited the economic structures established by their colonial oppressors, and simple political independence was not designed to serve their economic interests. They were stuck with monocultures and industries that rarely engaged in the refining and processing of raw materials.

Unlike their Western colonial predecessors, they could not just transfer the costs of industrialization and the establishment of welfare systems to other nations, and most were therefore caught in the "development trap," leading to ubiquitous foreign debt defaults to Western imperialists, and remaining in or reverting back to an exploited position in the hierarchy of global capitalism.

The capitalist mode of production was born and developed as a more and more globalized accumulation process. The international division of labor, the structure of production and consumption patterns in the periphery and the center, and the transfer of value within the system: all of these are necessary for capitalism to function on the world level.

The global accumulation process affects the specific economic develop-

21 Losurdo, Domenico (2016) *Class Struggle. A Political and Philosophical History*, pp. 319-320. New York: Palgrave Macmillan, 2016.

ment in each and every country in a center-periphery structured world-system—each country is subjugated to play a certain role to make the system function.

The periphery was, from the earliest stages of colonialism, placed in a role that fulfilled the needs of the center's accumulation, which blocked the development of Third World countries' productive forces and distorted their economies. This, in turn, made the economies in the center vital, further developing their productive forces. So long as the capitalist accumulation process continues smoothly on the global level, so long will its ruling class and the hegemonic power dominate the world-system, economically and politically.

In such a world-system, the Third World countries could not just break loose from the domination of the center. They had to diversify and develop their productive forces in order to fulfil the needs of their people, by importing technology. In order to do that, they had to interact with the global market. The revolutionary spirit alone was not enough to jump into a socialist mode of production. The best they could achieve was to establish some kind of transitional mode of production. To accomplish this, they had to establish and defend a state able to direct this process, and even that proved difficult in a world-system politically and militarily dominated by the US. To try to counter this pressure, they could cooperate with Third World countries in the same position and the bloc of "actually existing socialist" countries (I would rather use the term "transitional states"). However, even the transitional states were in a difficult position at the time. Already in the 1980s, the Soviet Union was forced to scale down assistance to Third World countries due to its own socioeconomic problems. The Soviet Union was caught up in an arms race which drained its resources, preventing their use elsewhere. The development of the productive forces of both the Soviet Union and the People's Republic of China was trailing behind the West, putting them under pressure on all fronts. Credits from the US-led World Bank and IMF became the last resort for countries in debt crisis. The countries of the Third World were subject to the conditions set by these institutions and had to accept structural adjustment reforms required by the World Bank and International Monetary Fund.

Hence, states seeking to develop a socialist mode of production had to defend themself, while at the same time try to develop the productive forces. To accomplish this task, Third World states have pursued a multiplicity of strategies, sometimes interacting with the capitalist system, and at other times, pursuing a strategy for a world revolution. As a result, some transitional states have been forced into isolation. Notwithstanding their socialist aspirations, political independence in most cases led to capitalist "developmentalist economics" by the end of the 20th century.

It is easy to conclude that this was inevitable and that the anticolonial movements should have foreseen the impending disaster. But they had little choice. Seizing state power was necessary to, at a minimum, change the balance of power in international relations. Up until the mid-1970s, global capitalism was actually under pressure. The struggle against colonialism and imperialism grew stronger as US neocolonialism penetrated the Third World, gradually replacing the old colonial powers. This contradiction, of imperialism versus anti-imperialism, interacted with the confrontation between the US and the bloc of transitional states.

Learning from Arghiri Emmanuel

Meeting Emmanuel in the late '70s and the beginning of the '80s, the anti-imperialist group I was a member of was ignited by the revolutionary spirit, hoping that the national liberation struggles would continue into an economic anti-imperialism and building socialist states in the Third World. This was also what we heard when we talked with cadres in the liberation movements that we supported in Africa, the Middle East, and Latin America. They were committed communists, waiting to take the next step in the struggle.

Emmanuel was less optimistic and was skeptical about such a project in the short run. The political and economic power of imperialism was too strong. Global capitalism was still a dynamic force developing the productive forces and dominating the world market. The newly liberated Third World states had first to develop their productive forces before they could take the first steps towards a socialist mode of production. To do this, they had to interact with the surrounding global capitalism in order to acquire the necessary technology, while also maintaining their political command in this transition period.

This stand was built on practical experience. Emmanuel had lived in the Belgian Congo from 1937-1941 and again from 1946-1960, working in a trading company and later managing construction work. He knew how the colonial economy functioned. In his last years in the Congo, Emmanuel was economic adviser for the elected president Patrice Lumumba. He advised Lumumba to not try to jump into a socialist mode production but first break the political power of the Belgian settlers in order to secure a state that served the interest of the poor—that is, the native Congolese population. In terms of the economy, his advice was to interact with both the "transitional states" and the capitalist world in order to get the knowledge and technology required to develop and diversify the productive forces of the Congo. When Emmanuel wrote that transnational companies could play a positive role in such a transition process, it was not because they are altruistic but because their investments for profit also implied a transfer of technology to a poor, underdeveloped country. Our anti-imperialist group was also at odds with this advice, as transnational capital symbolized the evils of imperialist exploitation, in our rather simplified and un-dialectical analysis of political economy.

Emmanuel was right and we were wrong. We did not have practical experience with economics in a Third World context, and our analysis of the balance of power between the forces of imperialism and that of socialism was far too optimistic. We thought that liberation with a socialist perspective would continue to gain strength and develop from national to economic liberation from the imperialist core. We underestimated the problems with changing the mode of production in a world dominated by capitalist economies. We underestimated the potential of development of global capitalism. We did not foresee the development of neoliberal globalization.

As it happened, the new global wave which came into being was not a world socialist revolution, but one of neoliberal globalization. Capitalism still had options for expansion—a new "spatial fix" in the international division of labor.

The "New International Economic World Order" came to nothing. The G77, the Non-Aligned Movement, and the UN-system were blunt in this regard. Formulated in the language of historical materialism, the overarching factor that ended the revolutionary wave of the long sixties, the shortcoming of the "transitional states" in both the Soviet and Chinese versions and in the new states in the Third World, was the inability to develop their productive forces to a sufficient degree and to break the dominance of the global capitalist market forces. Consequently, the neoliberal counter-offensive was able to achieve what the U. military could not in Vietnam—placing the Third World on its knees in the last decades of the 20th century.

The Rise and Fall of Neoliberalism

In the past fifty years, the economic geography of the world has changed in both the localization of productive activities, especially manufacturing, and in the size and composition of the flows of goods and services between countries and in global production chains, which is happening as never before in the history of capitalism. The outsourcing of hundreds of millions of industrial workplaces from the Global North to low wage countries in the South, made possible by new communications, computer, and logicists technologies, has completely changed the international division of labor. The effect on the "unequal exchange mechanism" has been both quantitative and qualitative. The size of the value transfer increased rapidly. The estimated size of unequal exchange in the late 1960s and '70s was around 300 billion dollars per year. In 1995, it is estimated to have been 1,750 billion, and in 2021 Hickey estimated it to 18,500 billion dollars. For the period 1995-2021, the estimate is 330,000 billion dollars in total.[22] From the time when Emmanuel wrote his book until today, unequal exchange has grown from 300 to 18,500 billion dollars per year—that is, by a factor of 6.

On the qualitative side, the industrialization of the Global South, based on exports to the consumer markets in the Global North, changed the dynamics of development in the capitalist world-system. The industrialization of a specific country was no longer dependent on having its own national consumption power. The geographical distance between production sites and consumption sites became less important. Production could take place where the factors were most favorable, and improved logistics in terms of shipping time and cost made the distance to the market less relevant.

The development of the productive forces also made possible the globalization of the production process itself. Each component could be produced where the conditions were optimal, and the assembly of the final commodity could take place in different locations near to, or indeed far from, the consumer. This changed global trade patterns. It was no longer only finished commodities being traded, but more and more subcomponents within and between firms. And, most importantly, unequal exchange was no longer based on the trade of raw materials, agricultural products, and low-end industrial products from the South against high-end industrial products from the North. The Global South became the site of industrial production in general, from shoes and T-shirts to advanced electronics and high-speed trains.

These changes in the accumulation process of global capitalism have had huge consequences for geopolitical developments. In the first phase of neoliberal globalization, from the late '70s until the millennium, transnational capital was on the offensive, and the US emerged as the hegemonic power in the world-system. It was superior in all aspects: economy, politics, military, and culture. The only former rival—the Soviet Union—was dissolved by neoliberal economics, which also penetrated deep into the Chinese economy, as it did into every country in the Global South through the demands for "structural adjustments" by the representatives of global capitalism.

However, it was not "the end of history." By the turn of the millennium,

22 See chapter 5.

the negative social consequences of neoliberalism began to weaken the political dominance of its institutions. The financial crisis of 2007-08 further strengthened the demand for state control of capital. The balance in the neoliberal contradiction tipped towards nationalism and the nation-state. China avoided severe consequences from the financial crisis primarily because its banking system was state-owned and not an integrated part of the global financial house of cards that had collapsed. China also quickly expanded investments in the state-owned sector to replace a flailing private capitalist sector. The financial crisis was a wake-up call to the Chinese leadership. Neoliberalism was no longer a dynamic force to develop the productive forces but was increasingly a problem in the form of economic stagnation, social inequality, and environmental problems. China began to shift the cycle of capital accumulation from being focused on the world market to more emphasis on domestic circulation, by tripling the wage level and through massive state programs for internal investment that have pulled hundreds of millions out of poverty in the countryside. After its encounter with neoliberalism, China emerged as a major economic power. China was able, for the first time in two hundred years, to break the polarizing dynamic of capitalism between the center and the periphery. It is a historical break of significant and decisive size. A nation of 1.4 billion people made the change from being one of the poorest countries on earth in 1949 to the leading industrial power in the world-system, with 35% of the world's gross production, compared with the US 12%.[23] The consequence was an increasing discordance between global capitalism and China's national project of development.

The inclusion of China in neoliberal globalization enabled an unintended stimulation of China's transitional mode of production, allowing it to become competitive, and even to surpass the hegemonic capitalist accumulation in some respects. Despite its integration into the neoliberal world-system since 1978, China has been able to break the spell of polarization and dependent industrialization by maintaining strong state capacity and planning instruments—all through the political governance of the Communist Party.

The South African Example

This was not the case in most of the countries of the Global South. The development in South Africa is an example. The African National Congress (ANC) became a leading movement in the struggle against the White settler regime up

23 Baldwin, Richard (2024). 'China is the world's sole manufacturing superpower: A line sketch of the rise.', *VoxEU*, 17 Jan 2024.

through the 1960s and 1970s. Most of the factors identified as being necessary for a revolution to succeed were present in South Africa: a dependent economy, a repressive state, and a well-developed culture of resistance. The ANC was ideologically closely connected to the South African Communist Party, which on its side was oriented towards the Soviet Union. The ANC led a struggle which was committed to socialist goals. In its Freedom Charter from 1955, the ANC spoke of visions of a society in which:

> The national wealth of our country, the heritage of South Africans, shall be restored to the people; The mineral wealth beneath the soil, the Banks and monopoly industry shall be transferred to the ownership of the people as a whole; All other industry and trade shall be controlled to assist the wellbeing of the people; All people shall have equal rights to trade where they choose, to manufacture and to enter all trades, crafts and professions.[24]

Hence, at the time, the ANC was considered a communist terrorist organization by the US. However, while the national liberation struggle in Guinea-Bissau, Mozambique, Angola, and Zimbabwe was settled in the 1970s, before the neoliberal counter-offensive, the struggle against the Apartheid regime dragged out into the '90s. The wave of anti-imperialist struggles in Africa with a socialist perspective was over. The Soviet Union and the People's Republics in Eastern Europe were being deconstructed and could not serve as strategic allies of the ANC. US hegemony was at its height. Neoliberal globalization had rolled over the Global South. In the early 1990s, there no longer was a window of opportunity for radical changes in the world-system.

Nevertheless, Mandela in January 1990 rejected reports that he had converted to capitalism. The United Democratic Front, a nationwide anti-apartheid coalition aligned with the ANC, released a one-paragraph statement from Mandela that said he wanted to clarify his stance on economic policy:

> The nationalization of the mines, banks and monopoly industries is the policy of the ANC, and a change or modification of our views in this regard is inconceivable. State control of certain sectors of the economy is unavoidable.[25]

Two years later, in January 1992, during his participation in the meeting of the World Economic Forum in Davos, Switzerland, Mandela changed his position concerning the economic policy for South Africa's future.

Tito Titus Mboweni (1959-2024), an anti-apartheid activist who left South Africa in 1980 to become ANC member in exile in Lesotho, and who had accompanied Mandela as an economic adviser in Davos, recalled what happened:

---

24 ANC (1955) The Freedom Charter.

25 *Tampa Bay Times* (1990) 'Mandela voices commitment to nationalization', *Tampa Bay Times*, 26.1.1990.

> "When we arrived in Davos, where Mr. Mandela was scheduled to speak, we were presented with a speech, prepared by some well-meaning folks at the A.N.C. office in Johannesburg that focused on 'nationalization as A.N.C. policy'," Mr. Mboweni recounted in a letter to the Sunday Independent newspaper in South Africa late last year. "We discussed this at some length and decided that the content was inappropriate for a Davos audience."
>
> "So I drafted a short message for the audience," he added. "That message was about how the A.N.C. intended to achieve social justice for the majority black people: decent housing, health care, decent education, public transport, access to clean water, sanitation and access to what I called 'the means of production', that is, the creation of a black business class. That is all. No capitulation."
>
> But as the five-day conference of high-level speed-dating wore on, Mr. Mandela soon decided he needed to reconsider his long-held views: "Madiba then had some very interesting meetings with the leaders of the Communist Parties of China and Vietnam," Mr. Mboweni wrote, using Mr. Mandela's clan name. "They told him frankly as follows: 'We are currently striving to privatize state enterprises and invite private enterprise into our economies. We are Communist Party governments, and you are a leader of a national liberation movement. Why are you talking about nationalization? It was those decisive moments which made him think about the need for our movement to seriously rethink the issue."[26]

The advice from the Chinese and Vietnamese communists were based on the difficult international situation for transitional states trying to build socialism in 1992 and their own deliberations on how to tackle neoliberal globalization.

Andrew Ross Sorkin continued the story, with a reference to Anthony Sampson.

> "They changed my views altogether," Mr. Mandela told Anthony Sampson, his friend and the author of Mandela: The Authorized Biography. "I came home to say: 'Chaps, we have to choose. We either keep nationalization and get no investment, or we modify our own attitude and get investment.'"[27]

It seems that Mandela had reached the conclusion that the prospect of turning the anti-apartheid struggle into a socialist transformation was unrealistic. The ANC's socialist convictions appeared outdated. What could be achieved at the time was to break the power of the White settler regime and dismantle the formal apartheid laws. The problem with Mandela's changed position was that the ANC was not a party with the qualities of the Chinese Communist Party. Mandela and the ANC did not manage to establish a transitional state, with the instruments capable of taming neoliberal globalization to the benefit of the South African workers and peasants. Instead, they had to conform to

---

26 Sorkin, Andrew Ross (2013) 'How Mandela Shifted Views on Freedom of Markets', *The New York Times*, December 9, 2013.

27 Ibid.

the demands of structural adjustment programs and embrace liberal democracy, which makes a virtue of not interfering with capitalist economics. This was what made the former terrorist Mandela a celebrated freedom fighter in the West.

Nelson Mandela won a triumphant victory in the first post-apartheid elections in 1994. The ANC became the ruling party, and Mandela became president. Titus Mboweni became Minister of Labour in Mandela's cabinet from 1994 to July 1998, then director of the South African Reserve Bank in 1999, and again Minister of Finance in 2018-21. In these positions, he facilitated the implementation of neoliberal economics in South Africa. There was no land reform, the mines were not nationalized, and so forth. Instead, water, electricity, and public transit were privatized. Popular uprisings and strikes were often violently crushed by the police. Only Mandela's prestige and the legacy of the anti-apartheid struggle kept the ANC in power. In 2010, Mboweni became, on the side of his government duties, an international adviser of Goldman Sachs International.[28]

Opening up to neoliberal globalization made the South African economy grow on average 3.2% annually from 1993 to 2012; however, this was far below China and even India. The income gap between White and Black South Africans has widened since the end of apartheid. While some Black South Africans have gained access to the privileges that were previously reserved for Whites, the vast majority of the Black population still lives in an informal apartheid system. Most of the land, mines, and companies remain in the possession of White South Africans. According to Bloomberg News, the average White household earns six times what a Black one does. Among young Black men, unemployment is close to 50%. Whites still hold nearly three-quarters of all management jobs.[29]

The trade unionists have become strong critics of the ANC. For example, the workers organized in the National Union of Metalworkers of South Africa (NUMSA) want to build a movement for socialism. New political organizations with a socialist orientation have been founded, such as the Economic Freedom Fighters (EFF) under the leadership of former ANC Youth League president Julius Malema, which has significant support in Black townships.

In the last election, in December 2024, the ANC lost its majority for the first time and formed a coalition government with the liberal Democratic Alliance, in opposition to the left wing of EFF and uMkonto we Sizwe Party. Sig-

28 *The Mail and Guardian* (2010) 'Tito Mboweni joins Goldman Sachs', *The Mail and Guardian*, 26.4. 2010.

29 BBC (2012) 'South Africa's census: Racial divide continuing', *BBC News*, 30.10. 2012.

nificant in the 2024 election was also that the voter turnout had dropped from 89% in the 1999 election to 58% in 2024.

The possibility for South Africa to change track and continue from national liberation to economic liberation is better today than in the situation Mandela faced in 1992. At the time, the Third World was on the defensive, and the balancing power of the Soviet Union had been dissolved. Today, the Global South is on the offensive and China is a world leader in industrial production. South-South trade is on the rise, and alternative banking and financial institutions are being built.

States in the Global South, like South Africa, despite still being intertwined in the US-led international order, are experiencing the decline, unpredictability, and the hypocrisy of Western emphasis on democracy and human values. They are drawn towards a multipolar world-system, and countries such as China, as more stable and reliable investment and trading partners.

The Emerging Multipolar World-System

What is unique in the emerging world-system is that countries from the former periphery are now taking an influential position in the global power game. To understand the contradictions of the multipolar world-system, we need to understand how these new poles came into being, as this determines their characteristics. The past continues to exist in the present. As mentioned above, first the decolonization process and then neoliberal globalization have transformed the Global South.

The change in the power structure of the world-system at the end of the Second World War, along with the transition from colonialism to neocolonialism, created a "window of opportunity" for liberation movements in what became the Third World. In Asia, India became independent in 1947, the Democratic People's Republic of Korea was founded in 1948, and the People's Republic of China was proclaimed in 1949. In Africa, Morocco and Tunisia gained independence in 1956, Ghana in 1957, Algeria in 1962, Kenya 1963, the Portuguese colonies Angola, Mozambique, Guinea-Bissau were liberated in the '70s, and so on. From the end of the Second World War and the subsequent tide of decolonization, over a hundred new nations gained independence. However, national liberation proved easier than ending imperialist exploitation. This was, on one hand, because of the lack of development of the productive forces in the Third World, and on the other because of the continuing economic, political, and military domination of the imperialist core countries, expressed through the structure of the world-system.

From the late 1970s, the capitalist offensive in the form of neoliberal globalization rolled over the Third World. The globalization of production triggered the rapid development of the productive forces, both qualitatively (computers, communications, and container transport) and quantitatively, in the form of the industrialization of Southeast Asia and Latin America, integrating hundreds of millions of new proletarians into the world economy. The globalization of production, new forms of transport logistics, and the liberalization of trade made the location of production near its market less important.

As described in preceding sections, neoliberalism gave capitalism decades of high profit for capital and cheap products for the consumers in the Global North. However, the aspects of contradictions are in constant struggle. In short, it was unavoidable that neoliberalism would encounter resistance. The rise of neoliberalism took place within the world-system of states, as an effort of transnational capital to avoid state interference and control of the movement of capital and goods. The contradiction between neoliberalism and nationalist governments reached a tipping point with the financial crisis of 2007–2008, which further strengthened the demand for a stronger state and control of capital.

With a Global South frustrated by the meagre economic results of the decolonization process and neoliberal globalization, it is no surprise that formations of South-South economic cooperation and political alliances arose and tried to counter the North-South division of the world-system. South-South trade is less unequal simply because the wage differences between Global South countries are less than between the Global North and South.

South–South Alliances

The Bolivarian Alliance for the Peoples of Our America (*Alternativa Bolivariana para los Pueblos de Nuestra América*, ALBA) was founded as an alternative to the Free Trade Area of the Americas (*Área de Libre Comercio de las Américas*, ALCA), which was the US attempt to introduce a free trade agreement for the entire Americas.[30] ALBA was initiated in 2001 by Hugo Chávez, the then president of Venezuela. It was a concrete attempt to solve the dilemma of trying to delink from the capitalist world market and being dependent on resources only available from it. ALBA was meant to make at least a partial delinking pos-

30 Hart-Landsberg, Martin (2009)' Learning from ALBA and the Bank of the South', *Monthly Review*, vol. 61, no. 4, September 2009; Hart-Landsberg, Martin (2010) 'ALBA and the Promise of Cooperative Developmen't, *Monthly Review*, vol. 62, no. 7 December 2010.

sible. It favored the expansion of the public sector, production for the domestic rather than for the world market, social benefits rather than profit, and an economy based on solidarity rather than competition. The financial crisis of 2007 made ALBA popular throughout Latin America. Venezuela and Cuba had already signed agreements for economic collaboration in 2004. Nine more countries have joined ALBA since then: Bolivia, Dominica, Ecuador, Grenada, Honduras, Nicaragua, Saint Lucia, Saint Vincent and the Grenadines, and Antigua and Barbuda (the latter renounced its membership in 2010 after a right-wing, US-backed military coup).

The member countries of ALBA are expected to exchange goods and services based on their resources and possibilities. Exchange is not meant to be according to the conditions of the world market, such as requiring payment in hard foreign currency. Venezuela, for example, delivers oil to Cuba in exchange for medicine and medical services. The countries also trade soybeans, rice, poultry, and dairy products. Steel works are built in Cuba to serve both countries. A joint shipping company is meant to strengthen cooperation within ALBA. Venezuela and Cuba have also signed treaties with Bolivia, helping the country expand its natural gas system. Cuba also provides aid to Bolivia's health and education sectors. On the Caribbean Island of Dominica, thousands of people have received eye surgery from Cuban medics who also train local doctors. In 2008, ALBA introduced its own currency, the SUCRE (*Sistema Unitario de Compensación Regional*, or "Unified System for Regional Compensation"). It was first used when Venezuela delivered rice to Cuba in 2010. Today, companies in Bolivia, Cuba, Ecuador, and Venezuela use it for their transactions within ALBA. In the long run, ALBA aims to become independent from the World Bank and the IMF, which have been responsible for implementing the neoliberal agenda across Latin America. The ALBA Bank grants low-interest loans to member countries, invests in industrial production and infrastructure, and finances schools and hospitals.

ALBA is largely financed by Venezuela's oil and promoted by its current left-leaning government. The instability of both oil prices and the political situation in the country have affected ALBA negatively. But ALBA has demonstrated that it is possible for Latin American countries to lay a foundation for common and progressive economic development. ALBA has proven that economic cooperation is possible between countries whose leaders don't necessarily share the same political ideology. Cuba, Venezuela, Bolivia, and Ecuador have governments committed to the direction of socialism. But ALBA also includes countries whose governments are social democratic and mainly aim to free themselves from US domination and free trade. The US, of course, is strongly opposed to ALBA.

Another Latin American initiative is the Bank of the South, established in 2007. Its goals are less ambitious than those of ALBA, but its reach is wider, since the bank includes the majority of South American countries. The Bank of the South was originally initiated by the governments of Venezuela and Argentina. Here, the agenda is also to achieve greater independence from the US.

BRICS

However, by far the most important initiative is BRICS, originally founded by five countries in 2009. In January 2025, the organization was enlarged, and it is now known as BRICS+, consisting of Brazil, China, Egypt, Ethiopia, India, Indonesia, Iran, the Russian Federation, South Africa, and the United Arab Emirates. The BRICS+ countries are very different geographically, socially, economically, and politically, and the aim of their collaboration is not socialism—far from it. However, they do have some things in common: they do not want to be incorporated into the global system on conditions set by the Global North; they understand that the current rules of the game do not benefit them but favor the US, Western Europe, and Japan; and they want to have a voice in decisions regarding global development. In 2014, BRICS+ founded the New Development Bank as an alternative to the IMF. As the BRICS+ countries decide to reorient their trade from North-South to South-South, they are also moving away from the dollar. They want to be able to trade in their own currencies and/or to develop a new common currency to promote more fair and easier trade, as this would reduce the losses due to the overvaluation of the US dollar exchange rate. With BRICS+ and their connected partners reaching 30% of global trade, such a shift could spark a large-scale sell off of US dollars.

Several things make BRICS+ different from previous Global South initiatives. The BRICS+ covers Asia, the Middle East, Africa, and Latin America. BRICS+ have 46% of the world's population. World Bank figures show that in 1994, the G7 countries (Canada, France, Germany, Italy, Japan, the UK, and the US) constituted 45.3% of world output, compared with 18.9% of world output in the BRICS+ countries. In 2025, the tables have turned: the BRICS+ now generates 36% of global GDP (PPP), while the G7 countries produce 29.3% of global GDP.[31]

31 World Bank (2025) GDP (ppp) (current international $) Data (Washington, DC: World Bank, 2024, 2025.

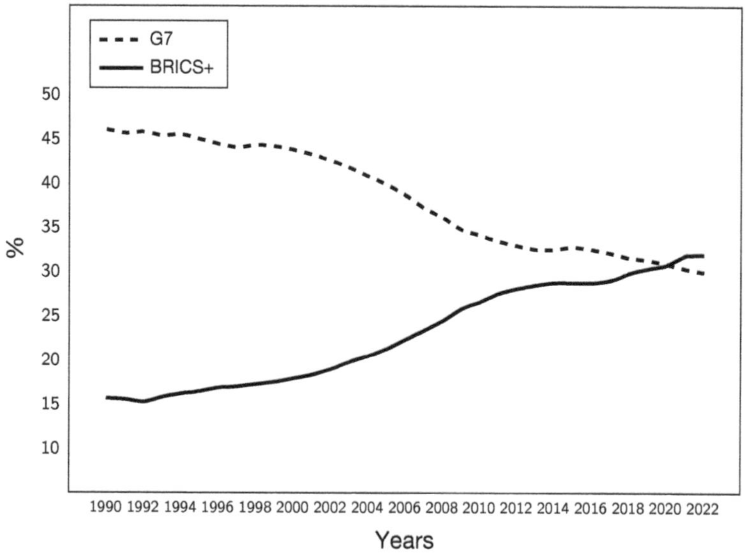

Figure VIII BRICS+ GDP (PPP) in world economy as from 1990 to 2022[32]

BRICS+ may not have the distinct socialist anti-imperialist spirit of the Tricontinental Movement, but it has the economic capacity to break loose from US-led imperialism and to build an alternative. This is backed by China's position as the world's leading industrial producer in both quantitative and qualitative terms, which is also very different from how the Soviet Union had been in the '70s, always lagging behind the West.

The Principal Contradiction

The principal contradiction in the era of neoliberalism was between transnational capital's globalization of production in the framework of a unipolar US-led world-system, as one aspect, and the national state, both in the Global North and South, attempting to regain control over economic development under the leadership of nationalist parties, ranging from conservatives and populist right- and left-wing parties to communists, in the remaining transitional states, as the other aspect. These two aspects have been transformed and concentrated into the current principal contradiction between declining US hegemony versus the

32 Duric, Ivan; Glauben, Thomas (2024). "BRICS: World Heavyweight in Agricultural Trade". Intereconomics. 2024, no. 3 page 160–166.

rise of China and an emerging multipolar world-system. This change was generated by the shift in the economic balance in the world-system as the result of forty years of neoliberal globalization.

Since the political leadership of transnational capital—the US—realized that it could no longer dominate the world-system by neoliberal economic means, it has refocussed its energies on geopolitical struggle by political and military means. The other aspect is the national states in the Global South, headed by China, united in the rejection of US hegemony, whatever the method.

As multipolarity gains strength, so does the resistance from the US, hence the increasing aggression of NATO and the trade wars and sanctions. The current war in Ukraine and Israel's war on Palestine are driven by the US's need to maintain control over both Europe and West Asia, and the corridors between Asia and the West. The US is still the dominant aspect in the principal contradiction, but China and multipolarity is the offensive aspect. China has plans and visions for the future, while US hegemony is increasingly struggling with economic and political crises.

The struggle between the aspects, together with a complex pattern of economic and political local contradictions in both aspects of the principal contradiction, constantly change the balance between the aspects. Each regional, national, and local struggle has to be seen in this pattern of contradictions. All political struggles in the world-system must take the conflict between declining US hegemony and the development of multipolarity into account when developing their strategy. Let's take a closer look at the two aspects.

The Decline of US Hegemony

The loss of economic superiority in terms of industrial production and world trade, and a weakening position in global finance, has changed US economic policy from promoting neoliberal globalization to the increasingly prevalent use of economic blockades, sanctions, and tariffs as a weapon in a geopolitical struggle to regain dominance. According to *The Washington Post*, the U.S. has imposed sanctions targeting a third of all nations with some kind of financial penalty.[33] On top of this, in April 2025 the US launched a global trade war. Through these policies, it is eroding the world market and the trust in dollars as world currency, both of which the US has relied on for the past century. The erosion of the world market is also hitting its partners in the imperial triad, the E.U and Japan,

33 *Washington Post* (2024), 'How four U.S. presidents unleashed economic warfare across the globe', (25 July 2024).

causing conflicts in their alliances. Through this tariff regime and through sanctioning so many countries, the US has convinced an increasing number of states to seek alternative economic and financial structures to the ones governed by the US.

Add to all this the political crisis in the US itself that splits the economic and political elite and cuts through the population. Trump's second presidency will accelerate the decline of US hegemony. The industrial-military-complex, the agricultural business, and the coal and oil industries support the Republican slogan "Make America Great Again" and its resultant policy of geopolitical confrontation. The tech giants, Google, Apple, and Amazon, and the electronics and automotive industries all wish for a return to neoliberal globalization, under the leadership of the US. However, you cannot turn back time. The Global South will not accept such an agenda. What unites the two political factions in the US is that they both want and need regime change in China and Russia to implement their plans.

The turn from neoliberal globalization to geopolitical confrontation has strengthened the military-industrial complex. US military spending is mainly paid for by printing dollars and issuing treasury bonds, but these are not as attractive as they once were. Add to this the BRICS+ policy of "de-dollarization" of global trade. The two pillars of US hegemony, which mutually support each other—military force and the dollar as world currency—are unstable.

The US uses the position of the dollar as world money to extract approximately one trillion dollars per year from the rest of the world.[34] For the global South, de-dollarization is a strategic goal, as the US has weaponized its financial domination based on the dollar. De-dollarization happens on two fronts: the use of dollars for payment in international trade and de-dollarization of bank reserves, investment and other financial transactions. World trade amounted to 23.8 trillion dollars in 2023, according to the World Trade Organization.[35] The vast majority of capital flows are financial, into and out of bonds, stocks, and the foreign exchange market. It must come to hundreds of trillions of dollars yearly.[36]

In October 2024, BRICS+ released a plan to transform the international monetary and financial system and challenge the dominance of the US dollar. It involves the creation of a BRICS Cross-Border Payment Initiative (BCBPI), in which members of the organization will use their national currencies to

34 Ross, John (2024) "What is the realistic strategy for "de-dollarisation"?", *MR Online*.

35 World Trade Organisation, WTO Stats.

36 Bank for International Settlements, 'OTC derivatives statistics at end-June 2023'.

trade. BRICS will likewise establish an alternative to the SWIFT system of interbank communication, which currently is overseen by the US and subject to weaponization. The intention is to not only de-dollarize trade but also to encourage investment in BRICS+ members and developing economies to be denominated in national currencies.[37]

De-dollarization is already unfolding in various countries' central bank reserves, where the share of dollars has slid to a two-decade low. China continues to sell US Treasury bonds, accumulated in the past decades of neoliberal globalization, in an effort to diversify its reserves and no longer rely on the US.

De-dollarization is most visible in commodity markets, where a large and growing proportion of energy is being priced in non-dollar-denominated contracts. Trade settlement in CNY is gaining ground outside of oil. too. The de-dollarization trend in the commodity trade is a boon for countries like India, China, Brazil, Thailand, and Indonesia, which can now not only buy oil at a discount but can also pay for it with their own local currencies. This reduces the need to maintain precautionary reserves of US dollars.[38]

It's no surprise that Trump has threatened BRICS+ with 100% extra tariffs if they try to de-dollarize or challenge the hegemony of the dollar as world money.[39] The Bank of China has been selling out its US Treasury securities in the past years. The total amount of US debt held by China has fallen to the lowest level as a percentage of GDP since China joined the World Trade Organization in 2001.

The US allies in the EU are increasingly being dragged into confrontation with the leading BRICS+ countries: Russia and China. At the end of the "Cold War," Germany and France began to cooperate with Russia, importing increasing amounts of energy and raw materials. The Nord Stream pipelines through the Baltic Sea supplied Europe with Russian gas, and the EU invested in industrial production in Russia. Trade and investment with China also expanded up until the Ukraine war, strengthening an independent EU position in the world-system. However, the turn in US policy from neoliberal globalization towards geopolitical confrontation changed all that. The US proxy war with Russia on Ukrainian soil disciplined the EU firmly back in the NATO fold. To be a dependable NATO partner, you are required to buy into the full tranche of US

37 Saaida, Mohammed (2024) 'BRICS Plus: de-dollarization and global power shifts in new economic landscape'.

38 J.P. Morgan, 'De-dollarization: Is the US dollar losing its dominance?'

39 Norton, Ben (2024) 'Trump threatens to punish de-dollarization: "I would not allow countries to go off the dollar"', *Geopolitical Economic Report*.

policy, including confrontation with China, support for Israel in the Middle East, and so on. After slavishly following orders from the US, NATO allies are repeatedly humiliated, for example by Trump going solo in negotiations with Russia. Furthermore, the US's various disruptions of the global market disproportionately impact the EU economies. Despite this, the EU, Japan, Australia, and New Zealand are clinging to the US, as they think it will preserve their position in the world-system; however, they will be dragged down by the descent of US hegemony.

The Rise of China

The other aspect in the principal contradiction is the rise of China, breaking two hundred years of imperialist value-transfer which has polarized the world-system. China's anti-imperialist struggle resulted in the formation of a socialist transitional state in 1949, which managed to survive both the Cold War and the offensive of neoliberalism. By keeping its state intact and thereby securing its institutions from neoliberal globalization, its engagement with the neoliberal world-system did not lead to renewed dependency on the capitalist center but instead to the development of its productive forces, enhancing the development of "socialism with Chinese characteristics." The size of China in terms of production, the development of advanced productive forces, and global trade make it the main driving force in the process of multipolarity. Multipolarity is not just an adjustment in the relations between the world powers. All the countries which constitute the new multipolarity belong to what was previously called the Third World—now the Global South. It can be seen as a revival of old organizations such as the Pan African Union, the Community of Latin American and Caribbean States, ALBA, and the G77, continuing through the formation of new ones, such as BRICS+. This creates multiple centers, depriving the current imperialist bloc of its power to determine the fate of the rest of the world.

The profile of the Global South is influenced by the political and economic history of the past century, first by the decolonization process and then by neoliberal globalization. The capitalist mode of production was still vital, and in the difficult last quarter of the 20th century, with the US as the hegemonic power, the Global South nations were sliding back into capitalism, engulfed in economic and political crises, sometimes dragged down by imperialist military intervention or civil war. This is the story of the Middle Eastern countries. Frustrated by the inability to develop a form of socialism, to solve the social problems, other political trends like political Islam became influential, for example in Algeria, Iraq, Syria, Iran, Afghanistan, South Yemen, and Palestine. This frustration over the inability to build socialism was also the case in the former Portuguese colonies in Africa: Angola, Mozambique, and Guinea-Bissau. The anti-apartheid struggle in South Africa also ended up in neoliberal capitalism.

However, the development of neoliberalism is a dialectical process. Transnational capital's globalization of production and consumption created a resistance against the consequences of neoliberalism in the form of different kinds of nationalism, longing for a strong state as a bulwark against the market forces. The turn in Russia from Yeltsin's capitulation to neoliberalism to the conservative nationalist policy of Putin's oligarchy capitalism is one example, and Modi's Hindutva nationalism in India is another. The trend of conservative national capitalism is widespread in the Global South: Turkey, Egypt, Iran, Saudi Arabia, and the Gulf states. Some, like India and Turkey, are trying to gain by balancing between the West, led by the US, and the new emerging multipolarity. In Latin America, we are seeing shifting left- and right-wing populist national regimes trying to cope with the challenges from capitalist globalization. With the economic and political history of the latter half of the 20th century in mind, it is no wonder that organizations—like BRICS+—which constitute the new multipolarity also have these conservative and populist trends.

The pursuit of individual goals creates friction within BRICS+. However, they are united in the effort to end the century-long dominance of the West. BRICS+ is not anti-capitalist. All members, except China, are explicitly capitalist, and even in China, capitalism still plays a role. Neither is BRICS+ anti-imperialist in the strict sense, but it is aiming to diminish the power of current US imperialism in the world-system. In that sense, the multipolar world-system is a step in the right direction, towards a more economically and politically equal world-order in which there is more space for the development of socialism, both by social movements in the capitalist states and by the transitional states. A multipolar world-system has the potential to take the next steps in a socialist direction, not least because it is driven by a huge, economically and politically influential transitional state: China.

Multipolarity is no wonderland, and the next steps will not come by themselves. As the crises of capitalism develop, it will also have an impact on capitalist states in the multipolar aspect of the principal contradiction. Capitalism will become increasingly irrational and even destructive. As it does not generate development, the capitalist states in the Global South will look for alternatives, and here China can be an example on how to handle the economic crises by expanding the role of the public sector to the benefit of common people. China used the dynamics of capitalism to develop its productive forces during the "Reform and Opening Up" period from 1978 by controlling the forces of capital. However, as capitalism lost its vitality, generating inequalities, dissolving social cohesion, and becoming increasingly unsustainable in relation to nature, its role had to be limited. This has become particularly evident since the 2007/8 financial crisis, after which some trends within "Reform and Opening Up" were modified to suit the change in global circumstances. The current "market socialism" is one more stepping stone crossing the river on the long transition towards socialism. The average rate of profit in the capitalist sector of the Chinese economy has fallen from 26% in 2007 to 13% in 2023, and, in parallel, net private investment as a share of gross domestic product has fallen from 23% in 2010 to 14% in 2023.[40] As the rate of profit in the capitalist sector has fallen, causing its investments in production to fall, we see an increase in investments in state-owned enterprises and in the public service sector in order to maintain overall demand and keep the economy in balance. This will cause the share of state-owned means of production to grow and gradually come to make up the majority of society's enterprises, and thus favourable conditions will be created for China's next step towards socialism. As the general crises of capitalism are deepening in the Global South, they are already looking towards China for solutions. China, with its development of productive forces both in quantitative and qualitative terms, is able to assist this transformation. China has invested billions in infrastructure in the Global South: building roads, railroads, dams, ports, and power plants. The latest investments have focused on communications technology and renewable energy. Unlike the US, E.U countries, the World Bank, and the IMF, China has not made special political and economic conditions a requirement for its loans, investments, aid, or trade. But China cannot change the world alone. Global South countries must develop their own economies working together. Currently the contradiction between declining US hegemony and the rise of China and the development of a multipolar world-system has made the transitional state an important anti-imperialist actor—not only on its own account, but also because it provides space for socialist movements globally.

South-South collaboration is not without problems. China's industrialization has created an enormous need for raw materials, some of it provided by countries in South America, Africa, and the Middle East. This natural wealth, which has historically been exploited by the imperialist countries, is now being used for the development of the Global South. However, this development must be based on mutual agreements and egalitarian relations that will benefit both the suppliers of raw materials and the industrialized nations in BRICS+.

40 Li, M. and Wei, L. (2024) 'Surplus Absorption, Secular Stagnation, and the Transition to Socialism: Contradictions of the U.S. and the Chinese Economies since 2000', *Monthly Review* vol.76 no. 5 pp. 18–20.

Just Another Imperialist Power?

China's exploration of minerals in Africa is sometimes mentioned as proof that China is just another imperialist power in the world-system. It might be that Chinese firms' conduct in Africa is carried out on the basis of profit. But that alone does not make China an imperialist power on par with the West. The rise of China, from one of the poorest countries in the world in 1949 to the "factory of the world," has been achieved by the hard work of its peasants and workers. Studies mentioned above indicate that China's position in the world-system is still more as an "exploited" than "exploiting" country.

Part of the Western Eurocentric left has portrayed China as engaged in an imperialist rivalry with the US. This is done without empirical evidence of such an economically exploitative role, and thereby dilutes the definition of imperialism as a useful concept. Empirical studies do not reveal that China, or other BRICS+ members for that matter, are part of the global imperialist structure, with large and long-lasting value transfers from weaker/and or neighbouring economies.[41]

The argument of Chinese imperialism is made on the basis of its expanding capital exports and its military buildup in the South Chinese Sea, in the face of an encirclement by US military bases and alliances. However, it is not China but the US which has 902 military bases abroad, with some four hundred of these surrounding China itself. China does not patrol in the Mexican Gulf, and China has not carried out any overseas military interventions in its history, while the US has intervened militarily in 101 countries.[42]

Pierre Rousset, writing in *International Viewpoint*, the journal of the Fourth International, declares that China is imperialist because it occupies significant maritime space in its region, governs Hong Kong, interferes in other countries via its Belt and Road Initiative, and has been known on occasion to use debt as a means of political-economic leverage.[43]China regained Hong

---

41 Roberts, Michael (2023) '50 Years of Dependency Theory', *The Next Recession*, November 4, 2023; Carchedi, Guglielmo and l Roberts, Michael (2021) The Economics of Modern Imperialism, *Historical Materialism* vol. 29, no. 4, page 23–69, 2021.; Ricci, Andrea (2019) Unequal Exchange in the Age of Globalization, *Review of Radical Political Economics* vol. 51, no. 2, 2019.

42 Tricontinental Institute (2024) 'Hyper-Imperialism: A Decadent New Stage', *Tricontinental Institute*, January 23, 2024.

43 Rousset, Pierre (2021) 'China: A New Imperialism Emerges', *International Viewpoint*, November 18, 2021.

Kong, which had been forcefully acquired by Britain during the First Opium War. The Belt and Road Initiative consists mainly of infrastructure projects to develop South-South trade, and Chinese loans are given on better terms than the IMF, and without demands for "structural adjustment."

The prominent US professor of political economy David Harvey even thinks that the tide has turned, and China exploits the West. In a review of Prabhat and Utsa Patnaik's book, *A Theory of Imperialism*, Harvey writes:

> Those of us who think the old categories of imperialism do not work too well in these times do not deny at all the complex flows of value that expand the accumulation of wealth and power in one part of the world at the expense of another. We simply think the flows are more complicated and constantly changing direction. The historical draining of wealth from East to West for more than two centuries, for example, has largely been reversed over the last thirty years.[44]

David Harvey's logic resembles the view of the US President Donald Trump. Remy Herrera, a research analyst at the National Center for Scientific Research (CNRS) at the Sorbonne in Paris and author of several books on the political economy of China, made the following observations in an interview, when asked the question:

> Interviewer: Since Trump's presidency, the United States has been waging a trade war against China in an attempt to reduce its trade deficit with China. However, in recent years, instead of decreasing significantly, the U.S. trade deficit with China reached \$419.4 billion in 2018 and \$382.9 billion in 2022, which are the top two deficits in history. Why is this happening? Is there unequal trade between China and the U.S., as the U.S. claims?
>
> Remy Herrera: The (almost) continuous widening of the trade balance between the two countries for several decades, largely unfavourable to the United States, constituted the pretext used by Washington to launch a trade war against Beijing. According to the U.S. administration, the deficit recorded by the United States in its trade of goods and services with China would provide "proof" that President Trump was right in declaring that the Chinese are extracting from the United States "hundreds of billions of dollars every year" and injecting them into China. It is undeniable that wealth is transferred from the deficit country (the United States) to the surplus country (China). But is it that simple? Is this logic solidly founded? What "wealth" are we talking about exactly in this debate?
>
> I mean that it is not so much a question of contesting the idea that China benefits from its trade relations with the United States, but rather of questioning the "fair" nature of these exchanges. This is a question that Marxist and other heterodox theorists have been asking for a long time. Unequal exchange, which is measurable using a variety of methods, reveals that, for a given volume exchanged, the total labor time provided by workers in one economy may turn out to be higher than that of workers in the partner country, thus causing a transfer of value from the first country to the second, which

44 Patnaik, Utsa and Patnaik, Prabhat (2016) *A Theory of Imperialism,* Columbia: Columbia University Press, 2016.

> thereby appropriates the value produced by the other country. Only taking into account the transfer of international value — which corresponds to the socially necessary work time required to produce a commodity — will reflect the true redistribution of wealth carried out between the two trading countries.
>
> In a scientific study that I had the honour of carrying out with fellow Chinese professors, we were able to seriously calculate the unequal exchange between the United States and China. These calculations are carried out using several different methods but lead to very similar results. These results confirm the existence, observable over the last four decades, of an unequal exchange between the United States and China; an unequal exchange which operates in favour of the United States and at the expense of China.
>
> The labor contents integrated into the products exchanged are different in the two countries: there are many more hours of labor incorporated in the goods and services that are exported by China to the United States than there are hours of labor embodied in goods and services that are exported from the United States to China. But, over this period of four decades, we can observe a very clear reduction in unequal exchange, without the latter disappearing completely, since we calculated that, just before the appearance of the Covid-19 pandemic, in goods moving between the two countries, approximately 6.5 hours of labor of Chinese workers are in fact exchanged for one single hour of labor of workers from the United States. And, on average, over the entire 40-year period, workers in China had to work more than 121 hours to obtain, in bilateral trade with the United States, one single hour of work from U.S. workers.
>
> Unequal exchange concerns most sectors of activity, which record transfers of value directed from China to the United States. This is especially the case for the textile, clothing and leather goods sector, for furniture and other supplies, but also for the sectors of electrical equipment and machinery, air transport, wooden items, rubber and/or plastic items, chemicals, and even accounting and management consulting activities.
>
> As a consequence, there is an unequal exchange to the detriment of China which persists, but there is also an erosion of the advantage of the United States in the exchange. And it is precisely, in our opinion, because there is a deterioration of the United States advantage that the U.S. administration, under the mandate of President Donald Trump, launched this trade war. In fact, a trade war is nothing other than the organization by the State of a commercial crisis. But the cure can be worse than the disease, and this is what has happened since the United States trade deficit, after having stabilized a little, began to increase again. Clearly, this trade war was an attempt by the administration led by President Trump to curb the slow, continuous erosion of the advantage of the United States, observed for decades in trade with its emerging rival, China.[45]

Remy Herrera's studies are confirmed by Minqi Li, who calculated that in 2017, China had a net labor loss in foreign trade (calculated as the total labor embodied in its exported goods and services minus the total labor embodied in its imported goods and services) equal to forty-seven million worker years, while the United States experienced a *net labor gain* in the same year of sixty-three million worker years.[46]

---

45 Herrera, Rémy (2024) China's economic development and role in international politics in the face of U.S. hostility. Interview by Tang Xiaofu for the Observers' Network, Beijing, published in May 2024. Here from. Workers World, June 29, 2024.

Jason Hickel and Dylan Sulivan in August 2025 summed up the reasons for the renewed hostility towards China:

> But over the past two decades, wages in China have increased quite dramatically. Around 2005, the manufacturing labour cost per hour in China was lower than in India, less than $1 per hour. In the years since, China's hourly labour costs have increased to more than $8 per hour, while India's are now only about $2 per hour. [...]
>
> These are positive changes for China—and specifically for Chinese workers—but they pose a severe problem for Western capital. Higher wages in China impose a constraint on the profits of Western firms that operate there or that depend on Chinese manufacturing for intermediate parts and other key inputs.
>
> The other problem, for the core states, is that the increase in China's wages and prices is reducing its exposure to unequal exchange. During the low-wage era of the 1990s, China's export-to-import ratio with the core was extremely high. In other words, China had to export very large quantities of goods in order to obtain necessary imports. Today, this ratio is much lower, representing a dramatic improvement in China's terms of trade, substantially reducing the core's ability to appropriate value from China.
>
> Given all this, capitalists in the core states are now desperate to do something to restore their access to cheap labour and resources. One option—increasingly promoted by the Western business press—is to relocate industrial production to other parts of Asia where wages are cheaper. But this is costly in terms of lost production, the need to find new staff, and other supply chain disruptions. The other option is to force Chinese wages back down. Hence, the attempts by the United States to undermine the Chinese government and destabilise the Chinese economy—including through economic warfare and the constant threat of military escalation. [...]
>
> The West turned decisively against China in the mid-2010s, at precisely the moment when the country began to raise its prices and challenge its position as a peripheral supplier of cheap inputs to Western-dominated supply chains.
>
> The second element that's driving US hostility towards China is technology. Beijing has used industrial policy to prioritise technological development in strategic sectors over the past decade, and has achieved remarkable progress. It now has the world's largest high-speed rail network, manufactures its own commercial aircraft, leads the world on renewable energy technology and electric vehicles, and enjoys advanced medical technology, smartphone technology, microchip production, artificial intelligence, etc. The tech news coming out of China has been dizzying. These are achievements that we only expect from high-income countries, and China is doing it with almost 80 percent less GDP per capita than the average "advanced economy". It is unprecedented.
>
> This poses a problem for the core states because one of the main pillars of the imperial arrangement is that they need to maintain a monopoly over necessary technologies like capital goods, medicines, computers, aircraft and so on. This forces the "Global South" into a position of dependency, so they are forced to export large quantities of their cheapened resources in order to obtain these necessary technologies. This is what sustains the core's net-appropriation through unequal exchange.
>
> China's technological development is now breaking Western monopolies, and may give

---

46 Minqi Li, "China: Imperialism or Semi-Periphery?" *Monthly Review* vol. 73, no. 3, page 57. July–August 2021.

other developing countries alternative suppliers for necessary goods at more affordable prices. This poses a fundamental challenge to the imperial arrangement and unequal exchange.[47]

The Contradictions of the Multipolar World-system

We need to find our bearings in history. Our starting point in developing a strategy must be the principal contradiction: the decline of the US versus the rise of China and a multipolar world-system. This means bringing China back into our view of the world, to see how China's policy affects our political perspectives and practice.

Anti-imperialism today cannot be the same as it was in "the long 1960s." History does not repeat itself; it moves ahead. So, we cannot just copy and paste the old strategy and praxis. In the anti-imperialist wave from the end of the Second World War and up through the decolonization process in "the long sixties," the main "agents of transformation" were the national liberation movements, often led by communist parties and supported by the bloc of socialist transitional states. These movements managed to gain national liberation, but only a few had the strength to establish durable socialist transitional states. In the current struggle against US hegemony, the primary agent is the transitional national state, primarily China. The struggle against imperialism and for socialism in the world-system can be seen as a multi-step sequence: first the movement, which takes state power, then the establishment of a transitional state that tries to develop the productive forces necessary for the transition to socialism, while struggling for survival in a world-system dominated by US hegemony.

In that effort, the transitional state seeks allied states opposed to Western dominance. One can see an analogy between China's policy of "New Democracy" in 1949, uniting "the working class, the peasantry, the urban petty bourgeoisie and the national bourgeoisie" to "enforce their dictatorship over the running dogs of imperialism,"[48] with the current alliance between transitional socialist orientated states and nationalist capitalist states in the Global South in order to stand against imperialism on the global level.[49]

---

47 Hickel, Jason and Sulivan, Dylan (2025) 'The real reason the West is warmongering against China', *Al Jazeera*, 3.8. 2025.

48 Tse-Tung, Mao (1949) On New Democracy, in *Selected Works* Vol. I, Beijing: Foreign Languages Press, 1965.

49 Rockhill, G. (2024) Gabriel Rockhill summarising the argument as presenting an analogy between the policy of New Democracy in China 1949 and the current strategy for a multipolar

BRICS+ is not an anti-capitalist organization. But it is a step in the right direction. The emerging multipolar world-system consists of a complex of contradictory currents—between hegemonic and counter-hegemonic, conservative and progressive, and capitalist and socialist forces. This is how the world looks. We have to keep in mind Marx's words, that no social order disappears before all the productive forces for which there is space have been developed. We are reaching this point. Then—as Marx continues—comes the period of social revolution.[50] The challenge is to navigate in this sea of interconnected contradictions.

In this struggle, it is important to remember that the motive force behind what happens at the state level is class struggle. Class struggle continues in the transitional state, as well as in the other states constituting the new multipolarity. Ignoring the contradictions between the oppressed and the oppressors, the exploited and the exploiters, is to deny the need of the working class to advance its struggle for socialism. On the other hand, we should not use class struggle to explain everything, without considering the foundation on which this class struggle takes place and where it leads.

As most of the nations in the multipolar world-system are capitalist, some even reactionary and conservative, they will be haunted by the structural crises of capitalism. We need to understand the dialectical relation between emerging multipolarity in the world-system and class struggle, both in the transitional states itself and in the conservative capitalist nationalist regimes in the Global South, such as in Russia, Iran, India, Egypt, or Turkey.

To reject that national capitalist states—even the conservative ones—in the Global South have a progressive part to play in the struggle against US unipolarity and to make the direct struggle for socialism by their working class the only acceptable alternative is to fail to consider the objective situation in the world-system. No matter how much we wish for it, there is not currently a strong, well-organized socialist movement of workers on the global level. Neither is there an existing International of Communist Parties or a "World Social Forum" of social movements of any significant strength. If we rely only on self-organized movements from below, then we do not have the forces to balance imperialism, and we are denying the very thing making "room" in the world-system for such movements to grow and organize.

---

world-system. 'Book and Series Launch: Torkil Lauesen's "The Long Transition Towards Socialism"', YouTube (2024).

50 Marx, Karl (1859) *A Contribution to the Critique of Political Economy*, Preface, Moscow: Progress Publishers, 1977.

The struggle against imperialism must be fought at the state level and at the level of the popular movements in combination. These must be seen as elements of the struggle that support and supplement each other. To develop a strategy in the complex pattern of contradictions, we must stick to the importance of the concept of the principal contradiction, as the point of departure of our analysis, and at the same time not neglect the feedback of the regional, national, and local contradictions.

The ongoing structural crises of the capitalist world-system make it unstable, causing sudden economic and political swings and seemingly odd alliances between transitional states and capitalist states. There are historical examples of such strange alliances. The transitional state of the Soviet Union entered a non-aggression pact with its arch-enemy—Nazi Germany—in 1939 to postpone a German invasion, gaining itself time for rearmament and mobilization. When the German invasion came anyway, the Soviets entered an alliance with the US and UK against Nazi Germany. In China, the communists entered an alliance with the Kuomintang (bourgeois nationalists) against the Japanese invasion, in spite of the fact that they had fought a life and death struggle against the Kuomintang for decades. The Soviets entered the pact with Nazi Germany to secure the existence of their transitional state. Likewise, Chinese communists made their strategic alliance to secure the national liberation struggle, the continued revolution, and eventually the establishment of the People's Republic of China. The use of the principal contradiction in the development of strategy can seem cynical. It can be difficult for revolutionaries in local struggles to be reconciled with these kinds of odd alliances. This is also the case today. Nevertheless, I think that the principal contradiction is a necessary and useful tool.

The same goes for the use of the theory of historical materialism. We must acknowledge the need to develop the productive forces in the Global South in order to enhance the transformation to socialism. The development of a multipolar world-system has unleashed the development of the productive forces from the constraints of US-led monopoly and finance capital, and can provide the foundations for a socialist transition in the longer run. So, in that sense, it is the establishment of a multipolar world-system, including the formation of BRICS+, which should be seen as a progressive step, and as a more reliable strategy than the wishful thinking of relying solely on some non-existing—or at least weak—proletarian international movement to be the driver of the much-needed transformation of the world-system.

The development of the productive forces in the Global South has placed them in a much better position to achieve this goal than such forces had in the sixties. The US is still the dominant aspect in the principal contradiction, but the South is on the offensive, encircling the center. While the transformative power of the Third World in the sixties was based on the "revolutionary spirit"—an attempted ideological dominance over economic development—the current transformative power of the Global South is based on its economic strength.

The current decline of US hegemony and strengthening of multipolarity in the world-system, even including those national conservative capitalist states, will open up "a window of opportunity" for the development of such movements—which is a precondition for the future transformation process towards socialism. The structural crises of the capitalist mode of production will not only appear in the Global North. They will also hit capitalism in the Global South, creating a political crisis in the ruling class, as it is unable to continue in the old way, thereby opening up the possibility for revolutionary class struggles. The structural crises of capitalism will put pressure on the national conservative regimes in the Global South for change, and the transitional states will stand out as concrete and realistic examples of what can be done to regenerate development. China's "transitional mode of production" has, in the past decade, already shown itself to be more effective than neoliberal economics in terms of generating development.

The objective conditions for advancing multipolarization are favourable. The realization of the transformation from capitalism towards socialism depends significantly on how China is able to manage multipolarity. Currently, the People's Republic of China has a strict policy of non-interference in other countries' internal affairs, reflected in its foreign policy at the state level. At the same time, the Communist Party of China has relations with communists, socialists, and progressive nationalist movements participating in class struggle in both the Global South and North. The balance between those positions is delicate and can change both as the struggle between the US-led West and the Global South deepens and as class struggles in the capitalist states in the Global North and South evolve. In the next decade, we will see the economic gap between North and South narrowing, strengthening multipolarity. Before the middle of the century, we might see that the balance has tipped in favour of a world-order based on a socialist mode of production, or at least a transitional mode of production. The coming years will be dangerous and critical; as the US sees its hegemony slipping away, it might turn to war, using NATO against its adversaries. The development of the proxy war in Ukraine and Palestine's liberation struggle will have a far-reaching influence on the overall world balance of power. The US is destabilizing the world-system, while China seems to be a stabilizing factor.

Things may develop faster than we expect. The next decades will be dramatic and dangerous. The transition will not be a tea party. We will see sudden changes in political alliances and, in this scenario, we need to stay on course and stick to a clear socialist perspective. If we can avoid major wars, the transformation from the capitalist mode of production to a socialist can be made rather smoothly; however, we are also working under time pressure due to the impact of the capitalist mode of production on the climate and the ecology of the planet in general. Much will depend on the BRICS+ holding together and its continued strength. As a communist, I can see the danger of relying on leaders such as Modi and Putin and states like Iran and Egypt. Certainly, the conservative and autocratic regimes are a weak link. Their policies, instability, and regional disputes may create openings for US interference. However, for the time being, they are cooperating to find alternative solutions to the rule of the US.

Trump's Counteroffensive

In September 2019, on the occasion of the 70th anniversary of the proclamation of the People's Republic of China, the Chinese State Council published a paper in which it stated that:

> Today's world is undergoing a level of profound change that has not been seen in a hundred years. Human society is full of both hope and challenges. Multipolarity, economic globalization, cultural diversity and information technology are extending their reach. Peace and development remain the themes of the times. At the same time, deep-seated problems are apparent throughout the world, with increasing instability and uncertainties. Building a global community of shared future and building a better world are the common aspirations of all peoples.
>
> China has entered a new era of development. China now has an impact on the world that is ever more comprehensive, profound and long-lasting, and the world is paying ever greater attention to China.[51]

With the decline of the US hegemony, the rise of China, and the development of a multipolar world-system, the world is undergoing profound changes not seen in the past hundred years. No wonder the US has pointed to China as the main enemy.

When Trump regained state power in the US in January 2025, he relaunched the policy of "Make America Great Again"—itself an acknowledgment that the US is in decline, but with the intention of a comeback. To make this happen, both the Democratic and Republican parties agree that the rise of China must be stopped. The problem they face is that China is much more

51 The State Council Information Office of the People's Republic of China (2019), 'China and the World in the New Era'.

powerful economically than the Soviet Union ever was.

The erosion and instability of the old US-led world order is becoming common sense. Trump's return to the Oval Office has accelerated this process. Joe Biden had already disciplined Europe fully back in the NATO fold through the US proxy war against Russia on Ukrainian (and Russian) soil. Europe even accepted significant economic losses, through cutting relations with Russia and through buying expensive liquid natural gas shipped from the US instead of cheap gas through the Nord Stream pipelines from Russia. Subsequently, Trump, by going solo on the question of the Ukraine war, has created a division in NATO between the US and its European partners, a division not seen since the establishment of the organization in 1949. The result is a stagnating Europe dissolving in confusion. Trump's domestic policy also contributes to the decline of US hegemony, as it splits both the ruling class and the working class and erodes the institutional framework of the state. It is difficult to predict where this will end.

In addition to the diplomatic chaos, Trump is also disrupting the global economy through the use of blockades, sanctions, and tariffs against friends and foes alike, destroying the economic order on which the US and Europe have thrived since the end of the Second World War. China has responded to the US tariffs with its own packages of tariffs and export controls on products essential for US supply chains. Other countries are searching for alternatives to their trade dependency on the US. Trump is waging these trade wars because the US no longer dominates the world economy, and he is trying to regain that position by weaponizing economic means, instead of relying on the country's privileged position in the more standard "competition" of the neoliberal world-system. It seems that Trump is trying to use the position of the US as the world's largest consumer market as a mechanism to squeeze tributes out of the rest of the world, in the form of tariffs to access the US market. The tariff-squeeze is backed up by different kinds of political and military threats. However, Trump's tariffs, economic sanctions, and blockades just contribute to erosion of the neoliberal world market which for half a century has been the goose laying golden eggs. Trump's policy accelerates the crises of imperialism. China can live without the US market, but US imperialism cannot do without the exploitation of low-wage labor in the Global South.

Trump and his administration are not doing all this out of ignorance. The US was also in economic problems in the 1970s due to a crisis of the dollar, in connection with the cost of the Vietnam War and the increase of oil prices by OPEC. However, the US was able to come out on top again through a new political-military strategy. US imperialism has always used a mixture of economic, political, and military means to dominate the world. Take relations with China as an example: the U.S. fought a war with China in Korea in the 1950s. The US enforced an economic blockade against the People's Republic of China from 1949 until 1971 and is now again encircling China with a ring of military bases and alliances. Despite the opening up of US-Chinese economic relations from 1978, China has had no illusions about the US intentions. Its ability to develop "socialism with Chinese characteristics" is entirely due to its break from imperialism through the first half of the 20th century, culminating in its revolution in 1949. The inspiration and implications of the rise of China for the Global South are not just in its economic achievements but its ongoing political and military struggle against imperialism.

The aim of Trump's tariff policy is to re-industrialize the US with high tech production. The US wants to reconstruct the international division of labor so that Global South again produces only low value-added goods while the rich nations in the core benefit from unequal exchange and monopoly rents through their control over high value-added technologies.[52] US Vice President JD Vance explained the policy in a speech about globalization at the annual American Dynamism Summit in Washington, DC, an event that brings together corporate executives and US government officials to facilitate contact and align political-corporate strategy:

> The idea of globalization was that rich countries would move further up the value chain, while the poor countries made the simpler things. You would open an iPhone box, and it would say "designed in Cupertino, California [...] the implication, of course, is that it would be manufactured in Shenzhen or somewhere else. And [...] some people might lose their jobs in manufacturing (in the U.S.), but they could learn to design or, to use a very popular phrase, learn to code [...] But I think we got it wrong. It turns out that the geographies that do the manufacturing get awfully good at the designing of things. There are network effects, as you all well understand. The firms that design products work with firms that manufacture. They share intellectual property. They share best practices [...] Now, we assumed that other nations would always trail us in the value chain, but it turns out that as they got better at the low end of the value chain, they also started catching up on the higher end. We were squeezed from both ends.[53]

This is a reference to China, which has decisively moved up the global value chain. Vice President Vance wants to reestablish the international division of labor from the past, where the periphery produces primary agricultural products, crude oil, and unprocessed minerals, alongside low value-added industrial goods such as textiles, shoes, and toys.

---

52 Vance, JD (2025) Vice President Vance remarks at the American Dynamism Summit, 18.3.2025.

53 Ibid., here from, Norton, Ben (2025) 'US VP JD Vance admits West wants Global South trapped at bottom of value chain', *Geopolitical Economy Report*, on March 26, 2025.

China's Foreign Minister Wang Yi commented on such ideas at the Munich Security Conference in February 2025:

> Whether it is the colonial system or the core-periphery structure, unequal orders are bound to meet their demise.[54]

Trump might get some EU firms to move their production facilities from Europe to the US, but he can't turn back the development of the productive forces in China. Trump's economic policy and the political and economic breakdown of the postwar international order are clear signs of US imperialism in crisis.

The Resistance from the Global South

Countering unequal exchange can offer the basis for a global coalition to create a new international order. However, the rule of imperialism and the effect of unequal exchange has divided the working class along hierarchical lines of nationality and citizenship. Hence, the main drivers of the struggle will be found in the Global South. They have the immediate material interest in getting rid of the unequal exchange.

In the 1970s, Samir Amin advised the countries in the Third World to delink from the imperialist economic system in order stop the value transfer of unequal exchange.[55] However, as Amin pointed out, delinking does not mean isolation—autarky—but the reorientation and subordination of international economic relations to the social and environmental needs of the peasants and working class. It requires a mutually complementary and reinforcing process between the class struggle in each country for the benefit of the working class, on one side, and the establishment of external global political conditions that make the restoration of national popular sovereignty possible, on the other. Building an anti-imperialist front on the state level, balancing US hegemony in the world-system, is an integral and fundamental part of the national liberation project. Putting an end to unequal exchange cannot be pursued in isolation and separately by individual countries. The driving force will be states trying to build socialism, and social and national liberation movements in the Global South.

---

54 Yi, Wang (2025) 'A Steadfast Constructive Force in a Changing World', Keynote Speech by Wang Yi, at the 61st Munich Security Conference, February 14, 2025. Here from, Norton, Ben, (2025) 'What is a 'multipolar' world? China says equality; Trump & Marco Rubio say imperial rivalry', *Geopolitical Economy Report*, on February 16, 2025.

55 Amin, Samir (1990) *Delinking, Towards a Polycentric World,* London: Zed Press, 1990.

In the 1960s and 1970s, we hoped that the Third World liberation movements would build socialist states that would cut off the pipelines of value transfer from South to North and thereby create a revolutionary situation in the imperialist center. We were too optimistic. The power of the capitalist world market was too strong. Capitalism, in the form of neoliberal globalization, still had an escape route.

In order to reduce the value transfer, the Global South must regain their economic sovereignty, which has been eroded by neoliberal globalization. They need to redirect their trade patterns from South-North to South-South. There might still be wage differences, but these will be much less than North-South differences. They also need to develop their productive forces in order to free themselves from dependency on Western technology.

China has succeeded in diminishing the imperial rent in the form of unequal exchange while simultaneously breaking through the technological monopoly of Western corporations. Chinese economists have calculated that:

> Between 1978 and 2018, on average, one hour of work in the United States was exchanged for almost forty hours of Chinese work. However, from the middle of the 1990s [...] we observed a very marked decrease in unequal exchange, without it completely disappearing. In 2018, 6.4 hours of Chinese labor were still exchanged for 1 hour of U.S. labor. [56]

In addition, the Global South needs to develop their own financial and banking systems to avoid dependency on the IMF and the World Bank and to weaken the US's capacity to weaponize the financial system using sanctions and blockades. Further, they need to adopt new means of international payment to reduce the power of the dollar in global markets. One example of such measures is the systems being developed by BRICS+.

We are reaching the point where the capitalist mode of production is no longer the most effective mode of production to develop the productive forces, and instead is becoming a globally destructive force, both in terms of human societies and the natural environment. At the same time *the transitional mode of production*, developed in the shadow of dominant capitalism and the hegemonic power of the US, has proved to be more effective in the development of the productive forces. The US can no longer compete with China, which is becoming the leading innovative economic power in the world. The leading capitalist countries are only creating conflicts and wars in their effort to uphold their hegemony, making it impossible to reach global solutions to the social and

---

56 Long, Zhiming; Feng, Zhixuan; Li, Bangxi and Herrera, Rémy (2020) 'U.S.-China Trade War. Has the Real "Thief" Finally Been Unmasked?', *Monthly Review*, Vol. 72 No. 5 October 2010, pp. 6-14.

ecological problems facing humanity.

We are approaching the point where the transitional modes of production can take the next step towards a socialist mode of production, releasing themselves from the remaining international bonds and internal methods of capitalism within the transitional mode of production. On the international level, this means delinking from imperialist financial institutions and expanding South-South trade and cooperation. On the national level, it means expanding the state-owned sector of the economy and other collective forms of production. Suspend the reliance on market forces in sectors like housing, health, education, and child and elder care. It will not happen next year, but in the next few decades. It will not happen automatically, but in a difficult and dangerous international and national class struggle, in which Emmanuel's ideas are highly relevant in order to analyze the situation and develop strategies.

Crisis and Revolution in the Global North

When the system becomes dysfunctional, irrational, and destructive, then a structural crisis occurs, and the possibility for the development of new mode of production arises on the basis of the old. As Lenin stated in 1920 in a letter to the Independent Social-Democratic Party of Germany:

> Every revolution (as distinguished from a reform) by its very nature implies a crisis, and a very deep crisis at that, both political and economic.[57]

Due to the instability of the world-system, it is difficult to predict the future, even in the short term. Having a personality as unpredictable as Trump as president of the US, does not make it easier. However, one thing is certain: the crises of the capitalist mode of production will be deepened.

Lenin defined the revolutionary situation:

> For a revolution to take place, it is usually insufficient for "the lower classes not to want" to live in the old way; it is also necessary that "the upper classes should be unable" to live in the old way.[58]

It seems to me that the majority of the working class in the Global North still want to defend their "old way of living," while it is increasingly the case that the ruling class cannot rule in "the old way" anymore.

---

57 Lenin. V.I. (1920) 'Draft (or Theses) of the R.C. P's reply to the letter of the Independent Social-Democratic Party of Germany', Lenin, V. I *Collected Works,* Vol. 30, p. 341. Moscow: Progress Publishers, 1965.

58 Lenin, V.I (1915) 'The Collapse of the Second International', *Collected Works,* Vol. 21, p. 213. Moscow: Progress Publishers, 1965.

We should defend the principles of public and free healthcare, education, unemployment support, etc., but not the "imperial mode of living," and the struggle has to be fought in a global context. An isolated national defence of the capitalist welfare state is a defence of a privileged position in global capitalism, and thus support for imperialism.

The majority of the working class in the imperialist North still identify themselves with the national interest of the imperialist national state, believing that it will defend the "imperial mode of living." This is reflected in the broad popular support for the NATO alliance.

The erosion of the capitalist welfare state can be seen as one of the causes of the rise in right wing populism, and even fascism, in the Global North. It is not unusual that a class losing its privileged position moves to the right. However, it is a losing game. The imperial mode of production cannot be defended, nor can it be universalized, as there is no exploitable periphery to mother Earth. Brand and Wissen state that:

> We are aware of the hegemonic character of the imperial mode of living—that is, the breadth and depth of its acceptance in society. In that mode, the Global North is attempting to maintain something that cannot be maintained, and something that cannot exist on a universal basis is expanded and universalized in many countries of the Global South. Therefore, in the face of growing upheaval and increasingly brutal externalizations, we recognize—politically and analytically—the urgent need for genuine alternatives that lead to a solidary mode of living, justice (both social and ecological), peace and democracy.[59]

In the coming decades, with a deepening economic and political crisis, it will be an important task to convince the working class that their long term interest is to join the anti-imperialist struggle, to put an end to global capitalism.

In that context, an important issue is how we relate to the crises of the capitalist system in the Global North. Most Western Marxists proclaim that the working class has to introduce a socialist system in order not to lose the benefits they had struggled so hard for in past generations.

But in fact, the relatively high living standard enjoyed by the majority is achieved by the exploitation of the Global South. This connection should not be hidden but made clear. There is no doubt which of these stories would be the most popular and would gain sympathy, but there is also no doubt about which is true. In 1920, at a time when the benefits from imperialism were much less than today, Lenin wrote:

> The Independents (in Germany) and the Longuetists (in France) do not understand and

59 Brand, Ulrich & Wissen, Markus (2021), *The Imperial Mode of Living—Everyday Life and the Ecological Crises of Capitalism,* p. 187. London: Verso, 2021.

> do not explain to the masses that the imperialist super profits of the advanced countries enabled them (and still enable them) to bribe the top stratum of the proletariat, to throw them some crumbs from the super profits (obtained from the colonies and from the financial exploitation of weak countries), to create a privileged section of skilled workers, etc.[60]

At the Second Congress of the COMINTERN in July 1920, Lenin elaborated on this.

> The workers' victory cannot be achieved without sacrifices, without a temporary deterioration of their conditions. We must tell the workers the very opposite of what Crispien (German delegate from the Independent Social-Democracy) has said. If, in desiring to prepare the workers for the dictatorship, one tells them that their conditions will not be worsened "too much", one is losing sight of the main thing, namely, that it was by helping their "own" bourgeoisie to conquer and strangle the whole world aristocracy developed. If the German workers now want to work for the revolution, they must make sacrifices and not be afraid to do so [...] to tell the workers in the handful of rich countries where life is easier (than in China), thanks to imperialist pillage, that they must be afraid of "too great" impoverishment, is counter revolutionary. It is the reverse that they should be told. The labour aristocracy that is afraid of sacrifices, afraid of "too great" impoverishment during the revolutionary struggle, cannot belong to the Party. Otherwise, the dictatorship is impossible, especially in West-European countries.[61]

This was never understood by the COMINTERN's West European parties. They did not explain to the workers the relation between the crises and the possibilities for revolution. Our aim in the capitalist crises is not to mitigate or mediate the economic and political effects because they hurt. We cannot save the system but fight it—move ahead beyond the system towards socialism. This lesson will be learnt as the crises drag on, the Global South gains strength, and the defence of the "imperial mode of living" turns out to be a blind alley.

The bourgeoisification of the working class and its support for imperialism is a historical development, a fact which opens up the possibility of a change in the position and attitude of the working class and maintains a future possibility of the class taking on their role as the gravediggers of capitalism.

In the solidarity movement with Palestine, we see local people standing shoulder to shoulder with Palestinians in diaspora. Refugees and migrant workers can be an anti-imperialist Trojan horse within the Global North. Due to their position in economic production and services, they are not powerless, and their affiliation with family and hope for the economic development of their home-

60 Lenin. V.I. (1920) 'Draft (or Theses) of the R.C. P's reply to the letter of the Independent Social-Democractic Party of Germany', Lenin, V. I, *Collected Works,* Vol. 30, p. 342. Moscow: Progress Publishers, 1965.

61 Lenin. V.I. (1920) 'Speech on the terms of admission into the Communist International', July 1920, in Lenin V. I, *Collected Works,* Vol. 31, pp. 248-249. Moscow: Progress Publishers 1965.

land in the Global South may be stronger than their loyalty to a state that barely tolerates their presence.

We need to develop a "solidary mode of living." Brand and Wissen state that:

> [...] in the formula that solidarity means—besides its inter-relational dimension—not to live at the cost of others and at the cost of nature, i.e. to overcome a mode of production that essentially rests on exploitation of human labour power and the destruction of the bio-physical foundations of life on earth. In that sense, solidarity has a highly institutionalised and structural dimension as it also implies to enable people and societies that they must not live at the expense of others and nature.[62]

However, the objective and subjective conditions for the struggle for a solidary mode of living differ depending on whether you are a beneficiary of the imperial mode of living or you are exploited by the mode of production—roughly speaking, whether you live in the Global North or South, though we should also take into consideration the growing middle and upper class in the South, and marginalized segments in the North.

The imperial mode of living is a manifestation and temporary solution of the contradiction within capitalism between expanding production and stagnating consumption, which is solved by externalization: imperialism. Consequently, the main opposition is to be found in the surrounding external areas wherein the exploitation of humans and nature take place. The resistance here is the driving force against imperialism.

In the short and middle term, the majority of the population in the Global North has an interest in defending the imperial mode of living, while the population in the South has the two options: trying to become integrated into the imperial mode of living or trying to develop a sustainable and solidary alternative. The first option will be in fierce competition with the states of the Global North. Choosing the second option will generate a life-and-death struggle of global capitalism.

To change the imperial mode of living, we need the participation of the vast majority of the world population, living in Asia, Africa, and Latin America. However, the struggle within "the belly of the beast" can play an important role. There are, and have always been, counterstreams of anti-imperialism, even in the North: acts of solidarity, resistance against imperialist wars, and support to liberation movements. Solidarity is more than words. Solidarity is something material you can hold in your hand. Solidarity is practical help in common strug-

---

62 Brand, Ulrich & Wissen, Markus (2020) 'The imperial mode of living and the political ecology of labour', paper presented at the Conference on International Solidarity and Relational Inequality, p. 4, Amsterdam, September 13, 2020.

gle. Solidarity is also changing our way of living, so we do not participate in the exploitation of others and harm our common environment.

9

The Transformation Towards Socialism on the National and Global Levels

OUR STRUGGLE SHOULD NOT BE LED BY UTOPIAN GOALS. We should understand it in the context of historical materialism. The recurrent debates about whether the Soviet Union, China, Cuba, or any state in the process of developing socialism is a worker's state or just some form of an elite-ruled authoritarian state are a mode of thinking that tries to fit the world into a preconceived ideal. It is as if one imagines an idyllic socialist society and contrasts the problematic reality associated with building socialism with the utopia fabricated in the mind. No matter how impressive the socialist progress would be, it will always remain below expectations.[1]

The transition from capitalism to socialism is a long process. In the same way, the transition to capitalism from feudalism was a process that took centuries, from the mercantilist Italian city-states, to the Dutch Empire, to the breakthrough of industrial capitalism in England at the beginning of the 19th century. Capitalism developed as a globalized process, and the process of the transition towards socialism is also global. However, it is not a sudden global simultaneous transformation. It contains many national revolutions. The struggle between capitalism and socialism has wavered back and forth since the mid-19th century. These historical circumstances do not eliminate the fact that the capital system has an end, although they have prolonged and complicated the process of transition. In history, the dialectical relationship between economic laws and class struggles creates tendencies but also, inevitably, countertendencies, and they interact with one another.

---

1 Kadri, Ali (2021) *China's Path to Development Against Neoliberalism*, p. 69. Singapore: Springer Press, 2021.

The transformation process has contained both socialist movements and states. The movements are a first step towards taking state power, but they are also a transformative power in themselves, changing our norms and values—for example, the movements of 1968.

The transformation process takes place within the framework of the world-system of states. Although the economy of capitalism is transnational, its political system has, throughout the course of history, been divided into national states. The nation-state is thus an inevitable component and factor in the transformation from capitalism to socialism.

As capitalism developed inside the feudal mode of production, so the socialist mode of production is developing in the bosom of capitalism. However, the capitalist mode of production could develop on a small scale, in every town and every marketplace inside feudal societies, while the socialist mode of production needs the larger scale of a national state to develop. It needs a comprehensive division of labor and political institutions to govern and plan production and distribution of the social product. It needs the power of the state to defend the socialist project in a world-system dominated by capitalism.

Throughout the 20th century, there have been numerous attempts to develop socialism within the framework of the national state. These socialist-oriented states inevitably came into conflict with the surrounding capitalist world. To uphold their national security and defend their project, these states were caught in the dilemma between supporting the world revolution, which in the long run is necessary for the success of building socialism, and the need to pursue more narrow national interests, to survive in the shorter run—exemplified by the Soviet strategy of "socialism in one country" and China today.

To see the transition as a long and global process is not only a matter of theory: it also has practical political implications. The current lack of confidence in socialism is to a great extent due to the disappointment with the experience of socialism in the Soviet Union, China, Eastern Europe, Cuba, Algeria, Vietnam, Mozambique, and so on. However, it was not socialism. It was a series of efforts to build socialism within the sea of capitalism. In fact, of these projects, only in the USSR under Stalin did the project itself claim that socialism had been established, in 1936.

The transformation towards socialism takes place within the framework of and in dialectical relations with capitalism. The different stages of the development of capitalism have had a huge impact on the attempts to build socialism.

The possibility of a successful and stable transition towards socialism will be limited if it only takes place in one country or global region. There has not yet been a socialist country at any point in time. Not in the Soviet Union nor in China or elsewhere. Socialism in one country has obviously not been a success, in terms of establishing a sustainable socialist-building project. A genuine and comprehensive transition from capitalism to socialism has to involve the majority of the world. Capitalism is a global system, and attempts to escape it, or resist it, by any nation-state have immediately been confronted economically, politically, and militarily by the surrounding dominating capitalist powers.

However, the road towards global socialism passes necessarily through national struggles. The national state is still the primary political framework in the world-system. With this in mind, any national struggle has to be fought with a clear understanding of the global perspective, therefore prioritizing internationalism in terms of both economic and political cooperation.

There have been many attempts to build socialism in the past. Their failure does not necessarily mean that their strategies were wrong, that the attempts were fruitless, or that the mission as such is impossible. The transformation from capitalism toward socialism is a long, ongoing historical process of effort, learning, and trials, as the capitalist mode of production runs out of options and declines. As the capitalist mode of production is reaching its limits in economic, political, and ecological terms, the transition towards socialism becomes urgent if we are not to end up in a chaotic collapse of capitalism.

The Transitional State and the World Revolution

The dialectic of the transitional state is represented by the nationalist development perspective and a global socialist perspective. An advanced socialist mode of production must be global, as its groundwork was laid by the capitalist mode of production, which is globalized both in terms of geography and accumulation processes. It is not globalization as such which is to blame for the inequality and destruction of planet Earth's ecology and climate; it is globalization of capitalism under US hegemony.

However, as mentioned above, the transformation process has to go through the national state. The national framework constitutes a historical constraint that must be considered as a necessity, not something we should make into a virtue. The Communist Party of China considers that China is in the "first (or primary) phase of socialism," a stage which still will take decades to complete. Rémy Herrera discussed the character of contemporary China in an interview:

The speeches of many current leaders of the Chinese Communist Party (CCP) suggest that China would still be in the "first phase of socialism," that is to say, in a stage considered essential for developing the productive forces and which would take a long time to reach its goal. According to them, the historical goal sought would indeed remain that of developed socialism — even if, it is true, the contours of the latter are far from being clearly and precisely defined. However, in Western countries, many researchers claim that these official political declarations claiming the persistence of socialism in China are only a facade, or the cover-up of a hidden form of capitalism, and that socialism is really dead and buried in China [...]

Moreover, even within the debates among Western Marxists, a clear majority of them affirm that the Chinese economy would henceforth be purely and simply capitalist. This is the case of certain well-known Marxists, such as David Harvey, who believes he has seen, since the 1978 reforms, "a neoliberalism with Chinese characteristics" where a particular type of capitalist market economy has incorporated more and more neoliberal devices operated in the framework of very authoritarian centralized control. This is also the case of Leo Panitch, for example, who analyzes the contemporary integration of China into the circuits of the world economy as the duplication by China of the role of "capitalist complement" formerly held by Japan, as a support that China would provide to the United States through capital flows allowing the latter to maintain its global hegemony, and as the trend towards the liberalization of financial markets in China leading to the dismantling of instruments of control of capital movements and undermining at the same time the bases of the power of the CCP. I do not agree with these researchers either. I defend the idea that today, the Chinese system still contains key elements of socialism, and the interpretation I give of its nature is compatible with socialism.

Thus, I read the Chinese political-economic system as a market socialism, or socialism with a market, based on some pillars which still distinguish it quite clearly from capitalism. I will cite, among these foundations: 1) the persistence of powerful and modernized planning; 2) a form of political democracy, obviously perfectible, but making collective choices possible; 3) extensive public services, conditioning political, social and economic citizenship; 4) ownership of land and natural resources that remains in the public domain; 5) diversified forms of ownership, adequate to the socialization of productive forces and boosting economic activity; 6) a general policy which consists of increasing labor remuneration more quickly compared to other types of income; 7) a desire for social justice displayed by public authorities in the face of rising social inequalities since 1978; 8) the priority given to the preservation of the environment, the protection of nature being now considered inseparable from social progress; 9) a conception of economic relations between States based on a win-win principle; and 10) political relations between States based on the search for peace and more balanced exchanges between peoples. Socialism "with Chinese characteristics" is not very far from this reading grid.

Is this state capitalism? [...] Rather than a state capitalism, which refers to the form of a "capitalism without capitalists" — the logical tendency of which will be to evolve towards a "capitalism with capitalists," [...] the system experienced by current China is rather similar, in my opinion, to that of an economy "with capitalists, but which is not capitalist." It is not a question of playing with words, but of remembering that the presence of capitalists in a given social formation does not mean, by this very fact, that such social formation is capitalist. Ultimately, the Chinese experience shows that the objective of the CCP was not to appropriate everything economically, but rather to keep political control over everything — which is not the same thing.[2]

Hence, China, or any other transitionary state, should *not* attempt to avoid contact with capitalist states, as the interaction with global capitalism is part of the transition process. It modifies capitalism and simultaneously presents an alternative to capitalism.

China must move ahead towards to socialism on the national road, as "socialism with Chinese characteristics," but keep in mind that a developed socialist mode of production has to be realized on the global level, as socialism writ large can only be sustainable if it solves the historically inherited problem of inequality between center and periphery in the world-system, as well as the global ecological and climate problems.

As we move ahead towards a more advanced stage of socialism, we will see the development of different socialisms with national characteristics, based on different histories and cultures. For the transitional state, it is important to keep a balance between the national interest and a socialist transformation of the world-system. Historically, this has been a problem in the socialist bloc. There are examples of excessive nationalisms in the relations between the Soviet Union and the East European countries and Yugoslavia, and most importantly the Sino-Soviet relations in the '60s. China's robust critique of Soviet revisionism in the '60s seems more a product of national contradictions with the Soviet Union than a part of the struggle against imperialism, seen in the light of China's own approach to the US in 1971 and the following "opening up" to global capitalism.

In the later years of Mao's leadership, Henry Kissinger, and later Nixon were invited to Beijing. In the following years, China developed a strategy built on an analysis of the world-system called the "Three Worlds Theory." In a conversation with Zambia's president Kenneth Kaunda in 1974, Mao defined the "Three Worlds" in this way:

> I hold that the U.S. and the Soviet Union belong to the First World. The middle elements, such as Japan, Europe, Australia and Canada, belong to the Second World. We are the Third World.[3]

---

2 Herrera, Rémy (2024) 'China's economic development and role in international politics in the face of U.S. hostility', Interview by Tang Xiaofu for the *Observers' Network*, Beijing, published in May 2024. Here from. *Workers World*, June 29, 2024.

3 Zedong, Mao (1974), 'On the Question of the Differentiation of the Three Worlds, excerpts of Mao Zedong's talk with President Kenneth Kaunda of Zambia. February 22, 1974.', in: *Mao Zedong on Diplomacy*, Beijing: Foreign Languages Press, 1998.

According to the theory, the two superpowers, the US and the Soviet Union, were fighting for world domination. In that confrontation, China declared that the Soviet Union was the aggressive part. The Soviet Union was no longer just "revisionist;" it was also "social imperialist." It was so dangerous that the Third World had to side with the Second World in supporting the US in its fight against "Soviet imperialism." However, was the Soviet Union "the most dangerous imperialist power" in the mid-1970s? There is no empirical evidence that the Soviet Union *relied* on imperialist exploitation to sustain its economy. On the contrary, they supported many Third World countries and remaining liberation struggles in, for example, South Africa, Palestine, and Nicaragua in the late '70s and into the '80s.

The "Three Worlds Theory" led China to support anti-Soviet movements in the Third World, for example the FNLA in the Angolan civil war, which was backed by Zaire, Apartheid South Africa, and the US, against the MPLA, which was supported by the Soviet Union and Cuba. China also fought a minor war with Vietnam, a close ally of the Soviet Union, in 1979.

I would argue that China allowed its ideological and national contradictions with the Soviet Union to determine its analysis of the principal contradiction in the world-system. This, however, is backwards: national and regional contradictions must be analysed in the context of the principal contradiction, if our related strategies are to prove effective.

Mao died in 1976, after more than 30 years as chairman of the Communist Party. During the following years, the "Three World Theory" slipped into the background of Chinese foreign policy as the economic and political crises in the Soviet Union deepened and neoliberalism gained force. With the comeback of Deng Xiaoping in 1978— whose reputation had been degraded during the Cultural Revolution—China began to develop a strategy based on the new principal contradiction in the world system: neoliberal globalization versus the national state. Nationalist disputes between transitional states in the future will not only benefit imperialism but will also increase the risk of nuclear warfare and will slow down solutions to the urgent environmental and climate problems. This would block the transition towards advanced global socialism.

Humanity has transitioned from scattered local places, then formed states and empires, and progressively moved towards a more and more globalized world-system, equipped with advanced productive forces, but we have developed a way of living that has damaged the planet, and acquired weapons with the ability to destroy human life. We have also contributed to the knowledge and ability to organize and manage the world-system as a whole, needed for an advanced social mode of production. The transformation of the relations of production towards socialism does not mean going back to productive forces organized only within a national framework. World unification has ceased to be an option. It has become a condition of our continuing existence.

Trying to develop socialism on the national level, the transitional states have kept the world revolution in mind. For the Soviet Union, it had top priority immediately after the revolution: organizing, hosting, and founding the COMINTERN. Lenin considered the continued process of the world revolution as necessary for the survival of the Soviet state and perceived it would happen within a few decades. After the Second World War, ambitions were more modest.

The idea to create an alliance between the socialist transitional states and the Global South against Western imperialism goes back to the Bandung Conference in 1955. The Soviet Union launched the strategy of "the non-capitalist road," a set of economic and political prescriptions to Third World countries where the "revolutionary democrats" held state power. Specific examples were Gamal Abdel Nasser's Egypt, where the Soviets assisted in building the Aswan Dam, and the Ba'ath Party in Syria and Iraq. The strategy argued that if this leadership is supported by local communists and by the socialist countries, it can bring about a non-capitalist transformation of the economy, preparing the way for later socialism. At the time of the revolutionary spirit of the Cultural Revolution in the 1960s, China tried to forge an "anti-revisionist" alliance with liberation movements and new Third World states. For example, China built a strategically important railway from the copper mine in Zambia to the ports in Tanzania. Occupying a third position among the transitional states, Yugoslavia promoted the Non-Aligned Movement. In the United Nations context, we see the formation of the Group of 77 from the Third World countries. Finally, there has been Cuba's ongoing, tireless efforts to assist socialist revolutions in the Third World, from Che Guevara to the present.

However, the nationalist and ideological contradictions and split between the Soviet Union and China in the sixties and seventies made it impossible to form a united front, between the socialist bloc and the Third World against the US imperialist system. The split in the camp of transitional states also weakened defences against the counter-offensive of neoliberalism in the following decades. The transitional states of the Soviet Union and Eastern Europe were dissolved, NATO split up Yugoslavia and created a widespread crisis of the idea of socialism.

A lesson from this is that the transitional states have to solve their national contradictions in ways which do not harm the unity against imperialism, in order to create the critical mass and momentum in the transformation from capitalism to socialism. The possibility of creating a multipolar world-system in the sixties was lost. The difference between then and now is that US hegemony is declining, and the transitional state of China has the capacity to assist the development of political and economic institutions that are viable and attractive alternatives to Western imperialism. What is still missing is a clear socialist agenda for this multipolar world-system.

For anti-imperialists in the Global North, an understanding of the dialectic of the transitional state, between national development and the pursuit of world socialism, is important as a guide on how to relate to the transitional states. We need to see the dilemmas and the balance between national development versus the mission of advancing socialism nationally and globally. In class terms, this is the contradiction between national class unity versus the class struggle nationally and globally. Anti-imperialists must defend transitional states against imperialism but also support movements struggling to advance the transition to socialism. We must push for a socialist transformation through class struggle to ensure that the socialist aspect dominates the national aspect in the contradictions of transitional states.

Advanced Socialism

To move onwards to an advanced socialist mode of production, we need, in addition to the "national characteristic of socialism," to develop the universal and global dimension of socialism. An advanced socialist mode of production has to be realized on the global level, as it has to solve the historically inherited problem of inequality between center and periphery in the world-system, as well as the global ecological and climate problems. What would such a change imply? It would mean getting rid of residual exploitative capitalist relations of production and patterns of consumption, all of which are in conflict with the global ecosystem. It would mean the development of common prosperity and the (re)development of commons, instead of privatization and extreme individualism; it is solidarity instead of competition. On the international level, investment and trade should promote global equality and sustainability. A global planned economy has to be introduced and managed by global political institutions.

Emmanuel did not believe in equalization within the capitalist mode of production:

> Under no circumstances can all of the [developing nations] become the United States, assuming that they want to. The United States is only the United States because the others are not. The level of development they have arranged considerably exceeds the global

> margins of the capitalist system worldwide: they are, in capitalist terms, overdeveloped. Naturally, they can only be overdeveloped because there are sufficient exploitable underdeveloped areas around them. It may still be possible to achieve this accelerated "extroverted" development in a particular small country, if the little international capital available is concentrated there. This will be because the others will not follow suit. For the whole of the Third World, such an attempt would be, apart from any value judgment, materially futile. The only way left to it is to set fire to the capitalist stage.[4]

Neither does Emmanuel believe it is possible to develop an advanced form of socialism on the national level—"socialism in one country." In a letter to Samir Amin, he writes:

> Nevertheless, if we consider the nation as a constraining reality that socialism itself cannot overcome and that it will take several generations to do so, I agree with you that the only way to unify the world is to first equalize the national levels through self-centered developments. But it certainly does not escape you that these "self-centred developments" will be to the detriment of the world optimum and cannot be done without friction. This shows once again that the national fact, which the Marxists had seriously underestimated, constitutes a source of contradictions in the world which the class struggle does not automatically resolve.[5]

As the Indian political economist Aritro Ghosh writes:

> Capitalism is a world-system and not an aggregation of national economies. A poor country will still be exploited by unequal terms in trade after a socialist revolution and the only way to break out of it is a third-world revolution whereby the whole swathe of poor countries forms a common union amongst themselves.[6]

To realize an advanced socialist mode of production requires not only that China move in that direction but also that the majority of states in the world-system join the effort. In the coming decades, we might see the development of different socialisms with national characteristics, based on different histories and cultures. However, it is essential to move on from the nationalist version towards global socialism, as the national component contains material for future national disputes which only benefit the remaining capitalist elements, increase the risk of nuclear warfare, and disturb the process of solving the urgent envi-

---

4 Emmanuel, Arghiri (1976) 'The Multinational Corporations and Inequality of Development', *International*. p. 763. *Social Science Journal*, vol. 28 no. 4, pp. 753-772. 1976. UNESCO. Paris 1976.

5 Among the papers found in Emmanuel's archive is a long, undated letter to Samir Amin with comments on the manuscript of Amin's book: Amin, Samir (1970) *L'accumulation a L'echelle Mondiale,* Paris et Dakar: Editions Anthropos, 1970. Amin's book was published in 1970; hence, the letter must be from before. This quote is from p.7. The document can be found online here: https://unequalexchange.org/2024/11/30/arghiri-emmanuels-letter-fo-samir-amin/.

6 Ghosh, Aritro (2025) 'The only way left to it is to set fire to the capitalist stage', Azaad Substack 10.2.2025.

ronmental and climate problems.

In the process of moving towards an advanced form of socialism, what then can be done to begin to solve the problem of global inequality? Not, it is understood, as some kind of global social democratic reforms; the social democratic capitalist welfare state is based on the value transfer of unequal exchange, and therefore cannot be extended to the global level. We cannot wait for the establishment of an advanced socialism to reduce global inequality. Reducing global inequality is part of the transition process. In the conclusion of his book *Unequal Exchange*, written in 1969, Emmanuel made this remark:

> Finally, wages being what they are, the whole problem lies in this question: who is going to pay the costs of the world optimum? If the very concept of a world economy has any meaning at all, and if it is not desired that the poor countries turn in on themselves and thereby cause a dangerous dislocation of the established division of labor, it will indeed be necessary to resolve to set up internationally at least such mechanisms of redistribution as already exist on the national scale. It will indeed be necessary to have an incomes policy on the international scale corresponding to what exists, however imperfectly, inside the nation. What the concrete content of this policy will be depends first and foremost on the social and political transformations that will come about within each country.[7]

Hickel and colleagues wrote in the conclusion of their study of the size of unequal exchange in 2023:

> Development and poverty eradication, and any plausible trajectory for reducing global inequality, requires a shift in the balance of power between North and South, such that the latter is able to reclaim its productive capacities to meet human needs. Toward this end, international wage floors and minimum resource prices could help reduce price inequalities and limit value transfers. Ending unequal exchange will also require ending structural adjustment conditions on finance, and democratising the institutions of global economic governance, so that Global South governments are free to use industrial, fiscal and monetary policy to pursue sovereign development and reduce their dependency on Northern capital. Such reforms are unlikely to be handed down from above, however. It will require a political struggle for national self-determination and economic sovereignty similar in scope to the anti-colonial movement of the 20th century.[8]

From being a dynamic developer of the productive forces, capitalism has today become a block on development. It has run out of geographic space and new proletarians to exploit, and it is on a collision course with the global ecosystem. Nor can the imperialist countries rely on a monopoly of high tech industrial

---

7 Emmanuel, Arghiri (1972) *Unequal Exchange: A Study of the Imperialism of Trade*, p. 270, New York: Monthly Review Press, 1972.

8 Hickel, Jason; Lemos, Morena Hanbury and Barbour, Felix: (2024) Unequal exchange of labour in the world economy. Page 5. *Nature Communications*| (2024) 15:6298, Springer Nature.

production to uphold their hegemony. They have been forced to turn from neoliberal economics to economic, political, and military warfare, eroding the very world market and political institutions which have served them well for half a century, in a desperate attempt to avoid losing their power.

The periphery today is in a better position to move ahead in economic liberation from imperialism compared with the Third World in the long sixties. The industrialization of the Global South has created the material possibilities for moving ahead towards socialism.

China, a former periphery state, has managed to break the polarizing dynamic of global capitalism and developed its productive forces to an advanced stage. The world-system is moving from unipolarity towards multipolarity, weakening capitalism's economic and political dominance. Today, China is one of the aspects in the current principal contradiction, with the ability more directly to determine its own development and influence the fate of humanity and the global ecosystem.

Crisis and Revolution in the Global North

What will the impact of this transformation process be in the short and middle term in our part of the world? It's difficult to predict the future when the world-system is so unstable, but the crises of capitalism will certainly deepen.

The instability in the world-system also affects the tools and options of the ruling class. They have turned away from neoliberal economic competition towards geopolitical struggle and militarism. The West against the rest. So, anti-imperialism has to be central in our struggle. You cannot fight capitalism without fighting imperialism. This is a vital lesson for activists and revolutionaries in the Global North, who might otherwise end up defending their privileged position in the global order.

An important task is to link the working class of the Global North with the anti-imperialist struggle. They must be convinced that their long-term interest does not lie with their imperialist national state and the "imperial mode of living" but in bringing an end to global capitalism, which has reached the point of threatening humankind's survival. They must understand that their standard of living and their welfare state are built upon the exploitation of the Global South.

This challenge is immense, but in recent years, we have seen anti-imperialist countercurrents develop. The genocide in Gaza since October 2023 has created a new generation of anti-imperialists in the Global North, not seen since the protests against the Vietnam war. The mobilization of solidarity with the Palestinian struggle is also a schooling in organization and a lesson in how the system works. Activists are learning the reality of the power instruments of the state, about the media, about imperialism in general. These lessons must be coupled with informed analysis to create effective strategies and praxis for this political moment. Anti-imperialists in the North are still a minority, but an important minority.

References

Abbas, Ferhat (1962) *La nuit coloniale, Presence africaine, 4th quarter*. Paris: René Julliard, 1962.

Allan, Roberts C (2009) *The British Industrial Revolution in Global Perspective*. Cambridge: Cambridge University Press, 2009.

— (2015) "The High Wage Economy and the Industrial Revolution: A Restatement." *Economic History Review*, vol. 68, No.1, pp 1-22. 2015.

Allianz (2014), Allianz *Wealth Report*. Nationale Zentralbanken und Statistikämter, Allianz SE. allianz.com

Amin, Samir (1970) *L'accumulation a l'echelle Mondiale: Critique de la theorie du sous-development*. Dakar/Paris: IFAN-Anthropos, 1970.

— (1973) *The End of a Debate*. Dakar: IDEP 1973. Also published in: Amin, Samir (1977) *Imperialism and Unequal Development, Essays by Samir Amin*. New York: Monthly Review Press, 1977.

— (1974) *Accumulation on a World Scale*. New York: Monthly Review Press 1974.

— (1976) *Unequal Development: An Essay on the Social Formations of Peripheral Capitalism*. Monthly. New York: Review Press, 1976.

— (1987) letter to Communist Working Group, Copenhagen dated 21.1. 1987. Private correspondence.

— (1990) *Delinking, Towards a Polycentric World*. London: Zed press, 1990.

— (2003) "World Poverty, Pauperization and Capital Accumulation", *Monthly Review*. Vol. 55, no. 5, p. 1-9.

— (2010). *The Law of Worldwide Value*. New York: Monthly Review Press, 2010.

— (2017) "The Sovereign Popular Project: The Alternative to Liberal Globalization." *Journal of Labor and Society*, vol. 20, no. 1, March 2017.

ANC (1955) *The Freedom Charter*: https://www.anc1912.org.za/the-freedom-charter-2/

Anthropocene Working Group (2019) *Results of Binding Vote by AWG.* May 21, 2019. Online: https://quaternary.stratigraphy.org.

Aschoff, Nicole (2015) The "Smartphone Society." *Jacobin*, no. 17, March 2015.

Baldwin Richard (2024). "China is the world's sole manufacturing superpower: A line sketch of the rise." *VoxEU,* 17 Jan 2024. CEPR. cepr.org/voxeu/columns/china-worlds-sole-manufacturing-superpower-line-sketch-rise

Baerresen, D. W. (1971) *The Border Industrialization Program of Mexico.* Texas: Health Lexington Books, 1971.

Banaji, Jairus (2024) "Arghiri Emmanuel (1911-2001)." *Historical Materialism.* https://www.historicalmaterialism.org/figure/arghiri-emmanuel-19112001/

Bank for International Settlements, 'OTC derivatives statistics at end-June 2023'. https://www.bis.org/publ/otc_hy2311.htm

Bargigli, Leonardo (2024) "An Inconvenient Truth About the Working Class in the West." Contropiano 25 August 2024. https://contropiano.org/interventi/2024/08/25/una-scomoda-verita-sulla-classe-operaia-in-occidente-0174954

BBC (2012) "South Africa's census: Racial divide continuing." 30.10. 2012. https://www.bbc.com/news/world-africa-20138322

Bettelheim, Charles (1952) "Le Problème de l'Emploi," Paris: UNESCO. 1952.

— (1969) "Débat sur l'impérialisme, rapports internationaux et rapports de classe." *Politique Aujourd'hui,* N° 12. Paris,1969.

— (1969) "Les travailleurs des pays riches et pauvres ont des interets solidaires," in *Le Monde,* November 11, 1969.

— (1972) "Theoretical Comments." In Emmanuel, Arghiri, *Unequal Exchange: A Study of the Imperialism of Trade.* New York: Monthly Review Press, 1972.

Bhattacharjee, Shikha Silliman (2016) "Precarious Work in the H&M Global Value Chain. A Report to the ILO." Geneva: ILO 2016.

Bizvibe (2017) Minimum Wages in Asia's Textile and Apparel Industry. https://blog.bizvibe.com/blog/textiles-and-garments/minimum-wages-asias-textile-apparel-industry

Brand, Ulrich & Wissen, Markus (2020) "The imperial mode of living and the political ecology of labour." Paper presented at the Conference on International Solidarity and Relational Inequality Amsterdam, September 13, 2020. https://soc21.nl/wp-content/uploads/2020/09/Wissen-Brand_The-imperial-mode-of-living_final.pdf

— (2021), *The Imperial Mode of Living – Everyday Life and the Ecological Crises of Capitalism.* London: Verso 2021.

Brown, Freya. (2011). Summary and review: "Marx's theory of price and its modern rivals" by Howard Nicholas. https://anti-imperialism.org/2014/01/25/summary-and review-marxs-theory-of-price-and-its-modern-rivals by-howard-nicholas-2011/ (Link expired).

Bukharin, Nicolai (1917) *Imperialism and World Economy.* London: Merlin Press. 1930.

Bunker, Stephen G. (1984) "Modes of Extraction, Unequal Exchange, and the Progressive Underdevelopment of an Extreme Periphery: The Brazilian Amazon 1600–1980." *American Journal of Sociology*, vol. 89, no. 5. 1984.

Carchedi, Guglielmo and l Roberts, Michael (2021) "The Economics of Modern Imperialism." *Historical Materialism* vol. 29, no. 4, pp. 23–69, 2021.

Castro, Fidel (1973) "Speech by Fidel Castro, 4th of January 1973." Latin American Network Information Center. Online: Castro Speech Data Base—Latin American Network Information Center, LANIC. https://wayback.archive-it.org/11176/20230808050541/http://lanic.utexas.edu/project/castro/db/1973/19730104.html

— (1979a) Speech delivered at the 34th Session of the United Nations General Assembly, in New York City, 12, October 1979. Here cited in 'On The Shoulders Of Giants. . . '1979 Address To The United Nations'—Fidel Castro', *Éirígí*, https://eirigi.org/latestnews/2019/8/13/on-the-shouldersfidel-castro-1979-address-to-united-nations.

— (1979b): "Fidel Castro speech to the UN in his position as chairman of the non-aligned countries movement 12 October 1979", https://web.archive.org/web/20110611014358/http:/lanic.utexas.edu/la/cb/cuba/castro/1979/19791012.html

— (1981) "Speech at the Conference of the Inter-parliamentarian Union in Havana, 15-23 August 1981." *Granma* 27 Sept. 1981. Havana Cuba.

Chi-Hsi, Hu (1975) *Mao-Tse-Tung et al Construction du Socialisme.* Paris: Le Seuil. 1975.

Clelland, Donald A (2012) "Surplus Drain and Dark Value in the Modern World-System". In *Handbook of World-Systems Analysis,* ed. Christopher Chase-Dunn and Salvatore Babones. London: Routledge. 2012.

— (2014) "Theoretical Conceptualization of Bright Value in Global Commodity Chains." https://drive.google.com/file/d/1y7Yvwhbi6CJJVoY0LW2fLfAxiCtX view

— (2014) "The Core of the Apple: Dark Value and Degrees of Monopoly in the Commodity Chains." *Journal of World-System Research,* vol. 20, no. 1. 2014.

— (2020) "Peeling to the Apple Core: Dark Value Drains at the Heart of High-Tech Mass Consumption, 2010-2020." Unpublished Paper provided by Wilma A. Dunaway.

Clemens, Michael Montenegro, Claudio and Pritchett, Lant (2009) "The Place Premium: Wage Differences for Identical Workers Across the US Border." Background Paper to the 2009 World Development Report (Policy Research Working Paper 4671). New York: World Bank. 2009.

Cole, G.D.H. and Postgate, Raymond (1949) *The Common People, 1746–1946.* London: Methuen and Co. 1949.

Communist Working Group (1986) *Unequal Exchange and the Prospects of Socialism.* Copenhagen: Manifest Press, 1986. New edition, Washington: Iskra books, 2025. Available free online at https://www.iskrabooks.org/unequal-exchange

— (2025) *Unequal Exchange and the Prospects of Socialism,* Washington: Iskra books, 2025. Available free online at https://www.iskrabooks.org/unequal-exchange

Danish Ministry of Employment (2021) "Satser for 2021. https://dst.dk/en/Statistik/emner/arbejde-og-indkomst/beskaeftigelse-og-arbejdsloeshed/loenmodtagere

Day, Roderic (2022) "[Masses, Elites, and Rebels: The Theory of "Brainwashing"](https://redsails.org/masses-elites-and-rebels/) 23.5.2022. RedSails.org: https://redsails.org/masses-elites-and-rebels/

Dedrick, J., Kraemer K. L., & Tsai T. (1999) "ACER: An IT company learning to use information technology to compete." *Center for Research on Information Technology and Organization, University of California*.

Delgado Wise, R., and S. Gaspar (2018) "Claves para descifrar la arquitectura de la globalización neoliberal: Exportación de fuerza trabajo e intercambio Desigual." In *La Globalización Neoliberal en Crisis,* edited by José Luis Calva, pp.159–186. Mexico: Juan Pablos.

Delgado Wis, Raúl (2022) "Imperialism, Unequal Exchange, and Labour Export." In Zak Cope (ed.), Immanuel Ness (ed) *The Oxford Handbook of Economic Imperialism.* Oxford: Oxford University Press 2022.

Donaldson, T (2016) "H&M to source more garments from Bangladesh." *Sourcing Journal,* March 14, 2016.

Dorninger, C. et al. (2021) "Global patterns of ecologically unequal exchange: Implications for sustainability in the 21st century." *Ecologic Economics.* Vol. 179, January 2021, 106824. Science Direct 2021.

Drahokoupil, Jan Andrijasevic, Rutvica and Sacchetto, Devi (eds.) (2016) *Flexible workforces and low profit margins: electronics assembly between Europe and China.* Brussel: European Trade Union Institute (ETUI) 2016.

Duhigg, Charles and Bradsher, Keith (2012) "How the U.S. Lost Out on iPhone Work." *New York Times,* January 22, 2012.

Duhigg, Charles (2012) Apple's Jobs to Obama. *New York Times,* January 23, 2012.

Dunaway, Wilma. A. (ed.) (2013) *Gendered Commodity Chains: Seeing Women's Work and Households in Global Production.* Stanford: Stanford University Press, 2013.

Duric, Ivan; Glauben, Thomas (2024) "BRICS: World Heavyweight in Agricultural Trade" *Intereconomics.* Volume 59, 2024 · Number 3. pp. 160–166. https://www.intereconomics.eu/contents/year/2024/number/3/article/brics-world-heavyweight-in-agricultural-trade.html#footnote-003

The Economist (2025) The Consequences of Success, *The Economist,* January 18, 2025. https://economist.com/china/2025/01/16/an-initiative-so-feared-that-china-has-stopped-saying-its-name

Edwards, Hodee Waldstein (1978) *Labor Aristocracy, Mass Base of Social Democracy.* Stockholm: Aurora Edition. 1978. Republished by Estuary Press in 2024.

— (1988) *Autobiography 1988: H. W. Edwards.* San Francisco: Estuary Press 2024.

Emmanuel, Arghiri (1944) "Apology." Translated By Daniel Williams. https://unequalexchange.org/2024/11/03/arghiri-emmanuels-apology/

— (1945) *Dialectic Materialism.* (In Greek, under translation to English.) Supplied by Catherine Emmanuel for the Emmanuel archive at IISG, Amsterdam.

— (1960) "Speech given by Mr. A. Emmanuel, at the M.N.C. banquet, on July 6, 1960, at the Stanley Hotel, in Stanleyville, in response to the speech of the Provincial President of the M.N.C.", Emmanuel's Association with Patrice Lumumba and His Expulsion from the Congo—Arghiri Emmanuel Association https://unequalexchange.org/2024/09/17/emmanuels-association-with-patrice-lumumba-and-his-expulsion-from-congo/

— (1960): "Telegram to Patrice Lumumba." https://unequalexchange.org/category/digital-archive/

— (1961) Analysis of the Congo's economy. Unpublished paper. https://unequalexchange.org/category/digital-archive/

Emmanuel, Arghiri & Bettelheim, Charles (1962) "Échange inégal et politique de développement," *Problèmes de planification*, No. 2, Sorbonne: Centre d'Étude de Planification Socialiste. Paris 1962.

— (1963) "Échange inégal", *Revue Problemes de Planification,* No. 2. Paris, 1963.

— (1964) « El Intercambio Desigual. « *Revue Economica,* La Havane, Fevrier, 1964.

— (1967) "Letter dated June 1967 to Mobuto." Emmanuel archive, IISG Amsterdam.

— (1969) "Letter to Samir Amin." (Translated from French) Among the papers found in Emmanuel's archive is a long undated response to Samir Amin with comments to the manuscript of Amin's book: *L'accumulation a L'echelle Mondiale* (Accumulation on World Scale). The Book was published in 1970; hence, the letter must be from before. There is no introduction in the document so maybe some pages are missing. The text starts rather abruptly with comments about the connection between wages and productivity. The letter (like all his letters) is not listed in Emmanuel's own CV and biography. This quote is from page 7 in the document. It can be accessed here: https://unequalexchange.org/category/digital-archive/

— (1970) "The Delusions of Internationalism." *Monthly Review,* Vol. 22, no.2. June 1970, pp. 13-19.

— (1972) *Unequal, Exchange, A Study of the Imperialism of Trade.* New York: Monthly Review Press 1972.

— (1972) "White Settler Colonialism and the Myth of Investment Imperialism." *New Left Review,* no. 73.pp. 35-57, London 1972.

— (1975) "Unequal Exchange Revisited." *IDS Discussion Paper No. 77* Institute of Development Studies, Sussex University, Brighton, UK.

— (1975) "Unequal Exchange, A Summary." Paper presented to a conference on trade at Sussex University UK.1975. https://unequalexchange.org/category/digital-archive/

— (1976) "Letter to Immanuel Wallerstein," 25.10 1975, From Emmanuel's personal archive at IISG, Amsterdam.

— (1976) "The multinational corporations and inequality of development." *Social Science Journal,* vol. 28, no. 4, pp.753-772. 1976. Paris: UNESCO. 1976. https://unesdoc.unesco.org/ark:/48223/pf0000019907

— (1976) "Europe-Asia Colloquium. For the use by the Commission on International Relations. Some guidelines for the "problematique" of world Economy." IEDES Dated 6.10.76 Manuscript found in Emmanuel's archive. at the IISG in Amsterdam.

— (1979) "The State in the Transitional Period." *New Left Review* no. 113-114, January-April 1979, pp.110-131. London 1979.

— (1982) *Appropriate or underdeveloped Technology?* London: John Wiley & Sons, Chichester 1982.

— (1984) *Profit and Crises.* London: Heinemann Books, 1984.

— (1984) "The Economic Crisis and the Ways to Get Out of It." Unpublished paper: https://unequalexchange.org/category/digital-archive/

— (1986) "Preface" to, Manifest Communist Working Group (1986) *Unequal Exchange and the Prospects for Socialism in a Divided World,* pp. 9-15. Copenhagen: Publishing House Manifest. 1986. Republish by Iskra Books, 2025.

Engels, Frederick (1845) *The Condition of the Working Class in England.* New York: Panther Books, 1969.

— (1847) "The Movements of 1847". In: *Marx & Engels Collected Works,* Volume 6. New York: International Publishers, 1975.

— (1858) "Letter to Marx, dated 7 October 1858, " In *Marx and Engels, Selected Correspondence,* p. 110. Moscow: Progress Publishers, 1965.

— (1859) "Review of Karl Marx: Critique of Political Economy," In *Marx and Engels Collected Works,* Volume. 16, p. 476. Moscow: Progress Publishers, 1976.

— (1882) "Letter to Kautsky, dated 12 September 1882", In, *Marx and Engels, Selected Works,* p. 678. Moscow: Progress Publishers, 1970.

— (1884) "The Dialectics of Nature." In, *Marx & Engels Collected Works, Vol. 25.* New York: International Publishers, 1975.

— (1884) *Engels, Paul & Laura Lafargue Correspondence,* Volume. I, p. 233. Moscow: Foreign Languages Publishing House, 1959.

ESG News (2024) "China Dominates Global Wind and Solar Energy Construction." *ESG* News, July 12, 2024. https://esgnews.com/china-dominates-global-wind-and-solar-energy-construction/

Exiobase: https://www.exiobase.eu

Fanon, Frantz (1961) *The Wretched of the Earth.* London: Penguin Books, 1961.

Feenstra, Robert C (1998) "Integration of Trade and Disintegration of Production in the Global Economy." *Journal of Economic Perspective*, vol. 12, no. 4. 1998.

Foster, J. B. and B. Clark (2004) "Ecological Imperialism: The Curse of Capitalism." *Socialist Register vol. 40.* 2004, pp.186–201.

— (2018) "Women, Nature, and Capital in the Industrial Revolution." *Monthly Review,* vol. 68, no. 8, January 2018. https://monthlyreview.org/articles/women-nature-and-capital-in-the-industrial-revolution/

Foster, John Bellamy (2022) "Ecological Civilization, Ecological Revolution: An Ecological Marxist Perspective." *Monthly Review* vol. 74, no. 5, October 2022. https://monthlyreview.org/2022/10/01/ecological-civilization-ecological-revolution/

Francis, G. & Sutcliffe, B. (1987) *The Profit System: The Economics of Capitalism.* New York: Penguin books, 1987.

Frank, A. G. (1966) "The Development of Underdevelopment." *Monthly Review* vol. 18, no. 4, pp.17–31.

— (1981) *Crisis in the Third World.* London: Heinemann. 1981

Fröbel, F, Heinrichs, J, Kreye, O (1980) *The New International Division of Labour.* Cambridge: Cambridge University Press, 1980.

Ghosh, Aritro (2025) "The only way left to it is to set fire to the capitalist stage." Azaad Substack 10.2.2025. https://azaaad.substack.com/p/the-only-way-left-to-it-is-to-set?utm_campaign=post&utm_medium=web

Gibson Bill (1980) "Unequal Exchange: Theoretical Issues and Empirical Findings." *Review of Radical Political Economics*, vol. 12 no.3, pp. 15-35.

Global Debt Monitor (2024) https://imf.org/external/datamapper/GDD/2024%20Global%20Debt%20Monitor.pdf

Glyn, Andrew and Sutcliffe, Bob (1972) *British capitalism, workers and the profits squeeze,* London: Penguin. 1972.

Gowan, Peter (1999) *The Global Gamble: Washington's Faustian Bid for World dominance.* London: Verso. 1999.

Gramsci, Antonio (1929-35) *Prison Notebooks, Vol. 2,* Notebook 4. New York: Columbia University Press, 1996.

Grossman, Gene M. and Rossi-Hansberg, Esteban (2006) "The Rise and Fall of Offshoring: It's Not Wine for Cloth Anymore." https://www.princeton.edu/~erossi/RO.pdf

Guevara, Che (1964) "Speech delivered March 25, 1964 at the plenary session of the United Nations Conference on Trade and Development" (UNCTAD) https://marxists.org/archive/guevara/1964/03/25.htm

— (1964) "Speech at 19th General Assembly of the United Nations in New York, December 11, 1964," in *The Che Reader,* New York: Ocean Press, 2005.

— (1964). "Remarks in Algeria to Jeunesse, December 23, 1964," Published in *«Revolución»,* December 26, Havana 1964.

— (1966) "Message to the Tricontinental," in: Ernesto 'Che' Guevara: *On Socialism and Internationalism,* p. 39. New Delhi: Left Word Books, 2020. https://thetricontinental.org/wp-content/uploads/2020/10/Che_Guevara_On_Socialism_and_Internationalism_EN.pdf

Hart-Landsberg, Martin (2009) "Learning from ALBA and the Bank of the South". *Monthly Review*, vol. 61, no. 4, September 2009.

— (2010) "ALBA and the Promise of Cooperative Development. " *Monthly Review,* vol. 62, no. 7 December 2010.

Hawkins, Amy (2024) "China building two-thirds of world's wind and solar projects. *The Guardian*, 11.7. 2024. https://theguardian.com/

world/article/2024/jul/11/china-building-twice-as-much-wind-and-solar-power-as-rest-of-world-report

Herman, Edward S.; Chomsky, Noam (1988) *Manufacturing Consent.* New York: Pantheon Books. 1988.

Herrera, Rémy (2024) "China's economic development and role in international politics in the face of U.S. hostility." Interview by Tang Xiaofu for *the Observers' Network*, Beijing, published in May 2024. Here from. Workers World, June 29, 2024. https://workers.org/2024/06/79439/

Hersh, Jonathan and Voth, Hans-Joachim (2009) "Sweet Diversity: Colonial Goods and the Rise of European Living Standards after 1492." *Economics Working Papers, no. 1163.* Universitat Pompeu Fabra 2009.

Hickel, J. (2020) *Less is More: How Degrowth Will Save the World.* UK: Random House, 2020.

— (2021), *The Divide.* United Kingdom: Left Book Club, 2021.

Hickel, J. Sullivan, D. & Zoomkawala, H (2121) "Plunder in the post-colonial era: quantifying drain from the global South through unequal exchange, 1960–2018." *New Political Economy* 26, March 2021 pp. 1–18.

Hickel, J. & Sullivan, D. (2023) "Capitalism, global poverty, and the case for democratic socialism." *Monthly Review.* Vol. 75, no. 3, 99–113, July-August 2023.

Hickel, Jason; Lemos, Morena Hanbury and Barbour, Felix: (2024) "Unequal exchange of labour in the world economy." *Nature Communications*| (2024) 15:6298, Springer Nature. https://www.nature.com/articles/s41467-024-49687-y

Hobsbawm, Eric J. (1957) "The British Standard of Living 1790–1850," *Economic History Review* 10, no. 1. pp. 46-68.

Hopkins, K. Terence and Wallerstein, Immanuel (2013) "Commodity Chains in the World-Economy Prior to 1800." *Review* (Fernand Braudel Center), vol. 10, no. 1 1986, pp. 157–170.

Horrell, Sara and Humphries, Jane (2018) "Women's Labour Force Participation and the Transition to the Male Breadwinner Family." *Economic History Review,* vol. 48, no. 1.

Hudson, M (2024) "As stock market crashes, is U.S. facing new financial crisis?" *Geopolitical Economic Report* (7 August 2024). https:

//mronline.org/2024/08/11/as-stock-market-crashes-is-u-s-facing-new-financial-crisis-economist-michael-hudson-explains

ILO (1974) *International Labour Review*, 1974, vol. 109, no. 5-6, pp. 422-9. Geneva: ILO. 1974.

— (2002) "Decent Work and the Informal Economy." *Report* no.6. Geneva: International Labour Organization 2002.

— (2011) "World of Work Report 2011." Geneva: International Labour Organization, 2011.

Ilonga, Héritier (2024) "Arghiri Emmanuel, the law of unequal exchange, and the failures of liberation in the DR Congo." *ROAPE*, 4 September. https://roape.net/2024/09/04/arghiri-emmanuel-the-law-of-unequal-exchange-and-the-failures-of-liberation-in-the-dr-congo-part-one/

— (2024) "Arghiri Emmanuel, the Free Republic of Congo, and socialism – not capitalism – first." *ROAPE* 11 September 2024. https://roape.net/2024/09/11/arghiri-emmanuel-in-the-congo-from-patrice-lumumba-to-antoine-gizenga-and-socialism-not-capitalism-first/

IMF, 2024 Global Debt Monitor, https://www.imf.org/external/datamapper/GDD/2024%20Global%20Debt%20Monitor.pdf

Intan Suwandi and John Bellamy Foster (2016) "Multinational Corporations and the Globalization of Monopoly Capital." *Monthly Review*, vol. 68, no. 3. July–August 2016.

Isaacson, W (2011) *Steve Jobs*. New York: Little Brown, 2011.

J.P. Morgan, 'De-dollarization: Is the US dollar losing its dominance?', https://www.jpmorgan.com/insights/global-research/currencies/de-dollarization

Joseph, G.G. and Tomlinson, M. (1991) "Testing the Existence and Measuring the Magnitude of Unequal Exchange Resulting from International Trade: A Marxian Approach." *Indian Economic Review*, New Series, vol 26 No. 2, July-December pp. 123-148. Department of Economics, Delhi School of Economics, University of Delhi.

Kadri, Ali (2021) *China's Path to Development Against Neoliberalism*. Singapore: Springer Press 2021.

Kaplinsky, Raphael (2005) *Globalization, Poverty and Inequality. Between a Rock and a Hard Place.* Cambridge: Polity Press 2005.

Kerswell, Timothy (2011) *The Global Division of Labour and Division in Global Labour* (Ph.D. thesis). Queensland University of Technology 2011.

Keynes, John Maynard (1936) *The General Theory of Employment, Interest, and Money.* Cambridge: MacMillan Cambridge University Press, 1973.

Knauss, Steven (2015), "Unequal exchange in the 21st Century." Unpublished paper.

Kraemer, Kenneth L. Linden, Greg and Dedrick, Jason (2011) "Capturing Value in Global Networks: Apple's iPad and iPhone." Paper. Irvine, Berkeley & Syracuse: University of California & Syracuse University, 2011. Kravis, I.B., A. Heston and R. Summers (1978) *International Comparisons of Real Product and Purchasing Power.* Baltimore, USA: Johns Hopkins University Press, 1978.

Kravis I.B. (1986) "The three faces of the international comparison project." *The World Bank Research Observer* vol. 1. No. 1, p.3–26. New York, The World Bank 1986.

Köhler, Gernot (1998) "Unequal Exchange 1965–1995." Paper presented at School of Computing and Information Management, Sheridan Collage, Canada, 1998.

— (1998). "The Structure of Global Money and World Tables of Unequal Exchange." *Journal of World-Systems Research.* Volume 4. No.2 Fall 1998. Pp. 145-168.

— (2004) *The Global Wage System.* Canada: Nova Science Pub Inc. 2004.

Lauesen, Torkil (1986) "Handelsbalansens Politiske Ekonomi." *Häften för Kritiska Studier.* Vol. 19 no. pp.41-49. Göteborg 1986.

Lauesen, Torkil and Cope, Zak (2016) "Introduction" to: Marx, Karl & Engels, F: *On Colonies, Industrial Monopoly & Working Class.* Kersplebedeb, Montreal 2016.

Lauesen, Torkil (2018) *The Global Perspective, Reflections on Imperialism and Resistance.* Montreal: Kersplebedeb 2018.

— (2018) "The Parasite State in Theory and Practice." *Labor and Society, no.* 21. 2018. pp. 285-300.

— (2021) *Riding the Wave, Sweden's Integration into the Imperialist World System.* Montreal: Kersplebedeb, 2021.

— (2023) Emmanuel and us. https://unequalexchange.org/2023/07/06/emmanuel-and-us/

— (2024a) "Scandinavian Imperialism," *Journal of Labor and Society*, No. 27, 2024.

— (2024b), *The Long Transition Towards Socialism and the End of Capitalism*, Washington: Iskra Books, 2024. Available free online at: https://www.iskrabooks.org/the-long-transition

Leibowiz, G. (2017) "Apple CEO. Tim Cook: this is the number one reason we make iPhones in China (it's not what you think)." *Inc*, 21 December 2017.

Lenin, V.I. (1907) "The International Socialist Congress in Stuttgart (August 1907)." In: Lenin, *Collected Works*, Vol. 13, p 77. Moscow Progress Publishers, 1964.

— (1915) "The Collapse of the Second International," In Lenin, *Collected Works*, Vol 21. Moscow: Progress Publishers, 1974.

— (1915) "The Collapse of the Second International." Lenin: *Collected Works* Vol. 21. Moscow: Progress Publishers, 1964.

— (1916) "Imperialism, the Highest Stage of Capitalism." In: Lenin, *Collected Works*, Vol. 22. Moscow: Progress Publishers, 1972.

— (1916). "Imperialism and the Split in Socialism." In Lenin, *Collected Works*, Vol. 23, pp. 105–120. Moscow: Progress Publishers, 1964.

— (1920) "Draft (or thesis) of the R.C. P's reply to the letter of the Independent Social-Democracy Pary of Germany." Lenin, V. I *Collected Works* Vol 30. Moscow: Progress Publishers, 1964.

— (1920) "Supplementary Theses" In: Lenin, *Collected Works*, Vol. 31, pp.144-151, Moscow: Progress Publishers, 1964.

— (1920) "Speech on the terms of admission into the Communist International, July 1920." In Lenin V. I *Collected Works*, Vol 31. Moscow: Progress Publishers, 1964.

— (1920) "Left-Wing" Communism: An Infantile Disorder." In: Lenin, *Collected Works*, Volume 31. Moscow: Progress Publishers, 1964.

— (1922) "The role and functions of the trade unions under the new economic policy," Lenin: *Collected Works* Vol. 33. Moscow: Progress Publishers. 1964.

Lent, Jeremy (2018) "What Does China's 'Ecological Civilization' Mean for Humanity's Future?" *Ecowatch*, February 9, 2018. https://ecowatch.com/china-ecological-civilization-2532760301.html

Liberations Support Movement (1969-1981) "Liberation Support Movement Pamphlet Collection." https://jstor.org/site/struggles-for-freedom/southern-africa/liberation-support-movement-pamphlet-collection/?so=item_title_str_asc

Li, Minqi (2021) "China: Imperialism or Semi-Periphery?", *Monthly Review* vol. 73, no. 3, July–August 2021.

Li, M. and Wei, L. (2024) "Surplus Absorption, Secular Stagnation, and the Transition to Socialism: Contradictions of the U.S. and the Chinese Economies since 2000." *Monthly Review* vol.76 no. 5. 2024.

Lipke, Juergen (2002) "Unequal Exchange and Ecological Consumption—a Quantitative Study of Dependency Structures in the World System" Thesis at the Zentrum fur Entwicklungslunder forschung. Geographisches Institut, Freie Universitet Berlin. https://wsarch.ucr.edu/wsnmail/2004/msg00000.html

Long, Zhiming; Feng, Zhixuan; Li, Bangxi and Herrera, Rémy (2020) "U.S.-China Trade War. Has the Real "Thief" Finally Been Unmasked?" *Monthly Review,* Vol. 72 No. 5 October 2010.

Losurdo, Domenico (2016) *Class Struggle. A Political and Philosophical History.* New York: Palgrave Macmillan, 2016.

Lukács, György (1920). *History & Class Consciousness.* London: Merlin Press. 1967. https://marxists.org/archive/lukacs/works/history/lukacs3.htm

Lumumba, Patrice (1960) "Letter to Emmanuel, dated 12 of November 1960." https://unequalexchange.org/category/digital-archive/

Luxemburg, Rosa. (1913) "The Accumulation of Capital: A Contribution the Economic Theory of Imperialism." In: Luxemburg: *The Complete Works of Rosa Luxemburg* Vol 2, London, Verso, 2015.

The Mail and Guardian (2010) "Tito Mboweni joins Goldman Sachs," *The Mail and Guardian* 26.4. 2010. https://mg.co.za/article/2010-04-26-tito-mboweni-joins-goldman-sachs/

Marini, Ruy Mauro (1974) *The Dialectics of Dependency*, ed. Amanda Latimer and Jaime Osorio. New York: Monthly Review Press, 2022.

Marx, Karl (1845) "The German Ideology, Part I: Feuerbach. Opposition of the Materialist and Idealist Outlook." In: Marx-Engels, *Collected Works,* Volume 5. Moscow, Progress Publishers, 1976.

Marx, Karl and Engels, Frederick (1848) "The Communist Manifesto." In Marx and Engels, *Selected Works,* Moscow: Progress Publishers 1970.

Marx, Karl (1853) "The Future Results of British Rule in India." In: Karl Marx & Frederick Engels: *Collected Works,* Volume 12. Moscow: Progress Publishers 1975.

— (1857) *Grundrisse.* New York and London: Penguin Books 1973.

— (1857) *Grundrisse (Principes d'une critique de l'economie politique.* Paris: l'eiade edition of Oeuvres de Karl Marx Economic 1968.

— (1859) *A contribution to the critique of political economy. Preface, with some notes by R. Rojas.* Moscow: Progress Publishers, 1977.

— (1861) "Economic Manuscripts, 1861–63, Theories of Surplus Value." In: Karl Marx & Frederick Engels: *Collected Works,* Vol. 32. Moscow: Progress Publishers, 1975.

— (1865) "Letter to Engels, dated July 31, 1865." In Karl Marx & Frederick Engels: *Collected Works,* volume 42, p. 173. Moscow: Progress Publishers, 1975.

— (1867) *Capital.* Volume I. Moscow: Progress Publishers, 1962.

— (1870) "Letter to S. Meyer and A. Vogt, dated April 9, 1870." In: *Marx and Engels, On Colonialism.* Moscow: Progress Publishers,1960.

— (1881) "Letter to N.F. Danielson, dated February 19, 1881". In: *Marx and Engels Correspondence.* Moscow: International Publishers, 1968.

— (1883) *Capital,* Volume II. Moscow: Progress Publishers, 1962.

— (1883) (Edited by Engels, F.) *Capital,* Volume III, A Critique of Political Economy. First Published in 1894. New York: International Publishers 1959. Here from: https://marxists.org

— (1883) *Theories of Surplus-Value.* Moscow: Progress Publishers, 1976.

Milberg, William (2008) "Shifting Sources and Uses of Profits: Sustaining US Financialization with Global Value Chains." *Economy and Society,* vol. 37, no. 3. 2008.

Milberg, William and Winkler, Deborah (2013) *Outsourcing Economics: Global Value Chains in Capitalist Development.* Cambridge: Cambridge University Press, 2013.

Moxon, Richard W. (1973) *Offshore Production in Less Developed Countries.* Harvard University. Diss., 1973.

Myrdal, Gunnar (1956) *An International Economy, Problems and Prospects.* London: Routledge and Kegan Paul Ltd, 1956.

— (1963) Economic *Theory and Underdeveloped Regions.* London: Harper & Row, 1963.

NACLA, "The Tri-Continental Conference and the Ben Barka Affair". Retrieved 2020-03-12. https://nacla.org/article/tri-continental-conference-and-ben-barka-affair

Nakajima, A., & Izumi, H. (1995) "Economic Development and Unequal Exchange among Nations: Analysis of the U.S., Japan, and South Korea." *Review of Radical Political Economics,* Vol.27, no.3, pp. 86-94.

Naughton, B. (2008) "A political economy of China's economic transition." In. Brandt. L & Rawski, T. G. (Eds.), *China's great economic transformation.* Cambridge: Cambridge University Press, 2008.

Nehru, Jawaharlal (1934) *Glimpses of World History.* New Delhi: Oxford University Press. 1982.

Ness, Immanuel (2023) *Migration as Economic Imperialism: How International Labour Mobility Undermines Economic Development in Poor Countries.* Cambridge: Polity Press, 2023.

Ngai, P. & Chan, J. (2012) "Global capital, the state, and Chinese workers: the Foxconn experience." *Modern China* vol 38, no. 4, pp. 383–410, 2012.

Nicholas, H. (2011). *Marx's theory of price and its modern rivals.* Houndsmills: Palgrave Macmillan. 2011.

Nkrumah, Kwame (1965) *Neo-Colonialism, the Last Stage of imperialism*, London: Thomas Nelson & Sons, Ltd., London 1965. https://marxists.org/ebooks/nkrumah/nkrumah-neocolonialism.pdf

Norton, Ben (2024) "Trump threatens to punish de-dollarization: 'I would not allow countries to go off the dollar." Geopolitical Economy: https://geopoliticaleconomy.com/2024/09/13/trump-threat-punish-dedollarization-dollar/

Nyerere, Julius K. (1972) "A Call to European Socialists" (November 1972). In: Nyerere, *Freedom and Development: A Selection from Writings and Speeches 1968-1973.* Dar es Salaam: Oxford University Press, 1973.

OECD (2019) "Pension Markets In: Focus 2019," Table A B.2.: https://oecd.org/daf/fin/private-pensions/PensionMarkets-in-Focus-2019.pdf

— (2023) Global value and supply chains. https://oecd.org/en/topics/global-value-and-supply-chains.html — (2023) "Charted: Hours Worked vs.

Salaries in OECD Countries": https://visualcapitalist.com/cp/hours-worked-vs-salaries-in-oecd-countries/

Orléans, Leo (1977). *La Science et la Technologie en République Populaire de Chine.* Geneva: OECD, 1977.

Ossome, L.& Sirisha, N. (2021) "The Agrarian Question Of Gendered Labour in Labour Questions" In: Jha, P., Chambati, W. & Ossome, L (eds.) (2021) *The Global South.* London Palgrave Macmillan, 2021.

Palloix, Christian (1969) "l'impérialisme et l'échange inégal," *l'Homme et la Société* N° 12, Paris, 1969.

Patnaik, Utsa and Patnaik, Prabhat (2016) *A Theory of Imperialism*, Columbia, Columbia University Press, 2016.

Pedregal, Alejandro and Lukic, Nemanja (2024) "Imperialism, Ecological Imperialism, and Green Imperialism: An Overview." *Journal of Labor and Society,* vol 27, no. 1, 2024, pp. 105–138.

Penn World Table version 10.01, Groningen Growth and Development Centre, University of Groningen. https://rug.nl/ggdc/productivity/pwt/

Pérez-Sánchez, L., Velasco-Fernández, R. & Giampietro, M. (2021) "The international division of labor and embodied working time in trade for the US, the EU and China." *Ecologic Economy*. No. 180, 106909, 2021.

Peters, Glenn P (2008) "From Production-Based to Consumption-Based National Emission Inventories," in *Ecological Economics* 65, no. 1, 2008 pp. 13–23; World Resources Institute.

Raffer, Kunibert (1987) *Unequal exchange and the evolution of the world system.* New York: Palgrave Macmillan, 1987.

— (2006) "Differences between inequalities and unequal exchange: comments on the papers by Chaves and Köhler." In: *Entelequia, revista interdisciplinar*, no. 2. 2006.

Ricci, Andrea (2019) "Unequal Exchange in the Age of Globalization," *Review of Radical Political Economics,* vol. 51, no. 2, 2019.

— (2021) *Value and Unequal Exchange in International Trade, The Geography of Global Capitalist Exploitation.* New York: Routledge, 2021.

— (2022) "Global locational inequality: Assessing unequal exchange effects." *Economy and Space* 2022, Vol. 54. NO.7, pp. 1323–1340. Roberts, Michael (2023) 50 years of dependency theory. The Next Recession,

November 4, 2023: https://thenextrecession.wordpress.com/2023/11/04/50-years-of-dependency-theory/

Robinson, William (2008) *Latin America and Global Capitalism. A Critical Globalization Perspective*. Baltimore: Johns Hopkins University Press. 2008.

Rockhill, G. (2024) Gabriel Rockhill summarising the argument as presenting an analogy between the policy of New Democracy in China 1949 and the current strategy for a multipolar world-system. 'Book and Series Launch: Torkil Lauesen's "The Long Transition Towards Socialism"', YouTube (2024), available online at https://www.youtube.com/watch?v=zaJbwuOd8LQ.

Romero-Robayo, Palacios; Pallares-Miralles and Whitehouse (2012) "World Bank Pension Indicators and Database." *Social Protection and Labor. Human Development Network*, World Bank, Washington, D.C. 2012.

Ross, John (2024) "What is the realistic strategy for "de-dollarisation"?", *MR Online,* https://mronline.org/2024/06/18/what-is-the-realistic-strategy-for-de-dollarisation/

Rousset, Pierre (2021) "China: A New Imperialism Emerges," *International Viewpoint,* November 18, 2021.

Saaida, Mohammed (2024) 'BRICS Plus: de-dollarization and global power shifts in new economic landscape'. https://brics-econ.arphahub.com/article/117828/

Say, Jean-Baptiste (1803) *A Treatise on Political Economy*. Lippincott, Grambo & Co. Philadelphia: 1855. Reprint by: Canada: Batoche Books, 2001.

Scholten, Joe (2022) "How China Strengthened Food Security and Fought Poverty with State-Funded Cooperatives," *Geopolitical Economy Report.* May 31, 2022. https://geopoliticaleconomy.com/2022/05/31/china-food-security-poverty-cooperatives/

Semmel, B (1960) *Imperialism and Social Reform, English Social-Imperial Thought 1895-1914.* New York: Anchor Books Doubleday and Company, 1960.

Smith, John (2011) "Imperialism and the Law of Value," *Global Discourse,* vol. 2, no. 1, 2011. https://globaldiscourse.wordpress.com/wp-content/uploads/2011/05/john-smith.pdf

— (2015) "Marx's Capital and the global crisis." Paper presented at Imperialism: Old and New Conference. New Delhi. https://researchgate.

net/publication/306381038_Marx's_Capital_and_the_Global_Crisis_-_revised_Delhi_paper

— (2016) *Imperialism in the Twenty-first Century.* New York: Monthly Review Press, 2016.

Sorkin, Andrew Ross (2013) "How Mandela Shifted Views on Freedom of Markets." *The New York Times,* December 9, 2013.

Stanley, Issac (2019) *Dreaming Revolution: Tricontinentalism, Anti-Imperialism and Third World Rebellion,* London: Routledge, 2019.

The State Council Information Office of the People's Republic of China (2019) "China and the World in the New Era." http://english.scio.gov.cn/2019-09/28/content_75252746.htm

Stefanoni, Pablo (2006). 'Bolivia a due dimensioni', *Il Manifesto,* 22 July 2006. https://peacelink.it/latina/a/17714.html

Suwandi, I Jonna, R. J. & Foster, J. B. (2019) "Global commodity chains and the new imperialism." *Monthly Review.* Vol. 70. No.10 March 2019.

Suwandi, I. (2019) *Value Chains: The New Economic Imperialism.* New York: Monthly Review Press, 2019.

Sweezy, Paul and Huberman, Leo. eds. (1965) *Paul Alexander Baran (1910–1964): A Collective Portrait.* New York: Monthly Review Press 1965.

Tampa Bay Times (1990) "Mandela voices commitment to nationalization," *Tampa Bay Times* 26.1.1990. https://tampabay.com/archive/1990/01/26/mandela-voices-commitment-to-nationalization/

Therborn, Göran (1996) "Dialectics of Modernity: On Critical Theory and the Legacy of Twentieth Century Marxism." *New Left Review,* 215 Jan/Feb. London 1996.

Tricontinental Institute (2024) "Hyper-Imperialism: A Decadent New Stage," *Tricontinental Institute,* January 23, 2024.

Tse-tung, Mao (1937) "On Practice." In: Tse-tung, Mao, *Selected Works.* Vol. I. Peking, Foreign Languages Press1965. — (1949) "On New Democracy," in: Tse-tung, Mao, *Selected Works* Vol. II. Foreign Languages Press, Beijing. 1965.

— (1963) "Where Do Correct Ideas Come From?" in: Tse-tung, Mao: *Four Essays on Philosophy*. Beijing: Foreign Languages Press 1963.

Uchatius, Wolfgang (2010) "Das Welthemd." Die Zeit, December 17, 2010. Here from: Tony Norfield, "The China Price," *Economics of Imperialism,*

June 4, 2011. https://economicsofimperialism.blogspot.com/2011/06/what-china-price-really-means.html

UN, Statistical Yearbook, (1978 & 1981) UN, *Monthly Bulletin of Statistics* No. 5, May 1984.

UNCTAD (2009), *Handbook of Statistics, 1980–2009.* New York & Geneva: United Nations. 2009.

— (2013), *World Investment Report 2013.* New York & Geneva: United Nations 2013.

— (2018) UNCTAD-Eora Global Value Chain (GVC) database. https://worldmrio.com/unctadgvc/

— (2023) UNCTAD-Eora Global Value Chain (GVC) database. https://worldmrio.com/unctadgvc

Union of Concerned Scientists (2023), 'Each Country's Share of CO2 Emissions', https://ucs.org/resources/each-countrys-share-co2-emissions

Vance, J.D. (2025) "Vice President Vance remarks at the American Dynamism Summit, 18.3.2025," https://www.youtube.com/watch?v=YAgoUvuyLik. Here from, Norton, Ben (2025) US VP JD Vance admits West wants Global South trapped at bottom of value chain. *Geopolitical Economy Report*, on March 26, 2025. https://geopoliticaleconomy.com/2025/03/26/jd-vance-west-global-south-global-value-chain/

Varga, E and Mendelsohn (ed.) (1939) *New Data for V.I. Lenin's 'Imperialism, the Highest Stage of Capitalism.* Moscow: Foreign Languages Publishing House, 1939.

Vernon, James (2007) Hunger: *A Modern History.* Cambridge: Belknap Press, 2007.

Visana, Vikram (2022) "Uncivil liberalism: labour, capital and commercial society," In: *Dadabhai Naoroji's political thought.* Cambridge: Cambridge University Press, United Kingdom 2022.

Washington Post (2024) "How four U.S. presidents unleashed economic warfare across the globe." *Washington Post*, 25 July 2024. https://washingtonpost.com/business/interactive/2024/us-sanction-countries-work/

Webber, M. J., & Foot, S. P. H. (1984). "The Measurement of Unequal Exchange." *Economy and Space*, Vol., no7, pp. 927-947.

Weber, Isabella M. (2021) *How China Escaped Shock Therapy: The Market Reform Debate.* New York: Routledge. 2021.

Wikipedia, 'List of countries by home ownership rate', https://en.wikipedia.org/wiki/Owner-occupancy

Williams, K.M. (1985) "Is "Unequal exchange" a mechanism for perpetuating inequality in the modern world system?" *Studies in Comparative International Development,* no.20, pp. 47–73 1985.

World Bank (2025) GDP (ppp) (current international $) Data (Washington, DC: World Bank, 2024, 2025. https://data.worldbank.org/indicator/NY.GDP.PCAP.PP.CD

World Population Review. (2024) US Trade Deficit by Country 2025. https://worldpopulationreview.com/country-rankings/us-trade-deficit-by-country

World Trade Organisation, WTO Stats, https://stats.wto.org/

Xiaoping, Deng (1978) "Carry Out the Policy of Opening to the Outside World and Learn Advanced Science and Technology from Other Countries." In: Xiaoping, Deng, *Selected Works.* Vol. 2, Beijing Foreign Languages Press, 1992. https://dengxiaopingworks.wordpress.com/selected-works-vol-2-1975-1982/

— (1985) "We Shall Expand Political Democracy and Carry Out Economic Reform." In: Xiaoping, Deng, *Selected Works* Vol. 3, Beijing: Foreign Languages Press 1992. https://marxists.org/reference/archive/deng-xiaoping/1985/7.htm

— (1986). "Interview with Mike Wallace of CBS 60 Minutes." CBS, September 2, 1986. Here from: *All Asia Times,* December 13, 2006. Retrieved from https://china.usc.edu.

Xing, Yuqing and Detert, Neal (2010) "How the iPhone Widens the United States Trade Deficit with the People's Republic of China." In: *ADBI Working Paper* no. 257. Asian Tokyo: Development Bank Institute, 2010.

Yi, Wang (2025) "A Steadfast Constructive Force in a Changing World," Keynote Speech by Wang Yi, at the 61st Munich Security Conference, February 14, 2025. Here from, Norton, Ben, (2025) What is a 'multipolar' world? China says equality; Trump & Marco Rubio say imperial rivalry. Geopolitical Economy. https://geopoliticaleconomy.com/2025/02/16/multipolarity-china-trump-marco-rubio-imperialism/

Young, Robert J.C. (2018). *Disseminating the Tricontinental.* London: Routledge. 2018.

www.ingramcontent.com/pod-product-compliance
Ingram Content Group UK Ltd.
Pitfield, Milton Keynes, MK11 3LW, UK
UKHW031047070526
12323UKWH00002B/153

9 798330 613342